SOUTHEAST
HOME LANDSCAPING

Fourth Edition

Other titles available in the *Home Landscaping* series:

CALIFORNIA

MID-ATLANTIC

MIDWEST
including South-Central Canada

NORTHEAST
including Southeast Canada

NORTHWEST

TEXAS

WESTERN

CRE▲TIVE
HOMEOWNER®

SOUTHEAST
HOME LANDSCAPING

Fourth Edition

54 Landscape Designs with 200+ Plants & Flowers for Your Region

ROGER HOLMES
RITA BUCHANAN

Technical Editor for Updated Edition: Mark Wolfe

About the Authors

Roger Holmes is the founding editor of *Fine Gardening* magazine. He co-edited the monumental Taylor's *Master Guide to Gardening* and other highly regarded gardening books, and produced the landscaping series of which this book is part.

Rita Buchanan is a lifelong gardener with degrees in botany and an encyclopedic knowledge of plants. She worked with Roger Holmes to edit *Fine Gardening* magazine and co-edit several books. She is the author of numerous award-winning books and is a contributor to many gardening magazines.

Southeast Home Landscaping, 4th Edition (2023) is a revised edition of *Southeast Home Landscaping, 3rd Edition* (2010), published by Creative Homeowner, an imprint of Fox Chapel Publishing Company, Inc. Revisions include new sections, updated information, and updated landscape designs with native plants.

SOUTHEAST HOME LANDSCAPING
WORDWORKS

EDITORS	Roger Holmes, Rita Buchanan
ASSISTANT EDITOR	Monica Norby, Sarah Disbrow
COPY EDITOR	Nancy J. Stabile, Sarah Disbrow
INTERIOR DESIGN	Deborah Fillion
ILLUSTRATORS	Frank Dyer
COVER AND INTERIOR DESIGN	Steve Buchanan (Portfolio of Designs); Michelle Angle Farrar, Lee Hov, Robert LaPointe, Rick Daskam, Teresa Nicole Green (Guide to Installation)

FOURTH EDITION

MANAGING EDITOR	Gretchen Bacon
EDITOR	Christa Oestreich
TECHNICAL EDITOR	Mark Wolfe
DESIGNER	Mary Ann Kahn

Southeast Home Landscaping, 4th Edition
ISBN 978-1-58011-588-9

Library of Congress Control Number: 2022946176

We are always looking for talented authors. To submit an idea, please send a brief inquiry to acquisitions@foxchapelpublishing.com.

Printed in China

Current Printing (last digit)
10 9 8 7 6 5 4 3 2 1

Creative Homeowner®, *www.creativehomeowner.com*, is an imprint of New Design Originals Corporation and distributed exclusively in North America by Fox Chapel Publishing Company, Inc., 800-457-9112, 903 Square Street, Mount Joy, PA 17552, and in the United Kingdom by Grantham Book Service, Trent Road, Grantham, Lincolnshire, NG31 7XQ.

Safety First

Though all concepts and methods in this book have been reviewed for safety, it is not possible to overstate the importance of using the safest working methods possible. What follows are reminders—do's and don'ts for yard work and landscaping. They are not substitutes for your own common sense.

- *Always* use caution, care, and good judgment when following the procedures described in this book.

- *Always* determine locations of underground utility lines before you dig, and then avoid them by a safe distance. Buried lines may be for gas, electricity, communications, or water. Start research by contacting your local building officials. Also contact local utility companies; they will often send a representative free of charge to help you map their lines. In addition, there are private utility locator firms that may be listed in your Yellow Pages. Note: previous owners may have installed underground drainage, sprinkler, and lighting lines without mapping them.

- *Always* read and heed the manufacturer's instructions for using a tool, especially the warnings.

- *Always* ensure that the electrical setup is safe; be sure that no circuit is overloaded and that all power tools and electrical outlets are properly grounded and protected by a ground-fault circuit interrupter (GFCI). Do not use power tools in wet locations.

- *Always* wear eye protection when using chemicals, sawing wood, pruning trees and shrubs, using power tools, and striking metal onto metal or concrete.

- *Always* read labels on chemicals, solvents, and other products; provide ventilation; heed warnings.

- *Always* wear heavy rubber gloves rated for chemicals, not mere household rubber gloves, when handling toxins.

- *Always* wear appropriate gloves in situations in which your hands could be injured by rough surfaces, sharp edges, thorns, or poisonous plants.

- *Always* wear a disposable face mask or a special filtering respirator when creating sawdust or working with toxic gardening substances.

- *Always* keep your hands and other body parts away from the business ends of blades, cutters, and bits.

- *Always* obtain approval from local building officials before undertaking construction of permanent structures.

- *Never* work with power tools when you are tired or under the influence of alcohol or drugs.

- *Never* carry sharp or pointed tools, such as knives or saws, in your pockets. If you carry such tools, use special-purpose tool scabbards.

The Landscape Designers

Kim Hawks is founder and owner of Niche Gardens, based in Chapel Hill, N.C., a national retail mail-order nursery specializing in nursery-propagated North American native plants, particularly those of the southeastern United States. Holder of a degree in horticulture from North Carolina State University, Ms. Hawks has written for gardening magazines and lectures widely on native plants, gardening, and garden design. Her designs appear on pp. 40–43, 48–51, 64–67, and 96–99.

Glenn Morris has designed southern landscapes for many years. Trained as a landscape architect at North Carolina State University, he specializes in homeowner-directed problem solving and has received an award for design excellence from the American Society of Landscape Architects. Mr. Morris has also written extensively about gardening and design. His designs appear on pp. 28–31, 36–39, 56–59, 80–83, 100–103, 108–111, and 112–115.

Stephen and Kristin Pategas own Hortus Oasis in Winter Park, Fla. They provide services in residential, commercial, and specialty garden design and consultation. Stephen is a registered landscape architect; Kristin is a horticul-turist and a Florida Certified Landscape Designer. In addition to creating award-winning landscape designs, Stephen and Kristin regularly contribute to magazines and appear on television gardening shows. Their designs appear on pp. 76–79.

Dan Sears is principal in the Sears Design Group of Raleigh, N.C., a firm specializing in residential land planning and landscape design. In 25 years as a landscape architect, he has won numerous regional and national design awards and has had many projects published in magazines and journals. Mr. Sears has been a member of the North Carolina Board of Landscape Architects. His designs appear on pp. 20–23, 32–35, 52–55 60–63, 68–71, 104–107, and 116–119.

Jimmy and Becky Stewart are professional gardeners in Atlanta, Ga., where they design and install residential gardens. As designers, they strive to create year-round interest in their gardens. As avid plant enthusiasts, they are constantly experimenting with new and different plants to see which do best in the Atlanta area. Their designs have been featured in many publications. Their designs appear on pp. 44–47, 88–91, 120–123, and 124–127.

Contents

About This Book

Of all the home improvement projects homeowners tackle, few offer greater rewards than landscaping. Paths, patios, fences, arbors, and—most of all—plantings, can enhance home life in countless ways, large and small, functional and pleasurable, every day of the year. At the main entrance, an attractive brick walkway flanked by eye-catching shrubs and perennials provides a cheerful send-off in the morning and welcomes you home from work in the evening. A carefully placed grouping of small trees, shrubs, and fence panels creates privacy on the patio or screens a nearby eyesore from view. An island bed showcases your favorite plants, while dividing the backyard into several areas for a variety of activities.

Unlike some home improvements, the rewards of landscaping can lie as much in the activity as in the result. Planting and caring for lovely shrubs, perennials, and other plants can afford years of enjoyment. And for those who like to build things, outdoor construction projects can be a special treat.

While the installation and maintenance of plants and outdoor structures are within the means and abilities of most people, few of us are as comfortable determining exactly which plants or structures to use and how best to combine them. It's one thing to decide to dress up the front entrance or patio, another to come up with a design for doing so.

That's where this book comes in. Here, in the Portfolio of Designs, you'll find inspiration for nearly two dozen common home landscaping situations, created by landscape professionals who live and work in the Southeast region. Drawing on years of experience, they balance functional requirements and aesthetic possibilities, choosing the right plant or structure for the task based on its proven performance in similar situations.

Complementing the Portfolio of Designs is the second section, Plant Profiles, which provides information on all the plants used in the book. The book's third section, the Guide to Installation, will help you to install and maintain the plants and structures described in the designs. The following discussions take a closer look at each section; we've also printed representative pages of the sections on pp. 9 and 10 and pointed out their features.

Portfolio of Designs

This is the heart of the book, providing examples of landscaping situations and solutions that are at once inspiring and accessible. Some are simple, others more complex, but each one can be installed in a few weekends by homeowners with no special training or experience.

For each situation, we present two designs, the second a variation of the first. As the sample pages ahead show, the first design is displayed on a two-page spread. A perspective illustration (called a "rendering") shows what the design will look like several years after installation, when the perennials and many of the shrubs have reached mature size. The rendering also shows the planting as it will appear at a particular time of year. (For more on how plantings change over the course of a year, see "Seasons in Your Landscape," pp. 12–15.) A site plan shows the positions of the plants and structures on a scaled grid. Text introduces the situation and the design and describes the plants and projects used.

The second design option, presented on the second two-page spread, addresses the same situation as the first but differs in one or more important aspects. It might show a planting suited for a shady rather than a sunny site; or it might incorporate different structures or kinds of plants (adding shrubs to a perennial border, for example). As for the first design, we present a rendering, site plan, and written information, but in briefer form. The second spread also includes photographs of landscapes in situations similar to those featured in the two designs. The photos showcase noteworthy variations or details that you may wish to use in the designs we show or in designs of your own.

Installed exactly as shown here, these designs will provide enjoyment for many years. But individual needs and properties will differ, so we encourage you to alter the designs to suit your site and desires. You can easily make changes. For example, you can add or remove plants and adjust the sizes of paths, patios, and fences to suit larger or smaller sites. You can rearrange groupings and substitute favorite plants to suit your taste. Or you can integrate the design with your existing landscaping. If you are uncertain about how to solve specific problems or about the effects of changes you are considering, consult with staff at a local nursery or with a landscape designer in your area.

PORTFOLIO OF DESIGNS

FIRST DESIGN OPTION

Plants & Projects
Noteworthy qualities of the plants and structures and their contributions to the design.

Summary
An overview of the situation and the design.

Concept Box
Summarizes an important aspect of the design; tells whether the site is sunny or shady and what season is depicted in the rendering.

Site Plan
Positions all plants and structures on a scaled grid.

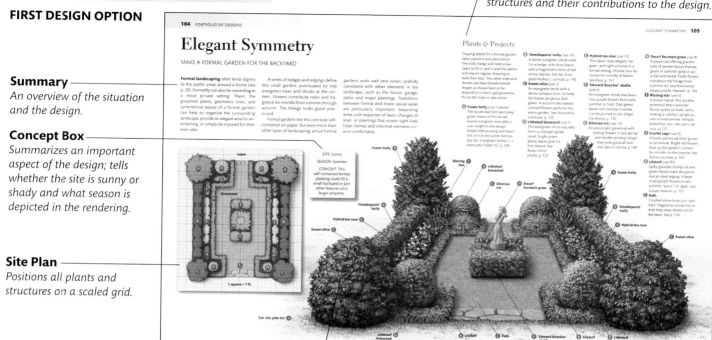

Rendering
Shows how the design will look when plants are well established.

Site Plan
Plants and structures on a scaled grid.

Variations on a Theme
Photos of inspiring designs in similar situations.

SECOND DESIGN OPTION

Summary
Addressing the same situation as the first design, this variation may differ in design concept, site conditions, or plant selection.

Concept Box
Site, season, and design summary.

Rendering
Depicts the design when plants are well established.

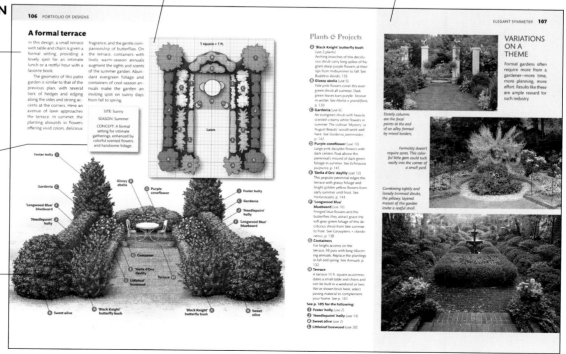

PLANT PROFILES

Choices
Selections here help you choose from the many varieties of certain popular plants.

Plant Portraits
Photos of selected plants.

Detailed Plant Information
Descriptions of each plant's noteworthy qualities and requirements for planting and care.

GUIDE TO INSTALLATION

Sidebars
Detailed information on special topics, set within ruled boxes

Step-by-Step
Illustrations show process; steps are keyed by number to discussion in the main text.

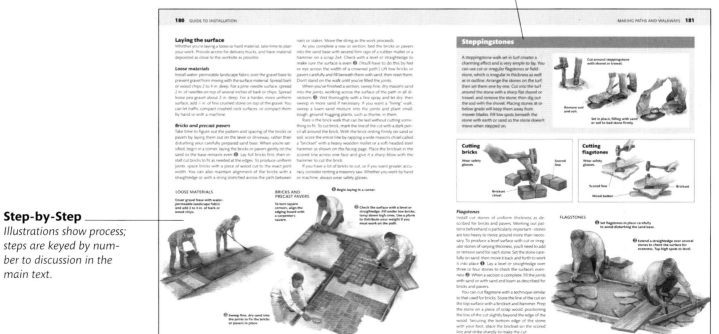

Plant Profiles

The second section of the book includes a description of each plant featured in the Portfolio. These outline each plant's basic preferences for environmental conditions, such as soil, moisture, and sun or shade, and give advice about planting as well as ongoing care.

Working with the book's landscape designers, we selected plants carefully, following a few simple guidelines: Every plant should be a proven performer in the region; once established, it should thrive without pampering. All plants should be available for purchase at nurseries and garden centers; if they're not in stock, they can be ordered, or you can ask the nursery staff to recommend suitable substitutes.

In the Portfolio section, you'll note that plants are referred to by their common name but are cross-referenced to the Plant Profiles section by their botanical name. While common names are familiar to many people, they can be confusing. Distinctly different plants can share the same common name, or one plant can have several different common names. Botanical names, therefore, ensure greatest accuracy and are more appropriate for a reference section such as this. Although you can confidently purchase most of the plants in this book from local nurseries using the common name, knowing the botanical name allows you to make sure that the plant you're ordering is actually the one that is shown in our design.

Guide to Installation

In this section you'll find detailed instructions and illustrations covering all the techniques you'll need to install any design from start to finish. Here we explain how to think your way through a landscaping project and anticipate the various steps. Then you'll learn how to do each part of the job: preparing the site; laying out the design; choosing materials; building paths, trellises, or other structures; amending the soil for planting; buying the recommended plants and putting them in place; and caring for the plants to keep them healthy and attractive year after year.

We've taken care to make installation of built elements simple and straightforward. Hardscape elements, such as paths, trellises, fences, and arbors, all use basic materials available from local suppliers, and they can be assembled by people who have no special skills or tools beyond those commonly used for home maintenance. The designs can easily be adapted to meet specific needs or to fit in with the style of your house or other landscaping features.

Installing different designs requires different techniques. You can find what you need by following the cross-references in the Portfolio to pages in the Guide to Installation, or by skimming the Guide. If you continue to improve your landscape by adding more than one design, you'll find that many basic techniques are reused from one project to the next. You might want to start with one of the smaller, simpler designs. Gradually you'll develop the skills and confidence to do any project you choose.

Most of the designs in this book can be installed in a weekend or two; some will take a little longer. Digging planting beds, building retaining walls, and erecting fences and arbors can be strenuous work. If you lack the time or energy for the more arduous installation tasks, consider hiring a teenager to help out. Local landscaping services can provide any of the services you need help with.

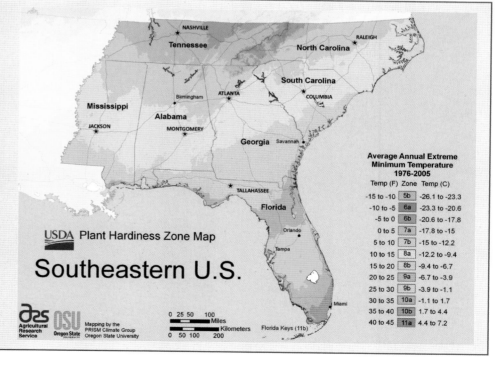

SOUTHEAST HARDINESS ZONES

This map is based on one developed by the U.S. Department of Agriculture. It divides the region into "hardiness zones" based on minimum winter temperatures. While most of the plants in this book will survive the lowest temperatures in the region, a few may not. These few are noted in the Plant Profiles descriptions, where we have usually suggested alternatives. When you buy plants, most will have "hardiness" designations, which correspond to a USDA hardiness zone on the map. A Zone 7 plant, for example, can be expected to survive winter temperatures as low as 0°F, and it can be used with confidence in Zones 7 and 8 but not in the colder Zone 6. It is useful to know your zone and the zone designation of any plants that you wish to add to those in this book.

USDA Plant Hardiness Zone Map

Southeastern U.S.

Average Annual Extreme Minimum Temperature 1976-2005		
Temp (F)	Zone	Temp (C)
-15 to -10	5b	-26.1 to -23.3
-10 to -5	6a	-23.3 to -20.6
-5 to 0	6b	-20.6 to -17.8
0 to 5	7a	-17.8 to -15
5 to 10	7b	-15 to -12.2
10 to 15	8a	-12.2 to -9.4
15 to 20	8b	-9.4 to -6.7
20 to 25	9a	-6.7 to -3.9
25 to 30	9b	-3.9 to -1.1
30 to 35	10a	-1.1 to 1.7
35 to 40	10b	1.7 to 4.4
40 to 45	11a	4.4 to 7.2

Agricultural Research Service

OSU Oregon State University

Mapping by the PRISM Climate Group Oregon State University

0 25 50 100 Miles
0 50 100 200 Kilometers

Florida Keys (11b)

Seasons in Your Landscape

One of the rewards of landscaping is watching how plants change through the seasons. During the dark winter months, you look forward to the bright, fresh flowers of spring. Then the lush green foliage of summer is transformed into the blazing colors of fall. Perennials that rest underground in winter can grow chest-high by midsummer, and hence a flower bed that looks flat and bare in December becomes a jungle in July.

To illustrate typical seasonal changes, we've chosen one of the designs from this book (see pp. 70–71) and shown here how it would look in spring, summer, fall, and winter. As you can see, this planting looks quite different from one season to the next, but it always remains interesting. Try to remember this example of transformation as you look at the other designs in this book. There we show how the planting will appear in one season and call attention to any plants that will stand out at other times of year.

The task of tending a landscape also changes with the seasons. Below we've noted the most important seasonal jobs to summarize the annual work cycle.

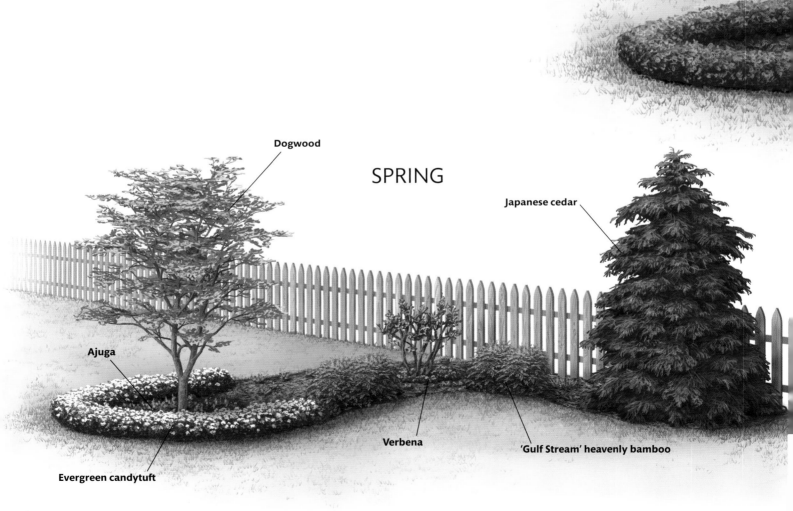

Dogwood

SPRING

Japanese cedar

Ajuga

Verbena

'Gulf Stream' heavenly bamboo

Evergreen candytuft

SUMMER

Butterfly bush

Veronica

Purple coneflower

Spring

The spring flower season begins in February across most of the Southeast and peaks in March and April, when the dogwoods and azaleas bloom, the lawns turn green, and the trees leaf out. In this garden, a pink dogwood is joined by spring-blooming perennials such as white evergreen candytuft, blue ajuga, and pink verbena. Meanwhile, summer-blooming plants are just starting to grow. The evergreen Japanese cedar and heavenly bamboo have traded their winter colors for plain green. Do a thorough cleanup in early spring. Remove last year's perennial flower stalks and foliage, cut ornamental grasses to the ground, prune shrubs and trees, renew the mulch, and neaten the edges between flower beds and lawn.

Summer

In summer, both evergreen and deciduous trees and shrubs grow new shoots covered with fresh foliage. Flowering perennials and shrubs such as the verbena, veronica, purple coneflower, and butterfly bush shown here add spots of color to the otherwise green landscape. To coax as many flowers as possible from these plants and to keep the garden tidy, cut or shear off older blossoms as they fade. Summer weather is typically hot and humid throughout this region, but droughts are not uncommon. Water new plantings at least once a week during dry spells, and water older plants, too, if the soil gets so dry that they wilt. Pull any weeds that sprout up through the mulch; this is easiest when the soil is moist.

Fall

The bright fall foliage and ripening berries of dogwoods and other trees and shrubs brighten the Southeast landscape in late October or November. Meanwhile, butterfly bush, verbena, and veronica continue blooming from summer into fall, joined in September or so by 'Autumn Joy' sedum, hardy chrysanthemums, and switchgrass. These fall flowers last for many weeks as the weather cools off and the days get shorter. You can leave grasses and perennial stalks standing all winter, if you choose, or clear them away whenever hard frosts or heavy rains turn them brown or knock them down. Toss the stems on the compost pile, along with any leaves that you rake up. After the first frost, replace any summer annuals with pansies or other cold-weather annuals, and plant tulips or other spring-blooming bulbs now. Fall rains usually soak the ground, so you can stop watering.

'Autumn Joy' sedum

Winter

In winter, when much of the landscape turns tan and brown, you appreciate evergreen plants such as the bronze Japanese cedar, crimson heavenly bamboo, emerald evergreen candytuft, and purple ajuga shown here. Welcome in winter, too, are clumps of rustling grass; dried perennial flower stalks; and shrubs and trees with handsome branch patterns, conspicuous buds or berries, or distinctive bark.

Normally, garden plants need little if any care in winter. If a heavy snow or an ice storm snaps or crushes some plants, you can trim away the broken parts as soon as it's convenient, but if plants get frozen during a severe cold spell, wait until spring to assess the damage before deciding how far to cut them back.

FALL

Butterfly bush

'Heavy Metal' switchgrass

Veronica

Hardy chrysanthemum

WINTER

Japanese cedar

Ajuga

Evergreen candytuft

'Gulf Stream' heavenly bamboo

As Your Landscape Grows

Landscapes change over the years. As plants grow, the overall look evolves from sparse to lush. Trees cast cool shade where the sun used to shine. Shrubs and hedges grow tall and dense enough to provide privacy. Perennials and ground covers spread to form colorful patches of foliage and flowers. Meanwhile, paths, arbors, fences, and other structures gain the patina of age.

Constant change over the years—sometimes rapid and dramatic, sometimes slow and subtle—is one of the joys of land-scaping. It is also one of the chal-lenges. Anticipating how fast plants will grow and how big they will eventually get is difficult, even for professional designers, and was a major concern in formulating the designs for this book.

To illustrate the kinds of changes to ex-pect in a planting, these pages show one of the designs at three different "ages." Even though a new planting may look sparse at first, it will soon fill in. And be-cause of careful spacing, the planting will look as good in 10 to 15 years as it does after 3 to 5. It will, of course, look differ-ent, but that's part of the fun.

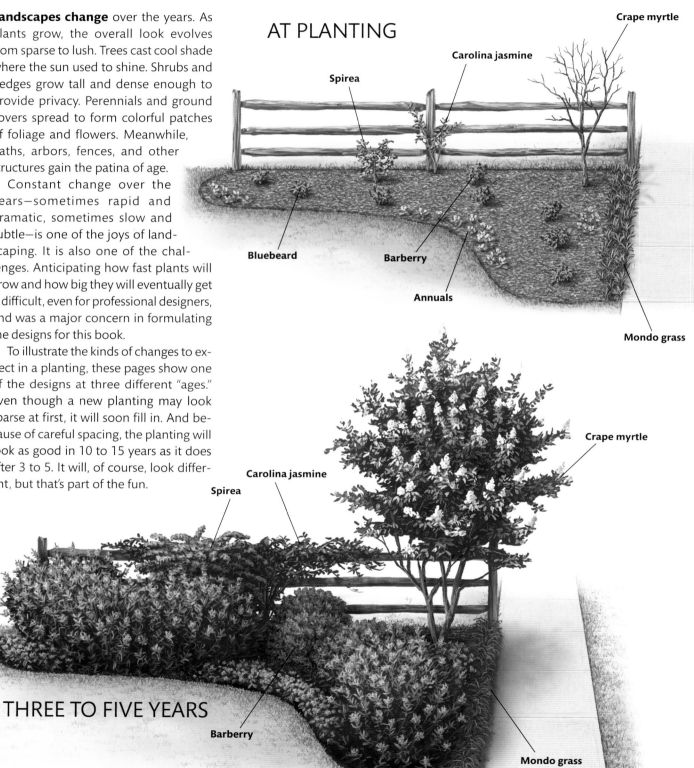

AT PLANTING

Crape myrtle

Carolina jasmine

Spirea

Bluebeard

Barberry

Annuals

Mondo grass

THREE TO FIVE YEARS

Spirea

Carolina jasmine

Crape myrtle

Barberry

Mondo grass

At Planting—Here's how the corner planting (pp. 38–39) might appear in spring immediately after planting. The fence and mulch look conspicuously fresh, new, and unweathered. The crape myrtle is only 4 to 5 ft. tall, with trunks no thicker than broomsticks. It hasn't leafed out yet. The spirea and barberries are 12 to 18 in. tall and wide, and the Carolina jasmine just reaches the bottom rail of the fence. Evenly spaced tufts of mondo grass edge the sidewalk. The bluebeards are stubby now but will grow 2 to 3 ft. tall by late summer, when they bloom. Annuals such as vinca and ageratum start flowering right away and soon form solid patches of color. The first year after planting, be sure to water during dry spells and to pull or spray any weeds that pop through the mulch.

Three to Five Years—Shown in summer now, the planting has begun to mature. The mondo grass has spread to make a continuous, weed-proof patch. The Carolina jasmine reaches partway along the fence. The spirea and barberries have grown into bushy, rounded specimens. From now on, they'll get wider but not much taller. The crape myrtle will keep growing about 1 ft. taller every year, and its crown will broaden. As you continue replacing the annuals twice a year, keep adding compost or organic matter to the soil and spreading fresh mulch on top.

Ten to Fifteen Years—As shown here in late summer, the crape myrtle is now a fine specimen, about 15 ft. tall, with a handsome silhouette, beautiful flowers, and colorful bark on its trunks. The bluebeards recover from an annual spring pruning to form bushy mounds covered with blooms. The Carolina jasmine, spirea, and barberry have reached their mature size. Keep them neat and healthy by pruning out old, weak, or dead stems every spring. If you get tired of replanting annuals, substitute low-growing perennials or shrubs in those positions.

TEN TO FIFTEEN YEARS

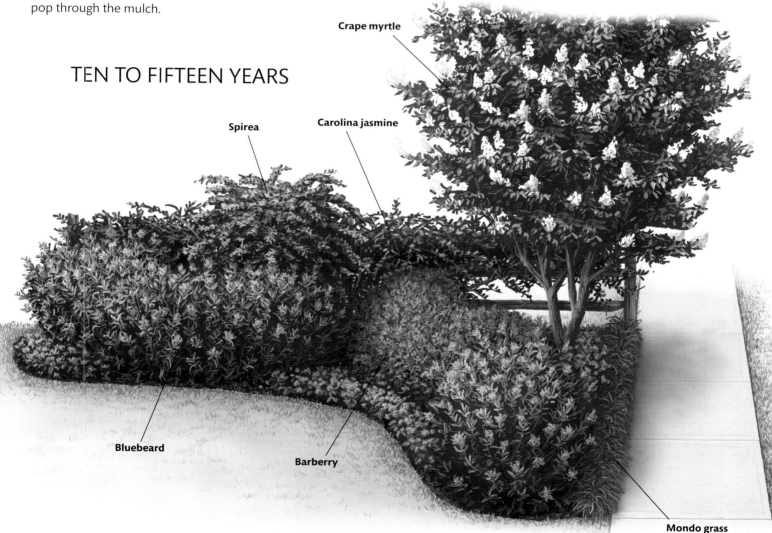

Crape myrtle

Spirea

Carolina jasmine

Bluebeard

Barberry

Mondo grass

Landscaping in an Unpredictable Climate

It's no secret that our dynamic climate is not the same today as it was 100, 50, or even 25 years ago. The thirty-year rolling temperature averages used to map USDA hardiness zones reveal cold winters moving steadily northward. Frost dates end earlier in spring and begin later in fall, extending the growing season. We've also experienced an increase in damaging storms and severe drought. On top of the infusion of beauty and the increase in property value, landscaping projects can also protect your property and neighborhood from the unpredictability of a changing climate.

This backyard plan includes pavers and plenty of low-level shrubs to reduce the amount of flooding that could occur. Reducing lawn space means there is less to mow and more space for plants to grow.

The projects in this book can help you build a more resilient landscape. Well-chosen, well-placed shade trees cool the home and reduce the energy used for air conditioning. Decreasing lawn area and increasing the area planted with layers of low-maintenance trees, shrubs, and perennials cuts back energy used on mowing, edging, and blowing, improves the soil's ability to absorb rainfall, and conserves water. Choosing native plants that are adapted to flooding and winds from tropical storms alleviates some of the risk of storm damage in coastal areas. Installing flagstone or pavers instead of a poured concrete slab patio or walkway means that more rainwater can soak into the ground rather than running off into the streets.

While the designs in this book were drawn up as easy-to-follow, broadly effective guides, you will gain even greater benefits by adapting the plant selections to your unique growing conditions. Consider the effects of intense rainfall, strong winds, severe drought, and inconsistent temperatures in your yard. If your property is exposed to wind, then choose deep-rooted, wind-resistant trees and shrubs. For flood-prone areas, plants must be able to withstand occasional root saturation or even partial submersion. Hedge against wild temperature swings by selecting a diverse mix of plants with cold and heat tolerance. In any case, following the landscape maintenance best practices outlined later in the book will help you establish strong, healthy plants.

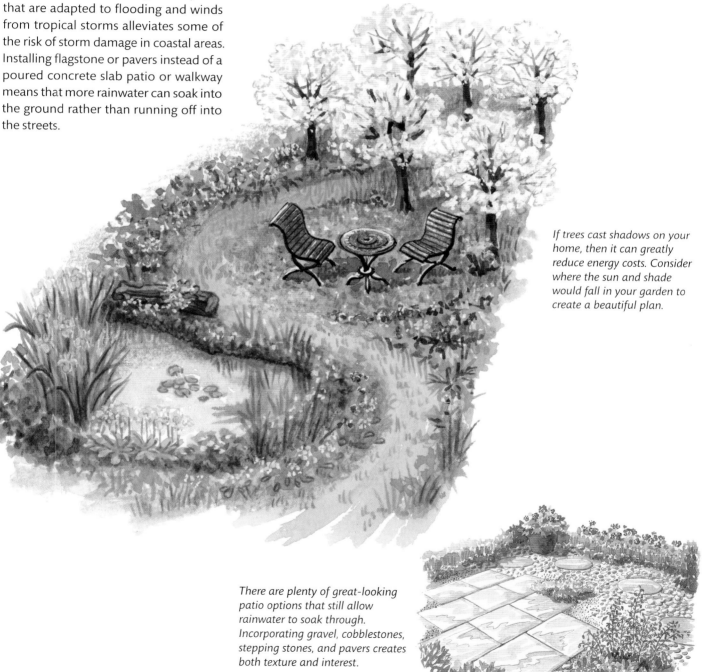

If trees cast shadows on your home, then it can greatly reduce energy costs. Consider where the sun and shade would fall in your garden to create a beautiful plan.

There are plenty of great-looking patio options that still allow rainwater to soak through. Incorporating gravel, cobblestones, stepping stones, and pavers creates both texture and interest.

Portfolio *of* Designs

This section presents designs for nearly two dozen situations common in home landscapes. You'll find designs to enhance entrances, decks, and patios. There are gardens of colorful perennials and shrubs, as well as structures and plantings to create shady hideaways, dress up nondescript walls, and even make a centerpiece of a lowly mailbox. Large color illustrations show what the designs will look like, and site plans delineate the layout and planting scheme. Texts explain the designs and describe the plants and projects appearing in them. Installed as shown or adapted to meet your site and personal preferences, these designs can make your property more attractive, more useful, and—most important—more enjoyable for you, your family, and your friends.

An Elegant Entry

MIX CLASSIC SYMMETRY AND COMFORTABLE PLANTS

A formal garden has a special appeal. Its simple geometry is soothing in a sometimes confusing world, and it never goes out of style. Traditional homes with symmetrical facades are especially suited to the elegant lines and balanced features of this design. The look is formal, but it is an easy formality featuring gentle curves, as well as straight lines, and plants whose tidy forms are produced by nature, not shears.

Unlike many formal gardens whose essentials can be taken in at a glance, this one imparts an air of mystery for visitors approaching from the street. A matching pair of crape myrtles at the corners of the property obscure that view, so that it's only when you approach the gate that the entire garden reveals itself.

A wide brick walkway creates a small courtyard with an eye-catching column of roses at its center. Neat rectangles of lawn are defined by beds of colorful annuals and perennials backed by the graceful curve of a low informal evergreen hedge. Distinctive evergreen shrubs and trees mark the corners of the design and stand guard near the front door. A picket fence reinforces the geometry of the overall design and adds a homey touch. A ground cover of low evergreen shrubs between sidewalk and fence looks good and makes this often awkward area easy to maintain.

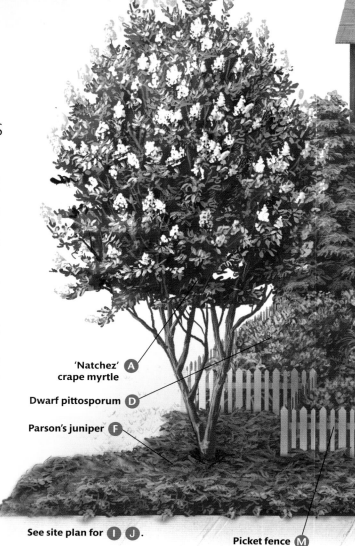

'Natchez' A
crape myrtle

Dwarf pittosporum D

Parson's juniper F

See site plan for I J.

Picket fence M

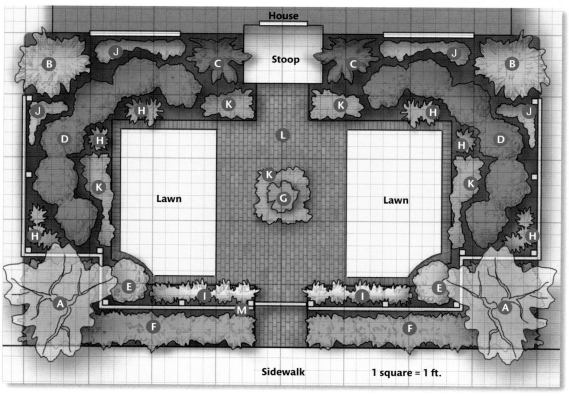

House

Stoop

Lawn

Lawn

Sidewalk   1 square = 1 ft.

B 'Yoshino' Japanese cedar

SITE: Sunny

SEASON: Summer

CONCEPT: A paved "courtyard" framed by tidy shrubs and pretty perennials creates a comfortably formal look on a small lot.

C Hollywood juniper   **L** Walk and mowing strip   **G** 'Blaze' climbing rose   **K** Annual salvia   **H** Daylily   **E** Indian hawthorn   **F** Parson's juniper

Plants & Projects

As formal gardens go, this one is very easy to maintain. The shrubs exhibit compact growth that need little pruning, and the perennials require little care.

A **'Natchez' crape myrtle** (use 2 plants)
These showy, multitrunked, small deciduous trees frame the garden with large clusters of crepe-papery white flowers blooming all summer, colorful leaves in fall, and handsome bark in winter. See *Lagerstroemia indica*, p. 150.

B **'Yoshino' Japanese cedar** (use 2)
A pair of these naturally cone-shaped, fine-textured evergreen trees mark the corners of the house. Foliage is rich green in summer, bronze in winter. See *Cryptomeria japonica*, p. 141.

C **Hollywood juniper** (use 2)
An uneven branching pattern gives this small evergreen tree an informal, sculptural look. It's narrow enough to fit on each side of the door. See *Juniperus chinensis* 'Torulosa', p. 149.

D **Dwarf pittosporum** (use 12)
This evergreen shrub makes a lush, dressy but informal hedge with shiny green leaves. Its creamy white flowers scent the air in early summer. See *Pittosporum tobira* 'Wheeleri', p. 158.

E **Indian hawthorn** (use 2)
Flowers cover the dark foliage of this low, spreading evergreen shrub in spring, followed by blue berries. Select any compact cultivar. See *Rhaphiolepis indica*, p. 159.

F **Parson's juniper** (use 22)
Rugged, gray-green evergreen shrubs edge the sidewalk, their horizontal branches held slightly above the ground. See *Juniperus davurica* 'Expansa', p. 149.

G **'Blaze' climbing rose** (use 1)
This cultivar will cover the central post with glossy green leaves and deep red flowers all summer. Buy a "rose post" at a nursery, or use an old column or other post. Plant salvias around the base. See *Rosa*, p. 161.

H **Daylily** (use 12)
Mix early- and late-blooming cultivars of this useful perennial. For this design, use orange- and yellow-flowered ones. See *Hemerocallis*, p. 144.

I **'Stella d'Oro' daylily** (use 10)
From early summer until frost, this hardy perennial's extended show of golden yellow flowers can't be beat. The grassy foliage is attractive, too. See *Hemerocallis*, p. 144.

J **Purple verbena** (use 24)
This perennial's clusters of purple flowers keep blooming from early summer to frost. See *Verbena bonariensis*, p. 166.

K **Annual salvia** (use a total of 60)
Red or purple flowers greet visitors for months. Autumn sage (see Salvia greggii, p. 163) is a good perennial substitute. See Annuals, p. 132.

L **Walk and mowing strip**
A wide brick walk (p. 176) creates a small courtyard. The brick mowing strip (p. 210) eases lawn maintenance.

M **Picket fence**
Paint or stain the fence to complement the house. See p. 198.

Graceful geometry

A curvaceous formality characterizes this welcoming design. Its outline is reminiscent of a classical amphitheater, with a variety of perennials and evergreen shrubs rising from the "stage" (lawn) in graceful ordered tiers. Making use of the existing walkway, the design relies entirely on plants for its elegant effect.

Evergreen foliage gives the planting its structure, while its eye-catching variety of leaf color and texture provides considerable interest. Flowers add color, starting with the fragrant spring blooms of daphne and dianthus, followed by the distinctive globes of hydrangea in early summer and crimson sage blossoms in summer and fall.

Take care during installation to lay out the curving beds precisely. The contrast between sheared hedges and looser "natural" hedges is pleasing to the eye, and it makes maintenance more manageable.

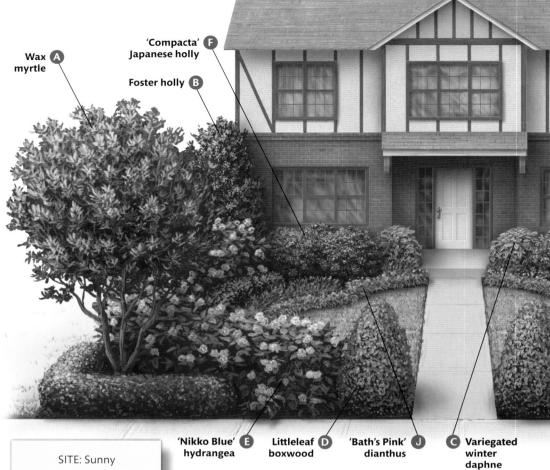

SITE: Sunny

SEASON: Summer

CONCEPT: Colorful curves demonstrate that formal doesn't have to mean rigid or square.

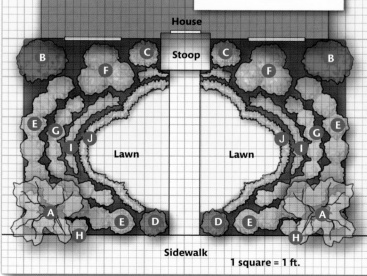

1 square = 1 ft.

Plants & Projects

Ⓐ Wax myrtle (use 2 plants)
Airy, open, multitrunked, evergreen trees with silvery bark and fragrant gray-green foliage. See *Myrica cerifera*, p.154.

Ⓑ Foster holly (use 2)
These slender evergreen trees are perfect for corners of the house. Lots of red berries. See *Ilex*, Evergreen hollies: *Ilex x attenuata* 'Foster #2', p. 146.

Ⓒ Variegated winter daphne (use 2)
Intensely fragrant white flowers on this compact evergreen shrub greet visitors at the door in spring. Glossy leaves are edged with gold. See *Daphne odora* 'Aureomarginata', p. 141.

Ⓓ Littleleaf boxwood (use 2)
A classic evergreen for the formal garden that can be sheared into any shape. In this design, it takes the form of two tall, glossy green cones, sentinels at the garden's entrance. See *Buxus microphylla*, p. 137.

Ⓔ 'Nikko Blue' hydrangea (use 18)
Thick, shiny green leaves of this deciduous shrub make a handsome "natural" hedge. Bears blue or pink snowball-like flowers in June. See *Hydrangea macrophylla*, p. 146.

Ⓕ 'Compacta' Japanese holly (use 6)
Leathery dark green leaves of this evergreen shrub contrast with the daphne; its mounding form fits below the windows. See *Ilex*, Evergreen hollies: *I. crenata*, p. 146.

Ⓐ **Wax myrtle**

Ⓑ **Foster holly**

Ⓖ **'Helleri' Japanese holly**

Ⓗ **Dwarf yaupon holly**

Autumn Ⓘ **sage**

Ⓔ **'Nikko Blue' hydrangea**

VARIATIONS ON A THEME

Whether expressed in geometry, repetition, or an unexpected way, formality can enrich a front yard.

Formal needn't mean square. This circular design comes as a pleasant surprise to a visitor entering through the modest gate at the top of the photo.

Ⓖ **'Helleri' Japanese holly** (use 16)
This evergreen shrub's neat mounds of matte green foliage are the right height to create a "layered" effect in front of the hydrangeas. See *Ilex*, Evergreen hollies: *I. crenata*, p. 146.

Ⓗ **Dwarf yaupon holly** (use 10)
An evergreen shrub that forms compact mounds of small, matte green leaves, ideal for a low hedge. See *Ilex*, Evergreen hollies: *I. vomitoria* 'Nana', p. 146.

Ⓘ **Autumn sage** (use 30)
This bushy, low-growing perennial brightens the planting from summer through fall with loose clusters of crimson flowers. See *Salvia greggii*, p. 163.

Ⓙ **'Bath's Pink' dianthus** (use 48)
Mats of grassy blue-gray foliage form an edging around the lawn. Bears wonderfully fragrant pink flowers in spring; sheared after bloom, the foliage looks fresh the rest of the year. See *Dianthus*, p. 141.

Your front yard may not be this extensive, but it can look equally stunning with a similar combination of curved paths and beds of naturalized daffodils.

Greeting Place

MAKE THE MOST OF A SMALL LOT WITH AN ENTRY GARDEN

A trend in many new neighborhoods is to crowd larger houses onto smaller and smaller lots. As a consequence, homeowners need to take advantage of every opportunity for landscaping and outdoor living their property offers. One area for doing so is the main entrance to your home.

This design makes imaginative use of the approach to the front door. Instead of a small bed of flowers by the driveway, generous beds planted with attractive trees, shrubs, and ground covers flank a spacious walkway. Made of precast pavers, the walk is really two small connected patios. Abutting the driveway, a semicircle affords ample room to get in and out of the car and to greet family and friends. Halfway to the house, a circular patio provides a place to enjoy the garden; there's even room for a bench, if you'd like.

The plants are chosen for a Florida setting, though a number will do well in other parts of the Southeast. Pink loropetalum blossoms greet visitors in spring; white African irises continue into summer. And lantana offers flowers most of the year. The evergreen trees and shrubs need little pruning and they won't outgrow their spaces. As the Japanese ligustrum matures, its shady canopy and scented white flowers will keep the entry inviting on hot summer afternoons.

Japanese ligustrum **(A)**
'Obsession' heavenly bamboo **(G)**
Asian jasmine **(I)**
Trailing lantana **(H)**
Asian jasmine **(I)**
Paving **(K)**

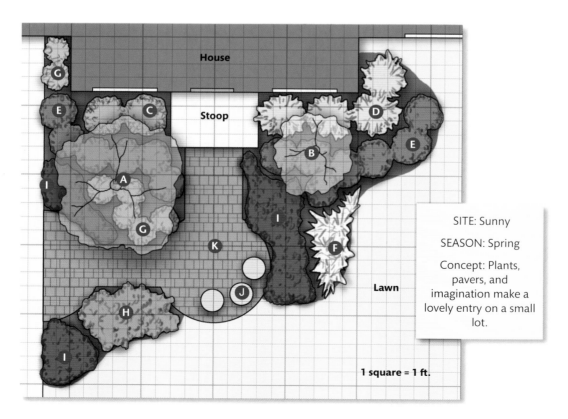

House
Stoop
Lawn

1 square = 1 ft.

SITE: Sunny

SEASON: Spring

Concept: Plants, pavers, and imagination make a lovely entry on a small lot.

C 'Bronze Beauty' cleyera

D 'Ruby' loropetalum

E 'Nana' yaupon holly

J Containers

E 'Nana' yaupon holly

I Asian jasmine

F White African iris

B Weeping yaupon holly

E 'Nana' yaupon holly

Plants & Projects

Little pruning is needed in this planting unless you'd like to coax more blooms from the loropetalum and lantana by deadheading or light pruning. Asian jasmine can be kept tidy by trimming it once in spring.

A Japanese ligustrum (use 1) An elegant tree for a narrow space. Slender trunks are topped with a crown of glossy evergreen foliage all year. In early summer the dark foliage showcases airy clusters of white flowers, and in fall, blue berries that attract birds. Grows quickly, keeping its attractive shape without pruning. See *Ligustrum japonicum*, p. 151.

B Weeping yaupon holly (use 1) The drooping branches of this small evergreen tree are clothed in small oval gray-green foliage.

Female hollies bear red berries. See Evergreen hollies: *Ilex vomitoria* 'Pendula', p. 146.

C 'Bronze Beauty' cleyera (use 2) This shrub is grown mainly for its smooth, heavily lacquered foliage. New leaves of this cultivar are bronze-tinted; mature leaves are a dark green. Flowers are small and inconspicuous. See *Ternstroemia gymnanthera* 'Bronze Beauty', p. 165.

D 'Ruby' loropetalum (use 4) An evergreen shrub, it produces layers of small rounded burgundy foliage and a lavish fringe of bright pink flowers in spring. See *Loropetalum chinense* var. *rubrum* 'Ruby', p. 152.

E 'Nana' yaupon holly (use 13) Popular as a small foundation plant or tall ground cover, this

evergreen holly grows about 3 to 5 ft. tall and wide. It keeps a pleasing rounded shape. Leaves are small and gray-green. See Evergreen hollies: *Ilex vomitoria*, p. 146.

F White African iris (use 5) From spring to early summer, lovely white flowers open above this perennial's dark green leaves. The swordlike foliage adds a dramatic vertical accent all year. See *Dietes vegeta*, p. 141.

G 'Obsession' heavenly bamboo (use 7) Low and compact, this evergreen shrub will fill in and make a good ground cover under the tree. Its fine-textured green-gold foliage turns orange in fall and bronzy red during winter. See *Nandina domestica*, p. 154.

H Trailing lantana (use 4) Masses of lavender flowers blanket this bushy perennial for much of the year. An occasional trimming encourages more blooms. See *Lantana montevidensis*, p. 150.

I Asian jasmine (use 15) This evergreen vine creates a dense mat of shiny leaves that smother weeds and tolerates some foot traffic. See *Trachelospermum asiaticum*, p. 166.

J Containers (use 3) Grow annuals in large pots to accent the planting. Shown here are complimentary bronze-leaf begonias with pink and white flowers.

K Paving If you don't want to trim precast pavers, consider concrete or a free-form flagstone design. See p. 176.

A lush entry in the shade

Less traditional than the previous design, and less expensive too, this entryway retains the existing walkway and uses lush, well-adapted plants, one of them a Florida native, to brighten a shady entrance.

All of these plants have naturally pleasing forms and maintain a size that won't overrun the small space. The ferns, mondo grass, and zebra ginger maintain a low profile that helps create a sense of spaciousness around the entryway. The taller lady palm and anise provide balance and structure near the house. Both are as undemanding and long-lived as they are beautiful. A garden bench provides a place to sit and enjoy the striking display.

Plants & Projects

Ⓐ Lady palm (use 1)
This exceptional small palm produces many reedlike stems adorned with dark, lustrous, richly patterned foliage. Lady palm may grow up to 7 ft. tall, but does so slowly. See *Rhapis excelsa,* p. 159.

Ⓑ Yellow anise (use 1)
Often sheared into hedges, this evergreen shrub also makes a nice specimen by itself. It has a pleasing conical shape and dark green leaves that smell like licorice when crushed. See *Illicium parviflorum,* p. 148.

Ⓒ Zebra ginger (use 1)
This bold shrub will brighten the doorstep with its enormous yellow-striped green leaves. Its white flowers bloom on long pendant stalks in the summer. See *Alpinia zerumbet* 'Variegata', p. 132.

Ⓓ 'Xanadu' philodendron (use 3)
With its compact mounding habit and large and shiny foliage, this evergreen shrub makes a handsome setting for the bench. See *Philodendron* 'Xanadu', p. 156.

Ⓔ Cast-iron plant (use 9)
This unusual perennial is a favorite ground cover. Its evergreen leaves are stiff, have a leathery sheen, and emerge from the ground like pickets. See *Aspidistra elatior,* p. 133.

Ⓕ Holly fern (use 11)
This extraordinary fern bears stiff, erect, dark green fronds with coarsely fringed margins.

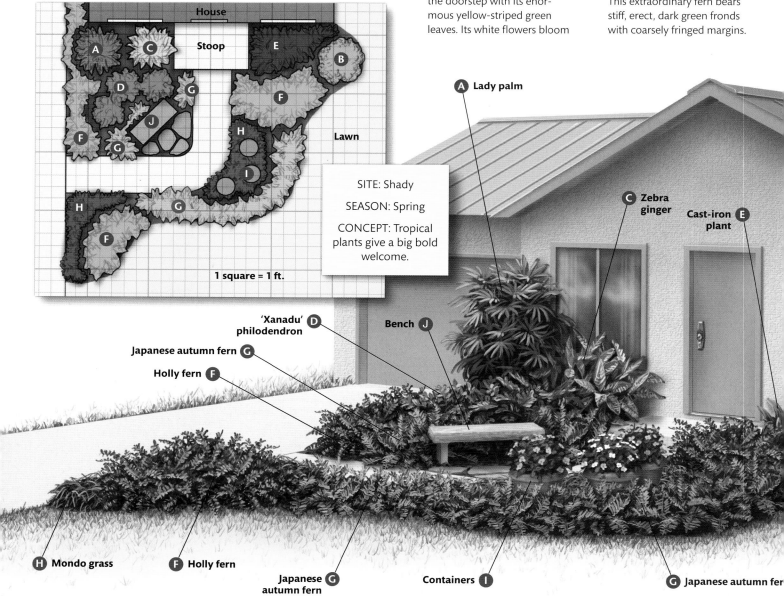

House

Stoop

Lawn

SITE: Shady

SEASON: Spring

CONCEPT: Tropical plants give a big bold welcome.

1 square = 1 ft.

Ⓐ Lady palm

Ⓒ Zebra ginger

Cast-iron plant Ⓔ

Ⓓ 'Xanadu' philodendron

Bench Ⓙ

Ⓖ Japanese autumn fern

Ⓕ Holly fern

Ⓗ Mondo grass

Ⓕ Holly fern

Ⓖ Japanese autumn fern

Containers Ⓘ

Ⓖ Japanese autumn fern

See Ferns: *Cyrtomium falcatum*, p. 142.

G **Japanese autumn fern** (use 14)
This fern's new growth is coppery red, gradually turning green with age. See Ferns: *Dryopteris erythrosora*, p. 142.

H **Mondo grass** (use 19)
Though not a true grass, this evergreen perennial has narrow dark green leaves that resemble unmowed turf. See *Ophiopogon japonicus*, p. 155.

I **Containers**
Impatiens in pastel colors fill terracotta pots in spring. Plant other annuals as the seasons change.

J **Pavers and bench**
Pavers provide a level footing for a stone bench. See p. 176.

A water garden and lush plantings turn an entry approach into a viewing platform.

VARIATIONS ON A THEME

These designs offer garden settings that are interesting in their own right, not just as accompaniments to a trip to the front door.

This formal design, right, suits its architectural setting; its split path permits a leisurely garden stroll.

A very colorful entry to a stuccoed bungalow, below, is capable of stopping traffic for a longer look.

B **Yellow anise**

F **Holly fern**

Southern Hospitality

MAKE A PLEASANT PASSAGE TO YOUR FRONT DOOR

Why wait until a visitor reaches the front door to extend a cordial greeting? An entryway landscape of well-chosen plants and a revamped walkway not only make the short journey a pleasant one, they can also enhance your home's most public face and help settle it comfortably in its surroundings.

The curved walk in this design extends a helpful "Please come this way" to visitors, while creating a roomy planting area near the house. The walk bridges a grassy "inlet" created by the free-flowing lines of the beds. The flowing masses of plants, lawn, and pavement nicely complement the journey to the door.

Two handsome trees and a skirting of shrubs form a partial screen between the walk and front door and the street. A striking collection of evergreens transforms a foundation planting near the house into a shrub border. Ground covers edge the walkway with pretty foliage, flowers, and berries. A decorative screen by the stoop marks the entry. Fragrant flowers and colorful foliage cover the screen year-round, enticing visitors to linger awhile.

The rest of the planting contributes to the all-season interest with flowers spring, summer, and fall (several fragrant). Colorful foliage and berries grace the autumn and winter months.

River birch **A**

'Emerald Heights' **E**
distylium

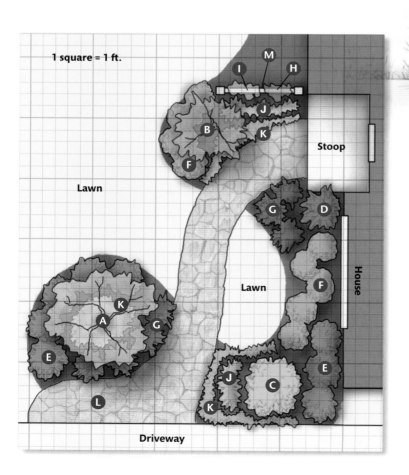

Walk **L**   Creeping willowleaf **G**
cotoneaster

1 square = 1 ft.

Lawn

Stoop

Lawn

House

Driveway

Plants & Projects

Preparing the planting beds and laying the walk are the main tasks in this design. The plantings require only seasonal cleanup and pruning once it's installed.

A **River birch** (use 1 plant)
The multiple trunks of this deciduous tree display pretty peeling bark. Leaves are glossy green in summer, colorful in fall. See *Betula nigra*, p. 134.

B **Japanese maple** (use 1)
This small deciduous tree will thrive in the shade of the taller birch, providing colorful delicate leaves and a graceful tracery of branches in winter. See *Acer palmatum*, p. 130.

C **Burford holly** (use 1)
This evergreen shrub is easily maintained in a conical form by shearing. Its large leaves are a great backdrop for a fine show of red winter

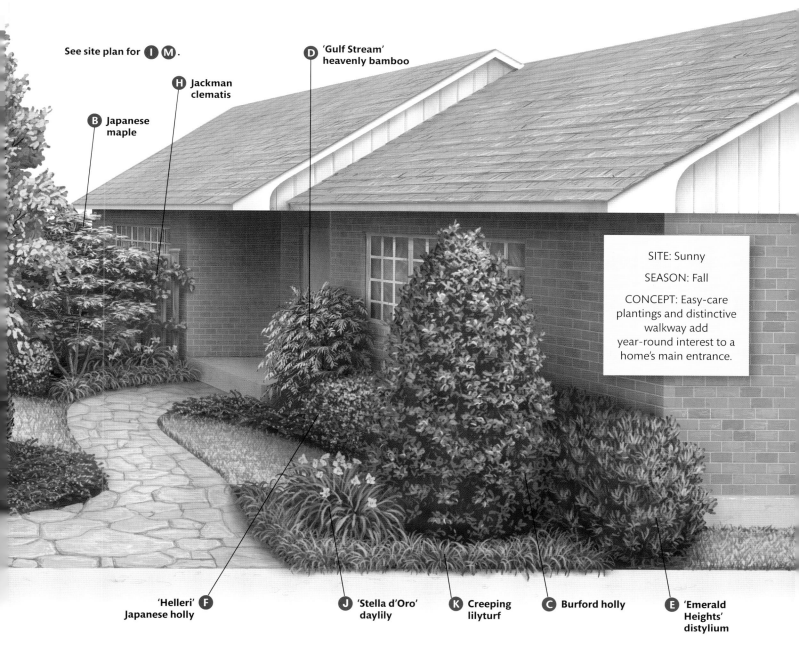

See site plan for **I** **M**.

H Jackman clematis

D 'Gulf Stream' heavenly bamboo

B Japanese maple

SITE: Sunny

SEASON: Fall

CONCEPT: Easy-care plantings and distinctive walkway add year-round interest to a home's main entrance.

F 'Helleri' Japanese holly

J 'Stella d'Oro' daylily

K Creeping lilyturf

C Burford holly

E 'Emerald Heights' distylium

---

berries. See *Ilex*, Evergreen hollies: *I. cornuta 'Burfordii'*, p. 146.

D **'Gulf Stream' heavenly bamboo** (use 1)
An evergreen shrub with leaves that change color each season. Non-fruiting cultivars are eco-friendly. See *Nandina domestica*, p. 154.

E **'Emerald Heights' distylium** (use 8)
This compact, dense, broadleaf, evergreen shrub makes an outstanding foundation plant with excellent resistance to pests and diseases. Late winter produces red flowers along the stem. See *Distylium*, p. XX

F **'Helleri' Japanese holly** (use 9)
This evergreen shrub won't outgrow its place under the windows, instead filling the space with mounds of small, shiny leaves. See *Ilex*, Evergreen hollies: *I. crenata*, p. 146.

G **Creeping willowleaf cotoneaster** (use 7)
An evergreen ground cover, this shrub displays dark purple leaves and red berries in winter. See *Cotoneaster salicifolius 'Repens'*, p. 141.

H **Jackman clematis** (use 1)
A vine that will cover the screen with violet-purple flowers in summer. See *Clematis* x *jackmanii*, p. 139.

I **Carolina jasmine** (use 1)
This evergreen vine offers something year-round. Fragrant yellow trumpet-shaped flowers greet visitors in early spring. Neat green leaves complement the blooming clematis in summer, then turn maroon for the winter. Prune annually. See *Gelsemium sempervirens*, p.143.

J **'Stella d'Oro' daylily** (use 11)
This cultivar is one of the longest-blooming daylilies, producing golden yellow flowers from late spring to frost. Even without the glowing flowers, this perennial's grassy light green foliage contrasts nicely

with the nearby lilyturf. See *Hemerocallis*, p. 144.

K **Creeping lilyturf** (use 44)
This evergreen perennial makes a grasslike mat of dark green leaves along the walk and under the birch. Small spikes of violet, purple, or white flowers appear in summer. See *Liriope spicata*, p. 152.

L **Walk**
Flagstones of random size and shape are ideal for the curved walk. See p. 176.

M **Screen**
A simple structure with narrow vertical "pickets," this is easy to make and sturdy enough to support the vines. See p. 198.

VARIATIONS ON A THEME

While they differ in many ways, each of these entryway landscapes looks just right for its house and site.

Neat as a pin, this entry features a brick courtyard, door-step garden, and a sweeping border lining a flawless lawn.

Magnificent live oaks and a lush shade garden create a fairy-tale approach to a cottage.

A curving stroll garden leads to this front door, its brick path lined with colorful annuals and perennials.

A shady welcome

If your entry is shady, receiving less than six hours of sunlight a day, try this planting scheme, which replaces the sun-loving plants from the previous design with others that prefer the shade. Overall, the emphasis is still on year-round good looks.

Shade brings out the best in southern plants. In spring, shown here, the planting is awash with flowers and fragrance. During the summer, the dogwoods make a lovely covered walkway to the front door, while shrubs, hostas, and ferns provide a cool display of attractive foliage. Much of the foliage carries on right through the winter; then the Lenten rose announces the arrival of spring and the cycle begins anew.

Plants & Projects

Ⓐ Dogwood (use 3 plants)
This is one of the finest small trees, with white flowers in spring and lovely green foliage that turns crimson in fall, when bright red berries ripen. You can prune the lower branches to create headroom for the passage to the door. See *Cornus florida*, p. 140.

Ⓑ 'Roseum Elegans' rhododendron (use 1)
This evergreen shrub is a stately presence at the corner of the house, with its glossy leaves and striking clusters of pink flowers in late spring. See *Rhododendron*, p. 161.

Ⓒ Chinese mahonia (use 1)
Leathery horizontal leaflets of this upright evergreen shrub stand out against the vertical pickets of the screen near the door. In early spring it produces fragrant golden yellow flowers, followed by showy clusters of blue berries. See *Mahonia fortunei*, p. 153.

See site plan for Ⓙ Ⓛ.

English boxwood Ⓓ

Chinese mahonia Ⓒ

Dogwood Ⓐ

Ⓔ Pink Gumpo azalea

Japanese painted fern Ⓖ

Walk Ⓚ

Lenten rose Ⓗ

Vinca Ⓘ

'Elegans' hosta Ⓕ

'Roseum Elegans' rhododendron Ⓑ

Ⓓ **English boxwood** (use 1) Sheared or pruned to a more "natural" shape, this evergreen shrub joins the mahonia in framing the entry. The dark green leaves exude a distinct fragrance. See *Buxus sempervirens*, p. 137.

Ⓔ **Pink Gumpo azalea** (use 11) These spreading evergreen shrubs are eye-catching from the street. Mounds of frilly pink flowers extend the season of bloom into early summer. See *Rhododendron*, Gumpo azaleas, p. 161.

Ⓕ **'Elegans' hosta** (use 12) The large, blue-gray, textured leaves of this perennial add color to the shade from spring until frost. White flowers are a bonus in summer. See *Hosta sieboldiana*, p. 144.

Ⓖ **Japanese painted fern** (use 12) The loveliest of ferns, its delicately colored deciduous fronds blend green, silver, and maroon. They add a lush look beneath the dogwoods. See Ferns: *Athyrium goeringianum* 'Pictum', p. 142.

Ⓗ **Lenten rose** (use 18) Among the first to flower in spring, this perennial's nodding cuplike blooms range from light green to rose, pink, or white When the flowers have faded, the evergreen foliage continues to justify the plant's prominent place in the garden. See *Helleborus orientalis*, p. 144.

Ⓘ **Vinca** (use about 130) Dark green shiny leaves and small blue flowers in spring give this creeping perennial ground cover a dainty look. It will soon carpet the beds. See *Vinca minor*, p. 167.

See p. 29 for the following:

Ⓙ **Carolina jasmine** (use 1)

Ⓚ **Walk**

Ⓛ **Screen**

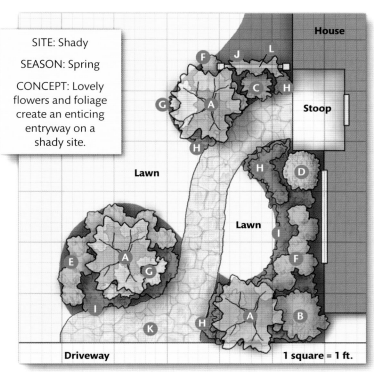

SITE: Shady

SEASON: Spring

CONCEPT: Lovely flowers and foliage create an enticing entryway on a shady site.

House

Stoop

Lawn

Lawn

Driveway

1 square = 1 ft.

A Foundation with Flair

FLOWERS AND FOLIAGE DRESS UP A RAISED ENTRY

A home with a raised entry invites down-to-earth foundation plants that anchor the house to its surroundings and hide unattractive concrete-block underpinnings. In the hospitable climate of the South, a durable, low-maintenance planting need not mean the usual lineup of clipped junipers. As this design shows, a foundation planting can be more varied, more colorful, and more fun.

Within the graceful arc of a low boxwood hedge is a balanced arrangement of shrubs in sizes that fit under windows and hide the foundation. Larger shrubs and a small tree punctuate the planting and contribute to the variety.

The predominantly evergreen foliage looks good year-round, and in spring and early summer it is a fine backdrop for a lovely floral display. White flowers sparkle on the trees and shrubs, with irises in blues, purples, and pinks at their feet. Twining up posts or over railings, the Star jasmine greets visitors with its deliciously scented creamy flowers.

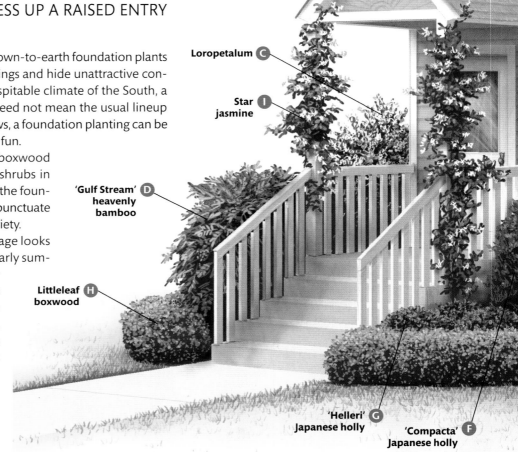

Loropetalum **C**

Star jasmine **I**

'Gulf Stream' heavenly bamboo **D**

Littleleaf boxwood **H**

'Helleri' Japanese holly **G**

'Compacta' Japanese holly **F**

Plants & Projects

Once established, the plants in this design require little maintenance beyond seasonal cleanup and a yearly pruning. To keep it tidy, the boxwood hedge will need trimming once or twice a year. Clear iris leaves as they fall.

A **Star magnolia** (use 1 plant) This small, multitrunked deciduous tree perfectly fits the corner of the house. Spring's fragrant white flowers are followed by dark green foliage that looks good all summer. See *Magnolia stellata*, p. 153.

B **Possumhaw** (use 1) Brightly colored berries decorate this deciduous shrub in fall and winter. The smooth green leaves are attractive in summer. (Also called winterberry holly.) See *Ilex decidua*, p.146.

C **Loropetalum** (use 1) | An elegant presence next to the stoop, this evergreen shrub has layers of arching branches

bearing lacy white flowers in spring and may bloom sporadically through the summer. See *Loropetalum chinense*, p. 152.

D **'Gulf Stream' heavenly bamboo** (use 3) | A colorful evergreen shrub with straight, unbranched stems and layers of lacy leaves tinged gold in spring, changing to summer green and turning orange-red in winter. It produces white flowers in the summer months. See *Nandina domestica*, p. 154.

E **Variegated pittosporum** (use 8) | This evergreen shrub brings a dressy look and year-round color with its rounded mounds of glossy gray-green leaves mottled with white. Creamy white flowers scent the air in early summer. See *Pittosporum tobira* 'Variegata', p. 158.

F **'Compacta' Japanese holly** (use 1) | Fill the corner next to the stoop with this handsome evergreen shrub. It can be shaped into a ball or cone by shearing. See *Ilex*, Evergreen hollies: *I. crenata*, p. 146.

G **'Helleri' Japanese holly** (use 3) Smaller than 'Compacta', this evergreen shrub won't outgrow its place, making tidy mounds of small, rounded, dull green leaves. See *Ilex*, Evergreen hollies: *I. crenata*, p. 146.

H **Littleleaf boxwood** (use 32) A classic sheared evergreen hedge defines the foundation garden; this compact shrub's small, glossy green leaves give it a fine texture. See *Buxus microphylla*, p. 137.

I **Star jasmine** (use 2) On early summer evenings you

can sit on the stoop and enjoy the fragrance of this evergreen vine's white flowers. Twining stems of glossy dark green leaves can climb and cover the posts. See *Trachelospermum jasminoides*, p. 166.

J **Siberian iris** (use 8) For graceful May flowers in shades of blue, yellow, or white, this perennial is a natural choice. After flowering, the erect grassy leaves contrast with the rounded pittosporum. See *Iris sibirica*, p. 148.

K **Bearded iris** (use 12) These perennials bear showier flowers than their Siberian cousins in a rainbow of colors. Blooms in midspring; stiff leaves are coarser and shorter than those of Siberian iris, but attractive. See *Iris*, p. 148.

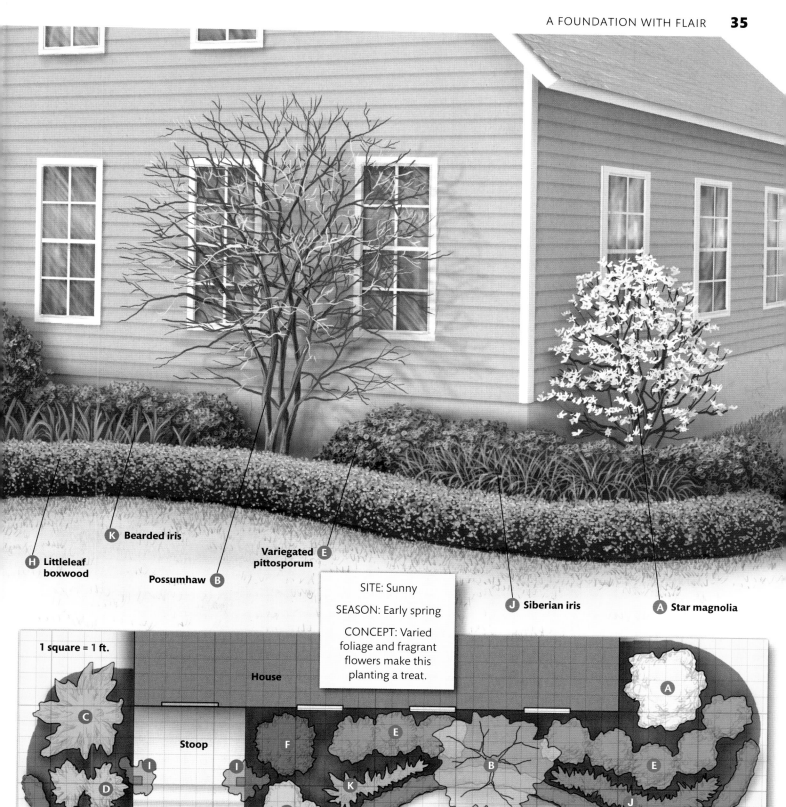

K Bearded iris

H Littleleaf boxwood

Possumhaw B

Variegated pittosporum E

J Siberian iris

A Star magnolia

SITE: Sunny

SEASON: Early spring

CONCEPT: Varied foliage and fragrant flowers make this planting a treat.

1 square = 1 ft.

House

Stoop

Steps

Sidewalk

Lawn

Setting for a shady porch

Porch sitting, one of summer's favorite pastimes, can be made even more pleasurable with this planting. Like the previous design, this one combines deciduous and evergreen plants and mixes handsome foliage and pretty flowers to look good in all four seasons. All the plants will thrive in a shady location.

The central Japanese maple screens the porch from the street without obstructing the view of sitters on the porch. Informal hedges of cherry laurel and holly skirt the porch foundation. Glossy-leaved gardenias flank the stoop behind small patches of annuals, and a grassy edging outlines the beds.

Fragrant flowers perfume the porch for months, beginning in earliest spring with witch hazel, followed by cherry laurel, and then gardenia in summer. Vine-covered porch posts and hanging pots of annuals scattered around the porch decking complete the cozy setting.

Annuals (in pots) **I**
Star **J** jasmine
Vernal **B** witch hazel
Gardenia **E**

Annuals **I**   Gardenia **E**
Lilyturf **H**
Japanese **A** maple
Variegated **G** Solomon's seal
Jackman **F** clematis
Dwarf yaupon **D** holly

Plants & Projects

Ⓐ Japanese maple (use 1 plant)
This small deciduous tree screens the porch even in winter with eye-catching sculptural branches. Choose a cultivar with cool green leaves in summer; they'll turn a vivid red in fall. See *Acer palmatum*, p. 130.

Ⓑ Vernal witch hazel (use 1)
Unusual spidery flowers appear on this deciduous native shrub in the earliest days of spring and waft their bewitching fragrance over the porch. Large leaves are golden in fall. See *Hamamelis vernalis*, p. 143.

Ⓒ 'Emerald Heights' distylium (use 5)
This compact, dense, broadleaf, evergreen shrub makes an outstanding foundation plant with excellent resistance to pests and diseases. See *Distylium*, p. XX.

Ⓓ Dwarf yaupon holly (use 5)
A small evergreen shrub that forms compact mounds of small gray-green leaves and stays just the right size for the base of the porch. See Ilex, Evergreen hollies: *I. vomitoria 'Nana'*, p. 146.

Ⓔ Gardenia (use 2)
Evergreen shrubs that flank the steps with low mounds of glossy leaves all year. The sweet scent of its white flowers will

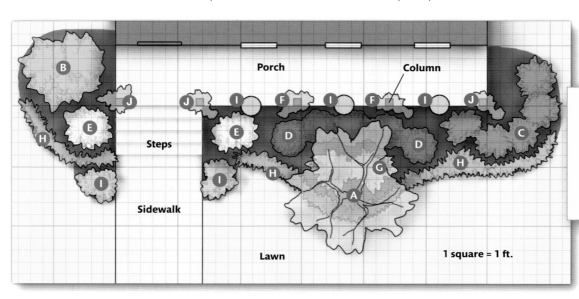

Porch   Column

B
J   **J**   **I**   **F**   **I**   **F**   **I**   **J**
E
H   **E**   **D**   **D**   **C**
Steps   **H**   **G**   **H**
I   **I**   **A**
Sidewalk

Lawn   1 square = 1 ft.

SITE: Shady

SEASON: Summer

CONCEPT: Foliage, flowers, and fragrance add to the pleasures of a sociable porch.

J Star jasmine

C 'Emerald Heights' distylium

beguile visitors in summer. 'Mystery' and 'August Beauty' are good cultivars for this spot. See *Gardenia jasminoides*, p. 142.

F **Jackman clematis** (use 2)
Large violet-purple summer flowers make this deciduous vine a natural choice for the central porch columns. See *Clematis x jackmanii*, p. 139.

G **Variegated Solomon's seal** (use 7)
Fragrant white bell-shaped flowers dangle beneath the arching stems and green-and-white leaves of this perennial in spring. See *Polygonatum odoratum* 'Variegatum', p. 158.

H **Lilyturf** (use 28)
Grasslike clumps of evergreen leaves make an attractive year-round edging. White or purple flowers in late summer. See *Liriope muscari*, p. 152.

I **Annuals**
Impatiens, begonias, and coleus provide year-round color in the beds and the porch baskets. See Annuals, p. 132.

See p. 32 for the following:

J **Star jasmine** (use 3)

VARIATIONS ON A THEME

Anything but boring, these designs illustrate some of the imaginative possibilities for foundation plantings.

This dramatic planting plays on the contrasts between foliage and flowers. Spiky agaves rise above the colorful flowers of low-growing verbena.

Pink azaleas light up this shady site. Additional evergreen shrubs and a carpet of mondo grass add year-round contrasting color and texture.

Simple and striking, in this planting a neat boxwood hedge corrals large, loose hydrangeas.

On the Street

GIVE YOUR CURBSIDE STRIP A NEW LOOK

Homeowners seldom think much about the area that runs between the sidewalk and street. At best this is a tidy patch of lawn; at worst, a weed-choked eyesore. Yet this is one of the most public parts of many properties. Planting this strip with attractive perennials, shrubs, and trees can give pleasure to passersby and visitors who park next to the curb, as well as enhancing the streetscape you view from the house. (This strip is usually city-owned, so check local ordinances for restrictions before you start a remake.)

It might help to think of this curbside strip as an island bed between two defined boundaries: the street and the sidewalk. These beds are divided further by a wide pedestrian walkway, providing ample room for visitors to get in and out of front and rear car doors. A pair of handsome evergreen trees form a gateway. The diagonal skew of this design keeps the symmetry of the plantings on either side from appearing staid. You can expand the beds to fill a longer strip, or plant lawn next to the beds.

This can be a difficult site. Summer drought and heat, pedestrian and car traffic, and errant dogs are the usual conditions found along the street. Plants have to be tough to perform well here, but they need not look tough. These combine colorful foliage and flowers for a dramatic impact from spring until fall. Evergreen foliage and clumps of tawny grass look good through the winter. The plantings beneath the trees won't grow tall enough to block your view of the street as you pull out of the driveway.

Japanese ligustrum Ⓐ

'Little Princess' spirea Ⓑ

'Crimson Pygmy' Japanese barberry Ⓒ

Ⓔ Dwarf fountain grass

'Stella d'Oro' Ⓕ daylily

Ⓓ 'Blue Pacific' shore juniper

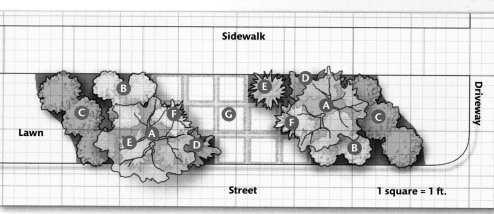

Sidewalk

Lawn

Driveway

Street

1 square = 1 ft.

Plants & Projects

Tough as they are, these plants will benefit from a generous bark mulch, which conserves moisture, helps control weeds, and makes the bed look neat. Prune the shrubs occasionally to keep them tidy and healthy. Divide the clumps of day-lilies when they get crowded.

A **Japanese ligustrum** (use 2)
The dark green, waxy leaves of this small broad-leaved evergreen tree are a perfect background for the fragrant white flowers it bears in early summer. Dark blue berries follow in fall and winter. Grows quickly; prune lower branches as necessary to accommodate visitors using the walk. See *Ligustrum japonicum*, p. 151.

B **'Little Princess' spirea** (use 6)
The small fine leaves and rosy pink flowers of this dainty deciduous shrub belie its tough nature. It will bloom happily for weeks in conditions next to the street in early summer. See *Spiraea japonica*, p. 164.

C **'Crimson Pygmy' Japanese barberry** (use 6)
The maroon leaves of this shrub turn crimson in late fall. Naturally forms a tidy mound. See *Berberis thunbergii*, p. 134.

D **'Blue Pacific' shore juniper** (use 2)
This low, trailing evergreen ground cover has handsome blue-green foliage that can stand up to street life. Makes a subtle carpet beneath the trees. See *Juniperus conferta*, p. 149.

E **Dwarf fountain grass** (use 2)
This perennial grass is a year-round presence. Fluffy flower spikes rise above neat clumps of arching green leaves in mid-summer. Flowers and foliage turn shades of gold and tan in autumn and last through the winter. See Pennisetum alopecuroides *'Hameln'*, p. 156.

F **'Stella d'Oro' daylily** (use 8)
This very popular perennial produces golden yellow flowers from late spring until frost; quite a feat considering that each flower lasts only a day. The grassy foliage is attractive, too. See *Hemerocallis*, p. 144.

G **Walk**
This design provides interest underfoot. Set the framework of pressure-treated 2x4s on a sand-and-gravel base (see p. 176); position the square precast concrete pavers in the center of each cell; and fill between paver and frame with crushed rock, tamped firm.

SITE: Sunny

SEASON: Summer

CONCEPT: Small but varied planting transforms an often neglected area and treats visitors and passersby to a colorful display.

A Japanese ligustrum

Dwarf fountain grass **E**

F 'Stella d'Oro' daylily

G Walk

B 'Little Princess' spirea

C 'Crimson Pygmy' Japanese barberry

VARIATIONS ON A THEME

Streetside gardening can be a challenge, but a thoughtful selection of tough plants can turn an awkward spot into a showpiece.

Annuals such as pansies and violas can be tucked in among perennials for additional springtime color along the street.

These brightly colored perennials and shrubs are a cheerful sight to drivers and sidewalk passersby alike.

A curbside planting can make a big, bold impression that greets visitors long before they arrive at your curb. This narrow bed consists of a row of rounded boxwoods punctuated by the slender trunks of crape myrtles.

Leafy oasis

Plants & Projects

This design features plants that thrive in shade, perfect for those cool, shady streets that make many neighborhoods so pleasant. Emphasizing foliage more than flowers, the effect is more subdued than the previous design, but still cheerful.

A pair of small trees once again anchor the design. They flower in early spring, followed by the azaleas and ajuga flanking the walk. A mix of rich green foliage, accented by the large blue leaves of the hostas, carries the planting through the summer and fall. The evergreen azaleas and ivy and the handsome form of the redbuds look good through the winter.

A Redbud (use 2 plants)
Small pink flowers line the branches of this small deciduous tree in early spring. Heart-shaped leaves turn gold in the fall. This fast-growing tree needs little pruning; just remove lower limbs. See *Cercis canadensis*, p. 138.

B Gumpo azalea (use 15)
These low, spreading evergreen shrubs form mounds of fine-textured foliage, an ideal background for the lovely display of frilly flowers that brighten the shade in late spring. Use pink or white cultivars, or both. See *Rhododendron*, p. 161.

C 'Elegans' hosta (use 12)
The huge, blue-gray, textured leaves of this perennial add cool color to the shade from spring until frost, contrasting with the finer-leaved azaleas. In late summer, white flowers peek just above the foliage. See *Hosta sieboldiana*, p. 144.

D Japanese spurge (use 100)
An ideal ground cover for semi-shade or shady areas. It has a low, shrubby growth habit and spreads by shallow lateral stems to form a dense mat of rich, deep green foliage. In early spring, tiny white flower spikes form at the branch tips. See *Pachysandra terminalis*, p. XX.

E Ajuga (use 50)
An excellent ground cover for partial shade, this evergreen perennial will quickly spread to carpet the areas next to the walk with dark green or multi-colored leaves. In late spring, the foliage is covered with erect spikes of tiny blue flowers. See *Ajuga reptans*, p. 131.

See p. 37 for the following:
F Walk

SITE: Shady

SEASON: Late spring

CONCEPT: Enhance the looks of a shady curb with lovely foliage and a spring flush of flowers.

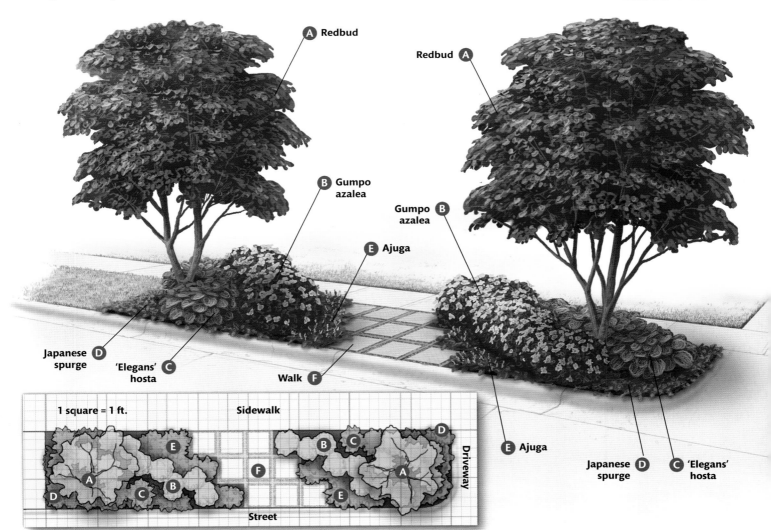

An Eye-Catching Corner

BEAUTIFY A BOUNDARY WITH EASY-CARE PLANTS

The corner where your property meets your neighbor's and the sidewalk is often a kind of grassy no-man's-land. This design defines that boundary with a planting that can be enjoyed by both property owners, as well as by passersby. Good gardens make good neighbors, so we've used well-behaved, low-maintenance plants that won't make extra work for the person next door—or for you.

Because of its exposed location, remote from the house and close to the street, this is a less personal planting than those in other more private and frequently used parts of your property. It is meant to be appreciated from a distance. Rising from low-growing plants at the edge of the lawn to the butterfly bush near the sidewalk, the design draws the eye when viewed from the house. An existing split-rail fence along the property line serves as a backdrop for the plants without hiding them from the view of neighbors or passersby. While not intended as a barrier, the planting also provides a modest psychological, if not physical, screen from activity on the street.

There's lots of bloom summer and fall, some of it fragrant, some bearing nectar that's attractive to butterflies. Flowing grasses and the evergreen foliage of shrubs and perennials carry the planting from late fall through winter. For early-spring color, consider planting daffodils among the daylilies, coneflowers, and other perennials, whose rising leaves will cover the fading bulb foliage after bloom.

Goldflame honeysuckle **C**

Chinese abelia **B**

Germander **J**

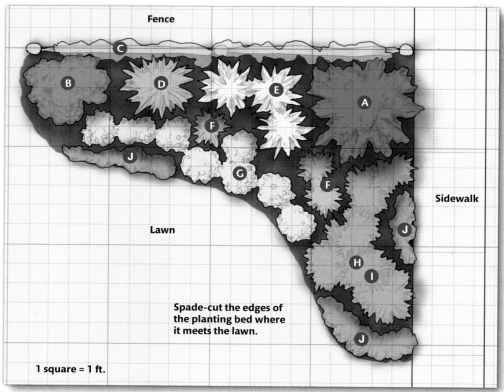

Fence

Lawn

Sidewalk

Spade-cut the edges of the planting bed where it meets the lawn.

1 square = 1 ft.

Plants & Projects

These rugged plants thrive on an open, sunny, dry site and require little care beyond seasonal pruning and removal of spent flowers. In spring, cut the fast-growing butterfly bush and the overwintered grasses close to the ground, shear the germander, and thin old growth out of the honeysuckle. During summer, snip off spent flowers from coneflower and lilies.

A **'White Profusion' butterfly bush** (use 1 plant)
The arching branches of this vase-shaped deciduous shrub carry long spikes of fragrant white flowers at their tips. Blooms from midsummer until fall. Butterflies are attracted to the flowers. See *Buddleia davidii*, p. 135.

D 'Shenandoah' switchgrass

F Dwarf fountain grass

E 'Golden Sword' yucca

A 'White Profusion' butterfly bush

I Asiatic lilies

J Germander

H Daylily

G 'Goldsturm' coneflower

Germander **J**

SITE: Sunny

SEASON: Summer

CONCEPT: A colorful planting that looks good year-round marks the property line in a neighborly fashion.

B **Chinese abelia** (use 1)
Another favorite of butterflies, this evergreen shrub bears white flowers with a delicious honeysuckle fragrance from early summer to frost. Its mound of glossy leaves contrasts with the grassy neighbors and turns purple-bronze in winter. If this plant isn't available, use glossy abelia (Abelia x grandiflora). See *Abelia chinensis*, p. 130.

C **Goldflame honeysuckle** (use 1)
Beginning in early summer, this evergreen vine covers the fence with fragrant pink-and-yellow flowers. The blue-green leaves provide cover and color through the winter. See *Lonicera* x *heckrottii*, p. 152.

D **'Shenandoah' switchgrass** (use 1)
A dense clumping perennial grass with a fairly upright growth habit. It produces attractive wispy, pink-tinged flower panicles above the foliage in summer. See *Panicum virgatum*, p. XX.

E **'Golden Sword' yucca** (use 3)
This shrubby perennial's sword-shaped evergreen leaves, striped with yellow and gold, bring a strong, spiky form to the corner planting. Tall stems bearing showy clusters of creamy flowers appear in June. See *Yucca filamentosa*, p. 169.

F **Dwarf fountain grass** (use 3)
Near the front of the planting, this perennial grass produces spreading mounds of green leaves that turn warm shades of orange and tan in autumn. Fluffy flower spikes appear in midsummer. See *Pennisetum alopecuroides* 'Hameln', p. 156.

G **'Goldsturm' coneflower** (use 8)
An improved version of the reliable old black-eyed Susan. In late summer an abundance of large, gold-and-brown, daisy-like flowers rise on stalks above clumps of dark green leaves. See *Rudbeckia fulgida*, p. 162.

H **Daylily** (use 6)
For a rugged planting of grassy, light green foliage and cheerful summer flowers, this hardy perennial can't be beat. Choose pink-flowered cultivars to blend with the germander and lilies. Use both early and late varieties to extend the season of bloom. See *Hemerocallis*, p. 144.

I **Asiatic lilies** (use 20) The large, trumpet-shaped flowers of these regal perennials add color all summer. Plant the bulbs among the daylilies, with which they'll coexist nicely. Choose white and purple cultivars for a spectacular effect. See *Lilium*, p. 151.

J **Germander** (use 12)
A great perennial for edging the bed, forming neat mounds of small, shiny evergreen leaves. In late summer, a profusion of tiny pink flowers make a soft pink haze over the foliage. See *Teucrium chamaedrys*, p.166.

VARIATIONS ON A THEME

On an acreage or a suburban lot, you can create a garden that welcomes wildlife and offers you a little slice of nature.

This corner planting shows what you can do with a small collection of colorful perennials and a fence. Brick makes an attractive edging in front of the bed and complements the red daylilies.

Nothing signals old-fashioned neighborliness like pink clematis and a white picket fence.

Large masses of brightly colored flowers don't so much catch the eye as grab it.

Simply shrubs

This design is simpler but no less attractive than the previous one. The crape myrtle flowers all summer long and has fall color and lovely bark. In spring, the Carolina jasmine is covered with deliciously fragrant, golden yellow flowers, and the spirea is a cloud of white. The shrubby bluebeard blooms for weeks in late summer and fall.

Daffodils, both large and small, join with other colorful bulbs in early spring. Seasonal plantings of annuals, replaced in spring and fall, bloom throughout the year.

This planting requires only routine pruning and cleanup. Prune the crape myrtle and bluebeard in winter, and the spirea and Carolina jasmine in early summer. Renew the mulch when you replant the annuals.

Plants & Projects

Ⓐ 'Natchez' crape myrtle
(use 1 plant)
Grown as a small multitrunked specimen, this deciduous tree bears large white flowers for months in summer. Its orangy red fall foliage and attractive bark add to the three-season show. See *Lagerstroemia indica*, p. 150.

Ⓑ 'Crimson Pygmy' Japanese barberry (use 3)
This deciduous shrub's maroon leaves turn crimson in fall, when they're joined by bright red berries. Its low, rounded form fits well beneath the crape myrtle. See *Berberis thunbergii*, p. 134.

Ⓒ 'Snowmound' spirea (use 1)
In May, the profusion of white flowers covering the arching branches of this deciduous

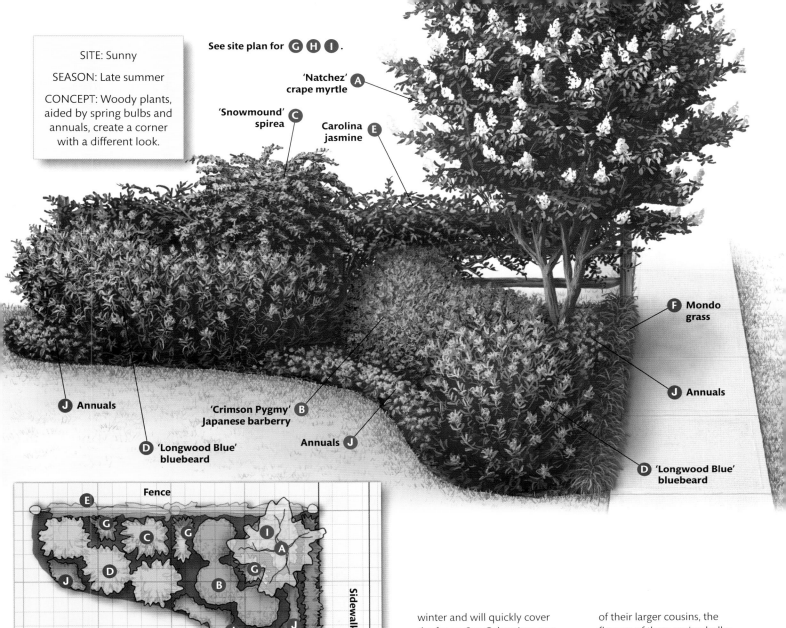

See site plan for **G** **H** **I**.

A 'Natchez' crape myrtle

C 'Snowmound' spirea

E Carolina jasmine

F Mondo grass

J Annuals

J Annuals

B 'Crimson Pygmy' Japanese barberry

D 'Longwood Blue' bluebeard

J Annuals

D 'Longwood Blue' bluebeard

Fence

E **G** **G** **C** **I** **A** **G** **D** **J** **B** **J** **J** **F** **D** **H**

Sidewalk

Lawn

1 square = 1 ft.

---

shrub truly do make it look like a mound of snow. Blue-green leaves and a neat form are attractive the rest of the season. See *Spiraea nipponica*, p. 164.

D **'Longwood Blue' bluebeard** (use 5)
Butterflies like the fringed blue flowers of this deciduous shrub; blooms from late summer to frost. Offers soft gray foliage, a tough nature, and a compact form that fits the front of the planting. See *Caryopteris x clandonensis*, p. 138.

E **Carolina jasmine** (use 1)
In early spring this tough, attractive evergreen vine gives a warm greeting to passersby with its fragrant, yellow, trumpet-shaped flowers. The slender leaves are maroon in winter and will quickly cover the fence. See *Gelsemium sempervirens*, p. 143.

F **Mondo grass** (use 60)
The thin, leathery, grassy leaves of this evergreen perennial create an attractive deep green edging along the sidewalk in all four seasons. See *Ophiopogon japonicus*, p. 155.

G **Regular daffodils**
(use 3 clumps of 12 each)
Tucked between the bare branches of deciduous shrubs, the cheerful yellow trumpet flowers of this hardy bulb are one of spring's most welcome sights. The shrubs' emerging leaves will hide the bulbs' foliage as it fades after bloom. See Bulbs: *Narcissus*, p. 136.

H **Miniature daffodils** (use 60)
Charming little reproductions of their larger cousins, the flowers of these spring bulbs will rise just above the mondo-grass foliage that edges the bed along the sidewalk. See Bulbs: *Narcissus*, p. 136.

I **Small bulbs** (use 50)
A colorful spring carpet of crocus, grape hyacinth, or glory-of-the-snow graces the area beneath the crape myrtle. Plant them 3 in. apart; any color will do. See Bulbs, p. 136.

J **Annuals** (use about 50, spaced 1 per sq. ft.)
Three patches of annuals edging the lawn and sidewalk add color to the planting all year. Plant ageratum and annual vinca for a summer show, and blue and yellow pansies for winter. See Annuals, p. 132.

A Postal Planting

MAKE YOUR DAILY MAIL RUN A PERENNIAL PLEASURE

For some, the lowly mailbox may seem a surprising candidate for landscaping. But posted like a sentry by the driveway entrance, the mailbox is highly visible to visitors and passersby. And it is one of the few places on your property that you visit nearly every day. A handsome planting like the one shown here pleases the passing public and rewards your daily journey, as well as that of your friendly letter carrier.

Plantings around mailboxes too often suffer from timidity—too few plants in too little space. This design makes a bold display, covering a good-size area with color for many months. The long-blooming perennials here are all well suited to the hot, sunny, and often dry conditions that prevail by most streetside mailboxes.

Mail arrives year-round, and no season is overlooked in this planting. Summer is the most colorful, with cheery flowers in blue, pink, red, and gold, highlighted by the yucca's eye-catching spires of creamy white blossoms. Sage, sedum, and asters continue the show through the fall. Then the evergreen foliage of many of the plants comes into its own, making the planting look fresh for visits through the winter and spring, when pink dianthus and blue phlox begin the cycle anew.

'Golden Sword' **A** yucca

Stone edging **J**

Plants & Projects

These are all tough, heat-tolerant plants, but they do best if you add a deep bark mulch to help conserve moisture. Maintenance is minimal. In early spring, cut back the old stems and renew the mulch. Then enjoy your trips to the mailbox.

A **'Golden Sword' yucca** (use 1 plant)
This shrubby perennial offers sword-shaped evergreen leaves striped with yellow and gold. Bears showy clusters of creamy flowers on tall stems in summer. See *Yucca filamentosa*, p. 169.

B **'Powis Castle' artemisia** (use 1)
A perennial that forms a large mound of lacy gray-green aromatic foliage. Can be evergreen in areas with mild winters. See *Artemisia*, p. 133.

C **'Cherry Chief' autumn sage** (use 1)
Loose clusters of cherry red flowers cover this bushy perennial from summer through fall. Evergreen in mild winters. See *Salvia greggii*, p. 163.

D **'Goldsturm' coneflower** (use 3)
This perennial makes a late-summer show of large, golden yellow, daisylike flowers with black centers, above a mound of dark green foliage. See *Rudbeckia fulgida*, p. 162.

E **'Appleblossom' yarrow** (use 6)
A tough perennial with aromatic, delicate-looking gray-green foliage. It bears flat clusters of tiny, clear pink flowers through the summer months. A fine companion for the neighboring sedum and autumn sage. See *Achillea*, p. 131.

F **'Autumn Joy' sedum** (use 3)
A perennial with interesting fleshy gray-green leaves topped by flat clusters of flowers that appear in August and mature from pink to rusty red as autumn progresses. See *Sedum*, p. 164.

G **Stoke's aster** (use 3)
From June to frost, this perennial produces pretty blue flowers atop evergreen foliage. See *Stokesia laevis*, p. 165.

H **'Bath's Pink' dianthus** (use 2)
Pick a few of this perennial's fragrant pink flowers on late-spring mail runs; enjoy the grassy evergreen foliage the rest of the year. See *Dianthus*, p. 141.

I **Moss phlox** (use 3)
Choose a pale blue-flowered variety of this evergreen perennial ground cover to creep around the yucca. Blooms prolifically for several weeks in spring. See *Phlox subulata*, p. 157.

J **Stone edging**
Keep the lawn and bed separate with an edging of small fieldstones, installed using the method described for installing a brick edging on p. 210.

SITE: Sunny

SEASON: Early summer

CONCEPT: Drought-tolerant perennials enhance your trips to the mailbox.

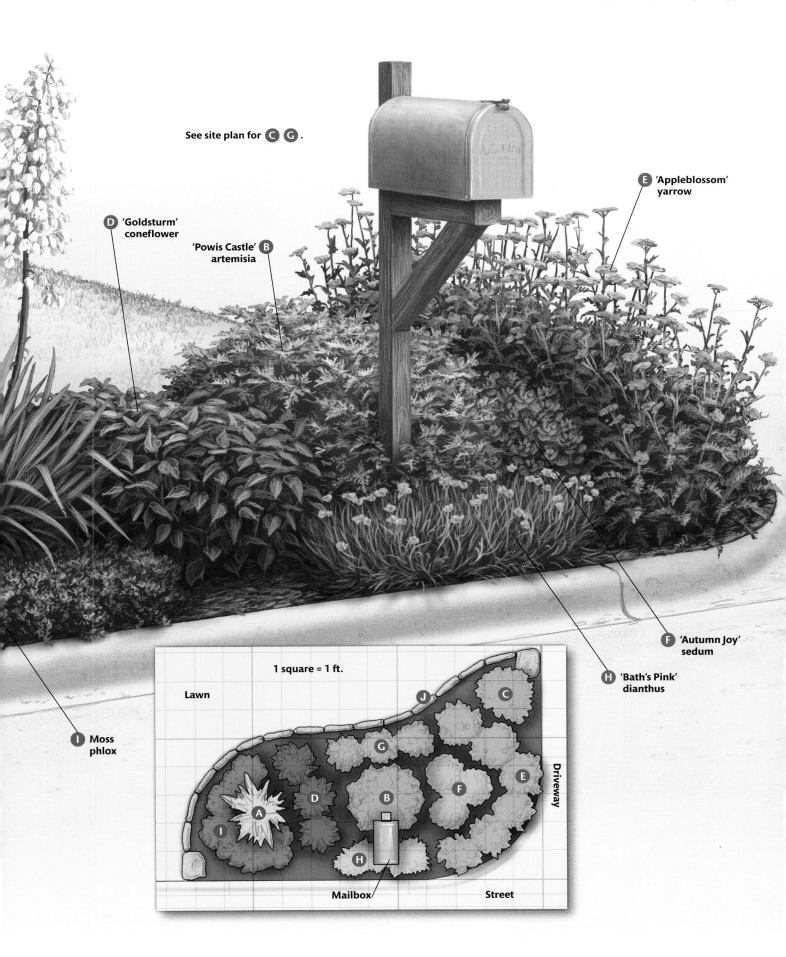

See site plan for **C** **G** .

D 'Goldsturm' coneflower

'Powis Castle' artemisia **B**

E 'Appleblossom' yarrow

F 'Autumn Joy' sedum

H 'Bath's Pink' dianthus

I Moss phlox

1 square = 1 ft.

Lawn

J

C

G

D

E

Driveway

B

A

F

I

H

Mailbox

Street

Mostly foliage

Foliage can create as much fanfare as flowers, with even less fuss. Here, a dark green carpet of mondo grass replaces the flowering ground covers in the previous design. Two forms of heavenly bamboo provide colorful foliage year-round and add to the variety of leaf textures offered by the sedum, sage, yucca, and artemisia that repeat from the previous design. The tall, spiky foliage of the spring-blooming irises alongside the mailbox looks good long after the elegant flowers have passed. Once established, these tough plants require only seasonal care and cleanup.

SITE: Sunny

SEASON: Late fall

CONCEPT: Foliage rivals flowers for eye-catching interest in this planting.

See site plan for **G**.

F 'Powis Castle' artemisia

E 'Golden Sword' yucca

B 'Obsession' heavenly bamboo

A 'Moon Bay' heavenly bamboo

H 'Autumn Joy' sedum

C Bearded iris

D Mondo grass

I Stone edging

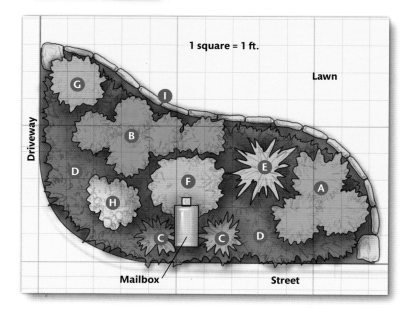

1 square = 1 ft.

Lawn

Driveway

Mailbox

Street

Plants & Projects

A **'Moon Bay' heavenly bamboo** (use 3 plants) A small evergreen shrub whose lacy leaves change color with the seasons: gold in spring, green in summer, and a lovely red or burgundy in fall and winter. Forms an upright clump about 2 ft. tall and rarely needs pruning. See *Nandina domestica*, p. 154.

B **'Obsession' heavenly bamboo** (use 5) Another dwarf cultivar, this evergreen shrub has a lower, more spreading growth habit than 'Moonbay', with the same striking foliage. See *Nandina domestica*, p. 154.

C **Bearded iris** (use 2) In midspring this perennial's large showy flowers

rise on stiff stalks above a clump of thick, swordlike green foliage. Choose a cultivar with blue flowers, which will stand out against the artemisia. See *Iris*, p. 148.

D **Mondo grass** (use 50 sprigs) Carpet the planting with the rich dark green, grassy leaves of this evergreen perennial, which will highlight the other plants. See *Ophiopogon japonicus*, p. 155.

See p. 44 for the following:

E **'Golden Sword' yucca** (use 1)

F **'Powis Castle' artemisia** (use 1)

G **'Cherry Chief' autumn sage** (use 1)

H **'Autumn Joy' sedum** (use 1)

I **Stone edging**

VARIATIONS ON A THEME

On the accompanying pages, we've featured designs that will enhance any mailbox. But the box itself can also be an attraction.

This streaky blue box is an excellent foil for the red-orange flowers of the honeysuckle twined around the post.

The colors of this box and post work nicely with the surrounding floral display.

White-flowering clematis highlights the old-fashioned charm of this antique postbox.

Landscaping a Low Wall

A COLORFUL TWO-TIER GARDEN REPLACES A BLAND SLOPE

Some things may not love a wall, but plants and gardeners do. For plants, walls offer warmth for an early start in spring and good drainage for roots. Gardeners appreciate the rich visual potential for composing a garden on two levels, as well as the practical advantage of working on two relatively flat surfaces instead of a single sloping one. If you have a wall, or have a place to put one, grasp the opportunity for some handsome landscaping.

This design places two complementary perennial borders above and below a wall bounded at one end by a set of stairs. While each bed is relatively narrow, when viewed from the lower level the two combine to form a border almost 10 ft. deep, with plants rising to eye level or more. The planting can be extended with the same or similar plants.

Building the wall that makes this impressive sight possible doesn't require the time or skill it once did. Nor is it necessary to scour the countryside for tons of fieldstone or to hire an expensive contractor. Thanks to precast retaining-wall systems, a knee-high do-it-yourself wall can be installed in as little as a weekend. More experienced or ambitious wall builders may want to tackle a natural stone wall, but anyone with a healthy back (or access to energetic teenagers) can succeed with a prefabricated system.

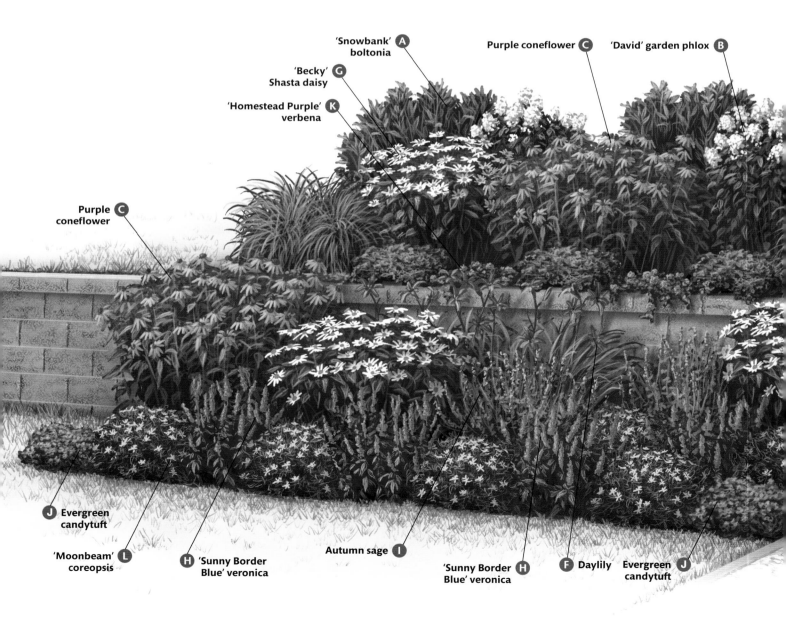

Plants & Projects

Drifts of blues, whites, yellows, and pinks, a dash of cherry red, and the flash of butterfly wings keep the garden popping with color from summer through fall. For more color in spring, plant small bulbs such as crocus or grape hyacinth throughout the beds. Care is basic: spring and fall cleanup, snipping spent flowers, and dividing a plant now and then.

A 'Snowbank' boltonia (use 2)
White daisylike flowers cover this tough perennial for three to five weeks in fall. An upright plant with fine blue-green leaves, it never needs staking. See *Boltonia asteroides*, p. 135.

B 'David' garden phlox (use 3)
A sturdy perennial topped with clusters of clear white, fragrant flowers in late summer. It forms a patch of upright stems clothed in healthy green leaves, mak-ing a pleasing backdrop for the plants in front of it. See *Phlox paniculata*, p. 156.

C Purple coneflower (use 9)
Thick flower stalks rise above this perennial's clump of dark green foliage in midsummer, displaying large daisylike blos-soms. Each flower has dark pink petals surrounding a dark central cone. Leave some seed heads for winter interest and the finches they attract. See *Echinacea purpurea*, p. 141.

D 'Caesar's Brother' Siberian iris (use 4)
The erect grassy leaves of this perennial provide an inter-esting spiky look along the wall, and the graceful flowers add deep purple color in late spring. See *Iris sibirica*, p. 148.

E Gold moneywort (use 4)
Planted at the feet of the irises, the bright yellow, coin-shaped leaves of this creeping perennial spill over the wall. Yellow flowers in summer complement the coreopsis in the lower bed. See *Lysimachia nummularia* 'Aurea', p. 153.

F Daylily (use 5)
Grassy foliage and colorful trumpet-shaped flowers, fresh every day, make this perennial a lovely centerpiece for the lower bed. Choose a cultivar with maroon flowers to blend with the pink coneflowers nearby, or mix several kinds and colors to give a longer blooming period. See *Hemero-callis*, p. 144.

G 'Becky' Shasta daisy (use 9)
This popular perennial's big white daisies bloom all sum-mer on sturdy stalks that never need staking. The shiny foliage looks good through the winter. See *Chrysanthemum* x *super-bum*, p. 139.

H 'Sunny Border Blue' veron-ica (use 6)
Lustrous green crinkled leaves topped with bright blue flower spikes make this peren-nial a cheerful recurring presence in the garden. It will bloom from early summer to frost if you clip off the spent flow-ers. See *Veronica*, p. 167.

I Autumn sage (use 2)
A bushy low-growing perennial with loose clusters of bright red flowers that keep coming all summer and fall. See *Salvia greggii*, p. 163.

J Evergreen candytuft (use 6)
An excellent evergreen pe-rennial for a wall, with a low, rounded form that falls loosely over the edge. It's topped with clusters of white flowers. See *Iberis sempervirens*, p. 146.

K 'Homestead Purple' verbena (use 2)
This perennial also trails over the edge of the wall and bears purple flowers from spring to frost if you clip off the spent blossoms. See *Verbena canadensis*, p. 167.

L 'Moonbeam' coreopsis (use 6)
Edging the lower bed, this perennial's tidy mound of fine foliage sparkles for months with small yellow flowers. See *Coreopsis verticillata*, p. 139.

M Retaining wall and steps
This 2-ft.-tall wall and the steps are built from a precast concrete block system. Select a color that complements your house. See p. 188.

N Path
Gravel is an attractive, informal surface, easy to install and to maintain. See p. 176.

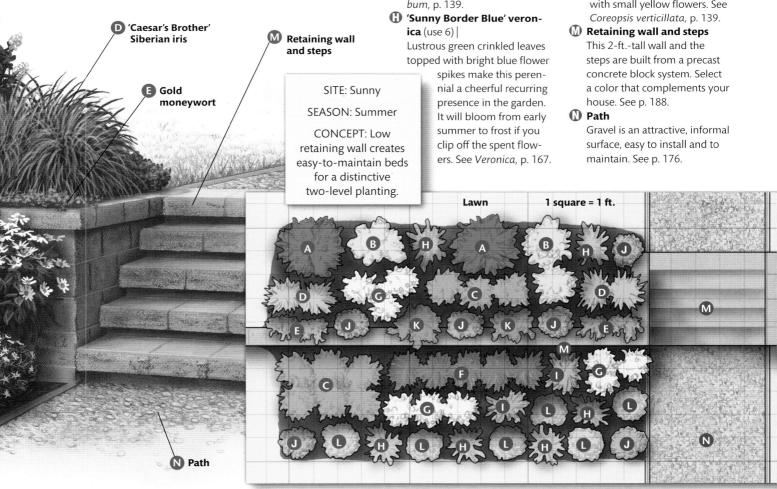

D 'Caesar's Brother' Siberian iris

E Gold moneywort

M Retaining wall and steps

SITE: Sunny

SEASON: Summer

CONCEPT: Low retaining wall creates easy-to-maintain beds for a distinctive two-level planting.

Lawn   1 square = 1 ft.

N Path

A late-season treat

This design adds flowers and colorful foliage to the wall garden to bolster its appeal in fall. The backbone of the fall planting remains the long-flowering summer perennials of the previous plan, but some new additions make autumn a satisfying encore to the summer show.

With flowers in blues and pinks, the new plants fit right into the overall color scheme. Bluebeard and pincushion flower attract butterflies, and the pink flowers of sedum are pretty accents at the garden edges. Blazing star's striking purple flower spikes have become distinctive seed heads by fall, when, along with the feathery plumes and golden leaves of dwarf fountain grass, they add mellow color to the scene.

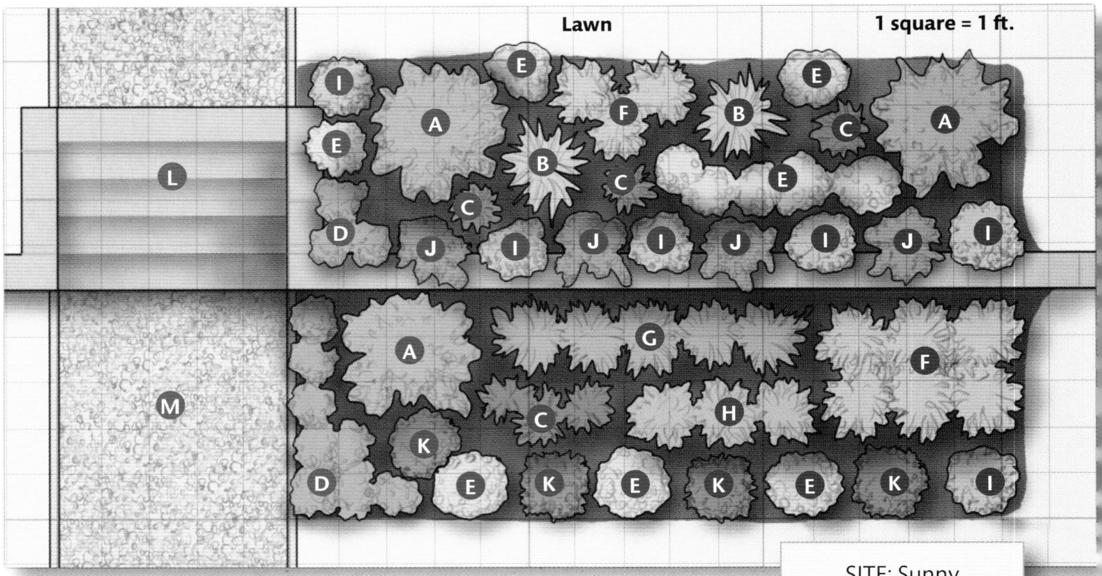

Lawn

1 square = 1 ft.

SITE: Sunny

SEASON: Early fall

CONCEPT: New additions enhance the wall garden's appeal during the autumn months.

A 'Longwood Blue' bluebeard

C Blazing star

B Dwarf fountain grass

E 'Butterfly Blue' pincushion flower

Purple F coneflower

J 'Homestead Purple' verbena

I Evergreen candytuft

L Retaining wall and steps

M Path

D 'Vera Jameson' sedum

C Blazing star

E 'Butterfly Blue' pincushion flower

G Daylily

H 'Becky' Shasta daisy

K 'Moonbeam' coreopsis

Plants & Projects

Ⓐ 'Longwood Blue' bluebeard
(use 3 plants)
The pretty blue fringed flowers on this deciduous shrub bloom from late summer to frost. Soft gray foliage makes a compact mound after the plant is cut back each spring. See *Caryopteris* x *clandonensis*, p. 138.

Ⓑ Dwarf fountain grass (use 2)
This perennial grass is most striking in fall, when its cascading mound of green leaves turns gold or tan beneath fluffy flower spikes held on arching stalks. Looks good far into winter, too. See *Pennisetum alopecuroides* 'Hameln', p. 156.

Ⓒ Blazing star (use 6)
This durable perennial's tall dense spikes of purple flowers are eye-catching from midsummer on. It combines beautifully with its garden neighbor and prairie companion, purple coneflower. Flowers are great for cutting and drying. See *Liatris spicata*, p. 151.

Ⓓ 'Vera Jameson' sedum (use 11)
A low-growing perennial next to the steps, where its distinctive purple-tinged succulent leaves can be appreciated close up. Flat clusters of pink flowers top the floppy stems in late summer and dry to a crisp brown in winter. See *Sedum*, p. 164.

Ⓔ 'Butterfly Blue' pincushion flower (use 11)
For lots of sky blue color near the steps, you can't beat this little perennial. Bloom begins in May and goes on until frost if you trim spent blossoms. See *Scabiosa columbaria*, p. 163.

See p.49 for the following:

Ⓕ Purple coneflower (use 9)

Ⓖ Daylily (use 5)

Ⓗ 'Becky' Shasta daisy (use 3)

Ⓘ Evergreen candytuft (use 6)

Ⓙ 'Homestead Purple' verbena (use 4)

Ⓚ 'Moonbeam' coreopsis (use 4)

Ⓛ Retaining wall and steps

Ⓜ Path

VARIATIONS ON A THEME

A low wall provides a wealth of landscaping opportunities: plantings above and below the wall as well as patios and walkways.

A retaining wall stepped back from the sidewalk, as shown here, creates a natural space for a garden on two levels. Plants that drape or cascade over the wall are particularly effective.

This stunning wall showcases roses and boxwoods. Apart from keeping the boxwoods closely pruned, maintenance is as minimal as the design.

Plantings surrounding this low wall set the stage for a path and small patio.

Gateway Garden

ARBOR AND PLANTINGS MAKE A HANDSOME ENTRY

Entrances are an important part of any landscape. They can welcome visitors onto your property; highlight a special feature, such as a rose garden; or mark the passage between two areas with different character or function. The design shown here can serve in any of these situations. A waist-high hedge of evergreen hollies creates a friendly, attractive barrier, just enough to signal the confines of the front yard. The simple wisteria-covered arbor provides welcoming access, particularly when it is enveloped in the pleasing aroma of the vine's striking flowers.

Curved planting beds face the house, defined by a lower, more informal hedge of evergreen azaleas. At one end, a holly forms a canopy for shade-loving astil- bes, with their feathery foliage and long summer display of white flower plumes. Flanking the arch, verbena adds months of purple flowers in summer and fall. Spring, however, offers the most bloom, with pink flowers covering the azaleas, low patches of moss phlox, and lavender flower clusters dangling from the wisteria like bunches of aromatic grapes.

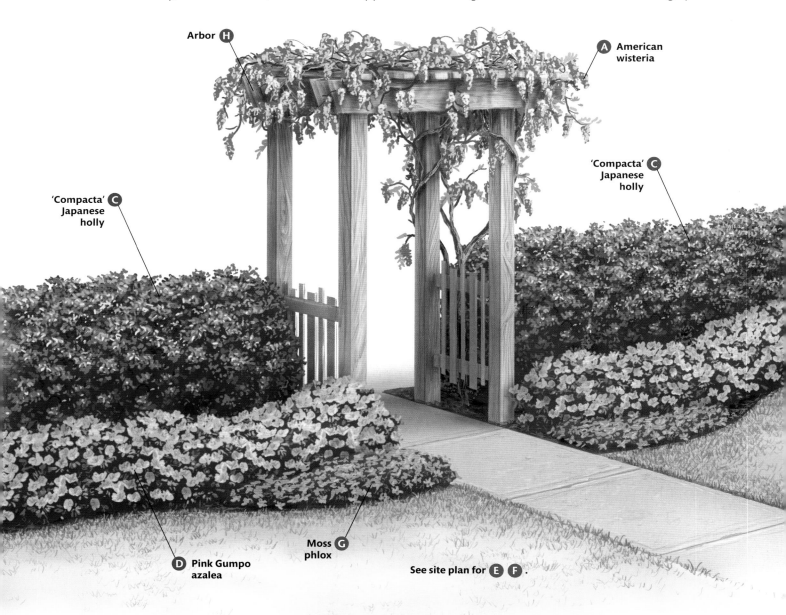

Arbor **H**

A American wisteria

'Compacta' **C** Japanese holly

'Compacta' **C** Japanese holly

D Pink Gumpo azalea

Moss **G** phlox

See site plan for **E** **F** .

Sidewalk

Existing walkway

Lawn

1 square = 1 ft.

B Yaupon holly

D Pink Gumpo azalea

SITE: Sunny

SEASON: Spring

CONCEPT: An arbor, hedge, and simple plantings define boundaries and provide an inviting entry.

Plants & Projects

On the planting plan shown here, the small bed could be tucked between the arbor and a driveway or the wall of a house. You can expand the design in either direction by extending the hedges and adding more perennials. The structures and plantings are easy to build, install, and care for. After the tree, hedges, and wisteria are trained and shaped to your taste, seasonal pruning will keep them tidy.

A **American wisteria** (use 1 plant) A vigorous deciduous vine with spectacular clusters of fragrant purple, blue, or white flowers in spring. Prune in midsummer to control its size and to stimulate abundant bloom. See *Wisteria frutescens*, p. 168.

B **Yaupon holly** (use 1) A small, tough, easy-to-grow evergreen tree with glossy dark green leaves and masses of red berries. Buy a multitrunked specimen and prune it for the best display of attractively crooked trunks and branches. See *Ilex*, Evergreen hollies: *I. vomitoria*, p. 146.

C **'Compacta' Japanese holly** (use 8) The dense twiggy habit and small evergreen leaves make this an excellent shrub for a sheared hedge, as we've shown here, or you can prune it more lightly for an informal effect. Either way, prune it in summer. See *Ilex*, Evergreen

hollies: *I. crenata*, p. 146.

D **Pink Gumpo azalea** (use 16) This low-growing evergreen shrub is well suited to the informal hedge that defines the curved edge of the bed. Clusters of large pink flowers arrive in late spring. Prune in early summer. See *Rhododendron*, p. 161.

E **White astilbe** (use 5) The white plumelike flowers of this hardy perennial shine out from the shade of the holly tree in summer. When not blooming, mounds of dark green, deeply divided leaves are an effective ground cover. See *Astilbe*, p. 133.

F **Purple verbena** (use 14) This perennial's clusters of small purple flowers seem to float in the air above mats of low foliage. Blooms from early summer to frost, attracting butterflies as a bonus. See *Verbena bonariensis*, p. 166.

G **Moss phlox** (use 10) Edging the walkway, this tough evergreen ground cover will creep under the azaleas to form a mat of prickly leaves covered with flowers in spring. Choose a pale pink cultivar that complements the azaleas. See *Phlox subulata*, p. 157.

H **Arbor** You can build this simple arbor in a weekend. Its 2x6 posts are sturdy enough to support the vigorous wisteria. You can stain it, or let the wood weather naturally. See p. 206.

VARIATIONS ON A THEME

Gateways mark boundaries and entice passage. These gates, with their hedges and plantings, provide transition between different areas on a property.

The unruly, if colorful, viny mop atop this gate makes an amusing contrast to the tidy evergreens and potted plants at its feet.

An impressive piece of architecture on its own, this entry arch is the right size and style for the wide, formal planting beds that flank it.

Elaborate and substantial borders funnel strollers toward a small gate in a large hedge.

Fancy a fence?

For many people, a picket fence and vine-covered arbor represent old-fashioned neighborly virtues. The fence here is a natural extension of the arbor presented in the previous pages. A narrower barrier than the hedge, it leaves room in the curving beds for larger shrubs and provides something for roses and jasmine vine to scramble over.

This design features camellias, whose flowers and evergreen foliage keep the entry beautiful all year. Trumpet creeper attracts hummingbirds to the arbor, while purple coneflower offers bright blossoms during the dog days of summer.

Plants & Projects

Ⓐ **Trumpet creeper** (use 2)
This vigorous deciduous vine will quickly cover the arbor with thick stems and large dark green leaves. Bears large clusters of coral-red flowers all summer long. See *Campsis radicans*, p. 137.

Ⓑ **Lady Bank's rose** (use 2)
Trained along the top of the fence, this climbing rose bears clusters of double yellow flowers that are a charming sight in spring. Glossy green leaves look good for many months. See *Rosa x banksiae*, p. 161.

Ⓒ **Star jasmine** (use 2)
This evergreen vine has stiff, woody stems that form bushy mounds against the fence. Sweetly fragrant white flowers bloom for weeks in early summer among glossy dark green leaves. See *Trachelospermum jasminoides*, p. 166.

Ⓓ **'Royal Purple' smoke tree** (use 1)
The dark purple foliage of this large deciduous shrub turns gold or orange in the fall. Bears

fluffy plumes of pink flowers in summer, a striking sight in combination with the purple leaves. Remove lower limbs to accommodate underplanting. See *Cotinus coggygria*, p.140.

E **Carolina jasmine** (use 2)
This tough evergreen vine spreads to form a ground cover beneath the smoke tree. Its fragrant yellow flowers are a treat in early spring. Prune as needed in midsummer to keep it from outgrowing its spot. See *Gelsemium sempervirens*, p. 143.

F **Camellia** (use 3)
These large evergreen shrubs are a handsome presence here, with their glossy dark green leaves and elegant white, pink, or rose flowers.

Combine different cultivars for color and to distribute bloom from late fall to spring. See *Camellia*, p. 137.

G **'Goldsturm' coneflower** (use 8)
An improved version of the reliable perennial sometimes called "black-eyed Susan," this cultivar has large, golden yellow, daisylike blooms with

black central cones. It produces masses of flowers in late summer above compact mounds of deep green foliage. See *Rudbeckia fulgida*, p. 162.

H **Vinca** (use about 12)
A perennial ground cover whose dense mats of shiny green leaves will quickly fill the space beneath the camellias and out to the walkway. Bears

small blue flowers in spring. See *Vinca minor*, p. 167.

I **Fence**
Alternating wide and narrow "pickets," this low fence varies slightly from the classic pattern but is easy to build. See p. 206.

See p. 53 for the following:

J **Purple verbena** (use 8)

K **Arbor**

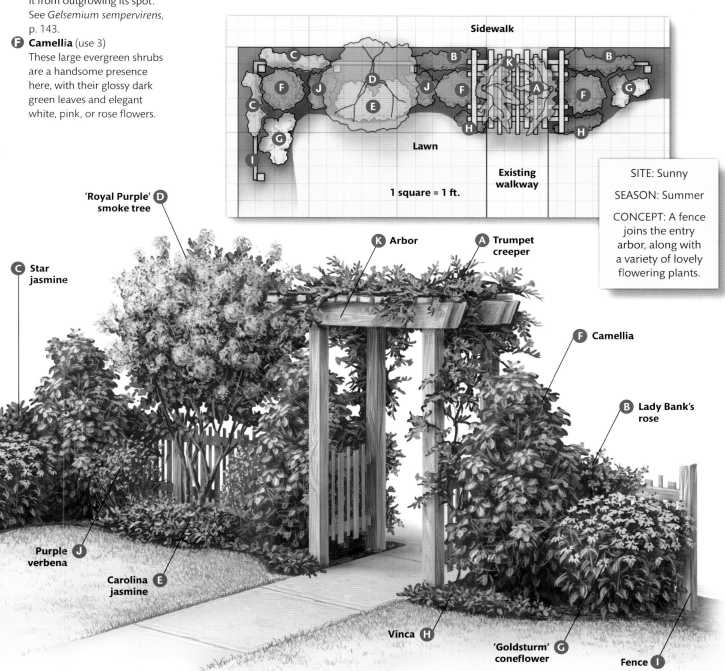

Sidewalk

Lawn

Existing walkway

1 square = 1 ft.

SITE: Sunny

SEASON: Summer

CONCEPT: A fence joins the entry arbor, along with a variety of lovely flowering plants.

'Royal Purple' **D** smoke tree

K Arbor

A Trumpet creeper

C Star jasmine

F Camellia

B Lady Bank's rose

Purple **J** verbena

Carolina **E** jasmine

Vinca **H**

'Goldsturm' **G** coneflower

Fence **I**

A Pleasant Passage

RECLAIM A NARROW SIDE YARD FOR A SHADE GARDEN

Many residential lots include a slim strip of land between the house and a property line. Usually overlooked by everyone except children and dogs racing between the front yard and the back, this often shady corridor can become a valued addition to the landscape.

In the design shown here, a flagstone path curves gently through a selection of trees, shrubs, and perennials to make a garden that invites adults, and even children, to linger as they stroll from one part of the property to another.

The wall of the house and a tall, opaque fence on the property line shade the space most of the day and give it a closed-in feeling, like a long empty hallway or a narrow room. The curved path makes the corridor seem wider, and the plants clustered at the bends create cozy "garden rooms." Entrances at each end are marked by pretty broad-leaved evergreens whose flowers entice visitors in early summer and fall. The handsome foliage and striking flowers of azaleas form the "walls" of the garden rooms. An edging of painted ferns, mondo grass, and astilbes adds color at their feet, while a magnolia about halfway along the path provides a light roof of fragrant flowers and flashing silvery leaves.

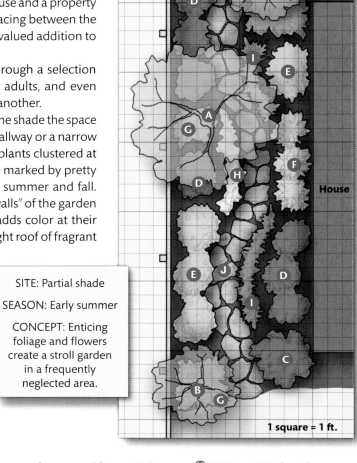

SITE: Partial shade

SEASON: Early summer

CONCEPT: Enticing foliage and flowers create a stroll garden in a frequently neglected area.

1 square = 1 ft.

Plants & Projects

Lay the flagstone path first, taking time to make graceful curves— they're instrumental in making the space seem larger than it is. Upkeep is minimal: just spring and fall cleanup, pruning shrubs to size and shape, and renewing the mulch every year or two.

A Sweet bay magnolia (use 1) Sheltering the path in the middle of the garden, this graceful deciduous tree blooms with fragrant, creamy white flowers in early summer. Its glossy silver-green leaves sparkle in the breeze and can be evergreen in areas with mild winters. See *Magnolia virginiana*, p. 153.

B Japanese ligustrum (use 2) These small trees mark the entrances to the garden with glossy evergreen leaves that showcase fragrant white flowers in early summer and dark blue-black berries in fall and winter. Grows narrowly upright, with multiple trunks. Remove the lower limbs. See *Ligustrum japonicum*, p. 151.

C 'Jean May' camellia (use 1) From late fall into early winter, this popular evergreen shrub produces masses of lovely pink double flowers. Glossy green leaves and compact upright form are attractive year-round. See *Camellia sasanqua*, p. 137.

D 'George Lindley Taber' azalea (use 7) Noted for its large, light pink spring flowers, this evergreen azalea also offers a loose, soft form that is pleasing beside the path throughout the year. See *Rhododendron*, p. 161.

E Plumleaf azalea (use 4) This deciduous shrub adds as much as a month of midsummer color—longer than most azaleas—with its large clusters of orange-red flowers. Delicately textured foliage shows well against the fence, too. See *Rhododendron prunifolium*, p. 161.

F Gold-dust aucuba (use 3) Large leathery green leaves speckled with bright yellow make this rugged evergreen a bright spot in the shade next to the house. See *Aucuba japonica 'Variegata'*, p. 134.

G Japanese painted fern (use 14) Lovely deciduous ferns add a lush, rich touch beneath the ligustrums, their delicately painted fronds blending green, silver, and maroon. See Ferns: *Athyrium goeringianum 'Pictum'*, p. 142.

H White astilbe (use 5) Mounds of dark green, deeply divided leaves of this perennial dress up the edge of the path all season and are a perfect backdrop for the plumelike flowers that appear in June. Choose a white-flowered cultivar. See *Astilbe*, p. 133.

I Mondo grass (use 1 per sq. ft.) The thin, leathery, grassy leaves of this evergreen perennial create an attractive ground cover edging the path. See *Ophiopogon japonicus*, p. 155.

J Path Providing just the right touch of informality, flagstones in random sizes trace a gracefully curving route through the planting. See p. 176.

A Sweet bay magnolia

B Japanese ligustrum

F Gold-dust acuba

D 'George Lindley Taber' azalea

G Japanese painted fern

B Japanese ligustrum

E Plumleaf azalea

H White astilbe

J Path

I Mondo grass

C 'Jean May' ca-mellia

A handsome brick-lined gravel walk, an attractive gate, window boxes, and vines create a passage of formal simplicity.

Evergreen privacy

If you like hedges and have a wide enough space to accommodate one, try this design. Here, a bank of evergreen wax myrtles helps enclose an equally appealing stroll garden. Other additions include crape myrtles at the entrances, white-flowering azaleas beside the house, holly ferns tucked along the hedge, and hostas with striking blue leaves edging the walk. For more color in spring, plant clusters of your favorite bulbs beneath the crape myrtles and wherever space allows along the path.

VARIATIONS ON A THEME

A narrow passage is a design challenge. These examples succeed in creating spaces you want to, rather than have to, walk through.

Shade-loving plants and a steppingstone path offer a slice of woodland in this passage.

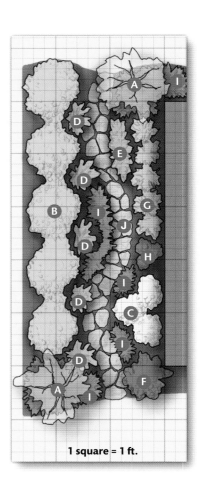

1 square = 1 ft.

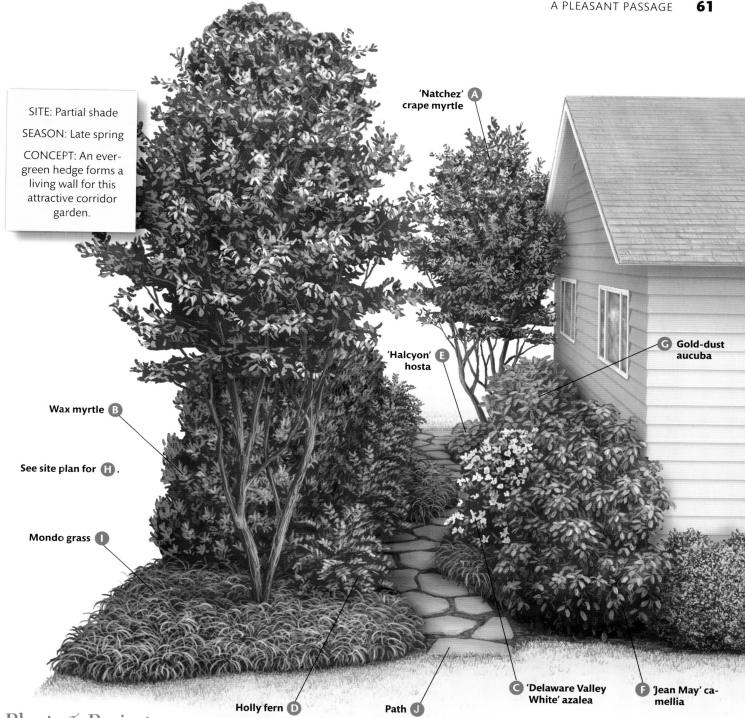

SITE: Partial shade

SEASON: Late spring

CONCEPT: An evergreen hedge forms a living wall for this attractive corridor garden.

'Natchez' **A** crape myrtle

G Gold-dust aucuba

'Halcyon' **E** hosta

Wax myrtle **B**

See site plan for **H** .

Mondo grass **I**

Holly fern **D**

Path **J**

C 'Delaware Valley White' azalea

F 'Jean May' camellia

Plants & Projects

A **'Natchez' crape myrtle** (use 2 plants)
A small deciduous tree with large clusters of crepe-papery white flowers all summer, bright fall color, and handsome flaking bark. Trim off lower limbs to better display plantings behind. See *Lagerstroemia indica*, p. 150.

B **Wax myrtle** (use 5)
This evergreen shrub's stems of slender, glossy aromatic leaves make a dense and tidy "natural" (not sheared) hedge. See *Myrica cerifera*, p. 154.

C **'Delaware Valley White' azalea** (use 3)
Its upright growth habit makes this evergreen shrub an excellent choice for the narrow spot between the house and path. Showy clusters of single white flowers light up the center of the garden in midspring. See *Rhododendron*, p. 161.

D **Holly fern** (use 5)
The shiny, coarse-toothed leaflets of this evergreen fern do look like holly leaves. Their color and texture make a nice contrast with the wax myrtles behind. See Ferns: *Cyrtomium falcatum*, p. 142.

E **'Halcyon' hosta** (use 5)
The leaves of this low-mounding perennial are powder blue in spring, darker blue in summer. In late summer, lilac-colored flowers wave above the foliage on slim stalks. See *Hosta*, p. 144.

See p. 56 for the following:
F **'Jean May' camellia** (use 1)
G **Gold-dust aucuba** (use 5)
H **White astilbe** (use 3)
I **Mondo grass** (use 1 per sq. ft.)
J **Path**

"Around Back"

DRESS UP THE FAMILY'S DAY-TO-DAY ENTRANCE

When people think of landscaping the entrance to their home, the public entry at the front of the house comes immediately to mind. It's easy to forget that the back door often gets more use. If you make the journey between back door and driveway or garage many times each day, why not make it as pleasant a trip as possible? For many properties, a simple planting such as the one shown here can transform the space bounded by the house, garage, and driveway, making it at once more inviting and more functional.

In a high-traffic area frequented by ball-bouncing, bicycle-riding children as well as busy adults, delicate, fussy plants have no place. This design employs durable plants, all of which look good year-round. The holly hedge links the house and the garage and separates the more private backyard from the busy driveway. A Japanese maple anchors the backyard planting, a composition of shrubs and perennials that is equally pleasing whether viewed on your way to and from the back door or while relaxing on a backyard deck or patio.

There are flowers in yellow, pink, white, and purple from spring through fall, including gardenias that fill the summer air with sweet scent and cheerful daylilies that bloom for months. And when the flowers fade in autumn, there is plenty of evergreen foliage to enjoy through the winter.

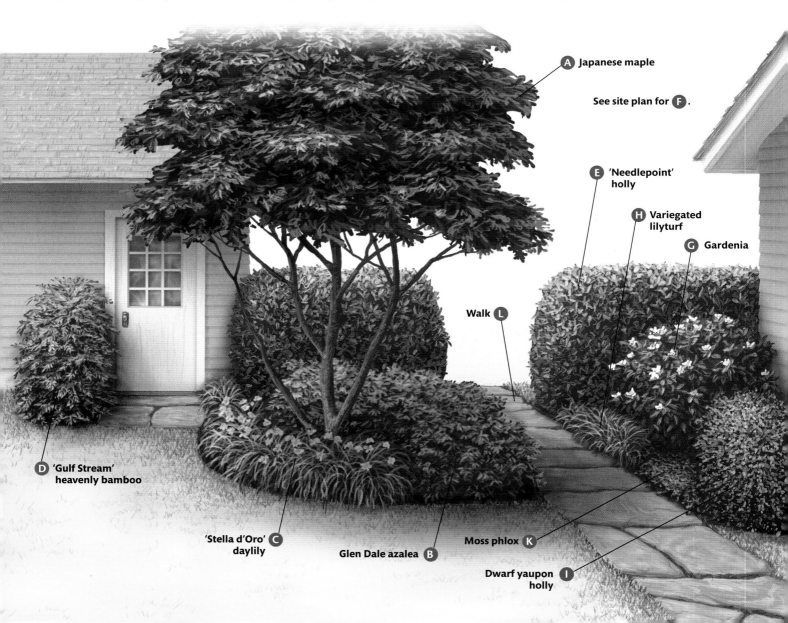

A Japanese maple

See site plan for **F**.

E 'Needlepoint' holly

H Variegated lilyturf

G Gardenia

Walk **L**

D 'Gulf Stream' heavenly bamboo

'Stella d'Oro' daylily **C**

Glen Dale azalea **B**

Moss phlox **K**

Dwarf yaupon holly **I**

Plants & Projects

If you don't need the path to the garage door shown here, extend the azaleas and heavenly bamboo to fill in near the garage, and plant additional lilyturf between the azaleas and holly hedge. Maintenance is not very demanding—just seasonal pruning and cleanup to keep the shrubs and perennials healthy, and periodic shearing to keep the hedge tidy.

A **Japanese maple** (use 1 plant)
A small deciduous tree with an attractive form and finely cut leaves. For striking summer color, choose from among the cultivars that have red leaves in that season as well as in the fall. See *Acer palmatum*, p. 130.

B **Glen Dale azalea** (use 3)
Lovely broad-leaved evergreen shrubs line the path beneath the maple tree. In spring they bear striking flowers in pink, white, red, or orange. See *Rhododendron*, p. 161.

C **'Stella d'Oro' daylily** (use 5)
Numerous golden yellow flowers (each lasting only a day) nod above this remarkable perennial's arching leaves from late spring until hard frost. See *Hemerocallis*, p. 144.

D **'Gulf Stream' heavenly bamboo** (use 2)
A colorful shrub with straight unbranched stems bearing layers of lacy evergreen leaves and white flowers in summer. The leaves change color from gold to green to red with the progress of the seasons. See *Nandina domestica*, p. 154.

E **'Needlepoint' holly** (use 5)
A tough evergreen shrub, ideal for shearing as a hedge, with shiny dark green leaves and a magnificent show of red berries in winter. See *Ilex*, Evergreen hollies: *I. cornuta*, p. 146.

F **'Diana' rose-of-Sharon** (use 1)
A deciduous shrub with eye-catching white flowers from July through September. Its size and colorful presence make it effective as an endpoint for this planting. See *Hibiscus syriacus*, p. 144.

G **Gardenia** (use 1)
Beloved in the Southeast for the sweet scent of its creamy white flowers, this evergreen shrub makes the trip down the path a pleasure in summer. Glossy dark green leaves look good all year. Plant 'Mystery' or 'August Beauty' here. See *Gardenia jasminoides*, p. 142.

H **Variegated lilyturf** (use 50)
This grasslike evergreen perennial makes a colorful edging along the lawn and path, with its dark green leaves striped in yellow and white. In late summer it bears small violet, purple, or white flowers. Space plants 1 ft. apart; they'll soon grow together. See *Liriope muscari* 'Variegata', p. 152.

I **Dwarf yaupon holly** (use 3)
A small evergreen shrub that forms compact mounds of small shiny leaves and stays just the right size for its spot between the path and the house. See *Ilex*, Evergreen hollies: *I. vomitoria* 'Nana', p. 146.

J **'David' garden phlox** (use 3)
This perennial offers sturdy upright stems of healthy green leaves topped for weeks in late summer with clusters of fragrant white flowers. See *Phlox paniculata*, p. 156.

K **Moss phlox** (use 7)
This evergreen perennial forms a dense mat of prickly foliage next to the path. In spring it is covered with pretty little flowers; a purple-flowered variety will look best in this planting. See *Phlox subulata*, p. 157.

L **Walk**
The texture, color, and irregular shape of this flagstone walk suit this planting well. Large stones look good and make a safe, even surface. See p. 176.

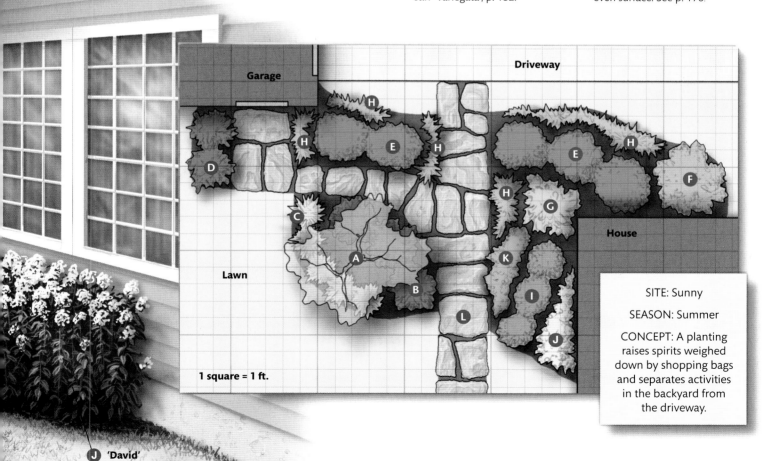

J **'David' garden phlox**

SITE: Sunny

SEASON: Summer

CONCEPT: A planting raises spirits weighed down by shopping bags and separates activities in the backyard from the driveway.

1 square = 1 ft.

A shady passage

This design features a simple vine-covered arbor that makes something special of the journey to and from the back door. (You can extend the arbor and the foundation planting of hydrangeas to suit your site.) A row of shrubs and a picket fence separate the driveway from the backyard.

Evergreen clematis forms a canopy on the arbor year-round, its white flowers adding a lovely fragrance in summer. The planting offers flowers from late winter through fall with few pauses. Hollies, heavenly bamboo, and lilyturf join the clematis to provide evergreen foliage that enlivens the area through the winter months.

Patio pots enhance an entry in no time, bringing plants right up to the back door.

VARIATIONS ON A THEME

Plantings like these can make any journey to the back door a pleasure.

A back entry can be as elegant as the front. This flagstone patio, columnar evergreens, and fragrant mounded lavender bring to mind landscapes of southern France.

A magnolia tree surrounded by hostas and other shade-loving ground covers is a simple way to enhance a walkway. The magnolia will be in bloom in springtime, when the hostas are just emerging.

Plants & Projects

Ⓐ Evergreen clematis
(use 1 plant per post)
The glossy green leaves of this vine cover the arbor year-round and serve as a handsome backdrop for the large white flowers that brighten and perfume the path in spring. See *Clematis armandii*, p. 139.

Ⓑ 'Obsession' heavenly bamboo (use 9)
This is a smaller version of the heavenly bamboo that anchors a corner of this planting (and is used in the previous design). Compact and bushy, it makes a colorful low hedge along the fence. The foliage turns bright crimson in winter. Needs little if any pruning. See *Nandina domestica*, p. 154.

Ⓒ 'Compacta' Japanese holly
(use 3)
Evergreen shrub that forms a dense mound of glossy leaves. Needs no pruning to maintain its tidy shape. See *Ilex*, Evergreen hollies: *I. crenata*, p. 146.

Ⓓ 'Nikko Blue' hydrangea (use 3)
This is a handsome cultivar of the

Arbor **I**

See site plan for **B** **K**.

Evergreen **A**
clematis

'Compacta' **C**
Japanese holly

C 'Compacta'
Japanese
holly

Herbs **H**

'Black Knight' **F**
butterfly bush

'Arp' **G**
rosemary

Evergreen **A**
clematis

Walk **L**   **J** Fence   **E** Lilyturf

D 'Nikko Blue'
hydrangea

popular deciduous shrub. Distinctive ball-shaped clusters of blue (or pink, depending on your soil) flowers cover the glossy foliage in summer. See *Hydrangea macrophylla*, p. 146.

E **Lilyturf** (use 40 or more)
A dark green form of this grassy evergreen ground cover is attractive year-round along the path. Purple or white flowers are showy in late summer. Space plants 1 ft. apart. See *Liriope muscari*, p. 152.

F **'Black Knight' butterfly bush** (use 1)
The arching branches of this vase-shaped deciduous shrub carry long trusses of fragrant, dark blue-purple flowers at their tips. Makes a fine focal point for the planting, blooming from midsummer through fall and attracting bevies of butterflies to the backyard. See *Buddleia davidii*, p. 135.

G **'Arp' rosemary** (use 1)
This well-known kitchen herb

is also a handsome evergreen shrub. Its gray-green, needlelike leaves are fragrant as well as tasty. Bears small blue flowers in late winter. See *Rosmarinus officinalis*, p. 161.

H **Herbs** (use 1 or more of each)
Anchored by the rosemary at

one end, this small garden of culinary herbs includes parsley, chives, basil, thyme, sage, and oregano.

I **Arbor**
A vine-covered wooden arbor shades the path from driveway toward back door. See p. 200.

J **Fence**
A picket fence complements the arbor and encloses the backyard. See p. 200.

See p. 61 for the following:

K **'Gulf Stream' heavenly bamboo** (use 1)

L **Walk**

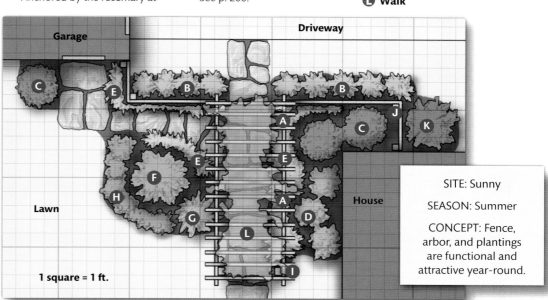

Garage

Driveway

House

Lawn

1 square = 1 ft.

SITE: Sunny

SEASON: Summer

CONCEPT: Fence, arbor, and plantings are functional and attractive year-round.

Angle of Repose

MAKE A BACK-DOOR GARDEN FOR A SHELTERED NICHE

Many homes offer the opportunity to tuck a garden into a protected corner. In the front yard, such spots are ideal for an entry garden or a display that showcases your house when viewed from the street. If the planting is in the backyard, as shown here, it can be a more intimate part of a comfortable outdoor room you can stroll around at leisure or enjoy from a nearby terrace or window.

This planting was designed with spring in mind, so we're showing that season here. (For a look at the planting later on, when perennials and shrubs take over the show, see p. 66.) Dozens of spring bulbs light up the corner from February through May, assisted by several early-blooming annuals, perennials, and handsome spring-flowered evergreen shrubs. Early flowers aren't the only pleasures of spring. Watch buds fatten and burst into leaf on the Japanese maple, and mark the progress of the season as new, succulent shoots of summer perennials emerge.

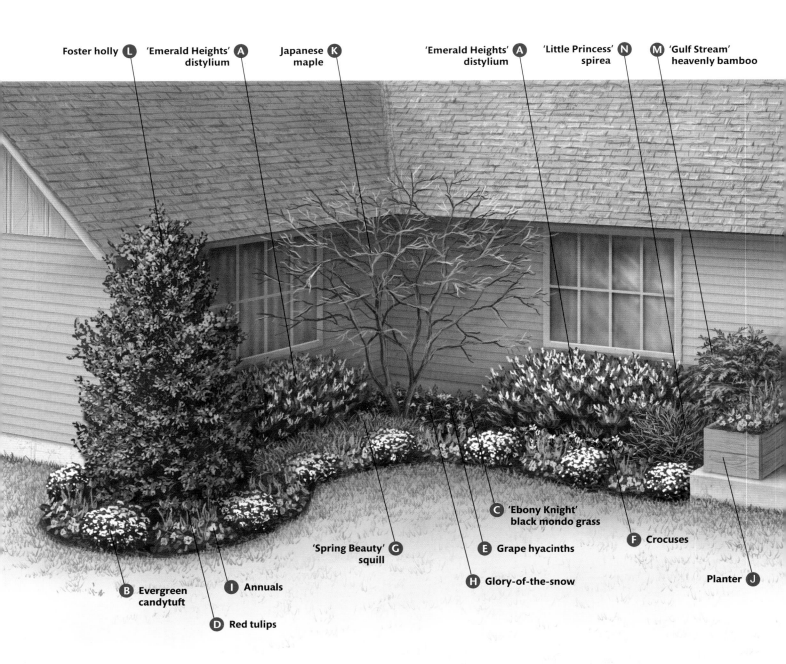

Foster holly **L**   'Emerald Heights' **A**
distylium   Japanese **K**
maple   'Emerald Heights' **A**
distylium   'Little Princess' **N**
spirea   'Gulf Stream' **M**
heavenly bamboo

C 'Ebony Knight'
black mondo grass

'Spring Beauty' **G**
squill   **E** Grape hyacinths   **F** Crocuses

H Glory-of-the-snow   Planter **J**

B Evergreen
candytuft   **I** Annuals

D Red tulips

Plants & Projects

Except for the red tulips, the bulb flowers in this planting are small, but they make a splash when blooming in masses. Their foliage will die back unnoticed among the perennial foliage that follows later in the season. Treat the tulips like pansies and other annuals—discard them after they bloom, and replant fresh tulip bulbs every fall.

Ⓐ **'Emerald Heights' distylium** (use 5 plants)
This compact, dense, broad-leaf, evergreen shrub makes an outstanding foundation plant with excellent resistance to pests and diseases. Late winter produces red flowers along the stem. See *Distylium*, p. XX.

Ⓑ **Evergreen candytuft** (use 8)
An excellent evergreen perennial for the edge of the garden, with a low, rounded form that is not too formal, topped with white flowers in early spring. Shear off the tops of the plants after the flowers fade. See *Iberis sempervirens*, p. 146.

Ⓒ **'Ebony Knight' black mondo grass** (use 28)
This evergreen grass makes an elegant carpet of thin, purple-black leaves, a striking setting for the small blue flowers of the spring bulbs sprinkled in the patch. See *Ophiopogon planiscapus*, p. 155.

Ⓓ **Red tulips** (use about 50)
Red tulips add vibrant color to the spring garden like no other plant. Repeated along the edge of the bed and in the planter, they look great with the yellow and blue pansies. Plant five bulbs between each clump of candytuft. Lots of different red cultivars are available; try different ones each year. See Bulbs: *Tulipa*, p. 136.

Ⓔ **Grape hyacinths** (use 30)
These little bulbs will spread happily beneath the maple tree, flecking the mondo-grass carpet with clusters of fragrant blue flowers. See Bulbs: *Muscari armeniacum*, p. 136.

Ⓕ **Crocuses** (use 40)
Plant generous clumps (six to eight per square foot) of these bulbs among the sedums (see p. 66), and enjoy their cup-shaped flowers in February. Use yellow or purple varieties, or both. See Bulbs: *Crocus*, p. 136.

Ⓖ **'Spring Beauty' squill** (use 10)
Clusters of bell-shaped flowers in a lovely shade of clear blue nod above the dianthus foliage in early spring. See Bulbs: *Scilla siberica*, p. 136.

Ⓗ **Glory-of-the-snow** (use 60)
Starry pale blue flowers with white centers will twinkle in the mondo grass as early as February. See Bulbs: *Chionodoxa luciliae*, p. 136.

Ⓘ **Annuals** (use about 4 dozen)
Alternating with the evergreen candytuft at the edge of the bed, yellow and blue pansies delight children (and adults) with their personable flowers. See Annuals, p. 132.

Ⓙ **Planter**
In spring this large planter offers a colorful array of tulips and pansies in a bed of blue-green dianthus foliage. You can build the 5-ft.-long, 2-ft.-wide planter yourself (see p. 200) or purchase one.

See p. 66 for the following:
Ⓚ **Japanese maple** (use 1)
Ⓛ **Foster holly** (use 1)
Ⓜ **'Gulf Stream' heavenly bamboo** (use 1)
Ⓝ **'Little Princess' spirea** (use 1)

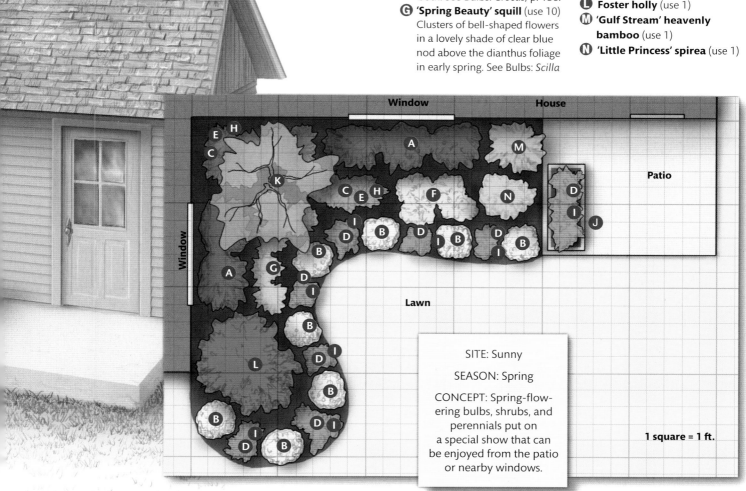

SITE: Sunny

SEASON: Spring

CONCEPT: Spring-flowering bulbs, shrubs, and perennials put on a special show that can be enjoyed from the patio or nearby windows.

1 square = 1 ft.

The scene in summer

There's no drop-off in interest or enjoyment as this planting moves from spring (shown on the previous pages) to summer and fall. Now perennials join woody plants in a tapestry of varied foliage accented by a succession of flowers in shades of white, blue, pink, and red.

Anchoring the planting is a lovely ornamental tree in perfect scale with the house. Foliage textures include a selection of delicate lacy leaves on the maple, heavenly bamboo, and spirea. Grassy dianthus and mondo grass contrast with the more robust foliage of the holly and cherry laurels. New annuals in the planter and edging the bed keep pace with the changing seasons.

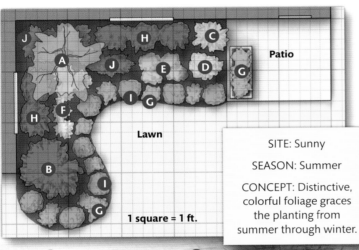

SITE: Sunny

SEASON: Summer

CONCEPT: Distinctive, colorful foliage graces the planting from summer through winter.

Plants & Projects

A **Japanese maple** (use 1 plant) This elegant small deciduous tree fills the corner beautifully with rich red leaves in summer as well as in fall; sculptural branches and attractive bark stand out in winter. (Many red-leaved cultivars are available.) See *Acer palmatum*, p. 130.

B **Foster holly** (use 1) The neat, narrow form and rich color of this broad-leaved evergreen tree add visual weight and balance to the end of the planting. This holly keeps its shape without pruning and bears lots of red berries. See *Ilex*, Evergreen hollies: *Ilex x attenuata* 'Foster #2', p. 146.

C **'Gulf Stream' heavenly bamboo** (use 1) An eye-catching evergreen shrub with pretty leaves that change color each season. Non-fruiting cultivars are eco-friendly. See *Nandina domestica*, p. 154.

D **'Little Princess' spirea** (use 1) This compact deciduous shrub's dainty leaves and neat form are just right for its spot by the planter. In early summer, pink flowers stand out against dark green foliage. See *Spiraea japonica*, p. 164.

E **'Autumn Joy' sedum** (use 4) The gray-green foliage of this tough plant contrasts nicely with the leaves of the cherry laurels. It gives a long and colorful show, with pale pink flower clusters that appear in August, maturing to dark pink and then rusty red. See *Sedum*, p. 164.

F **'Itsaul White' dianthus** (use 5) This perennial's marvelously fragrant white flowers appear in early summer. With a post-bloom shearing, the grassy blue-green foliage will look good through the winter. See *Dianthus*, p. 141.

G **Annuals** (use about 4 dozen) When the weather turns hot, replace pansies with blue ageratum and white annual vinca, filling the planter and the spaces along the edge of the bed. See Annuals, p. 132.

See p. 65 for the following:

H **'Emerald Heights' distylium**

I **Evergreen candytuft**

J **'Ebony Knight' black mondo grass**

B Foster holly Japanese maple **A** **H** 'Emerald Heights' distylium **C** 'Gulf Stream' heavenly bamboo

F 'Itsaul White' dianthus **E** 'Autumn Joy' sedum **G** Annuals

G Annuals **I** Evergreen candytuft **J** 'Ebony Knight' black mondo grass **D** 'Little Princess' spirea

VARIATIONS ON A THEME

These designs are set off by their L-shaped backdrops like actors before a stage set.

This sheltered corner, viewed from a picture window and reached through a glassed-in porch, is a perfect spot for a patio garden.

Elements of this garden sanctuary mirror the unique architectural features of the house, in particular the arches along the walls. A simple choice of plants enhances the air of tranquility in this private spot.

Assisted by shrubs and grasses, a wall provides an attractive, protected spot for a small patio and garden benches.

Down to Earth

HARMONIZE YOUR DECK WITH ITS SURROUNDINGS

A second-story deck is a perfect spot for viewing your garden and yard. Too often, however, the view of the deck from the yard is less pleasing. Perched atop skinny posts, towering over a patch of lawn, an elevated deck looks out of place, an ungainly visitor that is uncomfortable in its surroundings.

In the design shown here, attractive landscaping brings the deck, house, and yard into balance. Plants, combined with a simple homemade lattice skirting attached to the posts, form a broad pedestal of visual support for the deck. Framed by lovely maples, a planting of shrubs and perennials decreases in height from deck to lawn, making it easier for the eye to move between the levels.

In not too many years, the fast-growing native maples will cast shade over the deck. Next to the house, two sweet olives can stand on their own or tie into existing foundation plantings. In autumn their sweetly scented flowers will perfume the entire area. Across the front of the deck, a row of handsome oakleaf hydrangeas forms a hedgelike screen. The slender foliage of iris and sedge makes a grassy ruffle at their feet. Cherry laurels wrap around the corners in a flowing curve that broadens the deck's base when viewed from the lawn.

Grass paths lead to the area beneath the deck. Enclosed by the plantings and lattice, this area is ideal for storing garden tools, lawn furniture, and bicycles.

Red maple **A**

'Emerald Heights' **D**
distylium

SITE: Sunny

SEASON: Early summer

CONCEPT: A pleasing mix of woody plants and perennials leads the eye comfortably from ground to deck.

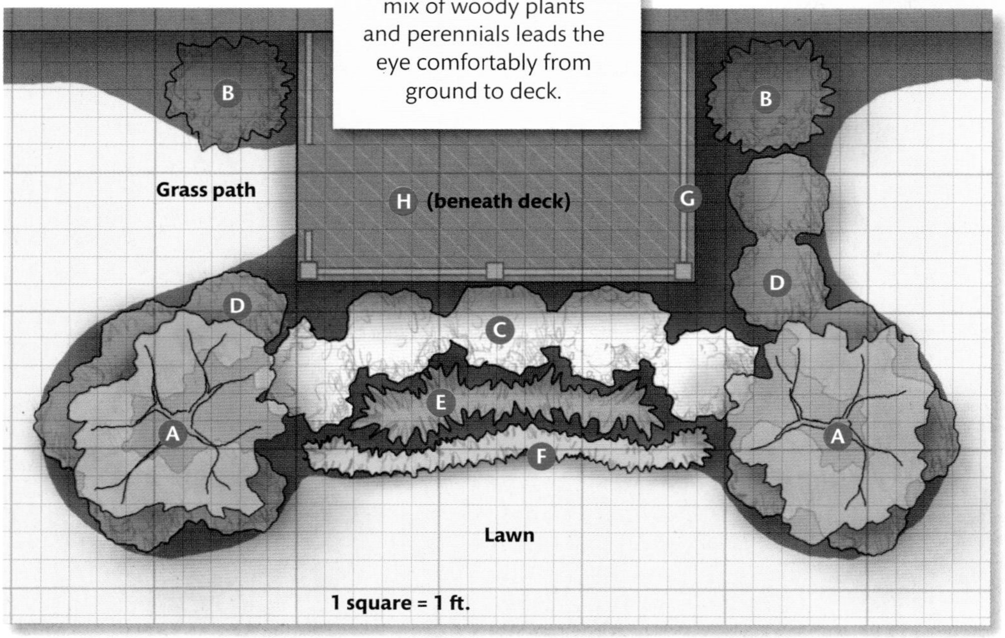

B

B

Grass path

H (beneath deck)

G

D

D

C

E

A

F

A

Lawn

1 square = 1 ft.

Plants & Projects

The lattice can be assembled and installed in a weekend, the planting in another. The curving bed is free-form, but it will look best if you take some care to make the curves "fair," with no awkward flat spots or pronounced bulges. The woody plants will take a few years to reach the sizes we've shown here. When the shrubs are small, mulching the beds with 3 to 4 in. of chipped or shredded bark will control weeds and retain moisture. Other than seasonal cleanup and pruning, the planting requires little maintenance.

A **Red maple** (use 2 plants)
A popular deciduous tree for its quick

G Lattice

Storage H
area

F Variegated
Japanese sedge

E Siberian iris

C Oakleaf hydrangea

D 'Emerald Heights'
distylium

Sweet olive B

growth and blazing red fall color. It is also colorful in spring, when the red flower clusters line the bare twigs. As the trees grow, remove lower limbs to accommodate the shrubs below and to encourage the trees to form a shady canopy over the deck. See *Acer rubrum*, p. 131.

B **Sweet olive** (use 2)
A slow-growing evergreen shrub with a dense compact form and glossy dark green leaves that resemble those of holly. Bears very sweet-scented flowers in late summer and fall. See *Osmanthus x fortunei*, p. 155.

C **Oakleaf hydrangea** (use 5)
Native to the South, this deciduous shrub offers colorful foliage that turns from pale

to dark green to red and purple as the season progresses. Papery flowers appear in spring until fall, giving way to cinnamon-colored bark in winter. See *Hydrangea quercifolia*, p. 146.

D **'Emerald Heights' distylium** (use 11)
This compact, dense, broadleaf, evergreen shrub makes an outstanding foundation plant with excellent resistance to pests and diseases. See *Distylium*, p. XX.

E **Siberian iris** (use 7)
The graceful flowers of this perennial add late-spring color to the front of the planting. The slender foliage looks good all summer. See *Iris sibirica*, p. 148.

F **Variegated Japanese sedge** (use 16)
This perennial's neat tufts of grasslike evergreen leaves, striped yellow and green, are an effective edging for the central bed. See *Carex morrowii* 'Aureo-variegata', p. 138.

G **Lattice**
Easy to make and attach to the deck posts, this lattice dresses up the deck when the shrubs are small (you might train morning glories on it) and provides a nice background for mature shrubs. See p.206.

H **Storage area**
For a durable tidy surface, cover the ground beneath the deck with 2 in. of crushed stone. Use a wooden edging to keep the stone out of the surrounding beds.

A terraced garden makes the transition up a slope from a low-lying lawn to this substantial deck.

Skirting a shady deck

This planting also integrates the deck with its surroundings, but it does so in a shady environment, produced perhaps by large trees nearby. The design includes a banquet of azaleas and rhododendrons that make a wonderful feast in spring, whether viewed from the deck or the lawn.

During the summer, a supporting cast of shade lovers provides lovely, if more subdued, color. Fall features the brilliant leaves of the maple; then the evergreen azaleas carry the planting through the winter.

VARIATIONS ON A THEME

Each of these plantings nicely merges its deck with the surroundings.

This well-thought-out design highlights, rather than hides, the handsome architecture of a second-story deck.

Perennials and dwarf evergreen shrubs make a seamless transition from the landscape to this deck.

Plants & Projects

Ⓐ **Japanese maple** (use 1 plant)
On a site with no need of additional shade, this small deciduous tree is a lovely accent. Choose a selection that has green leaves in summer and red or scarlet leaves in fall. See *Acer palmatum*, p. 130.

Ⓑ **Wax myrtle** (use 2)
Glossy aromatic leaves cover the slender stems of this graceful evergreen shrub. Birds like the gray berries that it bears in fall and winter. A fast grower, it will need yearly pruning to keep it from outgrowing its spot. See *Myrica cerifera*, p. 154.

Ⓒ **'George Lindley Taber' azalea** (use 6)
Large light pink flowers grace this shrub in spring. A vigorous plant, it grows quickly to produce a year-round evergreen screen for the storage area beneath the deck. See *Rhododendron*, p. 161.

Ⓓ **'Fiedlers White' azalea** (use 6)
Filling the corners between house and deck, these shrubs are a mound of white blossoms in spring and a lovely evergreen presence the rest of the year. See *Rhododendron*, p. 161.

Japanese maple **A**

L Lattice

M Storage area

Pink Gumpo azalea **F**

D 'Fiedlers White' azalea

Tassel fern **K**

Pink astilbe **I**

Dwarf Chinese astilbe **J**

G 'Elegans' hosta

B Wax myrtle

E 'Amagasa' Satsuki azalea

C 'George Lindley Taber' azalea

H 'Antioch' hosta

E 'Amagasa' Satsuki azalea (use 10)
A low evergreen shrub with a spreading form and deep pink flowers in late spring. See *Rhododendron*, p. 161.

F Pink Gumpo azalea (use 12)
Another low, spreading shrub. Mounds of its fine-textured evergreen foliage curve around the front edge of the planting. It bears clusters of large pink flowers in late spring. See *Rhododendron*, p. 161.

G 'Elegans' hosta (use 2)
A large perennial with the stature of a small shrub. Its huge blue, textured leaves look great with the nearby azaleas. White flowers bloom in summer. See *Hosta sieboldiana*, p. 144.

H 'Antioch' hosta (use 10)
Forming smaller but still impressive clumps, this hosta edges part of the bed with green-and-white leaves and has lavender flowers in summer. See *Hosta*, p. 144.

I Pink astilbe (use 6)
This perennial's dark green, deeply divided leaves make an effective transition from the azaleas behind them to the ferns in front. It bears plumes of pink flowers for weeks in early summer. Choose a tall cultivar for this spot in the design. See *Astilbe*, p. 133.

J Dwarf Chinese astilbe (use 10)
A smaller version of the previous plant, this perennial makes pretty patches of lacy foliage with pink flowers in late summer. See *Astilbe chinensis* var. *pumila*, p. 133.

K Tassel fern (use 12)
An evergreen fern with upright, finely divided, glossy green fronds. It adds a woodland feel to the front of the planting. See Ferns: *Polystichum polyblepharum*, p. 142.

See p. 69 for the following:

L Lattice

M Storage area

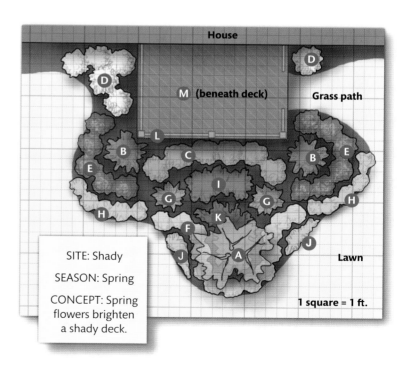

SITE: Shady

SEASON: Spring

CONCEPT: Spring flowers brighten a shady deck.

House

M (beneath deck)

Grass path

Lawn

1 square = 1 ft.

Make a Fresco of Flowers

A VERTICAL GARDEN BEAUTIFIES A BLANK WALL

Just as you enhance your living room by hanging paintings on the walls, you can decorate blank walls in your outdoor "living rooms." The design shown here transforms a nondescript garage wall into a living fresco, showcasing lovely flowers and foliage. Instead of a view of a plain wall, imagine gazing at this scene from a nearby patio, deck, or kitchen window. A vertical garden like this is also ideal where yard space is limited.

The simple composition spotlights three quite different plants, each striking in its own way. At one end, a deciduous shrub offers colorful leaves and fountain-like form. At the other, an evergreen tree provides balance and contrast with its narrow irregular form and bright green foliage. Between them, the wall sparkles all summer with red roses highlighted against a backdrop of healthy green leaves. Note how the off-center placement of the trellis on the wall combines with the narrow waist of the curving bed to draw the eye to the roses and blend the three main plants into a coherent whole.

A supporting cast of perennials performs admirably at the feet of the major players. Above a carpet of handsome foliage, these plants provide lovely flowers in red, blue, and white from spring to frost. The planting holds its own in winter, too, with a study in contrasts between the tree and shrub, one with rich evergreen foliage, the other an attractive bouquet of straight bare stems.

Mealy blue sage Ⓓ   **Hollywood juniper** Ⓑ   Ⓘ **Mowing strip**

Plants & Projects

Designed for a south- or west-facing wall that receives full sun, this planting uses tough plants that thrive in hot, dry conditions. They'll need regular watering for the first year (even in winter). Spread a layer of bark mulch to control weeds while the plants are young. From the second year on, the plants require only normal rainfall and little, if any, fertilizing.

Ⓐ **'Blaze' rose** (use 1 plant)
Long a favorite, this rose produces an abundance of small red blooms in spring and then off and on all summer. Foliage is healthy and shouldn't need spraying. As they grow, fix canes to the trellis with twist-ties. Each winter, cut a few of the older canes back to the ground. See *Rosa*, p. 161.

Ⓑ **Hollywood juniper** (use 1)
An uneven branching pattern gives this small evergreen tree an interesting, informal look. It is slow-growing and doesn't need pruning to keep it from crowding its space. The bright green foliage is a cheerful sight all year. See *Juniperus chinensis* 'Torulosa', p. 149.

Ⓒ **'Royal Purple' smoke tree** (use 1)
Foliage and flowers vie for top billing on this deciduous shrub. The dark purple leaves turn gold or orange in fall; pink flowers in fluffy plumes last weeks in summer and fall. Cut all stems back to 6-in. stubs each spring to produce a vase-shaped clump of straight, 5-ft.-long stems. See *Cotinus coggygria*, p. 140.

Ⓓ **Mealy blue sage** (use 9)
Through summer and fall, this perennial wildflower makes a carpet of glossy green foliage topped by slim spikes of blue flowers. (A medium blue cultivar will look best here.) See *Salvia farinacea*, p. 163.

Ⓔ **Autumn sage** (use 6)
This bushy, low-growing perennial forms an evergreen mass to balance the green juniper in winter, and its loose clusters of bright red or pink flowers keep coming from spring until fall. See *Salvia greggii*, p. 163.

Ⓕ **Bearded iris** (use 6)
This perennial produces elegant but short-lived flowers in spring, before the rose blooms. (Blue or white flowers will look best here.) The swordlike blue-green foliage is tough and at-tractive for months, sometimes evergreen in the Deep South. See *Iris*, p. 148.

Ⓖ **'Itsaul White' dianthus** (use 12)
Blue-green, grassy foliage and fragrant white flowers that bloom in spring with the rose make this a stunning perennial for the front of the planting. Shear the foliage after bloom and it will look good all year. See *Dianthus*, p. 141.

Ⓗ **Trellis**
This large trellis can be assembled in a few hours from 1x2s and 2x2s. Suspended on hooks, it is easy to remove to paint the wall. See p. 202.

Ⓘ **Mowing strip**
A brick edging neatly outlines the bed and makes mowing easier. See p. 210.

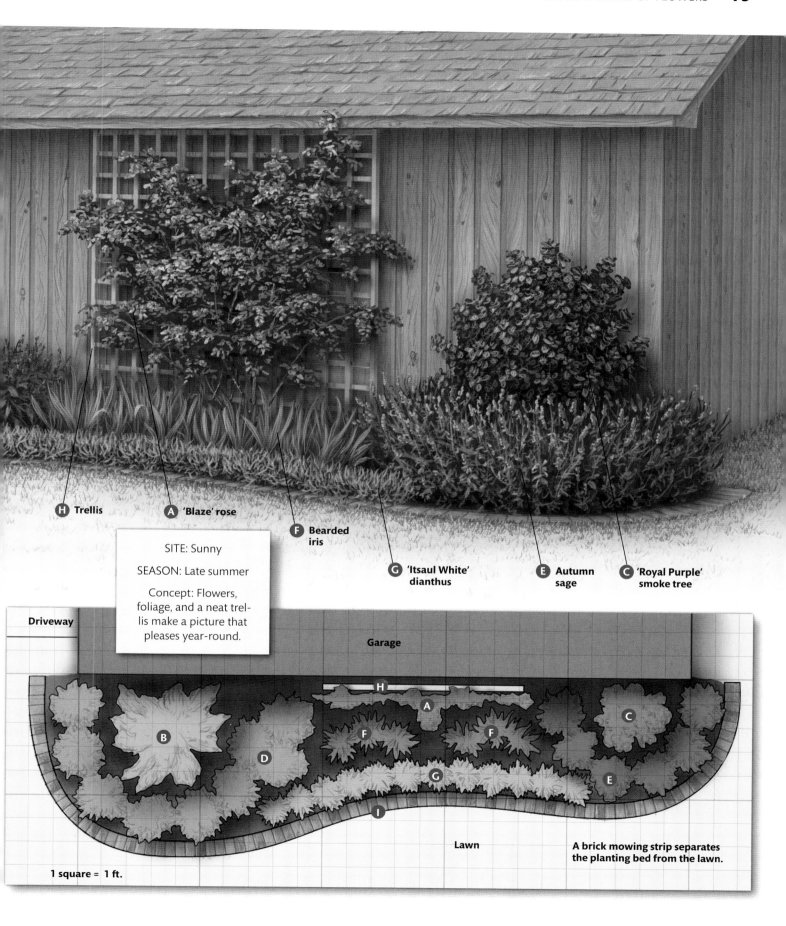

H Trellis

A 'Blaze' rose

F Bearded iris

SITE: Sunny

SEASON: Late summer

Concept: Flowers, foliage, and a neat trellis make a picture that pleases year-round.

G 'Itsaul White' dianthus

E Autumn sage

C 'Royal Purple' smoke tree

Driveway

Garage

H

A

F

B

F

C

D

G

E

I

Lawn

A brick mowing strip separates the planting bed from the lawn.

1 square = 1 ft.

A shady wall garden

A cooler, shadier site, such as an east- or north-facing wall, calls for a different palette of plants. The basic design remains the same as the previous one, but shade-tolerant shrubs, vines, and perennials replace the sun lovers.

Once again, the planting provides interest year-round. Scented flowers are present for months, beginning in late winter with sweet box and mahonia, followed by a summer-long display of honeysuckle on the trellis. Small bulbs in spring and hydrangea, lilyturf, and hostas in summer add to the show.

Varied foliage has its own eye-catching appeal in addition to providing a handsome backdrop for flowers. Winter is graced by evergreen foliage (which may turn purplish) and the mahonia's sky blue berries, which last until the mockingbirds eat them in spring.

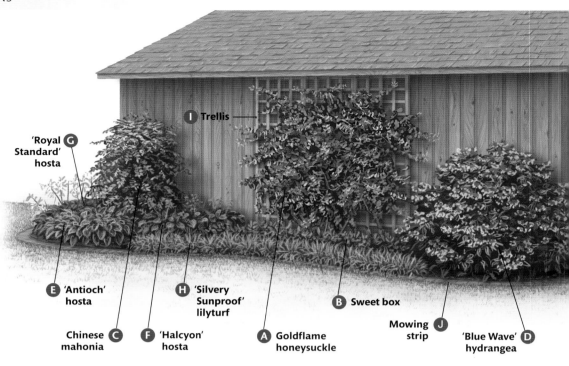

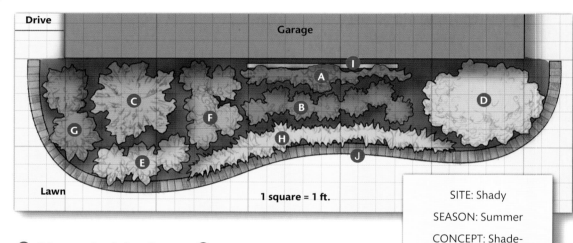

1 square = 1 ft.

SITE: Shady

SEASON: Summer

CONCEPT: Shade-tolerant perennials, vines, and shrubs make a showpiece of this wall on a cool, shady site.

Plants & Projects

A Goldflame honeysuckle (use 1 plant)
Cover the trellis with color and fragrance from spring through summer with this choice vine. Ruby red flower buds produce sweet-scented flowers that are pink outside, creamy white to yellow inside. The waxy blue-green leaves provide color through mild winters. See *Lonicera* x *heckrottii*, p. 152.

B Sweet box (use 7)
Small, sweetly scented, white flowers dot the shiny green foliage of this evergreen shrub in late winter. It will spread to form a solid carpet beneath the honeysuckle in about three years. See *Sarcococca hookeriana* 'Humilis', p. 163.

C Chinese mahonia (use 1)
The upright, straight-stemmed form of this evergreen shrub is ideal for this space. Dark blue-green leaves set off the fragrant yellow flowers in late winter and early spring. Pretty sky blue berries ripen in summer and last through the winter. See *Mahonia fortunei*, p. 153.

D 'Blue Wave' hydrangea (use 1)
A deciduous shrub with big, shiny green leaves and "lace-cap" summer flowers. Flowers will be pink or blue, depending on your soil. Plant about 50 grape hyacinth bulbs beneath it for spring color; fragrant purple flowers will bloom before the hydrangea leafs out. See *Hydrangea macrophylla*, p. 146.

E 'Antioch' hosta (use 3)
The green-and-white leaves of this tough perennial match the color, but contrast with the shape, of the nearby lilyturf. Lavender flowers are a bonus in midsummer. See *Hosta*, p. 144.

F 'Halcyon' hosta (use 5)
Forms broad clumps of distinctive foliage, powder blue in spring, darkening to blue-green in summer. Pale lavender flowers sway on slender stalks in midsummer. See *Hosta*, p. 144.

G 'Royal Standard' hosta (use 3)
This hosta forms large clumps of green leaves. Lilylike white flowers last for weeks in August and release a lovely sweet aroma on warm evenings. See *Hosta*, p. 144.

H 'Silvery Sunproof' lilyturf (use 15)
A perennial with green-and-white-striped leaves in grasslike clumps that make an attractive edging. Leaves are evergreen in mild winters. It has small purple flowers in late summer. See *Liriope muscari*, p. 152.

See p. 72 for the following:

I Trellis

J Mowing strip

VARIATIONS ON A THEME

Sometimes less is more. These three minimal approaches to a blank wall are as pleasing to the eye as are much more complex plantings.

A weathered wood fence, an architectural remnant, and a colorful hanging basket combine in a simple and artful way.

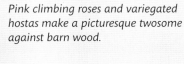

Pink climbing roses and variegated hostas make a picturesque twosome against barn wood.

A 'Ballerina' rose arches gracefully against a brick wall.

Garden by the Pool

ENHANCE YOUR POOLSIDE PLEASURES

The cool, blue water of a backyard swimming pool can be like a little slice of heaven in summer's heat and humidity. But too often the pool is surrounded by a slab of concrete and a chain-link fence—hardly an oasis. Because your pool is likely to be at the center of your home's outdoor activities, its setting should be a welcoming gathering place.

It doesn't take an enormous budget or a complete overhaul of the landscape to create a poolside oasis. The design shown here demonstrates that a relatively small project can work magic. The plantings, patio, and arbor help blend the pool more naturally with its surroundings while creating opportunities for entertaining and relaxation. If you're ambitious, you can easily extend the elements of the design around the pool. Or add to the setting over the years.

While creating an intimate setting near the pool, the design's height and depth look good from a distance, too. The plants are chosen for a Florida setting; consult with your nursery for suitable substitutes elsewhere in the region. All of them are low-maintenance broad-leaved evergreens with smooth rather than bristly or prickly leaves. They hold on to their foliage throughout the year, producing little litter. You won't be fishing leaves out of the water as you would with deciduous trees and shrubs. The plants that shed flowers after they bloom (loropetalum and cross vine) are positioned farthest from the pool.

> SITE: Sunny
>
> SEASON: Spring
>
> CONCEPT: A poolside patio and plantings offer a welcome retreat from the sun.

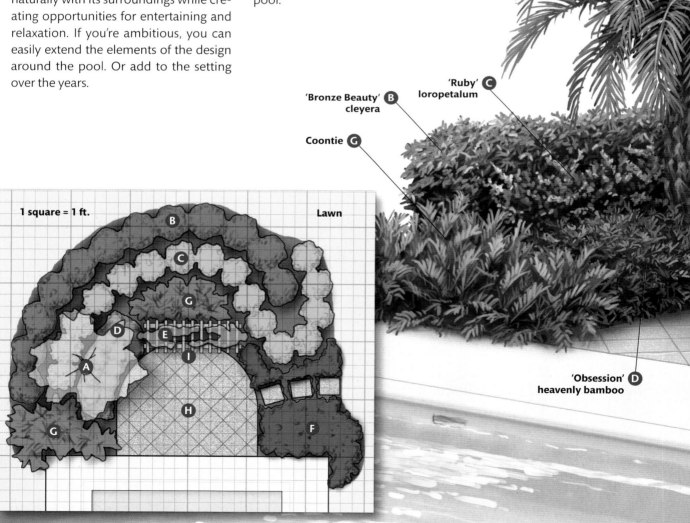

A Pindo palm

C 'Ruby' loropetalum

B 'Bronze Beauty' cleyera

G Coontie

D 'Obsession' heavenly bamboo

1 square = 1 ft.

Lawn

Plants & Projects

Building the arbor, installing the patio, and preparing the planting beds are strenuous tasks and may require frequent dips in the pool to complete. Once the plants are established, you'll have very little to do beyond seasonal pruning and cleanup.

A **Pindo palm** (use 1)
This sturdy palm will mature into a canopy of gray-green foliage 10 to 20 ft. high, held up by a stout trunk decorated with the bases of old leaf stalks. Yellow to orange fruits ripen in fall. They smell like pineapples and can be eaten from the tree or made into jam. See *Butia capitata*, p. 136.

B **'Bronze Beauty' cleyera** (use 12)
Growing 8 ft. tall, this glossy evergreen shrub doubles as a handsome privacy hedge and a striking backdrop for the pink flowers and burgundy foliage of the loropetalum. See *Ternstroemia gymnanthera* 'Bronze Beauty', p.165.

C **'Ruby' loropetalum** (use 16)
This evergreen shrub has arching branches bearing layers of small, rounded, burgundy leaves. Expect a burst of hot pink flowers in spring, and more bloom on and off from the summer through the fall. *Loropetalum chinense* var. *rubrum* 'Ruby', p. 152.

D **'Obsession' heavenly bamboo** (use 12)
Tiers of colorful, fine-textured evergreen foliage make this well-behaved shrub an excellent choice under the palm. See *Nandina domestica*, p. 154.

E **Cross vine** (use 2)
This twining vine will cover the arbor in lustrous dark green leaves all year. Older leaves may turn purple and red. In spring, hundreds of yellow and orange trumpet flowers open, providing a colorful focal point and a draw for migrating hummingbirds. Scattered bloom continues from summer to autumn. See *Bignonia capreolata*, p. 135.

F **Asian jasmine** (use 15)
A creeping evergreen vine that makes a thick, dark green carpet of fine, glossy, ivy-like leaves. It does not produce flowers. See *Trachelospermum asiaticum*, p. 166.

G **Coontie** (use 15)
A sculptural accent behind the bench and by the pool, this small cycad forms a clump of stiff evergreen leaves that resemble feathers. It bears interesting flower cones in summer. See *Zamia pumila*, p. 169.

H **Patio**
Shown here made of precast concrete pavers, the patio could be flagstones or a poured concrete extension of the pool surround. See p. 182.

I **Arbor**
Simple to build, this sturdy wooden arbor supports flowering vines and shades a wooden bench. See p. 203.

E Cross vine
I Arbor
B 'Bronze Beauty' cleyera
C 'Ruby' loropetalum
Patio H
G Coontie
Asian jasmine F

Palms by the pool

Palm trees are a natural next to water. This design makes spectacular use of native palms and other tropical plants that grow well in Florida. A bench swing and flagstone path scale down the cost and labor of the previous design without reducing its attractions. An old porch swing hanging from a simple post and beam structure provides a comfortable perch for relaxing with a book or enjoying the action in the pool.

The palms will provide a canopy of shade as they grow, and the evergreen grasses and shrubs will quickly add a sense of privacy. In spring and early summer, African irises bloom next to the bench. Their white petals open to reveal fine brush strokes of yellow and purple, worth viewing up close.

This design combines a rectilinear arbor and pool with soft mounds of colorful perennials. The arbor frames a dramatic view, which can be enjoyed from a hammock hung inside.

VARIATIONS ON A THEME

These poolside landscapes feature imaginative plantings and structures that complement the pools they surround.

This free-form pool and planting conjure a tropical lagoon. Flagstone decking and paths accommodate beds of exotic trees and shrubs.

Plants & Projects

Ⓐ **Sabal palm** (use 3)
This Southeast native plant provides a stately presence as well as a bit of shade. Large flower clusters appear in summer. See *Sabal palmetto*, p. 162.

Ⓑ **Hedge bamboo** (use 1)
An evergreen clumping bamboo, it has slender slightly weeping culms and small pointed leaves. See *Bambusa multiplex*, p. 134.

Ⓒ **Firebush** (use 3)
Abundant red flowers bloom all season above this evergreen shrub's dark green leaves. See *Hamelia patens*, p. 143.

Ⓓ **Cardboard plant** (use 1)
Dramatic as a single specimen, this evergreen cycad forms a large mound of leathery prehistoric-looking foliage. See *Zamia maritima*, p. 169.

E **Evergreen paspalum grass** (use 13)
This tropical grass forms a graceful waist-high mound of fine-textured yellow-green foliage. See *Paspalum quadrifarium*, p. 155.

F **White African iris** (use 11)
White flowers rise above fans of gray-green leaves when this perennial blooms in summer. Foliage stays crisp and fresh all year. See *Dietes vegeta*, p. 141.

G **'New Gold' lantana** (use 10)
Clusters of richflowers top this evergreen perennial almost year round in Florida. Their nectar attracts butterflies and night moths. See *Lantana* 'New Gold', p. 150.

H **'Super Evergreen Giant' lilyturf** (use 12)
This ground cover features attractive grassy dark green leaves. See *Liriope* 'Super Evergreen Giant', p. 152.

I **Bench swing**
You can make a swing support using the techniques for arbor posts shown on p. 193, but consult a builder to ensure stability. Ready-made bench swings are also available at garden centers or home stores.

J **Stepping stones**
Irregular flagstone pavers provide an attractive no-slip path to the swing. See p. 181.

SITE: Sunny

SEASON: Spring

CONCEPT: Tropical plants look at home beside a pool.

1 square = 1 ft.　　　　Lawn

Sabal palm **A**

'Super Evergreen **H**
Giant' lilyturf

C Firebush

B Hedge bamboo

I Bench swing

D Cardboard plant

'New Gold' **G**
lantana

White **F**
African iris

G 'New Gold' lantana

E Evergreen paspalum grass

J Steppingstones

Make a No-Mow Slope

A TERRACED PLANTING TRANSFORMS A STEEP SITE

A River birch

E 'Zabeliana' cherry laurel

B 'Savannah' holly

C Wax myrtle

G Daylily

D Forsythia

H Retaining wall

F Creeping willowleaf cotoneaster

Common features of houses like the one at left, steep slopes can be a land-scape nightmare. They're a chore to mow, and they can present problems of erosion and maintenance if you try to establish other ground covers or plantings. One solution to this dilemma is shown here—tame the slope by building a low retaining wall and planting the area with interesting low-care trees, shrubs, and perennials.

Steep slopes near the foundation are typically found around houses with walk-out basements or lower-level garages. Here, the low wall creates two terraces that mirror the curve of the driveway. On the lower level, shapely evergreens rise above a carpet of colorful daylilies. On the top level, massed ranks of deciduous and evergreen shrubs define the gentle curve of the remaining slope. Farther from the house an attractive tree punctu-ates the end of the wall. Low-growing shrubs spill down the hill, uniting the upper and lower planting terraces and marking the transition to the front lawn.

The planting provides good-looking flowers in spring and summer and hand-some foliage, pretty berries, and strik-ing bark in fall and winter. It is attractive whether viewed from above or below. Seen from the sidewalk, it frames the house and directs attention to the front entrance. It also screens the semiprivate area of drive and garage from the more public entrance. As the large shrubs grow, they overlap, tying the planting together and creating horizontal layers that fur-ther reduce the visual impact of the once-dominant slope.

The planting can easily be altered to accommodate existing foundation plants along the facade of the house. Or you can extend it to create a new foundation planting by adding more cherry laurels and cotoneasters, with perhaps a wax myrtle or two when you need some height.

Plants & Projects

Building the retaining wall, reshaping the slope, and preparing the planting beds is a big job—you might want to line up some energetic helpers or someone with a small earthmover. Once the plants are established, this design will provide years of enjoyment with a min-imum of maintenance. If you'd like extra flowers, plant small bulbs (crocus, grape hyacinth, small daffodils) in clumps of six or more.

A **River birch** (use 1 plant)
The multiple trunks of this fast-growing tree transform winter days with their exquisite bark, which peels back to reveal orange, tan, and creamy white layers. Medium green leaves cast a light summer shade. See *Betula nigra*, p. 135.

B **'Savannah' holly** (use 1)
This pyramidal tree with shiny evergreen leaves and red berries makes a fine accent by the garage. See *Ilex*, Evergreen hollies: *I. x attenuata*, p. 146.

C **Wax myrtle** (use 3)
An evergreen shrub with aromatic leaves and a graceful form. Birds like the clusters of gray berries in fall and winter. See *Myrica cerifera*, p. 154.

D **Forsythia** (use 6)
With cheery yellow flowers in early spring, this deciduous shrub covers lots of ground with its arching branches. Foliage is green in summer, purple in fall. See *Forsythia x intermedia*, p. 142.

E **'Zabeliana' cherry laurel** (use 4)
Narrow, glossy dark green leaves and a spreading habit make this a choice evergreen shrub to dress up the foundation. In midspring it's covered with fragrant white flowers. See *Prunus laurocerasus*, p. 159.

F **Creeping willowleaf cotoneaster** (use 12)
This tough, low-growing evergreen shrub is an excellent ground cover for a slope—its stems root where they touch ground, holding the soil in place. Bears white flowers in spring, red berries in fall, and its shiny leaves turn purple in cold weather. See *Cotoneaster salicifolius* 'Repens', p. 141.

G **Daylily** (use about 3 dozen)
For an extended show of lovely lilylike flowers, combine early- and late-blooming cultivars of this useful perennial in your favorite colors. Its grassy foliage and cheerful blooms make a bright informal edging for the drive. See *Hemerocallis*, p. 144.

H **Retaining wall**
Using a precast concrete wall system, you can build a curved wall like the one shown here in a weekend. See p. 188.

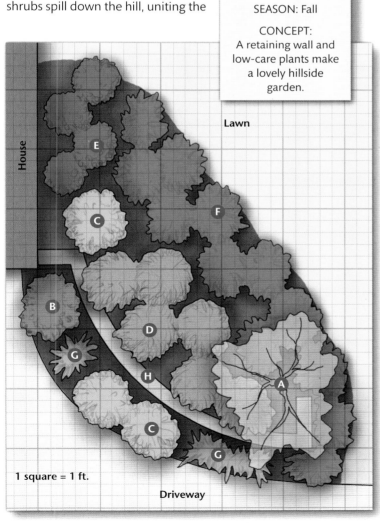

SITE: Sunny

SEASON: Fall

CONCEPT: A retaining wall and low-care plants make a lovely hillside garden.

Lawn

House

1 square = 1 ft.

Driveway

Design for a shady slope

If your slope is shaded by the house or a large tree nearby, here's a design similar to that on the previous pages but with a selection of shade-tolerant trees, shrubs, and perennials.

Once again, evergreen and deciduous foliage gives the planting a year-round presence. But spring (shown here) is the prettiest season, beginning with dogwood blossoms and early bulbs. At the base of the wall, the delicate fiddleheads of the ferns emerge. Then all the shrubs chime in—papery white hydrangea blossoms, striking trusses of pink rhododendrons, and, right by the lawn and drive where you can enjoy them best, the fragrant white flowers of the drooping leucothoe.

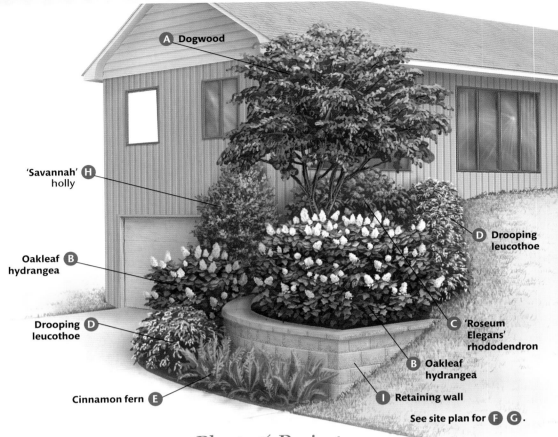

Site: Shady

Season: Late spring

Concept: Shade-tolerant plants make a handsome display on a shady site.

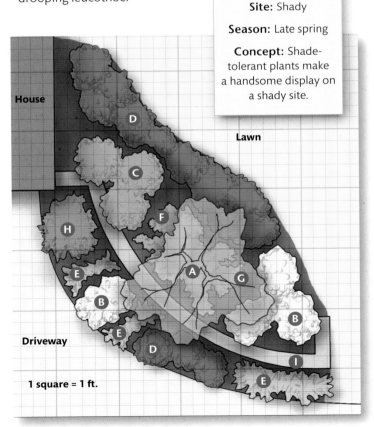

1 square = 1 ft.

Plants & Projects

Ⓐ Dogwood (use 1 plant)
This small deciduous tree is a central focal point with beauty in every season: white flowerlike bracts in spring, lovely light green foliage that turns crimson in fall, and bright red winter berries. Remove the lower limbs to accommodate nearby shrubs. See *Cornus florida*, p. 140.

Ⓑ Oakleaf hydrangea (use 4)
Oakleaf-shaped leaves and attractive reddish bark distinguish this deciduous shrub. It forms a handsome thicket at the base of the slope, with white flowers in spring and purple to red fall foliage. See *Hydrangea quercifolia*, p. 146.

Ⓒ 'Roseum Elegans' rhododendron (use 3)
This fast-growing evergreen shrub graces the top of the slope with its glossy leaves and rosy pink May flowers. See *Rhododendron*, p. 161.

Ⓓ Drooping leucothoe (use 13)
A spreading evergreen shrub whose mounds of dark green foliage are a perfect companion for the rhododendrons.

Fragrant white spring flowers. See *Leucothoe fontanesiana*, p. 151.

Ⓔ Cinnamon fern (use 24)
The interesting fiddleheads of this hardy fern unfurl into broad, pale green, plumelike fronds that create a woodland feel at the base of the wall. Fronds turn gold, then brown, in autumn. See Ferns: *Osmunda cinnamomea*, p. 142.

Ⓕ English ivy (use about 100)
Fill any open ground in the planting with this ground-covering evergreen vine. Spaced about 16 in. apart, it carpets the area with a dense mat of glossy green, lobed leaves. See *Hedera helix*, p. 144.

Ⓖ Bulbs
Scatter crocus, squill, grape hyacinth, and small daffodils among the shrubs for bright spring color. Plant groups of three to six bulbs per square foot. See Bulbs, p. 136.

See p. 81 for the following:

Ⓗ 'Savannah' holly (use 1)

Ⓘ Retaining wall

VARIATIONS ON A THEME

How you tame a slope depends on your purpose as well as your ingenuity.

A terraced vegetable garden puts the produce at a handy height for care and harvesting.

A simple, but lovely, combination of paving and plants transforms the gently sloping entrance to this modest house.

This splendid border makes superb use of its sloping site. Walking along its edge, a visitor is rewarded with something of interest on every sight line, from foot-height to tree top.

A Tropical Corner

SHOWCASE EXOTIC FOLIAGE AND FLOWERS

A Sabal palm

E Star jasmine

B 'Acoma' crapemyrtle

Firebush C

G 'New Gold' lantana

I Purple verbena

F White African iris

G 'New Gold' lantana

D Plumbago

H Asian jasmine

Tropical plants lend themselves to superlatives: exquisite flowers, luxuriant foliage, profuse bloom, magnificent structure, extraordinary texture, alluring fragrance. Everything about them is out of the ordinary, with the exception of where they can grow. If you live in Florida or along the Gulf Coast, you can reliably grow many tropical plants outdoors and enjoy their extravagant display year after year.

The vibrant tropical planting shown here could be used in any sun-drenched spot on your property. We've shown it wrapping the corner of a garage; the eye-catching foliage and flowers bring interest to a usually drab area. Three palms form the backbone of this simple design, creating an instant tropical look. Under their canopies, a small tree and a handful of shrubs and perennials display interesting leaf textures and splashes of color throughout the seasons. A climbing vine trained on one of the palms completes this tropical picture.

Most tropical plants revel in the high humidity that accompanies heat in Florida. In the torrid months of summer, lush palm foliage offers a cool contrast against heat-soaked cement or stucco walls. And when many garden plants simply give up the ghost, heat-loving firebush, plumbago, and verbena put out a bounty of flowers. In the winter months, when temperatures dip, the palms will still be luxuriant, and the plumbagos and lantanas will be covered in blossoms, reminding you that balmy days are just ahead.

Plants & Projects

These tropical plants need little care beyond regular watering and annual cleanup.

Ⓐ **Sabal palm** (use 3)
This native palm puts out a healthy crown of fan-to-featherlike gray-green leaves. The richly textured trunk is handsome too, and a great support for flowering vines. See *Sabal palmetto*, p. 162.

Ⓑ **'Acoma' crapemyrtle** (use 1)
Dense clusters of white crepe-papery flowers light up this small tree in late spring. Dark green deciduous leaves turn bright colors in fall, and flaking bark is attractive in winter. See *Lagerstroemia indica* x *fauriei* 'Acoma', p. 150.

Ⓒ **Firebush** (use 1)
This large evergreen shrub showcases brilliant scarlet flowers against bright green foliage. Berry clusters are showy too, ripening from green to yellow to red to black. See *Hamelia patens*, p. 143.

Ⓓ **Plumbago** (use 2)
The slender stems and small green leaves of this shrub are hidden for months under a cover of sky blue flowers. The heavy bloom is even more eye-catching when the scarlet firebush is in flower. See *Plumbago auriculata*, p. 158.

Ⓔ **Confederate jasmine** (use 1)
This vigorous vine will clamber to the top of the palm, dressing it in small, oval, leathery leaves.

In spring, masses of starry white flowers perfume the air. See *Trachelospermum jasminoides*, p. 116.

Ⓕ **White African iris** (use 19)
This perennial ground cover forms clumps of spearlike leaves that are arranged in lovely fans. From spring to early summer each leafy clump sends up slender branched stalks bearing white-petaled flowers tattooed in pastel shades. See *Dietes vegeta*, p. 141.

Ⓖ **'New Gold' lantana** (use 18)
This colorful perennial forms a durable mat of dark evergreen leaves buried in clusters of tiny orange-yellow flowers. Butterflies love them. See *Lantana* 'New Gold', p. 150.

Ⓗ **Asian jasmine** (use 8)
The small, oval leaves of this twining vine are dark green and glossy, providing a bold contrast beside gold lantana. See *Trachelospermum asiaticum*, p. 166.

Ⓘ **Purple verbena** (use 3)
From summer to fall, this upright evergreen perennial sports showy purple flowers and the colorful butterflies they attract. See *Verbena bonariensis*, p. 166.

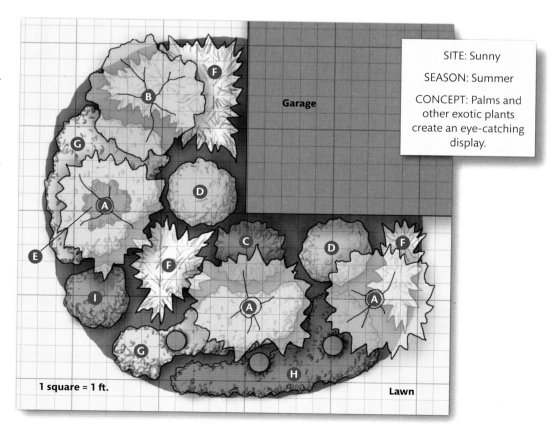

SITE: Sunny

SEASON: Summer

CONCEPT: Palms and other exotic plants create an eye-catching display.

Garage

1 square = 1 ft.

Lawn

Exotics in the shade

You can bring dazzling color to darker corners of your property too. This design features the colorful, shimmering foliage of tropical gingers and other exotic shade-loving specimens. Some of these plants produce splashes of brilliant flowers that lighten even the deepest shade.

At the center of this planting is an elegant small palm with slender stems and sleek dark fronds. Adding height along the wall is a trellis supporting a fragrant flowering vine.

A collection of spectacularly sculpted and textured shrubs, perennials, ferns, and grasses vie for attention throughout the border. But few plants grab the spotlight like the zebra ginger, with its vibrantly striped foliage and its elaborate wands of white flowers in summer.

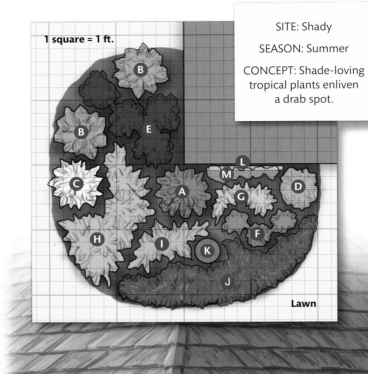

1 square = 1 ft.

SITE: Shady

SEASON: Summer

CONCEPT: Shade-loving tropical plants enliven a drab spot.

Lawn

Plants & Projects

Ⓐ Lady palm (use 1)
Considered one of the most beautiful of all palms. Slender stems bear large fronds of lustrous, dark green, deeply cut leaves that look like giant hands. See *Rhapis excelsa*, p. 159.

Ⓑ Blue ginger (use 2)
This jungle specimen has fleshy roots and dark green linear leaves arranged in spirals along stems that rise 5 to 8 ft. tall. Luscious-looking clusters of deep violet flowers bloom each autumn. See *Dichorisandra thyrsiflora*, p. 141.

Ⓒ Zebra ginger (use 1)
Named for its brilliantly striped foliage, this striking evergreen perennial contributes clusters of lightly fragrant bell-shaped

L Trellis

M Star jasmine

D Jacobinea

Lady palm Ⓐ

Ⓑ Blue ginger

'Xanadu' Ⓔ philodendron

Zebra ginger Ⓒ

Holly fern Ⓗ

Japanese autumn fern Ⓘ

Ⓖ Cast-iron plant

Ⓚ ZZ

Ⓙ Mondo grass

'Polly' dwarf Ⓕ African mask

flowers in summer. See *Alpinia zerumbet* 'Variegata', p. 132.

D **Jacobinea** (use 1)

In summer, this shrub's large coarse leaves are topped with showy pink flowers that look like feather dusters. See *Justicia carnea*, p. 149.

E **'Xanadu' philodendron** (use 4)

A beautiful foliage plant, this philodendron has a tidy growth habit and large, reflective, deeply lobed leaves. See *Philodendron* 'Xanadu', p. 156.

F **'Polly' dwarf African mask** (use 3)

A small evergreen perennial with oversized foliage colored green and purple and etched with silver veins. See *Alocasia* x *amazonica* 'Polly', p. 132.

G **Cast-iron plant** (use 9)

This perennial ground cover forms an upright clump of dark green strappy leaves that resemble polished leather. See *Aspidistra elatior*, p. 133.

H **Holly fern** (use 8)

Glossy, coarse-textured leaves distinguish this dark green fern. It makes a handsome companion to the finely textured autumn fern. See Ferns: *Cyrtomium falcatum*, p. 142.

I **Japanese autumn fern** (use 5)

The feathery fronds of this dark green woodland fern are coppery red when new. See *Dryopteris erythrosora*, p. 142.

J **Mondo grass** (as needed)

This perennial features neat low mounds of very fine blades. Plant on 10-in. centers. Over time they spread into a soft and dense shag carpet. See *Ophiopogon japonicus*, p. 155.

K **ZZ** (use 3)

Plant this African beauty in a colorful pot for yet another eye-catching accent. It doesn't flower, but the glossy, succulent foliage is highly decorative. See *Zamioculcas zamiifolia*, p. 169.

L **Trellis**

This simple wooden structure is easy to build and attach to a wall. See p. 202.

See p. 85 for the following:

M **Confederate jasmine** (use 1)

VARIATIONS ON A THEME

If your climate isn't quite tropical, you can still have exotic flowers and lush foliage with a tropical "feel."

Container plants provide a tropical accent when weather is warm, and can be moved indoors when it isn't.

Combined with other colorful flower and foliage plants, these red-orange cannas add a tropical note to this patio.

A Beginning Border

FLOWERS AND A FENCE MAKE A TRADITIONAL DESIGN

A mixed border can be one of the most delightful of all gardens. Indeed, that's usually its sole purpose. Unlike many other types of landscape plantings, a traditional border is seldom yoked to any function beyond that of providing as much pleasure as possible. From the first neat mounds of foliage in the spring to the fullness of summer bloom and autumn color, the mix of flowers, foliage, textures, tones, and hues brings enjoyment.

This border is designed for a beginning or busy gardener, using durable plants that are easy to establish and care for. Behind the planting, screening out distraction, is a simple fence. The border is meant to be viewed from the front, so tall plants go at the back. The arrange-

ment is symmetrical but not repetitive; the plants on each side of the center-line are different but of similar size and shape.

The plants here provide three seasons of staggered bloom and attractive foliage to carry interest through the winter months. Spring highlights include striking purple and yellow flowers of verbena and daylily and elegant white irises. During the long months of summer and fall, butterflies flit among the blue flowers on the butterfly bush and pincushion flower, and stately lilies join raucous coneflowers and daisies. Winter offers evergreen foliage of rosemary and Shasta daisy and the silvers and golds of the butterfly bush and flowing grass.

'Arp' C rosemary

Bengal tiger F canna

'Homestead Purple' J verbena

Plants & Projects

The plants chosen here all perform admirably in the high heat and humidity of the region, conditions that can pose problems for many traditional border plants. Removing spent flowers and seasonal pruning (cutting stems to the ground) are the main chores. Don't cut back the grass until spring, or you'll miss its buff and brown winter hues. And be sure to mark where the lilies are planted with labels, so you won't damage them in spring cleanup. Place a few stepping-stones in the bed for easy access. For a larger border, just plant more of each plant to fit the space, or repeat parts of the design.

A Evergreen clematis
(use 1 plant)
Clambering along the top of the fence, the glossy leaves of this evergreen vine create a shimmering backdrop. Large white flowers add fragrance in spring. Stretch thin wires between eye-bolts fixed to the fence to help

the vine climb. See *Clematis armandii*, p. 139.
B 'Nanho Blue' butterfly bush
(use 1)
A fine focal point, with arching branches tipped with long trusses of fragrant blue flowers from midsummer until fall. Underplant with daffodils and evergreen ajuga for additional color from spring through winter. See *Buddleia davidii*, p. 135.
C 'Arp' rosemary (use 1)
A small, bushy evergreen shrub whose needlelike silver-green leaves have a delicious aroma and taste. Tiny blue flowers appear in late winter and last through spring. See *Rosmarinus officinalis*, p. 161.
D 'Shenandoah' switchgrass
(use 1)
A dense clumping perennial grass with a fairly upright growth habit. It produces attractive wispy, pink-tinged flower panicles above the fo-

liage in summer. See *Panicum virgatum*, p. XX.
E Oriental lilies (use 2 clumps of 3 bulbs each)
In late summer these much-loved perennials will scent the entire border with the rich perfume of their large elegant flowers. Try one clump of 'Stargazer', with white-edged crimson blooms, and one of 'Casablanca', with pure white flowers. See *Lilium*, p. 151.
F Bengal tiger canna (use 3)
Stunning, large, yellow-and-green-striped leaves are eye-catching from spring through fall. Bears equally spectacular orange flowers in midsummer. See *Canna* 'Pretoria', p. 137.
G 'Coronation Gold' yarrow
(use 1)
This perennial's flat heads of bright gold flowers bloom for months atop gray-green ferny foliage. An attractive contrast to the nearby switchgrass. See *Achillea*, p. 131.

H 'Becky' Shasta daisy (use 3)
Big white daisies with yellow centers bloom all summer on this perennial's sturdy stalks. The foliage is dark green and shiny year-round. See *Chrysanthemum* x *superbum*, p. 139.
I Purple coneflower (use 3)
Mirroring the Shasta daisy, this perennial's daisylike flowers are dark with a dark center. Blooms in midsummer. See *Echinacea purpurea*, p. 141.
J 'Homestead Purple' verbena
(use 6)
This low-growing, evergreen, ground-cover perennial blooms steadily from late spring to frost if spent blossoms are removed. Its rosy purple flowers look lovely next to the white daisies. See *Verbena canadensis*, p. 167.
K 'White Swirl' Siberian iris
(use 1)
These rugged perennials form clumps of graceful grassy foliage at the front of the border,

N Fence

B 'Nanho Blue' butterfly bush

E Oriental lilies

D 'Shenandoah' switchgrass

A Evergreen clematis

G 'Coronation Gold' yarrow

L 'Stella d'Oro' daylily

I Purple coneflower

M 'Butterfly Blue' pincushion flower

H 'Becky' Shasta daisy

K 'White Swirl' Siberian iris

but the distinctive large white flowers are the main attraction. See *Iris sibirica*, p. 148

L **'Stella d'Oro' daylily** (use 3) Fresh golden yellow flowers appear daily from late spring to frost on this remarkable perennial. The healthy grasslike foliage complements that of the iris. See *Hemerocallis*, p. 144.

M **'Butterfly Blue' pincushion flower** (use 6) This perennial's tidy mounds of bright green foliage are covered with round blue flowers on wiry stems from late spring to frost (if you remove the spent flowers). Aptly named, butterflies like them. See *Scabiosa columbaria*, p. 163.

N **Fence** Clean arching lines and decorative finials atop the posts transform this simple, 6-ft.-high fence into a worthy backdrop for a handsome planting. p. 204.

SITE: Sunny

SEASON: Summer

CONCEPT: Even a novice can make a flower border flourish. A simple fence, carefree plants, and a ready-made design make this border both fetching and fail-safe.

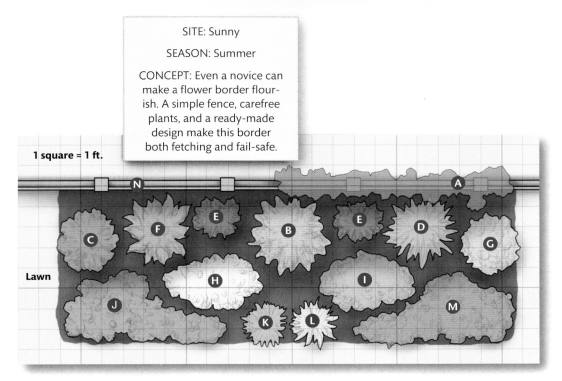

1 square = 1 ft.

Lawn

Now, add annuals

Here we've altered the design on the previous pages to include a large planting of annuals. The Southeast region's long growing season and mild winters allow two completely different plantings of annuals a year. The cool-season planting is depicted in the rendering at right, shown in the spring after the old perennial foliage has been cut back in anticipation of new growth.

As the spring and summer progress, the perennials reappear and fill in the border (as shown in the site plan). The continual color provided by the flowers and foliage of the annuals fills any gaps in the sequence of perennial bloom during the summer and fall. And it enlivens the winter garden immeasurably.

Planted in November, the cool-season annuals (and the neighboring daffodils) produce attractive foliage and flowers through May. Then it's time to replace them with warm-season annuals, colorful heat lovers that perform until November, when the cycle begins again.

See site plan for **E** and **G** through **M**.

O Fence   F 'Arp' rosemary   Daffodils B

Ajuga C   'Becky' K   Iceland poppies A   Dusty A   Violas A   Pansies A
          Shasta daisy   miller

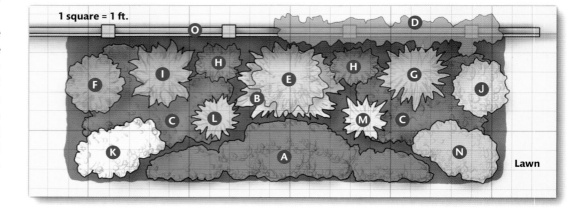

1 square = 1 ft.   Lawn

Plants & Projects

A Annuals
(use about 3 dozen plants) Buy cool-season annuals in the fall. Check the labels and choose compact varieties that stay under 1 ft. tall. Space the plants about 1 ft. apart; they will soon grow together. The popular cool-season annuals shown here include dusty miller, with silver-gray foliage; pansies, with large blue flowers; dwarf snapdragons, with white flowers; Iceland

poppies, with peachy pink flowers; and violas, with yellow flowers that resemble pansies flowers but are smaller. When the weather turns hot, replace the cool-season annuals with salvias, pentas, lantanas, gomphrenas, zinnias, or other types of hot-season annuals. Work some compost into the soil every time you replace the annual planting, and add some fresh mulch, too. See Annuals, p. 132.

B Daffodils (use 12)
Daffodils add color to the back of the border in spring, when the butterfly bush has been cut short and the perennials in the border are still dormant. 'Ice Follies' has lovely large flowers that open pale yellow and turn creamy white. Substitute other spring bulbs if you prefer. See Bulbs: *Narcissus*, p. 136.

C Ajuga (use 1 per sq. ft.)
This low-growing perennial makes a good "filler" that

spreads under and around other plants, offering bright blue flowers in spring and glossy evergreen foliage. 'Catlin's Giant' is a vigorous, fast-growing cultivar with large purple-bronze leaves. See *Ajuga reptans*, p. 131.

See p. 88 for the following:

D Evergreen clematis (use 1)

E 'Nanho Blue' butterfly bush (use 1)

F 'Arp' rosemary (use 1)

D Evergreen clematis

N Purple coneflower

A Dwarf snapdragons

SITE: Sunny

SEASON: Spring

CONCEPT: Mixing perennials and annuals makes a border even more colorful and interesting all year.

G **'Shenandoah' switchgrass** (use 1)

H **Oriental lilies** (use 2 groups of 3 bulbs each)

I **Bengal tiger canna** (use 3)

J **'Coronation Gold' yarrow** (use 1)

K **'Becky' Shasta daisy** (use 2)

L **'White Swirl' Siberian iris** (use 3)

M **'Stella d'Oro' daylily** (use 3)

N **Purple coneflower** (use 2)

O **Fence**

VARIATIONS ON A THEME

Whether your taste runs to ornamental grasses or formal English perennial gardens, there are countless ways to create an attractive border.

Borders offer small-scale pleasures among their bounty, rewarding closer looks as well as overall appreciation.

This small, shady border is the equal of its larger, sun-drenched cousins in beauty and interest.

Striking grasses are at once a focal point and a backdrop for other plants in this large border.

Patio Oasis

A FREE STANDING PATIO OFFERS OPEN-AIR ACTIVITIES

In warm climates, outdoor living can be a year-round pleasure. But many homes extend an invitation to the great outdoors only as far as a porch, deck, or patio attached to the house. The design shown here, a free-floating patio integrated with plantings, expands the possibilities for open-air gatherings to other spots on your property. Situated in an open expanse of lawn, it becomes a focal point and gathering spot. Positioned along the perimeter of the property, it defines the boundary in a neighborly way. Tucked into an out-of-the-way corner, it serves as a quiet refuge from noisier activities. Wherever you place it, the patio and plantings will provide an attractive destination and an enjoyable view for those who stay behind.

In this simple design the patio is large enough to accommodate a gathering of eight comfortably. A small pond and fountain is soothing to look at and to listen to. Planted close to the patio, a small tree will provide some shade as it grows, and several large shrubs at the back of the border impart a sense of privacy without closing off the views. Shrubs at the front harbor a large terra-cotta pot with a trellis supporting a flowering vine.

The plants are chosen for Florida's climate, but many will do well elsewhere in the region. They include vibrant flowers that serve as lightning rods for butterflies, hummingbirds, and other wildlife. Gold and purple lantanas will be in bloom nearly year-round, joined throughout the season by a continuous supply of flowers in fiery reds, rich golds, and electric blues and whites.

A Japanese ligustrum

J 'Amethyst' passionflower

C Firespike

B Firebush

F Blue porterweed

I 'New Gold' lantana

D Mexican bush sage

G 'Silky Gold' milkweed

I 'New Gold' lantana

K Patio

Plants & Projects

The patio and plantings can be installed in a couple of weekends. Once the plants are established, they'll need little care beyond regular watering and seasonal cleanup.

A **Japanese ligustrum** (use 1)
A fast-growing evergreen tree with great structural appeal. Handsome crooked trunks are topped with smooth, pointed, polished leaves, and panicles of fragrant, creamy white flowers from spring to summer. See *Ligustrum japonicum*, p. 151.

B **Firebush** (use 2)
Masses of bright red flowers top this showy evergreen shrub from spring to fall, maturing into shiny black berries. As autumn approaches, the large, bright green leaves become tinged with red. See *Hamelia patens*, p. 143.

C **Firespike** (use 3)
This tropical evergreen shrub has upright, rigid stems and glossy deep-green leaves with wavy margins. From winter through spring each stem is topped with a stunning foot-long panicle of tubular crimson flowers. Hummingbirds returning south appreciate this nectar pit stop. See *Odontonema cuspidatum*, p. 154.

D **Mexican bush sage** (use 7)
This beautiful plant adds soft texture and color to the border because every part of it is covered with fuzz. Velvety white flowers with purple calyces bloom in spikes above wooly stems and downy gray-green leaves. This evergreen perennial blooms best in the fall and spring. It also attracts bees, butterflies, and sometimes hummingbirds. See *Salvia leucantha*, p. 163.

E **Purple verbena** (use 1)
This evergreen perennial fills a vertical space in the garden. Its stiff thin stems and narrow see-through leaves are topped for months with small pompoms of purple flowers. See *Verbena bonariensis*, p. 166.

F **Blue porterweed** (use 13)
Ideal as a low hedge around the patio, this Florida native evergreen shrub offers gray-green foliage and slender blue flower spikes that will attract butterflies. See *Stachytarpheta jamaicensis*, p. 164.

G **'Silky Gold' milkweed** (use 11)
This is a pure gold form of everyone's favorite butterfly magnet. It blooms from spring through autumn on sturdy stalks that are lined with narrow, medium-green leaves. See *Asclepias curassavica* 'Silky Gold', p. 133.

H **Trailing lantana** (use 8)
This low-spreading evergreen perennial produces rich dark green leaves and lavish clusters of tiny lavender flowers. Each flower cluster is a landing pad for butterflies and moths. See *Lantana montevidensis*, p. 150.

I **'New Gold' lantana** (use 12)
For months, rich, clear orange-yellow flowers top this shrubby perennial. (Nearly year-round in Florida.) Another great nectar source for butterflies and night moths. See *Lantana* 'New Gold', p. 150.

J **'Amethyst' passionflower** (use 1)
Grown in a pot with a stake for support, this evergreen twining vine bears deeply lobed dark green leaves and knockout purple flowers. The leaves provide food for the larvae of Gulf fritillary butterflies. See *Passiflora* x 'Amethyst', p. 156.

K **Patio**
Precast pavers form the patio and edge for the little pool. Both inexpensive and durable, pavers are also easy to install. See p. 182.

L **Water feature**
Garden centers stock small fiberglass pools and simple fountains that are easy to install. See p. 184.

SITE: Sunny

SEASON: Spring

CONCEPT: A small patio and garden will make an inviting destination most anywhere on your property.

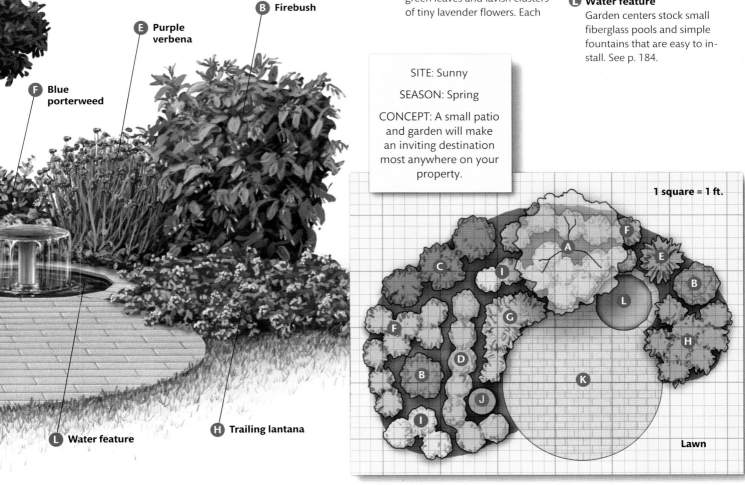

E Purple verbena
B Firebush
F Blue porterweed
L Water feature
H Trailing lantana
1 square = 1 ft.
Lawn

Shady oasis

If your yard is shaded by a large tree or nearby building, you might try this design featuring palms and other tropical plants that appreciate a little shade (and regular watering).

Like the previous design, this one creates a self-contained spot for entertainment and relaxation. Instead of the bountiful flowers of sun-loving plants, these trees, shrubs, ferns, and perennials have outstanding qualities in form and foliage. The contrasting forms, textures, and colors play off one another and off the bold patterns of the irregular flagstones.

SITE: Shady

SEASON: Spring

CONCEPT: A self-contained garden is an entertainment spot for a shady site.

1 square = 1 ft.

Lawn

Plants & Projects

A Yaupon holly (use 1)
A small broad-leaved evergreen tree with a vase-shaped growth habit, contoured trunks, and a dense crown of leathery leaves. Female hollies produce masses of bright red berries that last into winter. See *Ilex*, Evergreen hollies: *I. vomitoria*, p. 146.

B Lady palm (use 3)
Lustrous, dark green palm fronds on reedlike stems make this slow-growing palm an outstanding choice for a small patio. Well-established clumps can reach heights of 7 ft. See *Rhapis excelsa*, p. 159.

C Yellow anise (use 6)
This adaptable evergreen shrub should be on everyone's wish list of hedges. It wears a thick coat of yellow-green elliptical foliage reaching all the way to the ground. When the leaves are cut or crushed, they release a licorice scent. See *Illicium parviflorum*, p. 148.

D Zebra ginger (use 1)
This bold evergreen shrub will electrify any planting with its yellow-and-green striped leaves and long clusters of strikingly colored bell-shaped flowers. You can cut the flowers to enjoy indoors, too. See *Alpinia zerumbet* 'Variegata', p. 132.

E Cast-iron plant (use 17)
Dark green, swordlike leaves of this perennial create a bold silhouette against the stripey yellow anise leaves. Dependably evergreen. See *Aspidistra elatior*, p. 133.

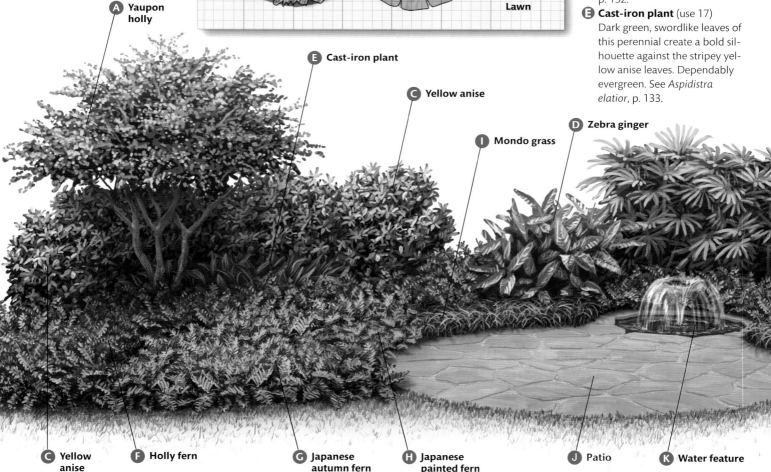

A Yaupon holly
E Cast-iron plant
C Yellow anise
I Mondo grass
D Zebra ginger
C Yellow anise
F Holly fern
G Japanese autumn fern
H Japanese painted fern
J Patio
K Water feature

F **Holly fern** (as needed)
Prized for its coarse, shiny foliage, this unusual-looking fern is a beautiful companion to more traditional feathery types. Plant 24 in. apart. See Ferns: *Cyrtomium falcatum*, p. 142.

G **Japanese autumn fern** (use 12)
This gorgeous plant displays coppery new growth among bright green leaves. See Ferns: *Dryopteris erythrosora*, p. 142.

H **Japanese painted fern** (use 3)
A delicate, low-growing fern with silvery fronds edged in maroon. See Ferns: *Athyrium nipponicum* 'Pictum', p. 142.

I **Mondo grass** (as needed)
This evergreen woodland perennial resembles grass but never needs mowing. Plant 10 in. apart. It spreads quickly into a soft carpet of ultra-thin leaf blades. See *Ophiopogon japonicus*, p. 155.

J **Patio**
Try flagstones, as shown here, for a different texture and feel than precast pavers. See p. 181.

See p. 93 for the following:

K **Water feature**

B **Lady palm**

E **Cast-iron plant**

F **Holly fern**

VARIATIONS ON A THEME

Located away from the house, these patios and plantings afford opportunities for relaxation and entertaining.

Nestled in a lushly green, shady spot, engagingly mismatched garden furniture and several colorful potted plants offer a comfortable retreat.

Backed by small trees and the giant leaves of elephant's ears, sitters here can enjoy the view and pleasant sound of a small fountain.

This formal patio provides ample space for large gatherings.

Garden in the Round

CREATE A PLANTING WITH SEVERAL ATTRACTIVE FACES

Plantings in domestic landscapes are usually "attached" to something. Beds and borders hew to property lines, walls, or patios; foundation plantings skirt the house, garage, or deck. Most are meant to be viewed from the front, rather like a wall-mounted sculpture in raised relief.

On the other hand, the planting shown here is only loosely moored to the property line, forming a peninsula jutting into the lawn. It is an excellent option for those who want to squeeze more gardening space from a small lot, add interest to a rectangular one, or divide a large area into smaller "outdoor rooms." Because you can walk around most of the bed, plants can be displayed "in the round," presenting different scenes from several vantage points

in the yard.

Without a strong connection to a structure or other landscape feature, a bed like this (or its close cousin, the island bed, which floats free of any anchors) requires an active sensitivity to scale. To be successful, the bed must neither dominate its surroundings nor be lost in them. The combination of large and small, subtle and bold plants is attractive when viewed up close or from a distance, and there's always something to admire as you stroll by.

Spring is the most colorful season, with lots of lovely flowers and new foliage. But evergreen shrubs, summer-flowering perennials, handsome fall foliage, and eye-catching winter berries provide interest through the rest of the year.

Saucer magnolia **A**

'Halcyon' hosta **B**

Plants & Projects

If you want more flowers, it's easy to add them to this planting. For spring bloom, plant small bulbs in any open space beneath the wax myrtles and daffodils among the perennials. Follow the bulbs with annual impatiens beneath the wax myrtles. You can also substitute annuals for some of the heavenly bamboo along the edge of the bed. Plant pansies in the fall for a winter show and sun-loving annuals in the spring for summer display.

A **Saucer magnolia** (use 1 plant)
A classic small deciduous tree, it offers large showy white, pink, or purple flowers in early spring. Large leaves, attractive bark, and pleasing form round out the year. Trim off the lower limbs to accommodate plants below. See *Magnolia* x *soulangiana*, p. 153.

B **'Halcyon' hosta** (use 12)
A shade-loving perennial, it forms a pool of colorful leaves beneath the magnolia, powder blue in spring, darkening to

blue-green in summer. See *Hosta*, p. 144.

C **'Obsession' heavenly bamboo** (use 15)
A small shrub whose evergreen leaves change from gold to green to red from spring to winter. It forms a compact mound and rarely needs pruning. See *Nandina domestica*, p. 154.

D **Wax myrtle** (use 2)
Sizable evergreen shrubs with slender stems and glossy leaves provide year-round privacy along the property line. Female plants bear clusters of gray berries in fall and winter. See *Myrica cerifera*, p. 154.

E **Lenten rose** (use 7)
Some of the very first flowers to appear in early spring are this evergreen perennial's nodding, cup-shaped blooms in pink, rose, white, or greenish shades. The large lobed leaves complement the slender foliage of the wax myrtles. See *Helleborus orientalis*, p. 144.

F **Creeping phlox** (use 17)
A perennial ground cover with fragrant flowers in spring and evergreen foliage. It will spread among the Lenten rose in front of the wax myrtles. See *Phlox stolonifera*, p. 156.

G **Bengal tiger canna** (use 3)
A striking perennial with a lush tropical look. Large yellow-and-green-striped leaves and eyecatching orange flowers from early summer to fall. See *Canna* 'Pretoria', p. 137.

H **'Caesar's Brother' Siberian iris** (use 3)
The erect grassy leaves of this perennial contrast with the rounded forms of spirea and pincushion flower. Bears elegant deep purple flowers in late spring. See *Iris sibirica*, p. 148.

I **'Snowmound' spirea** (use 1)
A deciduous shrub that is aptly named for its look in spring when covered with clusters of pure white flowers. Its neat

mound of arching stems and dark blue-green foliage is attractive the rest of the season. See *Spiraea nipponica*, p. 164.

J **Double Japanese aster** (use 7)
This easy perennial forms an upright clump of small leaves and produces numerous, tiny, white double flowers with yellow centers in summer and again (if cut back) in fall. See *Kalimeris pinnatifida*, p. 149.

K **'Butterfly Blue' pincushion flower** (use 7)
For months of misty blue color (and lots of butterflies) in the middle of the bed, you can't beat this little perennial. Round flowers on wiry stems appear in late winter and go right on until frost if you keep picking off spent blossoms. See *Scabiosa columbaria*, p. 163.

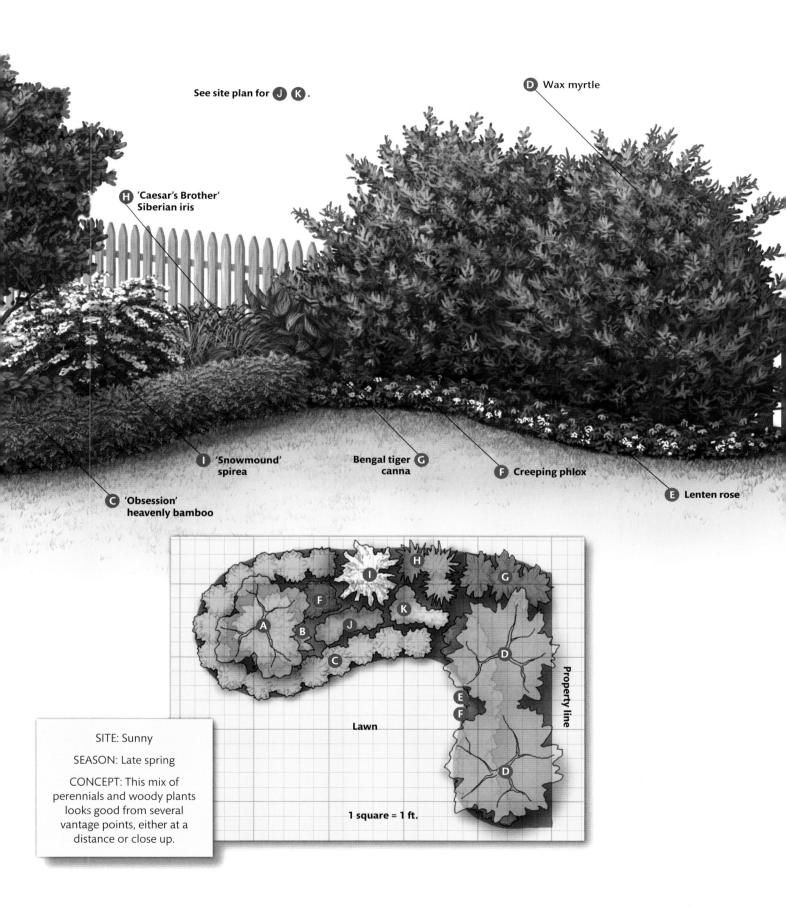

See site plan for **J** **K** .

D Wax myrtle

H 'Caesar's Brother' Siberian iris

I 'Snowmound' spirea

G Bengal tiger canna

F Creeping phlox

E Lenten rose

C 'Obsession' heavenly bamboo

SITE: Sunny

SEASON: Late spring

CONCEPT: This mix of perennials and woody plants looks good from several vantage points, either at a distance or close up.

Property line

Lawn

1 square = 1 ft.

Favoring fall

This planting is designed to lift your spirits after a long, hot summer. Butterfly bush, chrysanthemum, veronica, and verbena will all be blooming in the fall, in shades of blues, purples, pinks, and whites. The tall, elegant ornamental grass, sedum, and coneflowers add rich golds, tans, and bronzes to this scene.

This design will shine in other seasons as well. The pink dogwood will be the focal point of the spring garden, joined by a carpet of purple ajuga and white candytuft. There are plenty of flowers during the summer; several attract clouds of butterflies as a bonus. Colorful dried foliage and seed heads complement evergreen foliage in winter.

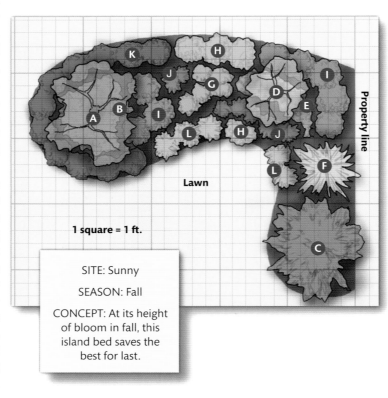

1 square = 1 ft.

Lawn

Property line

SITE: Sunny

SEASON: Fall

CONCEPT: At its height of bloom in fall, this island bed saves the best for last.

Plants & Projects

A **Dogwood** (use 1 plant)
A small deciduous tree offering spring flowers, light green foliage that turns crimson in fall, and bright red berries in autumn. Buy a pink-flowered cultivar. See *Cornus florida*, p. 140.

B **'Burgundy Glow' ajuga** (use 25)
A perennial ground cover with foliage mixing shades of purple, green, and white. Spikes of blue flowers add color beneath the dogwood in spring. See *Ajuga reptans*, p. 131.

C **'Yoshino' Japanese cedar** (use 1)
The fine-textured foliage of this handsome, fast-growing evergreen tree is bright green in summer, bronzy in winter. See *Cryptomeria japonica*, p. 141.

D **'White Profusion' butterfly bush** (use 1)
The arching branches of this deciduous shrub carry long clusters of fragrant white flowers at their tips. It blooms in summer and fall, providing a focal point for the bed and

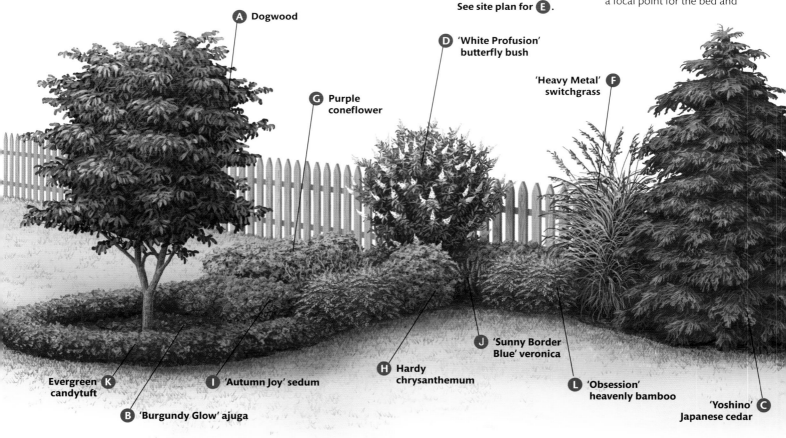

A Dogwood

D 'White Profusion' butterfly bush

See site plan for **E** .

F 'Heavy Metal' switchgrass

G Purple coneflower

J 'Sunny Border Blue' veronica

H Hardy chrysanthemum

K Evergreen candytuft

I 'Autumn Joy' sedum

L 'Obsession' heavenly bamboo

C 'Yoshino' Japanese cedar

B 'Burgundy Glow' ajuga

nectar for butterflies. See *Bud-dleia davidii*, p. 135.

E **'Homestead Purple' verbena** (use 6)
A low-growing and spreading perennial with evergreen foliage. Blooms steadily from summer until late fall, bearing round clusters of rosy purple flowers that look lovely beneath the white butterfly bush. See *Verbena canadensis*, p. 167.

F **'Heavy Metal' switchgrass** (use 1)
A stiff, metallic-blue grass with flower panicles that turn beige in fall. The foliage color turns an attractive amber color in winter. See *Panicum virgatum*, p. XX.

G **Purple coneflower** (use 5)
A durable prairie perennial that bears dark pink daisylike flowers with dark centers above a mound of dark foliage. Blooms in summer; dried seed heads last through the winter. See *Echinacea purpurea*, p. 141.

H **Hardy chrysanthemum** (use 4)
A much-loved perennial, its broad mound of aromatic foliage is covered with small, clear pink or white blossoms in fall. See *Dendranthema*, p. 141.

I **'Autumn Joy' sedum** (use 8)
Flat-topped pale pink flower clusters appear above this perennial's fleshy foliage in August. They mature to dark pink and are attractive through the winter. See *Sedum*, p. 164.

J **'Sunny Border Blue' veronica** (use 5)
The lustrous green, crinkled leaves of this perennial are topped with bright blue flower spikes from early summer to frost if you clip off spent flowers. See *Veronica*, p. 167.

K **Evergreen candytuft** (use 11)
An evergreen perennial with a loose rounded form. It is covered with bright white flowers in spring and may bear some scattered blooms in fall. See *Iberis sempervirens*, p. 146.

See p. 96 for the following:

L **'Obsession' heavenly bamboo** (use 5)

VARIATIONS ON A THEME

Large or small, a garden you can stroll around offers multiple attractions.

Tree roses add height and a touch of formality to a narrow island bed.

With large shrubs, roses, grasses, perennials, and ground covers, this island packs a lot into a relatively small space.

This garden-in-the-round is a striking study in foliage textures. When in bloom, the azaleas in the central bed transform the planting's character.

Create a "Living" Room

A PATIO GARDEN PROVIDES PRIVACY AND PLEASURE

A patio can become a true extension of your living space with the addition of plants to screen views and to create an attractive setting. In this design, plants and wooden screens at one end of the patio form a "wall" of three-dimensional and constantly changing floral motifs. The handsome brick floor accommodates a family barbecue or a large gathering. Together, plants and patio nicely commingle the "indoors" with the "outdoors."

Scale is particularly important when you're planting near the house. The small flowering cherry tree will grow large enough to cast welcome shade on the patio without overwhelming the house. The two staggered screen panels are large enough to block views from neighboring yards; covered with the evergreen foliage and lovely flowers of honeysuckle, they blend right into the planting. (Hummingbirds also love the honeysuckle's flowers, and songbirds like to dine on its berries.)

Evergreen shrubs are an attractive presence year-round and provide, along with the tree and vines, lovely flowers and fragrance from early spring to fall. Perennials add striking accents of flowers and foliage—flamboyant bronze cannas, cheery daylilies, and aromatic geraniums with pretty pink flowers.

The design can be adapted to suit patios in a range of sizes. (The drawing extends into the foreground to indicate this possibility.) Just extend the planting of gardenias and pittosporums along the house and, if you like, repeat part or all of the large "wall" planting along the edge of the patio or at the other end.

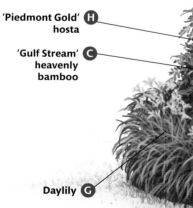

Yoshino cherry **A**

Trumpet **B**
honeysuckle

Screen **K**

'Piedmont Gold' **H**
hosta

'Gulf Stream' **C**
heavenly
bamboo

Daylily **G**

Plants & Projects

The patio and fence are sizable projects, but their rewards are large. Check local codes before building the fence. You'll need to cut some bricks for the angled edges, but the interesting shape is worth it. Once established, the plants require little maintenance beyond seasonal cleanup and simple pruning.

A **Yoshino cherry** (use 1 plant)
This lovely small deciduous tree brings shade to the patio. Fragrant pink or white flowers cluster along its bare branches in early spring; green leaves turn yellow in fall. See *Prunus* x *yedoensis*, p. 158.

B **Trumpet honeysuckle** (use 2)
This vigorous evergreen vine will quickly cover the screen panels with glossy blue-green leaves. Trumpet-shaped coral, red, or yellow flowers decorate the vine in early summer and appear off and on the rest of the season. See *Lonicera sempervirens*, p. 152.

C **'Gulf Stream' heavenly bamboo** (use 6)
A shrub with true four-season appeal. Its slender erect stems bear evergreen leaves that change color from gold to green to red with the seasons. In summer, the bush produces clusters of white flowers. See *Nandina domestica*, p. 154.

D **Dwarf pittosporum** (use 7)
This evergreen shrub brings a lush, dressy look to the patio with its neat mounds of shiny dark green leaves. Creamy white flowers scent the air in early summer. See *Pittosporum tobira* 'Wheeleri', p. 158.

E **'Radicans' gardenia** (use 9)
A dwarf form of the popular evergreen shrub beloved for the sweet, heavy scent of its creamy white flowers. Its low mounds of glossy dark green leaves spill onto the patio, and the flowers perfume the air for weeks in summer. See *Gardenia jasminoides*, p. 142.

F **Bronze canna** (use 8)
The large, lush purple-bronze leaves and showy red or orange flowers keep this popular heat-loving perennial colorful from early summer until fall. See *Canna*, p. 137.

G **Daylily** (use 18)
For an attractive edging of grassy light green foliage and cheerful summer flowers, this durable perennial can't be beat. Sizes vary and flower colors cover the spectrum; you can mix cultivars to extend bloom through most of the summer. See *Hemerocallis*, p. 144.

H **'Piedmont Gold' hosta** (use 3)
Brighten the shady spot beneath the cherry tree with this perennial's large, golden yellow, heart-shaped leaves. Forms a big clump of foliage, topped with white flowers for a few weeks in mid- to late summer. See *Hosta*, p. 144.

I **Bigroot geranium** (use 9)
Mounds of this perennial's deeply lobed, aromatic leaves edge the patio year-round. (It may die back in cold winters.) It bears pink flowers in late spring; leaves turn red to purple in winter. See *Geranium macrorrhizum*, p. 143.

J **Patio**
Brick pavers edged with 4x4 landscape timbers make a handsome durable patio that goes with almost any architectural style. See p. 182.

K **Screens**
These tall panels provide privacy, while gaps between the boards allow air to circulate among the plants. See p. 204.

House

K F

G

B G

C C I

F K

B A

H E

C

D

G

Lawn

1 square = 1 ft.

E

D

J

SITE: Sunny

SEASON: Early summer

CONCEPT: Planting provides privacy and colorful, fragrant ambiance on the patio.

F Bronze canna

E 'Radicans' gardenia

I Bigroot geranium

'Radicans' gardenia E

Dwarf D pittosporum

Dwarf pittosporum D

Patio J

VARIATIONS ON A THEME

Plants enrich outdoor living by defining spaces both large and small as well as by their beauty.

Roses in bloom present the perfect occasion for this spontaneous garden room.

A fence provides privacy as well as a scaffold for a lovely patio-side planting.

This spacious patio, with its shade tree and low edgings, is almost, but not quite, part of the nearby woods.

Private patio in the shade

If your patio is already blessed with a cool canopy of shade, perhaps from a large tree nearby, consider this planting. The basic design is the same as on the previous pages, but here a garden of shade-loving shrubs and a small understory tree afford screening and ambiance for those on the patio.

The light and airy dogwood is unsurpassed for a patio accent in a shady setting. The deciduous oakleaf hydrangea performs all year round, as do the evergreen shrubs and ground covers that complete the planting. Together they provide a pleasing range of leaf textures and colors. In spring, the planting bursts with flowers in pink and white that delight the eye and freshen the air on the patio with delicious scent.

Plants & Projects

Ⓐ **Dogwood** (use 1 plant)
A popular native, this small deciduous tree produces clouds of white or pink flowers in spring and dark green foliage that turns red in fall, when it is joined by a crop of red berries. See *Cornus florida*, p. 140.

Ⓑ **'Roseum Elegans' rhododendron** (use 4)
Tall enough to serve as a privacy screen for the patio, this evergreen shrub is a stately presence with glossy leaves and pink flowers in late spring. See *Rhododendron*, p. 161.

Ⓒ **Oakleaf hydrangea** (use 1)
An all-season performer, this deciduous shrub offers white flowers in late spring, colorful foliage in fall, and pretty peeling bark in winter. It grows

See site plan for **G**.

B 'Roseum Elegans' rhododendron

Dogwood **A**

Oakleaf **C** hydrangea

Drooping leucothoe **E**

Gumpo azalea **F**

Florida leucothoe **D**

Gumpo azalea **F**

Drooping leucothoe **E**

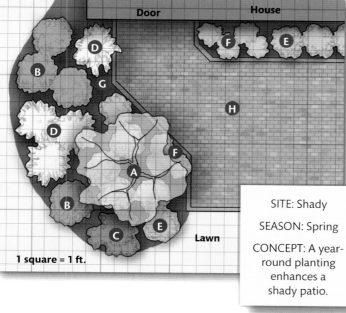

Door   House

SITE: Shady

SEASON: Spring

CONCEPT: A year-round planting enhances a shady patio.

1 square = 1 ft.

Lawn

large enough to help screen the patio in summer. See *Hydrangea quercifolia*, p. 146.

D **Florida leucothoe** (use 4)
One of the best evergreen shrubs for shade, with arching stems of willowy light green leaves. In spring, its bell-shaped white flowers waft a honey fragrance over the patio. This is a vigorous plant; an annual pruning will keep it in bounds. See *Leucothoe populifolia*, p. 151.

E **Drooping leucothoe** (use 8)
A lower-growing, spreading cousin of Florida leucothoe, with fragrant white flowers in spring and mounding dark green foliage that turns pur-plish in winter. See *Leucothoe fontanesiana*, p. 151.

F **Gumpo azalea** (use 7)
The small evergreen leaves give this low, spreading shrub a fine texture. Clusters of frilly pink mor white flowers cover the foliage in late spring. See *Rhododendron*, p. 161.

G **Ground cover**
(use 1 per sq. ft.)
When the plants are young, fill bare ground in the bed with evergreen ground covers such as vinca (*Vinca minor*, p. 167) or creeping phlox (*Phlox stolonifera*, p. 156). As the other plants grow to the sizes shown above, the shade will diminish or kill the ground covers.

See p. 100 for the following:
H Patio

Elegant Symmetry

MAKE A FORMAL GARDEN FOR THE BACKYARD

Formal landscaping often lends dignity to the public areas around a home (see p. 28). Formality can also be rewarding in a more private setting. There, the groomed plants, geometric lines, and symmetrical layout of a formal garden can help to organize the surrounding landscape, provide an elegant area for entertaining, or simply be enjoyed for their own sake.

A series of hedges and edgings define this small garden, punctuated by tidy evergreen trees and shrubs at the corners. Flowers contribute color and fragrance for months from summer through autumn. The foliage looks good year-round.

Formal gardens like this one look self-contained on paper. But even more than other types of landscaping, actual formal gardens work well only when carefully correlated with other elements in the landscape, such as the house, garage, patio, and major plantings. Transitions between formal and more casual areas are particularly important. Separating areas with expanses of lawn, changes of level, or plantings that screen sight lines helps formal and informal elements coexist comfortably.

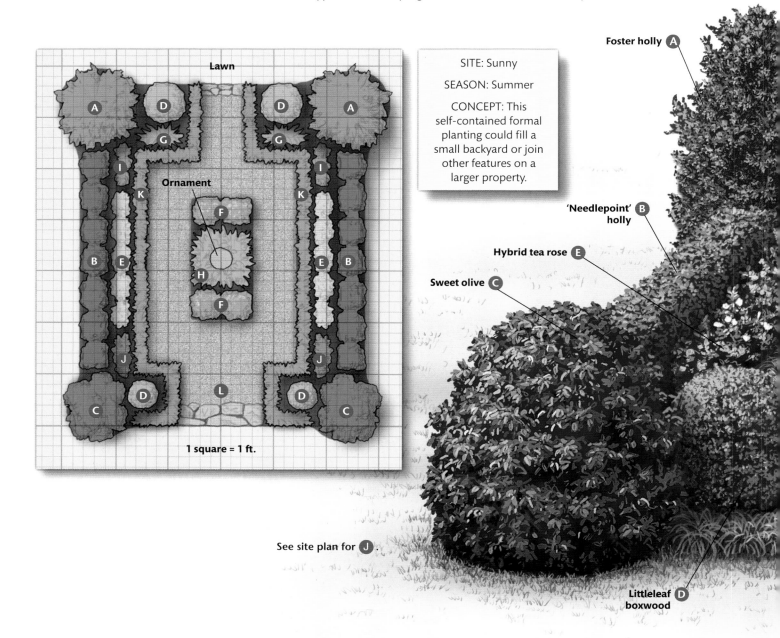

Lawn

Ornament

SITE: Sunny

SEASON: Summer

CONCEPT: This self-contained formal planting could fill a small backyard or join other features on a larger property.

1 square = 1 ft.

See site plan for **J**.

Foster holly **A**

'Needlepoint' holly **B**

Hybrid tea rose **E**

Sweet olive **C**

Littleleaf boxwood **D**

Plants & Projects

Shaping plants for a formal garden takes patience and persistence. The holly hedge will need a few years to fill in, and it and the abelia will require regular shearing to look their best. The other trees and shrubs can have loosely formal shapes as shown here or be sheared to a more rigid geometry. Prune the roses in late winter.

Ⓐ Foster holly (use 2 plants)
The pyramidal form and deep green leaves of this broad-leaved evergreen tree add visual weight to the design. Needs little pruning and bears lots of rich red winter berries. See *Ilex*, Evergreen hollies: *I. x attenuata* 'Foster #2', p. 146.

Ⓑ 'Needlepoint' holly (use 14)
A dense evergreen shrub ideal for a hedge, with shiny leaves and a magnificent show of red winter berries. See *Ilex*, Evergreen hollies: *I. cornuta*, p. 146.

Ⓒ Sweet olive (use 2)
An evergreen shrub with a dense compact form. Its holly-like leaves are glossy dark green. In autumn the sweetly scented flowers perfume the entire garden. See *Osmanthus x fortunei*, p. 155.

Ⓓ Littleleaf boxwood (use 4)
This evergreen shrub naturally forms a compact globe. Small, bright green, glossy leaves give it a fine texture. See *Buxus microphylla*, p. 137.

Ⓔ Hybrid tea rose (use 10)
The classic rose, elegant, fragrant, and right at home in a formal setting. Choose your favorites for months of bloom. See *Rosa*, p. 161.

Ⓕ 'Edward Goucher' abelia (use 4)
An evergreen shrub that bears rosy purple flowers from early summer to frost. Dark green leaves turn bronze in winter. Can be pruned to any shape. *See Abelia*, p. 130.

Ⓖ Siberian iris (use 10)
An aristocratic perennial with striking flowers in late spring and slender arching foliage that looks good all summer. See *Iris sibirica*, p. 148.

Ⓗ Dwarf fountain grass (use 8)
A perennial offering graceful tufts of slender leaves that are green in summer, gold or tan in fall and winter. Fluffy flowers rise above the foliage from summer on. See *Pennisetum alopecuroides* 'Hameln', p. 156.

Ⓘ Blazing star (use 6)
A prairie native, this durable perennial bears lavender flower spikes on leafy stems, making a colorful, upright accent in midsummer. Attracts butterflies, too. See *Liatris spicata*, p. 151.

Ⓙ Scarlet sage (use 8)
A bushy perennial often grown as an annual. Bright red flowers heat up the garden's corners for months in the summer. See *Salvia coccinea*, p. 163.

Ⓚ Lilyturf (use 90)
Spiky grasslike clumps of evergreen leaves make this perennial an ideal edging. It bears small purple flowers in late summer. Space 1 ft. apart. See *Liriope muscari*, p. 152.

Ⓛ Path
Crushed stone looks just right here. Flagstones across the entries help keep stones out of the lawn. See p. 176.

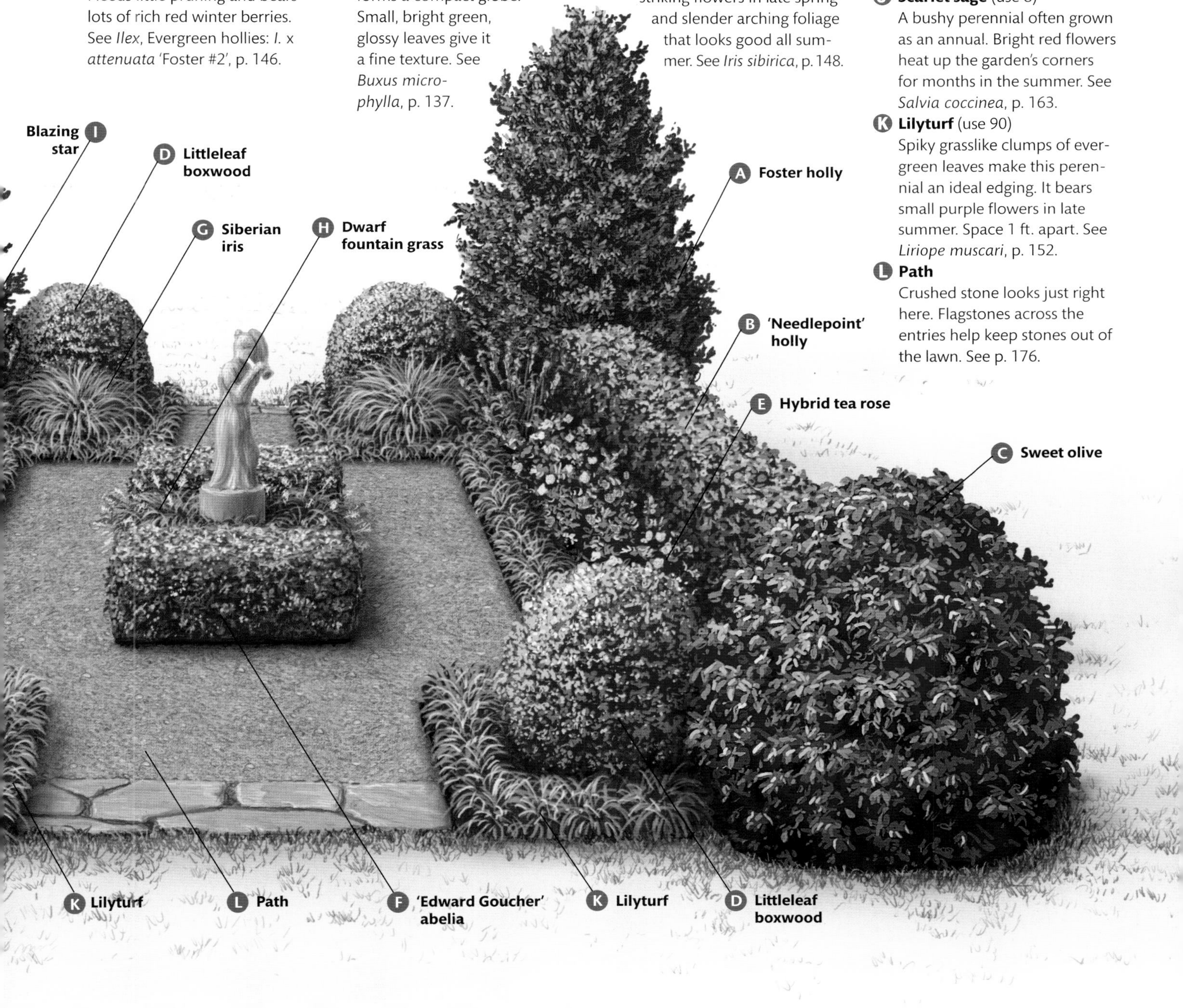

Blazing star **Ⓘ**
Ⓓ Littleleaf boxwood
Ⓖ Siberian iris
Ⓗ Dwarf fountain grass
Ⓐ Foster holly
Ⓑ 'Needlepoint' holly
Ⓔ Hybrid tea rose
Ⓒ Sweet olive

Ⓚ Lilyturf
Ⓛ Path
Ⓕ 'Edward Goucher' abelia
Ⓚ Lilyturf
Ⓓ Littleleaf boxwood

A formal terrace

In this design, a small terrace with table and chairs is given a formal setting, providing a lovely spot for an intimate lunch or a restful hour with a favorite book.

The geometry of this patio garden is similar to that of the previous plan, with several tiers of hedges and edging along the sides and strong accents at the corners. Here an avenue of lawn approaches the terrace. In summer, the planting abounds in flowers offering vivid colors, delicious

fragrance, and the gentle companionship of butterflies. On the terrace, containers with lively warm-season annuals augment the sights and scents of the summer garden. Abundant evergreen foliage and containers of cool-season annuals make the garden an inviting spot on sunny days from fall to spring.

SITE: Sunny

SEASON: Summer

CONCEPT: This formal setting for intimate gatherings is enhanced by colorful scented flowers and handsome foliage.

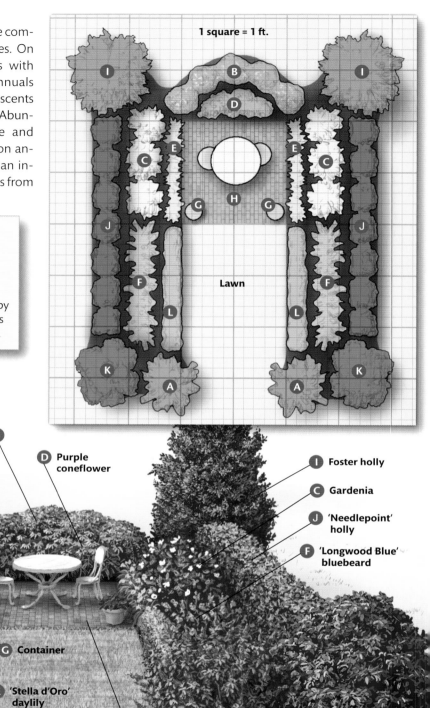

1 square = 1 ft.

Lawn

Foster holly I

Gardenia C

'Longwood Blue' bluebeard F

'Needlepoint' holly J

Glossy abelia B

D Purple coneflower

I Foster holly

C Gardenia

J 'Needlepoint' holly

F 'Longwood Blue' bluebeard

G Container

E 'Stella d'Oro' daylily

Terrace H

L Littleleaf boxwood

K Sweet olive

A 'Black Knight' butterfly bush

'Black Knight' butterfly bush A

K Sweet olive

Plants & Projects

(A) 'Black Knight' butterfly bush
(use 2 plants)
Arching branches of this deciduous shrub carry long spikes of fragrant deep purple flowers at their tips from midsummer to fall. See *Buddleia davidii*, 135.

(B) Glossy abelia (use 5)
Pale pink flowers cover this evergreen shrub all summer. Dark green leaves turn purple- bronze in winter. See *Abelia* x *grandiflora*, p. 130.

(C) Gardenia (use 6)
An evergreen shrub with heavily scented creamy white flowers in summer. The cultivar 'Mystery' or 'August Beauty' would work well here. See *Gardenia jasminoides*, p. 142.

(D) Purple coneflower (use 10)
Large pink daisylike flowers with dark centers float above this perennial's mound of dark green foliage in summer. See *Echinacea purpurea*, p. 141.

(E) 'Stella d'Oro' daylily (use 12)
This popular perennial edges the terrace with grassy foliage and bright golden yellow flowers from early summer until frost. See *Hemerocallis*, p. 144.

(F) 'Longwood Blue' bluebeard (use 10)
Fringed blue flowers and the butterflies they attract grace the soft gray-green foliage of this deciduous shrub from late summer to frost. See *Caryopteris* x *clandonensis*, p. 138.

(G) Containers
For bright accents on the terrace, fill pots with long-blooming annuals. Replace the plantings in fall and spring. See Annuals, p. 132.

(H) Terrace
A terrace 10 ft. square accommodates a small table and chairs and can be built in a weekend or two. We've shown brick here; select paving material to complement your home. See p. 182.

See p. 105 for the following:

(I) Foster holly (use 2)

(J) 'Needlepoint' holly (use 14)

(K) Sweet olive (use 2)

(L) Littleleaf boxwood (use 20)

VARIATIONS ON A THEME

Formal gardens often require more from a gardener—more time, more planning, more effort. Results like these are ample reward for such industry.

Stately columns are the focal points at the end of an alley formed by mixed borders.

Formality doesn't require acres. This colorful little gem could tuck easily into the corner of a small yard.

Combining tightly and loosely trimmed shrubs, the pillowy, layered masses of this garden invite a restful stroll.

A Shady Hideaway

CREATE A FRAGRANT OASIS IN A CORNER OF YOUR BACKYARD

C 'Nellie R. Stevens' holly

B Goldflame honeysuckle

A Carolina jasmine

K Arbor

D Saucer magnolia

L Paving

I Mealy blue sage

J Dwarf fountain grass

H 'Powis Castle' artemisia

G 'Emerald Heights' distylium

One of life's little pleasures is sitting in a shady spot reading a book or newspaper or just looking out onto your garden, relishing the fruit of your labors. If your property is long on lawn and short on shade, a bench under a leafy arbor can provide a cool respite from the cares of the day. Tucked into a corner of the property and set among attractive shrubs, vines, and perennials, the arbor shown here is a desirable destination.

Carefully selected and placed plants create a cozy enclosure. In addition to the vines covering the arbor, evergreen shrubs behind and to each side of it afford year-round screening. Plantings in front of the arbor reinforce the seclusion but don't obscure your view of the rest of the property. As they mature, the magnolia and smoke tree will give the planting a "woodsier" feel.

Whether you're strolling around the planting or relaxing beneath the arbor, you can enjoy flowers and fragrance from spring through fall. Bloom begins early with the magnolia and Carolina jasmine. Summer is full of flowers and the creatures attracted to them. Fragrant blossoms of honeysuckle and butterfly bush, the fluffy plumes of smoke tree, and the graceful spikes of mealy blue sage linger until the first hard frost in fall. Take a moment to savor the aromatic foliage of artemisia; this perennial stays fresh looking almost year-round.

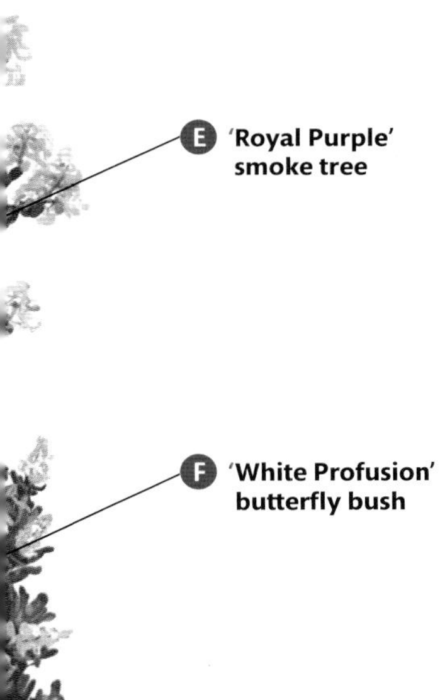

Plants & Projects

The arbor, paving, and plants can be installed in a few weekends. Pruning is the main chore in this planting. You'll need to trim the bottom limbs from the magnolia and smoke tree. The vines and shrubs will need yearly pruning, mostly to control their size.

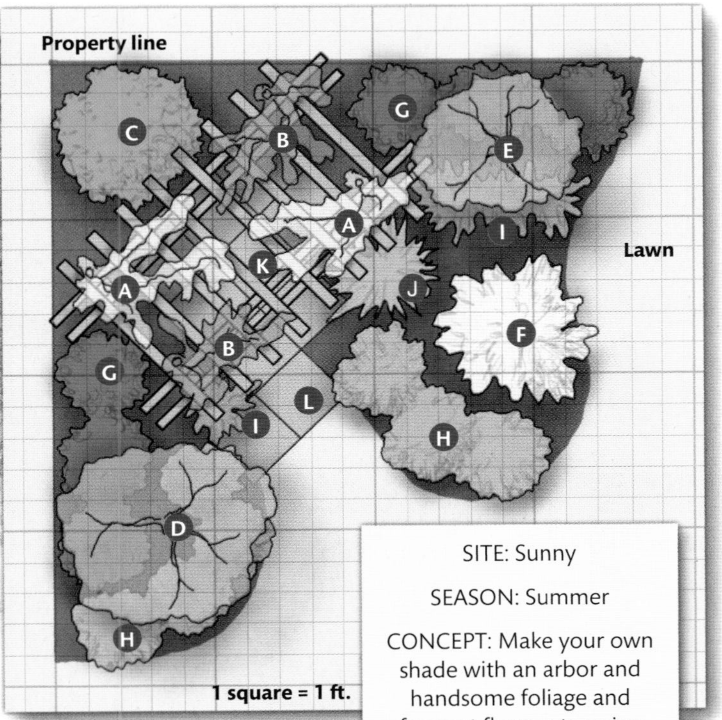

A Carolina jasmine
(use 2 plants)
An evergreen twining vine with fragrant bell-shaped flowers in early spring and slender dark green leaves that turn maroon in winter. See *Gelsemium sempervirens*, p. 143.

B Goldflame honeysuckle
(use 2)
A fast-growing vine providing summer color, fragrance, and shade. Blooms heavily in early summer, then off and on into fall. Its flowers are yellow on the inside, creamy pink on the outside. The handsome blue-green leaves shelter the arbor through the winter. See *Lonicera x heckrottii*, p. 152.

C 'Nellie R. Stevens' holly (use 1)
This tough, fast-growing evergreen holly screens the back of the arbor. Heavy crops of dark red berries sparkle on the dark waxy leaves if there is a male Chinese holly nearby. See *Ilex, Evergreen hollies*, p. 146.

D Saucer magnolia (use 1)
This popular deciduous tree offers fine form, handsome gray bark, and large oblong leaves. Distinctive white, pink, or purple flowers appear in early spring. Remove the lower branches to accommodate the plants beneath. See *Magnolia x soulangiana*, p. 153.

E 'Royal Purple' smoke tree
(use 1)
Pruned to a tree form by removal of the lower branches, this deciduous shrub provides colorful leaves from spring through fall and fluffy pink flowers in summer and fall. See *Cotinus coggygria*, p. 140.

F 'White Profusion' butterfly bush (use 1)
Arching branches of this deciduous shrub are tipped with fragrant white flowers from midsummer through fall. See *Buddleia davidii*, p. 135.

G 'Emerald Heights' distylium
(use 6)
This compact, dense, broadleaf, evergreen shrub makes an outstanding foundation plant with excellent resistance to pests and diseases. Late winter produces red flowers along the stem. See *Distylium*, p. XX.

H 'Powis Castle' artemisia
(use 7)
This perennial's mounds of aromatic lacy silver foliage set off the colors of the neighboring sage and cherry laurel. See *Artemisia*, p. 133.

I Mealy blue sage (use 12)
From early summer until frost, this perennial adds abundant color with spikes of blue flowers. Glossy green foliage makes attractive clumps. See *Salvia farinacea*, p. 163.

J Dwarf fountain grass (use 1)
In summer, arching green leaves and fluffy flower spikes bring a contrast in texture to the planting. In autumn and winter, this perennial grass is tan or gold; its dry leaves rustle musically next to the bench. See *Pennisetum alopecuroides* 'Hameln', p. 156.

K Arbor
This substantial structure can be built in a weekend. If you use cedar or cypress, you can let it weather to a handsome silver-gray color. See p. 203.

L Paving
Precast concrete pavers make an attractive, sturdy surface for the bench. Choose a color that will complement the flowers or foliage. See p. 176.

E 'Royal Purple' smoke tree

F 'White Profusion' butterfly bush

Property line

Lawn

1 square = 1 ft.

SITE: Sunny

SEASON: Summer

CONCEPT: Make your own shade with an arbor and handsome foliage and fragrant flowers to enjoy while you relax.

A gazebo makes a special garden retreat. Surrounding this one are river birches in beds of spring-flowering bulbs and azaleas. As the trees leaf out, they create an even more private haven.

VARIATIONS ON A THEME

What a treat to steal a quiet moment in a shady spot surrounded by lovely plants.

Roses shelter this simple, rustic arbor made of peeled posts.

Tucked among trees and extensive plantings, this arbor creates an outdoor room large enough for several people.

A cool spot for a nice site

If your site is hot and dry, the planting shown here is for you. Like the design on the previous pages, this one creates a cool, private retreat, but it does so with plants that tolerate heat and drought.

The plants in this design produce abundant flowers, but the foliage is perhaps even more compelling. Their texture and color is outstanding—broad leaves, narrow leaves, plump and succulent, thin and flowing leaves in gold, bronze, maroon, blue, silver, and a range of greens. The honeysuckle has it all: evergreen leaves and lovely fragrant flowers. Enjoy the hummingbirds drawn to its flowers; then be serenaded by songbirds dining on the berries that follow.

Plants & Projects

Ⓐ **Trumpet honeysuckle**
(use 2 plants)
This vigorous evergreen vine produces trumpet-shaped coral, red, or yellow flowers for most of the summer. See *Lonicera sempervirens*, p. 152.

Ⓑ **Pink anemone clematis**
(use 2)
Clouds of fragrant pink dogwoodlike flowers appear in profusion on this deciduous vine in spring. See *Clematis montana* 'Rubens', p. 139.

Ⓒ **Cleyera** (use 1)
Evergreen shrub with colorful leaves makes a year-round screen behind the arbor. Large red berries heighten fall and winter interest. See *Ternstroemia gymnanthera*, p. 165.

Ⓓ **'Goldflame' spirea** (use 5)
Deciduous shrub with arching stems and bright gold foliage that turns red in fall; pale pink summer flowers. See *Spiraea japonica*, p. 164.

Arbor **L**

Bronze canna **G**

'Shenandoah' **F**
switchgrass

B Pink anemone
clematis

A Trumpet
honeysuckle

See site plan for **C** .

'Moonshine' **I**
yarrow

'Goldflame' **D**
spirea

'Stella d'Oro' **K**
daylily

'Autumn Joy' **H**
sedum

Blue fescue **J**
grass

'Crimson Pygmy' **E**
Japanese barberry

E **'Crimson Pygmy'**
Japanese barberry (use 7)
Low deciduous shrubs edge the
front of the planting; maroon
leaves turn crimson in fall. See
Berberis thunbergii, p. 134.

F **'Shenandoah' switchgrass**
(use 2) A dense clumping perennial grass with a fairly upright growth habit. It produces
attractive wispy, pink-tinged
flower panicles above the foliage in summer. See *Panicum
virgatum*, p. XX.

G **Bronze canna** (use 12)
A large perennial with lush
bronze leaves and showy summer flowers in bright colors.
See *Canna*, p. 137.

H **'Autumn Joy' sedum** (use 6)
The gray-green succulent foliage of this perennial is topped
by flat flower clusters that mature from pale pink to rusty red
during late summer to fall. See
Sedum, p. 164.

I **'Moonshine' yarrow** (use 6)
Flat clusters of lemon yellow
flowers bloom for weeks in
summer atop this perennial.
The lacy and aromatic gray-
green foliage nicely sets off the
colors of the nearby plants. See
Achillea, p. 131.

J **Blue fescue grass** (use 3)
A perennial whose fine blue
leaves form neat tufts that
look great against the cannas
and barberries. Foliage lasts
through winter. See *Festuca
ovina* var. *glauca*, p. 142.

K **'Stella d'Oro' daylily** (use 20)
This popular perennial edges
the front of the planting with
grassy light green foliage and
cheerful golden yellow flowers
from mid-June until fall. See
Hemerocallis, p. 144.

See p. 109 for the following:

L **Arbor**

M **Paving**

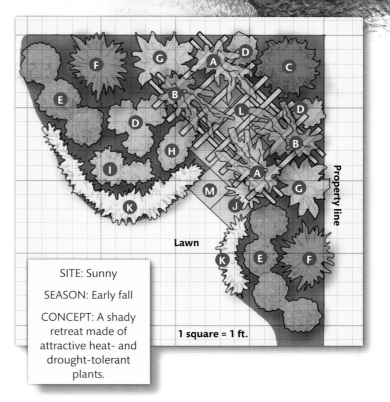

SITE: Sunny

SEASON: Early fall

CONCEPT: A shady
retreat made of
attractive heat- and
drought-tolerant
plants.

1 square = 1 ft.

Property line

Lawn

Back to Nature

CREATE A WOODED RETREAT IN YOUR BACKYARD

The open spaces and squared-up property lines in many new subdivisions (and some old neighborhoods as well) can make a home-owner long for the seclusion of a wooded landscape. It may come as a surprise that you can create just such a retreat on a property of even modest size. With a relatively small number of carefully placed trees and shrubs, you can have your own backyard nature park.

Trees and shrubs take time to reach the siz-able proportions we associate with a wood-land. The plants in this design were chosen in part because they make an attractive setting in their early years, too. Here we show the young planting a few years after installation. On the following pages you'll see the planting as it appears at maturity.

The grassy peninsula extending into the planting is an open "room" in the early years, with the juvenile trees and shrubs function-ing as a large mixed border. While the woody plants are small, a selection of durable peren-nials and wildflowers provides a focal point for the planting. Arrayed along the front of the bed, colorful perennials enliven the summer months. Two low-growing native wildflowers, both self-seeding annuals, carpet the ground between the small trees and shrubs.

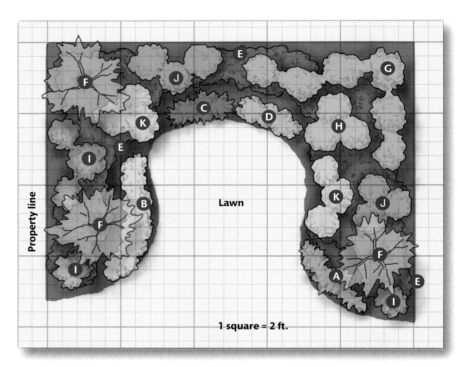

1 square = 2 ft.

Loblolly pine **F**

K 'Black Knight' butterfly bush

I Oakleaf hydrangea

B 'Goldsturm' coneflower

I Oakleaf hydrangea

E Annual wildflowers

Plants & Projects

Although this is a large planting, you can install it in several weekends. The biggest job is tilling and amending the soil of the entire area for planting; the healthy vigorous growth of the plants will repay the effort. Annual maintenance includes pruning away dead or damaged branches of the trees and shrubs and cleaning up the spent flowers and foliage of the perennials and wildflowers in spring and fall.

While the young trees and shrubs are growing, the plants described here will provide their full range of attractions in just a few years. You can arrange the perennials as shown here or intermix them, using a few plants of each perennial in each of the three areas. Include some daylilies, scarlet sage, or Siberian iris if you want more variety. Space any of these perennials about 2 ft. apart.

Ⓐ **Blazing star** (use 8 plants)
Spikes of small purple flowers rise on tall leafy stalks above a small mound of stiff grassy foliage in midsummer. Flowers attract butterflies and look good in dried arrangements. There are white-flowered cultivars, too; combine white with purple if you choose. See *Liatris spicata*, p. 151.

Ⓑ **'Goldsturm' coneflower** (use 8)
Bears dozens of large, golden yellow, "black-eyed Susans" in late summer. Let the seeds ripen to feed the birds in winter. It forms a large mound of rich green foliage that is attractive all season. See *Rudbeckia fulgida*, p. 162.

Ⓒ **Northern sea oats** (use 5)
A clump-forming ornamental grass with wide, light green leaves and, from midsummer on, interesting seed heads that dance in the wind. Cut the foliage back in spring so you can enjoy its lovely russet or tan color in winter. See *Chasmanthium latifolium*, p. 138.

Ⓓ **Purple coneflower** (use 5)
This prairie perennial produces an irregular mound of coarse dark green leaves topped by stiff branching flower stalks that carry large pink daisylike flowers with dark centers in midsummer. There are white-flowered cultivars too, and both pink and white would look good here. Leave some seed heads for winter interest and the finches they attract. See *Echinacea purpurea*, p. 141.

Ⓔ **Annual wildflowers** (sow seeds)
You can use native wildflowers to form a low ground cover under trees and shrubs. Annual phlox (*Phlox drummondii*), with pink, red, or white flowers, and Indian blanket (*Gaillardia pulchella*), with red-and-yellow flowers, are shown here. Both grow less than 1 ft. tall, so they won't shade or compete with the young shrubs. Both bloom from early summer through most of the season, attracting butterflies. These plants bear seeds and die in the fall; new seedlings will sprout the next spring. See Annuals, p. 132.

See p. 115 for the following:
Ⓕ **Loblolly pine** (use 3)
Ⓖ **Burford holly** (use 6)
Ⓗ **Winterberry holly** (use 3)
Ⓘ **Oakleaf hydrangea** (use 5)
Ⓙ **Chokeberry** (use 6)
Ⓚ **'Black Knight' butterfly bush** (use 6)

SITE: Sunny

SEASON: Summer

CONCEPT: Mixed planting across the back of a lot attracts birds and wildlife. Shown here just a few years after installation.

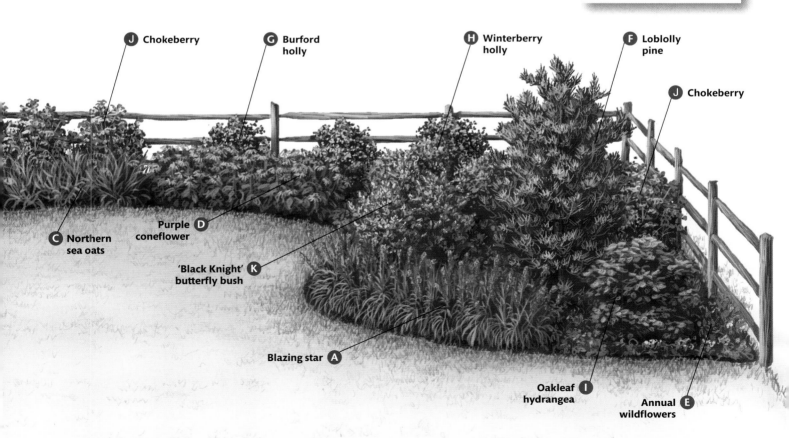

Ⓙ Chokeberry
Ⓖ Burford holly
Ⓗ Winterberry holly
Ⓕ Loblolly pine
Ⓙ Chokeberry
Ⓒ Northern sea oats
Purple coneflower Ⓓ
'Black Knight' Ⓚ butterfly bush
Blazing star Ⓐ
Oakleaf hydrangea Ⓘ
Annual Ⓔ wildflowers

This lovely garden contrasts effectively with the woodland beyond the rose-covered gate.

VARIATIONS ON A THEME

On an acreage or a suburban lot, you can create a garden that welcomes wildlife and offers you a little slice of nature.

A wide gravel path accommodates several people on a comfortable stroll through this planting.

Even on a small lot, a mature nature garden can evoke a larger woods. Potted plants and topiaries are a playful reminder of the domesticity nearby.

The mature woodland

Change and growth are the essence of living things, but when plants are small, it's not easy to imagine what they'll look like in about 15 years. So we've done it for you.

The grassy peninsula is now a small woodland meadow framed by sturdy trees rising up to 30 ft. Beneath them, shrubs that once seemed to stand too far apart create leafy masses 6 to 8 ft. tall, providing the sense of enclosure and privacy you longed for. Birds and small wildlife abound.

Along the sunny edge of the planting, the perennials continue to provide their colorful summer display. Where sun penetrates between the shrubs, the same native annuals cover the ground; in shadier spots they've been replaced by vinca or other low-growing shade-tolerant ground covers.

SITE: Sunny

SEASON: Fall

CONCEPT: After about 15 years, the planting is a private shady woodland retreat.

Plants & Projects

A **Loblolly pine** (use 3 plants)
This fast-growing evergreen tree is a regional favorite, ideal for this planting. Cone-shaped at first, it assumes a handsome open layered form. Trim off lower branches to accommodate shrubs below. See *Pinus taeda*, p. 157. Equally suitable here would be longleaf pine (*Pinus palustris*) or Eastern white pine (*Pinus strobus*), both discussed on p. 157.

B **Burford holly** (use 6)
A large shrub or small tree, this evergreen forms a tall screen across the back corner of the yard. Its leathery, glossy green leaves make a great backdrop for the magnificent show of red berries. See *Ilex*, Evergreen hollies: *I. cornuta* 'Burfordii', p. 146. You could substitute 'Nellie R. Stevens' *holly* or American holly (*I. opaca*). See p. 146 for both.

C **Winterberry holly** (use 3)
An abundance of bright red berries shine through the fall and winter days after this upright deciduous shrub drops its leaves. Dark green foliage turns yellow in fall. Plant one male cultivar as a pollinator to ensure a good berry crop. See *Ilex verticillata*, p. 148.

D **Oakleaf hydrangea** (use 5)
This native deciduous shrub is eye-catching year-round. Clusters of papery flowers that appear in spring change color and last through fall. Dark green leaves turn red and purple in fall. Peeling bark in shades of cinnamon and rust ornament the winter scene. See *Hydrangea quercifolia*, p. 146.

E **Chokeberry** (use 6)
Another four-season performer, this deciduous shrub offers shiny dark green leaves and small white flowers in spring, crimson foliage in fall, and a crop of small red berries all through the winter. A good companion for the hollies. See *Aronia arbutifolia*, p. 132.

F **'Black Knight' butterfly bush** (use 6)
Butterflies love this deciduous shrub, and you will, too. The arching branches carry long clusters of fragrant deep purple flowers from summer into fall. See *Buddleia davidii*, p. 135.

See p. 113 for the following:

G **Blazing star**

H **'Goldsturm' coneflower**

I **Northern sea oats**

J **Purple coneflower**

K **Annual wildflowers**

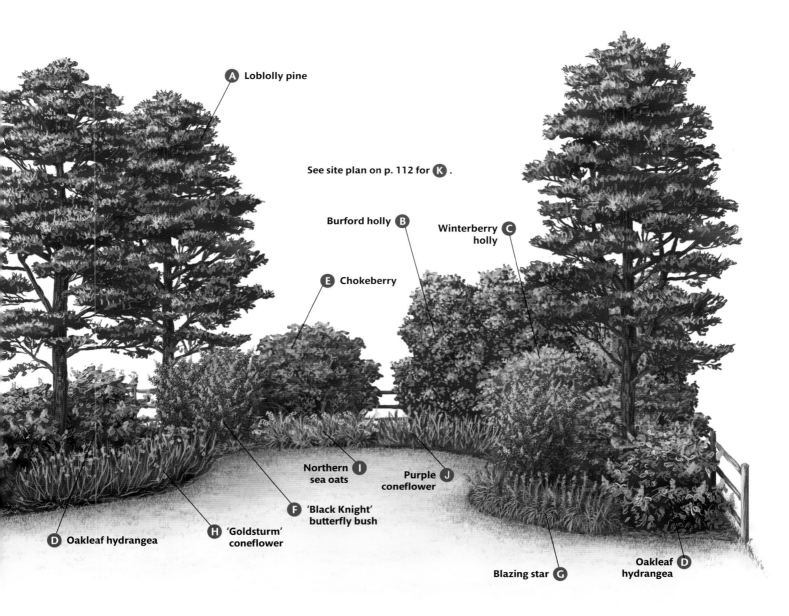

See site plan on p. 112 for **K** .

Loblolly pine **A**

Burford holly **B**

Winterberry holly **C**

E Chokeberry

Northern sea oats **I**

Purple coneflower **J**

F 'Black Knight' butterfly bush

H 'Goldsturm' coneflower

D Oakleaf hydrangea

Blazing star **G**

Oakleaf hydrangea **D**

Splash Out

MAKE A HANDSOME WATER GARDEN IN A FEW WEEKENDS

A water garden adds a new dimension to a landscape. It can be the eye-catching focal point of the entire property, a center of outdoor entertainment, or a quiet out-of-the-way retreat. A pond can be a hub of activity—a place to garden, watch birds and wildlife, raise ornamental fish, or stage an impromptu paper-boat race. It just as easily affords an opportunity for some therapeutic inactivity; a few minutes contemplating the ripples on the water's surface provides a welcome break in a busy day.

A pond can't be easily moved, so choose your site carefully. Practical considerations are outlined on pp. 142–145 (along with instructions on installation); think about those first. Then consider how the pond and its plantings relate to the surroundings. Before plopping a pond down in the middle of the backyard, imagine how you might integrate it, visually if not physically, with nearby plantings and structures.

The plantings in this design are intended to settle the pond comfortably into an expanse of lawn. The soil excavated during construction of the pond forms a mound along one side, a subtle change of elevation that adds a surprising amount of interest to a flat site. Seen from a distance, the trees, shrubs, ornamental grasses, and perennials that frame the pond resemble an island bed. Viewed from a comfortable seat at water's edge, however, the mound and plantings provide enclosure, privacy, and a sense of being on the island looking at its flora and fauna.

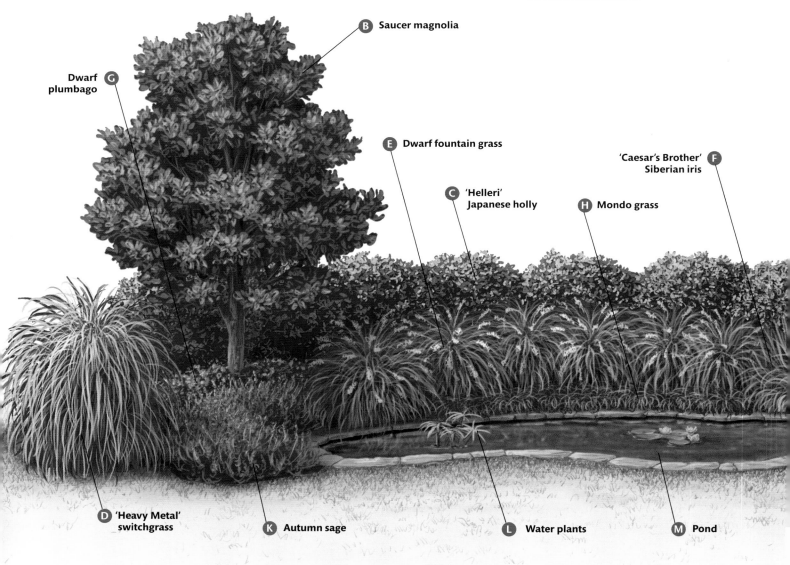

B Saucer magnolia

Dwarf plumbago G

E Dwarf fountain grass

'Caesar's Brother' Siberian iris F

C 'Helleri' Japanese holly

H Mondo grass

D 'Heavy Metal' switchgrass

K Autumn sage

L Water plants

M Pond

Plants & Projects

Once established, the plants take pretty good care of themselves. The pond, however, requires more attention to keep a healthy balance of water plants and fish (if you have them) in order to maintain oxygen levels and to keep algae in check. Consult local or mail-order suppliers to help you get the right mix.

A **Japanese maple**
(use 1 plant)
A small deciduous tree with lovely form and finely cut leaves. Choose a cultivar that has red leaves in summer. See *Acer palmatum*, p. 130.

B **Saucer magnolia** (use 1)
A deciduous tree prized for its large velvety leaves, handsome gray bark, and (of course) the large showy white, pink, or purple flowers it bears in early spring. See *Magnolia* x *soulangiana*, p. 153.

C **'Helleri' Japanese holly**
(use 9)
Planted on the back slope of the soil mound, this compact evergreen shrub makes a fine informal hedge. See *Ilex*, Evergreen hollies: *I. crenata*, p. 146.

D **'Heavy Metal' switchgrass**
(use 1)
A stiff, metallic-blue grass with flower panicles that turn beige in fall. The foliage color turns an attractive amber color in winter. See Panicum virgatum, p. XX.

E **Dwarf fountain grass** (use 6)
Broad mounds of grassy leaves echo the larger holly hedge behind this perennial. Its green leaves and flower spikes are gold and tan through the winter. See *Pennisetum alopecuroides* 'Hameln', p. 156.

F **'Caesar's Brother' Siberian iris** (use 3)
A perennial with striking blue-purple flowers in late spring and good-looking slender green leaves the rest of the season. See *Iris sibirica*, p. 148.

G **Dwarf plumbago** (use 12)
A perennial ground cover with small indigo blue flowers in summer and fall and smooth dark green leaves that turn maroon in fall. See *Ceratostigma plumbaginoides*, p. 138.

H **Mondo grass** (use 12)
The grassy leaves of this evergreen perennial ground cover edge the pond with dark green through all four seasons. See *Ophiopogon japonicus*, p. 155.

I **'Ebony Knight' black mondo grass** (use 20)
The slender purple-black foliage of this evergreen perennial carpets the ground beneath the maple in striking contrast to the adjacent green-and-gold moneywort. See *Ophiopogon planiscapus*, p. 155.

J **Moneywort** (use 15)
This fast-spreading perennial ground cover has bright green coin-shaped leaves and pretty yellow summer flowers. See *Lysimachia nummularia*, p. 153.

K **Autumn sage** (use 7)
Bushy perennial makes a bright red accent beside the pond all summer and fall. Glossy foliage can be evergreen in mild winters. See *Salvia greggii*, p. 163.

L **Water plants** (use 1 each)
Plant a dwarf water lily, a dwarf lotus, and a dwarf papyrus in pots; then set the pots in the pond. (See p. 185.) Add some oxygenating plants to keep the water clear and to sustain fish. See Water plants, p. 168.

M **Pond**
Installing a pond is arduous but simple work, requiring a weekend or two of energetic digging and a commercially available pond liner. Fieldstone disguises the liner edge and lends a natural look to the pond. See p. 184.

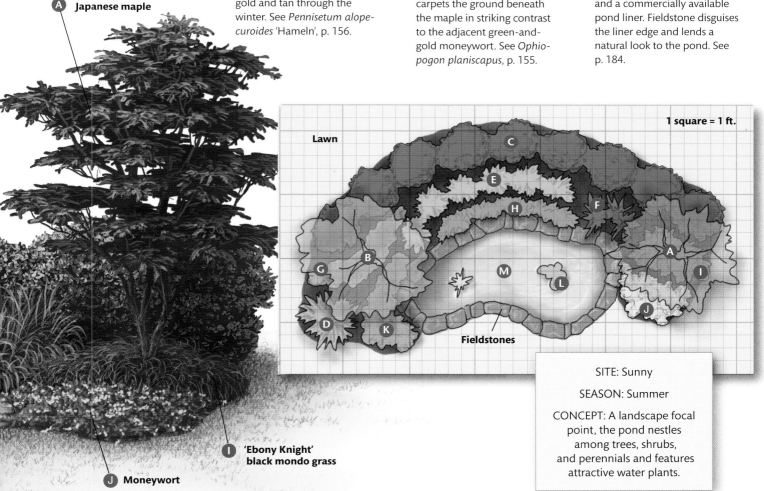

A Japanese maple

I 'Ebony Knight' black mondo grass

J Moneywort

1 square = 1 ft.

Lawn

Fieldstones

SITE: Sunny

SEASON: Summer

CONCEPT: A landscape focal point, the pond nestles among trees, shrubs, and perennials and features attractive water plants.

Mini-pond

This little pond provides the pleasures of water gardening for those without the space or energy required to install and maintain a larger pond. Within its smaller confines you can enjoy one or more water plants as well as a few fish. You might install a small fountain or, as shown here, opt for a simple reflecting pool.

Pond and plantings can stand alone in an expanse of lawn, but they will look their best integrated into a larger scheme. For instance, the scale is just right for use as the focal point of a patio planting.

We've selected plants that dangle and droop, mound and arch to create contours and contrasts that are similar to those in the previous design but on a more intimate scale. The varied foliage and colorful flowers suggested here make an attractive display in all four seasons.

Plants & Projects

Ⓐ Pink Gumpo azalea
(use 7 plants)
Low, spreading shrubs make neat mounds of small ever-green leaves that are an excellent backdrop for a late-spring display of distinctive pink flowers. See *Rhododendron*, p. 161.

Ⓑ Germander (use 3)
A perennial that forms a low mound of small shiny evergreen leaves. Bears tiny pink-purple flowers in late summer. See *Teucrium chamaedrys*, p. 166.

Ⓒ Northern sea oats (use 1)
This perennial grass has wide green leaves topped from mid-summer by clusters of flat seed heads that droop gracefully beside the pool. Winter color is a lovely warm tan. See *Chasmanthium latifolium*, p. 138.

Ⓓ Hardy chrysanthemum
(use 3)
An heirloom perennial to brighten autumn days, forming a broad mound covered with small blossoms in late fall. Choose from cultivars with pink, white, or yellow flowers. See *Dendranthema*, p. 141.

Ⓔ 'Moonbeam' coreopsis
(use 8)
A durable perennial with delicate-looking foliage and pale yellow flowers that bloom from June to September. See *Coreopsis verticillata*, p. 139.

Ⓕ Variegated Japanese sedge
(use 8)
Neat low tufts of grassy ever-green leaves, striped yellow and green, make this perennial grass ideal for a transition to adjacent lawn. See *Carex morrowii* 'Aureo-variegata', p. 138.

Ⓖ Creeping lilyturf (use 9)
This perennial spreads quickly to form a flowing mat of grassy leaves that stay dark green all year. Bears small lavender flower spikes in summer. See *Liriope spicata*, p. 152.

Ⓗ Pond
A small pond like this can be made with a molded fiberglass shell or plastic liner like the one in the previous design. Select edging stones in scale with the pond. See p. 184.

See p. 117 for the following:

Ⓘ 'Heavy Metal' switchgrass
(use 1)

Ⓙ Dwarf plumbago (use 12)

Ⓚ 'Ebony Knight' black mondo grass (use 5)

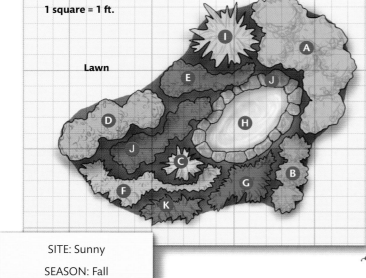

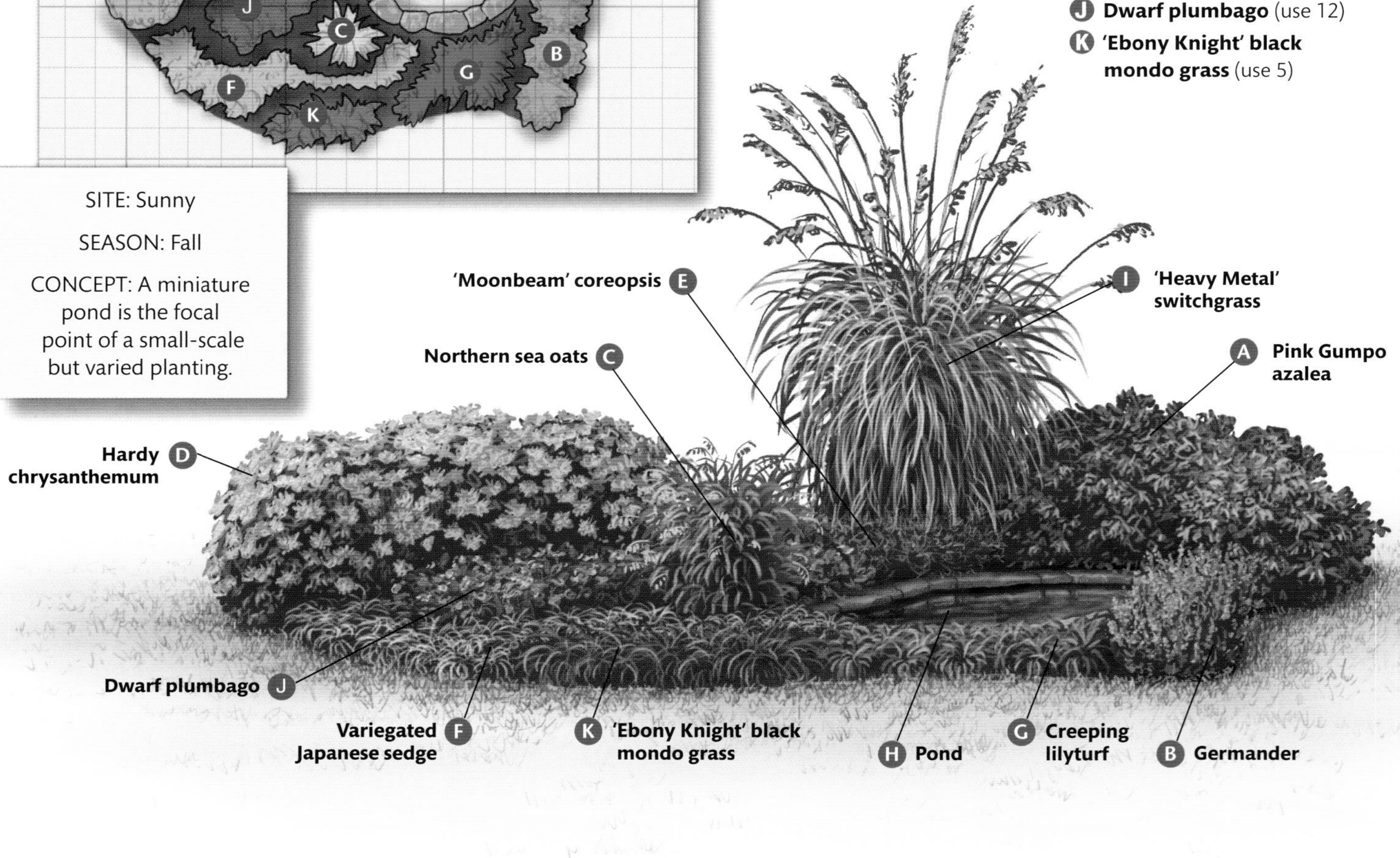

1 square = 1 ft.

Lawn

SITE: Sunny

SEASON: Fall

CONCEPT: A miniature pond is the focal point of a small-scale but varied planting.

'Moonbeam' coreopsis Ⓔ

Northern sea oats Ⓒ

Ⓘ 'Heavy Metal' switchgrass

Ⓐ Pink Gumpo azalea

Hardy Ⓓ chrysanthemum

Dwarf plumbago Ⓙ

Variegated Ⓕ Japanese sedge

Ⓚ 'Ebony Knight' black mondo grass

Ⓗ Pond

Ⓖ Creeping lilyturf

Ⓑ Germander

VARIATIONS ON A THEME

A water feature can be difficult to design and construct, but it can be a marvelous addition to any landscape.

At the corner of a patio, this pond enhances the enjoyment of a morning cup of coffee or a gathering of friends in the evening.

Natural contours, native plants, and irregular stones effectively blend this large pond with its surroundings.

Tucked into a corner by a window, this small pond can be enjoyed from inside the house as well as outside.

Under the Old Shade Tree

CREATE A COZY GARDEN IN A COOL SPOT

This planting is designed to help homeowners blessed with a large shade tree make the most of their good fortune. A bench is provided, of course. What better spot to rest on a hot summer day? But why stop there? The tree's high, wide canopy affords an ideal setting for a planting of understory shrubs and perennials. The result is a woodland garden that warrants a visit any day of the year.

The planting roughly coincides with the pool of shade cast by the tree. Evergreen shrubs and masses of mostly evergreen perennials extend around the perimeter. You can position the large mahonias to provide privacy, screen a view from the bench, or block early-morning or late-afternoon sun. Smaller plants (hostas, sedge, and other perennials) are placed nearer the path and bench, where they can be appreciated at close range.

The planting is colorful in spring, when the blossoms of Lenten rose are joined by fragrant yellow mahonia flowers and the scented white blooms of daphne. Pretty as these flowers are, the real attraction here is foliage. As summer heats up, the little woodland is a cool oasis of leaves in a range of textures and colors that brighten the shade. Bands of gold edge the blue-green leaves of hosta and the dark green daphne foliage, while golden flecks sparkle on the aucuba's leathery leaves.

Because most of the plants are evergreen, the display continues year-round. As fall shifts to winter, the tracery of bare branches of the shade tree is nicely balanced by the evergreen tapestry below.

Plants & Projects

For best results, thin the tree canopy, if necessary, to produce dappled rather than deep shade. Also remove limbs to a height of 8 ft. or more to provide headroom. The tree's roots compete for moisture with anything planted nearby. The plants here normally do well in these conditions, but need watering during any prolonged dry spells. Also, mulch generously and add fresh mulch every year or two. (For more on planting under a shade tree, see p. 210 and 217.) If desired, you can fill in bare spots between the shrubs with ajuga, foamflower, or creeping phlox, all of which spread quickly.

A Chinese mahonia
(use 7 plants)
A large evergreen shrub forming an erect clump of stout stems and leathery dark green foliage. Fragrant yellow spring flowers produce showy blue fruit clusters that attract birds. See *Mahonia fortunei*, p. 153.

B Gold-dust aucuba (use 3)
These striking evergreen shrubs with shiny, leathery green leaves flecked with bright yellow provide a colorful backdrop for the bench. See *Aucuba japonica* 'Variegata', p. 134.

C Prostrate Japanese plum yew
(use 7)
A low-growing evergreen shrub that spreads to form a wide, fine-textured cushion of dark green needles that contrasts handsomely with the mahonia. See *Cephalotaxus harringtonia* 'Prostrata', p. 138.

D Variegated winter daphne
(use 1)
The intensely fragrant bursts of starry white flowers that appear on this compact evergreen shrub will scent the entire area in spring. Glossy green leaves edged with gold are lovely near the path. See *Daphne odora* 'Aureomarginata', p. 141.

E Lenten rose (use 20)
In early spring this evergreen perennial bears nodding, cuplike blooms on a clump of large, shiny dark green leaves. Flower colors range from white to rose to shades of pink and green. See *Helleborus orientalis*, p. 144.

F Cast-iron plant (use 7)
This tough evergreen perennial thrives with little light or water. It will spread to form a mass of stiff green leaves at the base of the tree trunk. See *Aspidistra elatior*, p. 133.

G Japanese sacred lily (use 10)
An evergreen perennial forming an arching clump of swordlike leaves. Insignificant yellow flowers produce red berries. See *Rohdea japonica*, p. 161.

H 'Frances Williams' hosta (use 3)
A stately presence, this hardy perennial offers huge yellow-edged blue-green leaves with a seersucker texture. White flowers float on stiff stalks above the foliage in mid- to late summer. See *Hosta*, p. 144.

I Variegated Japanese sedge (use 10)
This perennial's neat low tufts of grasslike evergreen leaves, striped yellow and green, create a colorful ground cover along the path. See *Carex morrowii* 'Aureo-variegata', p. 138.

J Gold moneywort (use 25)
A quickly spreading perennial ground cover, it has golden yellow, coin-shaped leaves. It bears little yellow flowers in summer. See *Lysimachia nummularia* 'Aurea', p. 153.

K Path
Wood chips make an easy, informal surface for the short path and "clearing" in front of the bench. See p. 176.

SITE: Shady

SEASON: Summer

CONCEPT: A shade garden beneath a venerable old tree makes a lovely spot for sitting or strolling.

Prostrate Japanese **C** plum yew

Gold moneywort **J**

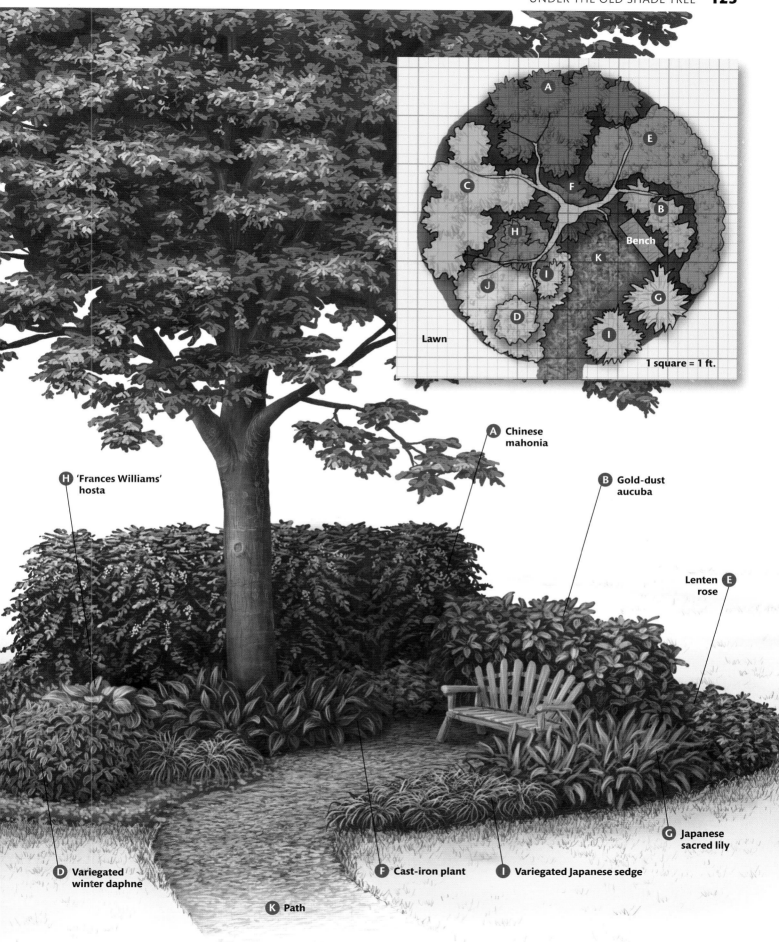

A Chinese mahonia

B Gold-dust aucuba

H 'Frances Williams' hosta

Lenten **E** rose

D Variegated winter daphne

F Cast-iron plant

I Variegated Japanese sedge

G Japanese sacred lily

K Path

Lawn

Bench

1 square = 1 ft.

VARIATIONS ON A THEME

Plant your own shade tree or take advantage of a venerable specimen to create a special garden spot.

Sometimes a special tree, like this charismatic old redbud, almost demands the presence of benches at its feet.

A piney woodland

A mature pine tree—its lower limbs either shed naturally or trimmed off, its upper branches forming a graceful spreading crown—can shelter a distinctive shade garden. Casting lighter shade and with less competitive roots than many shade trees, it allows a wider range of understory plants.

This planting replaces several tall shrubs in the previous design with ferns to produce the feel of an open woodland. There are flowers and fragrance in spring; the astilbes and hostas add mid- to late- summer bloom; and there is still plenty of evergreen foliage.

If you prefer more screening than provided here, work in a clump of mahonias or gold-dust aucuba. As in the previous design, fill gaps with ajuga, foamflower, or creeping phlox.

Plants & Projects

Ⓐ **Variegated lacecap hydrangea** (use 1 plant)
This deciduous shrub makes a fine accent next to the bench. Its shiny green leaves are edged with creamy white stripes. Blue or pink flowers are scattered in lacy clusters. Blooms in summer. See *Hydrangea macrophylla* 'Mariesii Variegata', p. 146.

Ⓑ **Tassel fern** (use 15)
Planted in a large mass, the glossy evergreen fronds of this fern contrast with the nearby hosta and plum yew foliage. It forms impressive clumps. See Ferns: *Polystichum polyblepharum*, p. 142.

Ⓒ **Japanese autumn fern** (use 5)
Fronds of this fern start out copper-colored in spring and mature to a rich green. It forms narrow, erect clumps. May stand up through mild win-

A collection of shade trees and large, screening shrubs is an ideal spot for a simple gravel patio.

Under the dappled light of this river birch, rose bushes receive enough sun to bloom abundantly.

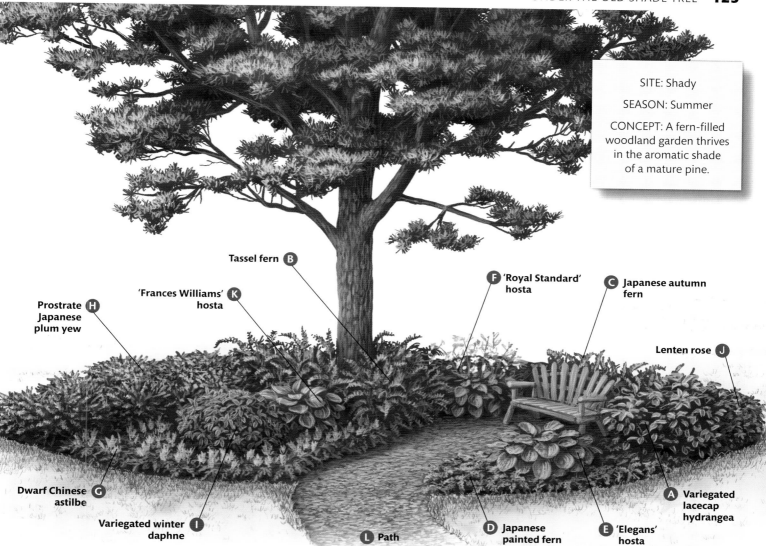

SITE: Shady

SEASON: Summer

CONCEPT: A fern-filled woodland garden thrives in the aromatic shade of a mature pine.

Tassel fern **B**

F 'Royal Standard' hosta

C Japanese autumn fern

'Frances Williams' hosta **K**

Prostrate Japanese plum yew **H**

Lenten rose **J**

Dwarf Chinese astilbe **G**

Variegated winter daphne **I**

L Path

D Japanese painted fern

E 'Elegans' hosta

A Variegated lacecap hydrangea

ters. If frozen to the ground, it recovers in spring. See Ferns: *Dryopteris erythrosora*, p. 142.

D **Japanese painted fern** (use 9)
One of the prettiest foliage plants, with delicately painted fronds blending green, silver, and maroon, this deciduous fern is displayed in front of the bench, where you can really enjoy it. See Ferns: *Athyrium goeringianum* 'Pictum', p. 142.

E **'Elegans' hosta** (use 1)
The huge, blue-gray, textured leaves of this perennial are a marvelous centerpiece among the ferns. White summer flowers are a bonus. See *Hosta sieboldiana*, p. 144.

F **'Royal Standard' hosta** (use 3)
Placed next to the bench, where you can get full benefit from the scent of its large white August flowers. Large, medium green leaves look healthy and

glossy from spring to fall. See *Hosta*, p. 144.

G **Dwarf Chinese astilbe** (use 15)
In late summer, fluffy spires of tiny mauve flowers blanket this low-growing perennial. Used here as a ground cover, its lacy foliage complements the deeply cut ferns nearby and sets off the hosta and daphne planted in its midst. See *Astilbe chinensis* var. *pumila*, p. 133.

See p. 120 for the following:

H **Prostrate Japanese plum yew** (use 7)

I **Variegated winter daphne** (use 1)

J **Lenten rose** (use 20)

K **'Frances Williams' hosta** (use 3)

L **Path**

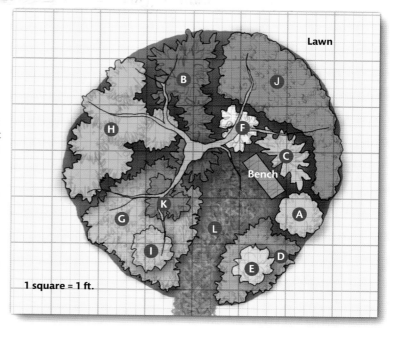

Lawn

1 square = 1 ft.

At Woods' Edge

SHRUB BORDER BORROWS A BACKDROP FROM NATURE

The woodlands and forests of the Southeast are treasured by all who live in the region. Many subdivisions, both new and old, incorporate woodland areas, with homes bordering landscapes of stately trees and large shrubs. (In some older neighborhoods, mature trees on adjacent lots create almost the same woodland feeling.)

The planting shown here integrates a domestic landscape with a woodland at its edge. It makes a pleasant transition between the open area of lawn, with its sunny entertainments, and the cool, secluded woods beyond. The design takes inspiration from the buffer zone of small trees and shrubs nature provides at the sunny edge of a wood, and it should have the same attraction to birds and wildlife

(and the people who enjoy them) as its natural counterpart does.

Small deciduous trees, rising to about 15 ft., mingle with lower-growing shrubs and a carpet of perennial ground covers and spring-blooming bulbs. A path accommodates quiet woodland strolls and provides access to the larger woods beyond.

Whether viewed from the path or the distant house, the planting is attractive all year. Spring offers a range of lovely flowers in white and pink, though chances are you'll find something in bloom any time of the year. Summer puts on a lush show of handsome foliage dappled with flowers. Brilliant leaves light up the fall display, while colorful bare branches and evergreen foliage distinguish the winter scene.

Sweet bay **B** magnolia

'Diana' **A** rose-of-Sharon

Path **M**

Plants & Projects

Even though this design calls for relatively few plants in a large area, preparing the entire planting bed by tilling and amending the soil will pay off in the long run with healthy vigorous growth (see p. 166). A deep mulch of bark or pine straw and regular watering the first summer will speed establishment. Then, devote a weekend each spring and fall to mulching and basic pruning.

A **'Diana' rose-of-Sharon**
(use 1 plant)
An updated version of an old-fashioned favorite, this deciduous shrub puts forth large pure white flowers that are a treat from July through September. See *Hibiscus syriacus*, p. 144.

B **Sweet bay magnolia** (use 1)
This graceful tree blooms with fragrant white flowers in early summer. Its silvery green leaves provide flickering color in a breeze and can remain on the tree through mild winters. See *Magnolia virginiana*, p. 153.

C **Glossy abelia** (use 3)
Pale pink flowers stand out against the glossy green leaves of this evergreen shrub from early summer to frost. See *Abelia* x *grandiflora*, p. 130.

D **Coral bark maple** (use 1)
A four-season tree for the path, an attractive vase shape, scarlet fall foliage, and striking coral-red bark to brighten winter days. See *Acer palmatum* 'Sango Kaku', p. 130.

E **Fringe tree** (use 1)
A small, slow-growing deciduous tree, bushy and typically multistemmed. In May, clusters of spicy-smelling frilly white flowers dangle from every branch. See *Chionanthus virginicus*, p. 139.

F **'Magnoliaeflora' Japanese camellia** (use 1)
An evergreen shrub with glossy leaves and elegant, semidouble, light pink flowers that bloom much of the winter and spring. See *Camellia japonica*, p. 137.

G **'Hummingbird' summersweet** (use 3)
A compact deciduous shrub with wonderfully fragrant white flowers in midsummer and golden fall foliage. See *Clethra alnifolia*, p. 139.

H **Oakleaf hydrangea** (use 1)
A four-season deciduous shrub with papery flowers in late spring, distinctive leaves that are red and purple in fall, and reddish bark for the winter. See *Hydrangea quercifolia*, p. 146.

I **Loropetalum** (use 1)
This evergreen shrub forms layers of arching branches that bear lacy white flowers in spring and may bloom sporadically through summer. See *Loropetalum chinense*, p. 152.

J **'Delaware Valley White' azalea** (use 7)
This evergreen shrub is ideal for the front of the planting, where its large white spring flowers are in full display. See *Rhododendron*, p. 161.

K **Autumn cherry** (use 1)
This small deciduous tree produces a cloud of light pink flowers in late fall and again in early spring. See *Prunus subhirtella* 'Autumnalis', p. 158.

L **Ground-cover** "fillers"
Fill in between the shrubs and trees with evergreen ground covers such as ajuga, creeping phlox, dwarf plumbago, vinca, or ferns, and patches of spring-blooming bulbs. As the woody plants mature, some ground covers may be shaded out.

M **Path**
Simply extend the mulch on the beds to form a path, or install a gravel base if drainage is a concern. See p. 176.

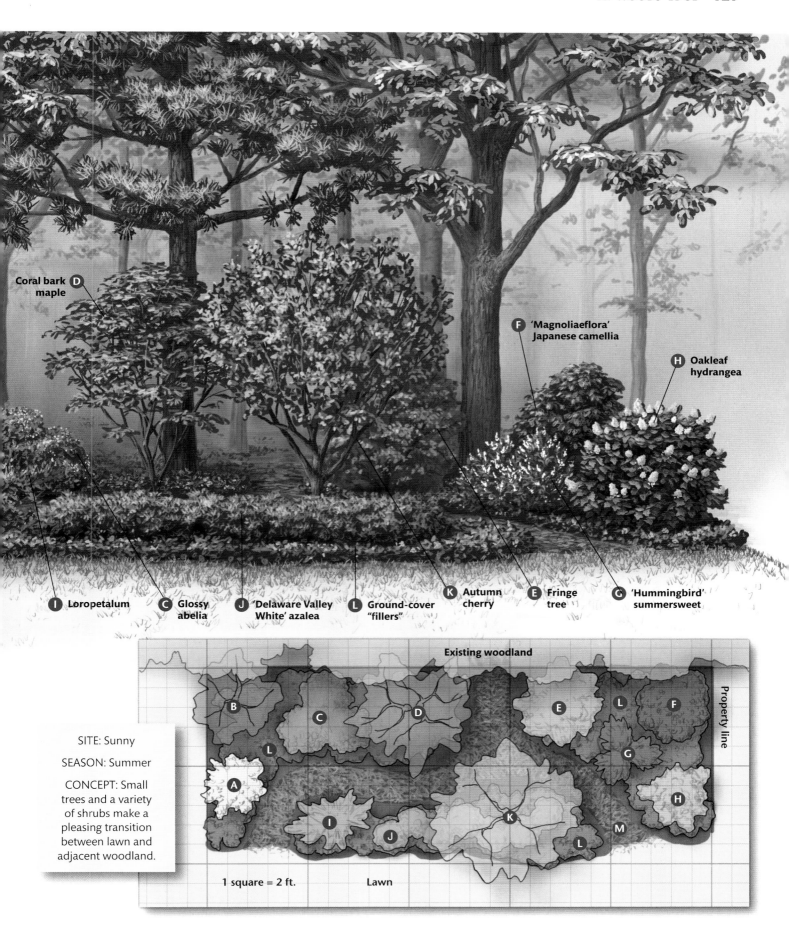

Coral bark D
maple

F 'Magnoliaeflora'
Japanese camellia

H Oakleaf
hydrangea

I Loropetalum   C Glossy
abelia   J 'Delaware Valley
White' azalea   L Ground-cover
"fillers"   K Autumn
cherry   E Fringe
tree   G 'Hummingbird'
summersweet

Existing woodland

Property line

SITE: Sunny

SEASON: Summer

CONCEPT: Small
trees and a variety
of shrubs make a
pleasing transition
between lawn and
adjacent woodland.

1 square = 2 ft.   Lawn

Scented shade

If your lot is on the shady side of a woodland, try this design (shown here in early spring). The layout is much the same in both plantings, but here smaller shade-tolerant trees and shrubs replace some of the previous design's sun lovers.

Once again there are flowers, foliage, berries, and colorful bark to please year-round. The decorative maple moves to the front, where it receives the most sun. Deciduous plants predominate and in fall produce a splendid array of golds, yellows, reds, and purples. The planting's most distinctive feature, however, is fragrance, provided in abundance from early to late spring and again in late summer and fall.

The ground covers listed in the main plan will also perform well in shade, but you might grow more ferns. Consider adding a bench along the path to provide a restful place to sit.

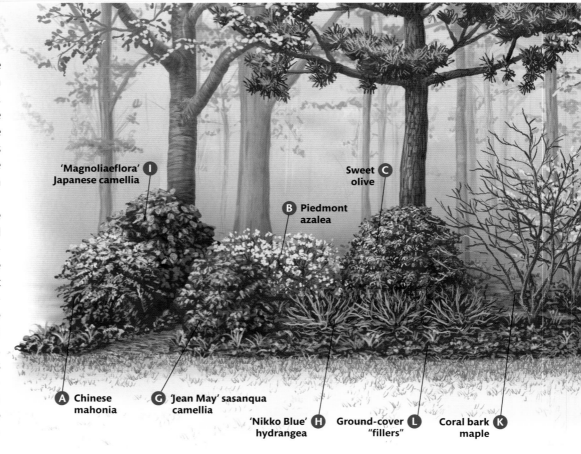

'Magnoliaeflora' **I** Japanese camellia

Sweet **C** olive

B Piedmont azalea

A Chinese mahonia

G 'Jean May' sasanqua camellia

'Nikko Blue' **H** hydrangea

Ground-cover **L** "fillers"

Coral bark **K** maple

SITE: Shady

SEASON: Very early spring

CONCEPT: Selected for a shady site, these trees and shrubs entice strollers to the shrub border with fragrant flowers and bright fall foliage.

Plants & Projects

A **Chinese mahonia**
(use 3 plants)
An evergreen shrub with holly-like foliage, fragrant yellow flowers in early spring, and bird-attracting blue berries. See *Mahonia fortunei*, p. 153.

B **Piedmont azalea** (use 3)
Fragrant white or pink blooms appear in spring on this native deciduous shrub. See *Rhododendron canescens*, p. 161.

C **Sweet olive** (use 1)
This compact shrub bears sweet-scented white flowers in late summer and fall on dense evergreen foliage. See *Osmanthus* x *fortunei*, p. 155.

D **'Arnold Promise'**
witch hazel (use 1)
Fragrant flowers of clear yellow appear in early spring on this small deciduous tree. Fall foliage is gold. See *Hamamelis* x *intermedia*, p. 143.

E **Winterberry holly** (use 3)
A deciduous native shrub with yellow fall foliage. Use one male and two females, so the female plants will bear bright red berries that attract birds. See *Ilex verticillata*, p. 148.

F **'Henry's Garnet'**
Virginia sweetspire (use 5)

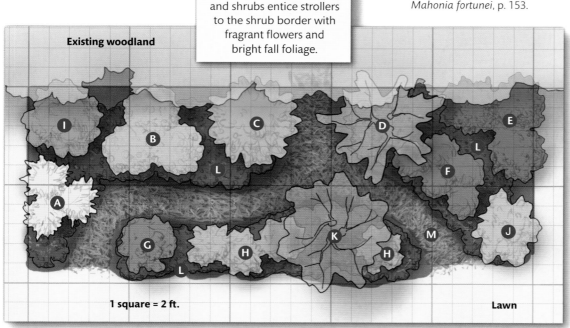

Existing woodland

I
B
A
G
L
C
L
H
K
H
D
F
L
E
M
J

1 square = 2 ft.

Lawn

D 'Arnold Promise'
witch hazel

Winterberry **E**
holly

M Path   **J** Oakleaf
hydrangea

F 'Henry's Garnet'
Virginia sweetspire

VARIATIONS ON A THEME

Ranging from simple passages to extensive gardens, there are many possibilities for a planting adjacent to a woodland.

Azaleas and dogwoods extend this garden right into the woods for a bright springtime show.

Made of bent tree branches and filled out with roses, this rustic structure signposts the path into a woods.

Glossy green leaves of this deciduous shrub turn a deep scarlet in fall. Bears fragrant white flowers in early summer. See *Itea virginica*, p. 149.

G 'Jean May' sasanqua camellia (use 1)
From fall into winter, this compact evergreen shrub welcomes strollers with lovely double pink flowers displayed against glossy leaves. See *Camellia sasanqua*, p. 137.

H 'Nikko Blue' hydrangea (use 4)
Pink or blue snowball-shaped flower clusters cover this deciduous shrub in midsummer. The smooth glossy leaves look great all season. See *Hydrangea macrophylla*, p. 146.

See p. 124 for the following:

I 'Magnoliaeflora' Japanese camellia (use 1)

J Oakleaf hydrangea (use 1)

K Coral bark maple (use 1)

L Ground-cover "fillers"

M Path

A wooden fence atop a low stone wall marks a distinct boundary between a garden and dense woods.

Plant Profiles

Plants are the heart of the designs in this book. In this section you'll find descriptions of all the plants used in the designs, along with information on planting and maintaining them. These trees, shrubs, perennials, grasses, bulbs, and vines have all proven themselves as dependable performers in the region. They offer a wide spectrum of lovely flowers and fruits, handsome foliage, and striking forms. Most contribute something of note in at least two seasons. You can use this section as an aid when installing the designs in this book and as a reference guide to desirable plants for other home landscaping projects.

Using the plant profiles

All of these plants are proven performers in many of the soils, climates, and other conditions commonly found in the region. But they will perform best if planted and cared for as described in the Guide to Installation. In these descriptions and recommendations, the term "garden soil" means soil that has been prepared for planting by digging or tilling and adding some organic matter, so that it's loose enough for roots and water to penetrate easily. Here also, "full sun" means a site that gets at least eight hours a day of direct sun throughout the growing season. "Partial sun" and "partial shade" both refer to sites that get direct sun for part of the day but are shaded the rest of the time by a building, fence, or tree. "Full shade" means sites that don't receive direct sunlight.

The plants are organized here alphabetically by their botanical name. While many plants are sold by common name, botanical names help ensure that you get what you want. If you're browsing, page references direct you to the designs in which the plants appear.

Abelia

ABELIA. Evergreen shrubs that bear countless small flowers over a very long season from early summer until frost and attract many butterflies. Lustrous pointed leaves are dark green in summer, purple-bronze in winter. Chinese abelia, *A. chinensis* (p. 40), has sweet-scented white flowers. 'Edward Goucher' abelia (p. 105) has rosy purple flowers. Glossy abelia, *A.* x *grandiflora* (pp. 107, 124), has pale pink flowers. All need full or partial sun and grow 3 to 6 ft. tall and wide, with arching limbs. Prune annually in early spring to keep the plants compact and neat.

Acer palmatum

JAPANESE MAPLE. Neat, small deciduous trees with delicate-looking leaves that have jagged edges. There are many kinds, growing 10 to 25 ft. tall and wide, with foliage that is green, bronze, or red in summer and red or scarlet in fall. They need shade from the midday sun and rich, moist soil covered with a layer of mulch. Water deeply once a week during dry weather. These maples grow slowly, so buy the biggest tree you can afford. Prune only to remove weak, damaged, or crossing limbs. Pages: 28, 34, 61, 65, 66, 70, 117.

Acer palmatum 'Sango Kaku'

CORAL BARK MAPLE. A small deciduous tree, reaching 15 ft. or taller, with twigs that turn bright coral-red in winter and early spring. Lobed leaves are light green in summer, scarlet in fall. Needs full or partial sun and rich, moist soil covered with a layer of mulch. Pages: 124, 127.

Abelia

Acer palmatum
JAPANESE MAPLE

Acer rubrum

RED MAPLE. An adaptable native that makes a good shade tree. Grows fast and reaches 40 ft. or taller. Deciduous leaves with three pointed lobes turn bright red in the fall. Clusters of small red flowers dangle from the bare twigs in early spring. Needs full sun. Native to swampy sites but adapts to drier soil. Page: 68.

Achillea

YARROW. Long-blooming perennials with flat clusters of small flowers on stiff stalks 2 to 3 ft. tall and finely divided gray-green leaves that have a pungent aroma. 'Appleblossom' (p. 44) has pink flowers. 'Coronation Gold' (pp. 88, 91) bears bright yellow-gold flowers. 'Moonshine' (p. 111) has lemon yellow flowers. All need full sun. Cut off old flower stalks when the blossoms fade. Divide every few years in spring or fall.

Ajuga reptans

AJUGA. A low, mat-forming perennial used as a ground cover. Erect 6-in. spikes densely packed with blue flowers are very showy for a few weeks in spring. Glossy evergreen foliage is typically green, but 'Burgundy Glow' (p. 98) has multicolored purple, green, and white leaves, and other cultivars have dark purple-bronze leaves. Prefers partial shade but tolerates full sun in sites with moist soil. After flowers fade, cut them off with a string trimmer, lawn mower, or hedge shears. Spreads quickly and will invade a lawn unless you keep cutting along the edge or install a mowing strip. Pages: 39, 90.

Acer rubrum
RED MAPLE

Achillea 'Appleblossom'
YARROW

Achillea 'Coronation Gold'
YARROW

Acer palmatum 'Sango Kaku'
CORAL BARK MAPLE

Ajuga reptans 'Burgandy Glow'
AJUGA

Alocasia x *amazonica* 'Polly'
DWARF AFRICAN MASK

Alpinia zerumbet 'Variegata'
ZEBRA GINGER

Aronia arbutifolia
CHOKEBERRY

Alocasia x *amazonica* 'Polly'

DWARF AFRICAN MASK. A colorful dwarf version of an evergreen perennial, it has large, tropical foliage that often resembles elephant ears. This cultivar bears dark green arrow-shaped leaves up to 1 ft. long, featuring silver veins and purple undersides. Leaf stalks emerge directly from the ground, forming a clump 18 in. wide and up to 24 in. tall. In Zones 9 and 10, the foliage disappears during winter, reappearing when evening temperatures reach the 70s. Not hardy farther north. Prefers well-drained moderately fertile soil and is happiest with only morning sun. Remove dead foliage to reduce bacterial soft rot and fungal diseases. The sap is mildly irritating. Page: 87

Alpinia zerumbet 'Variegata'

ZEBRA GINGER. An evergreen perennial that brightens shady spots in a tropical garden. Grows from ginger-scented rhizomes to form clumps of long, strap-like, yellow-and-green-striped leaves on strong but slender stems. In summer it bears pendant clusters of slightly fragrant bell-shaped white flowers with yellow-and-red-striped lips. Flowers can be cut for indoor arrangements. Grows well in deep or partial shade. Also adapts to full sun. Remove frost-damaged leaves in spring and apply water and fertilizer monthly until bloom. Not hardy north of Zone 9. Pages: 26, 86, 94.

Annuals

Gardeners in the Southeast use annuals generously to provide bright patches of colorful flowers throughout the year. You can buy inexpensive six-packs or flats of the most popular annuals at any garden center or nursery. They're fast-growing plants that bloom abundantly for months, and when they're finished blooming, or become ragged, it's easy to uproot them and replace them with something else. One of the fun things about growing annuals is that you can try different kinds from year to year, choosing varieties with small or large flowers in a wide range of colors, on plants that range in height from 6 to 30 in.

Annuals can be divided into two groups. Cool-season annuals are planted when the weather starts to cool in fall. They live through the winter, perhaps blooming off and on, and put on a show in spring, before hot weather starts. This group includes pansies, snapdragons, foxgloves, Iceland poppy, dianthus, and dusty miller. Hot-season annuals are planted after the last frost in spring. They grow and bloom throughout the heat of summer, usually continuing until the first hard frost in fall. This group includes coleus, pentas, lantana, salvia, gomphrena, impatiens, vincas, ageratum, and begonias. (See pages 21, 25, 27, 35, 43, 65, 66, 90.)

Some kinds of annual wildflowers, such as Indian blanket (*Gaillardia pulchella*) and annual phlox (*Phlox drummondii*), are easily grown from seed (pp. 113, 115). Prepare the soil for planting and sow the seeds in late fall or early spring. Water as needed to keep the seeds and little seedlings from drying out. They will grow quickly in the spring, bloom in early summer, then set seed and die in late summer or fall. Once established, they self-sow and bloom year after year, as in the roadside plantings that are so popular throughout the Southeast.

Aronia arbutifolia

CHOKEBERRY. A deciduous native shrub that grows erect to about 10 ft. tall and 8 ft. wide, with white flowers in late spring, crimson fall foliage, and small red berries that last all winter. Grows in sun or shade, in almost any soil. Carefree. Pages: 113, 115.

Artemisia 'Powis Castle'

'POWIS CASTLE' ARTEMISIA. A shrubby perennial that forms a dome-shaped mound 2 to 3 ft. tall and 4 to 5 ft. wide. The finely divided gray-green leaves have a pleasant aroma and are evergreen in mild winters. Needs full sun. Tolerates dry sites. Prune hard every spring, cutting stems back by about one-half. Pages: 44, 46, 109.

Artemisia 'Powis Castle' ARTEMISIA

Asclepias curassavica 'Silky Gold'

'SILKY GOLD' MILKWEED. Often planted to attract monarch butterflies, this evergreen perennial offers a new twist on the beloved milkweed. Small, star-shaped flowers form clusters of pure yellow-gold, instead of the traditional orange-yellow, from spring to autumn. Grows into an upright bushy plant 3 ft. tall and half as wide, bearing narrow pointed leaves. Adult butterflies feast on the flower nectar; caterpillars prefer the foliage, often leaving flowers perched on naked stalks. But don't worry, plants recover quickly, ensuring more foliage and flowers for you and food for future generations of butterflies. Aphids also love milkweed, but resist spraying them with anything stronger than a blast of water or mild soap spray. Grows in full sun and a wide range of soils. Root hardy in Zones 9 and 10. Page: 93.

Aspidistra elatior CAST-IRON PLANT

Aspidistra elatior

CAST-IRON PLANT. An unusual perennial with stiff, dark evergreen leaves about 24 in. tall and 4 in. wide. Flowers are inconspicuous. Spreads slowly to form a dense, weed-proof patch. Grows well in full or partial shade. Substitute hostas in Zone 6. Carefree. Pages: 26, 87, 95, 120.

Astilbe

ASTILBE. Among the best perennials for shady or partly shady sites, astilbes feature fluffy plumes of tiny flowers in summer and healthy, glossy, compound leaves all season. There are many kinds of hybrid astilbes that grow from 18 to 42 in. tall and have white, pale pink, rose, or red flowers in early to midsummer (pp. 53, 56, 59, 71). A related plant, the dwarf Chinese astilbe, *A. chinensis* var. *pumila* (pp. 71, 123), grows only 1 ft. tall and has lovely mauve flowers in August.

All astilbes prefer rich, moist, well-drained soil. They definitely need shade from the midday sun and tolerate full shade. Cut off flower stalks when the blooms turn brown (or leave them in place, if you like the looks of the dried flowers). Cut foliage to the ground in late fall or early spring. Divide every three to five years in spring or late summer, using a sharp spade, ax, or old pruning saw to cut the tough woody rootstock into a few large chunks.

Asclepias curassavica 'Silky Gold' MILKWEED

Astilbe

Aucuba japonica 'Variegata'
GOLD-DUST AUCUBA

Bambusa multiplex
HEDGE BAMBOO

Berberis thunbergii 'Crimson Pygmy'
JAPANESE BARBERRY

Betula nigra
RIVER BIRCH

Aucuba japonica 'Variegata'

GOLD-DUST AUCUBA. An evergreen shrub with thick, erect stems. Grows 6 to 10 ft. tall, at least 5 ft. wide. Large, toothed, leathery leaves are dark green speckled with yellow dots. Female plants bear cherry red berries, if there's a male plant nearby. One of the best shrubs for dark shady sites. Prune in late winter, if desired. Pages: 56, 59, 120.

Bambusa multiplex

HEDGE BAMBOO. Non-invasive evergreen bamboo that grows quickly to heights of 10 to 25 ft., screening a two-story house in two seasons. Ideal as a tall privacy hedge in areas too small for shade trees. Grows in clumps of erect, 1-in. stems (culms) bearing pairs of lance-shaped leaves at each node. As the culms mature and thicken, they "knock" in the wind, adding another dimension to the landscape. For more color, try 'Alphonse Karr', a cultivar with yellow and green-striped culms. Hedge bamboo prefers full sun, ample water, and fertile well-drained soil. Young culms can be easily removed if they creep out of bounds. Plants are also sold as B. glaucescens. Hardy in Zones 8 to 10. Page: 78.

Berberis thunbergii 'Crimson Pygmy'

'CRIMSON PYGMY' JAPANESE BARBERRY. A deciduous shrub that grows naturally into a broad, low, cushionlike mound about 2 ft. tall and 3 to 5 ft. wide. Valued for its shape and its foliage, which is dark maroon all summer, turning crimson in late fall. Needs full sun (foliage turns green if it doesn't get enough sun) and well-drained soil. Pruning is not needed, but you can shape it by shearing if you want to. Pages: 37, 42, 111.

Betula nigra

RIVER BIRCH. A deciduous tree with very attractive beige, tan, or coppery bark that peels loose and curls back like the pages of a book that's gotten wet. The leaves are glossy green all summer and turn tan or gold in fall. Grows 1 to 2 ft. a year, reaching 60 ft. tall and almost that wide when mature. Needs full sun. Prefers moist soil but adapts to drier sites. Subject to various diseases and insects, but usually the damage is minor. Train young trees to eliminate narrow crotches, which often break apart in ice storms. Pages: 28, 81.

Bignonia capreolata

CROSS VINE. A native vine of quilted, lance-shaped, evergreen leaves. In spring the entire plant turns into a mass of beautiful trumpetlike yellow to orange flowers with reddish throats, a welcome sight for winter-weary eyes and a source of nectar for migrating hummingbirds. Scattered bloom continues through the growing season. Train the vine on fences, trellises, or arbors for a colorful focal point. If left unattended, this vigorous climber can reach a height of 30 ft. Prune as needed, at least annually. Grows in full sun to partial shade and likes a moist but well-drained soil. Page: 77.

Bignonia capreolata
CROSS VINE

Boltonia asteroides 'Snowbank'

'SNOWBANK' BOLTONIA. A perennial wildflower that blooms for many weeks in fall, bearing thousands of small white asterlike blossoms. Forms an erect clump of many stems. Grows 3 to 4 ft. tall, 2 to 4 ft. wide. Foliage is pale green and stays healthy all summer. Needs full or partial sun. Cut stems back partway in late spring to reduce height of clump, if desired. Cut to the ground in winter. Divide every few years in early spring. Page: 49.

Boltonia asteroides
'Snowbank'

Buddleia davidii

BUTTERFLY BUSH. A fast-growing deciduous shrub that blooms from midsummer through fall. Arching shoots form a vase-shaped clump. Spikes of small white, pink, lilac, blue, or purple flowers form at the end of each stem. The flowers have a sweet fragrance and really do attract butterflies. 'Black Knight' (pp. 63, 107, 113, 115), with dark blue-purple flowers, and 'White Profusion' (pp. 40, 98, 109), with pure white flowers, grow 6 to 8 ft. tall and wide and have dark green foliage. 'Nanho Blue' (pp. 88, 90) has medium blue flowers and gray-green foliage and grows only 4 to 5 ft. tall and wide. All kinds need full sun and well-drained soil. Cut old stems down to 1-ft. stubs in early spring to promote vigorous growth and maximum flowering.

Buddleia davidii
'White Profusion'
BUTTERFLY BUSH

Recommended bulbs

Chionodoxa luciliae, Glory-of-the-snow

Sprays of starlike blue, white, or pink flowers on 6-in. stalks in February. Plant bulbs 3 in. deep, 3 in. apart. Pages: 43, 65.

Crocus, Crocus

Cup-shaped flowers on 4-in. stalks in February. Available in white, yellow, lilac, and purple. Plant bulbs 4 in. deep, 4 in. apart. Pages: 43, 65, 82.

Muscari armeniacum, Grape hyacinth

Grapelike clusters of sweet-scented purple flowers last for several weeks in midspring. Plant bulbs 3 in. deep, 3 in. apart. Grassy foliage appears in fall, dies down in late spring. Pages: 43, 65, 82.

Narcissus, Daffodil, jonquil, and narcissus

Bright yellow, white, or bicolor flowers, often fragrant, on stalks 6 to 18 in. tall. Different kinds bloom in sequence from January through early April. Plant bulbs 4 to 6 in. deep, 4 to 6 in. apart, depending on their size. Miniature daffodils (p. 43) such as yellow 'Baby Moon' have flowers about 2 in. wide and short leaves that are inconspicuous after the flowers fade. Full-size daffodils such as white 'Ice Follies' (pp. 43, 90) have flowers 3 to 4 in. wide and long floppy leaves.

Scilla siberica, Squill

Loose clusters of bell-shaped flowers on 5-in. stalks in March. 'Spring Beauty', the most popular cultivar, has clear blue flowers. Plant bulbs 3 in. deep, 3 in. apart. Pages: 65, 82.

Tulipa, Tulip

Large flowers in bright or pastel shades of all colors but blue, held on stalks 6 to 20 in. tall. Different kinds bloom between February and April. Plant bulbs 4 to 6 in. deep, 4 to 6 in. apart. Page: 65.

Tulipa
TULIP

Narcissus
DAFFODIL

Butia capitata
PINDO PALM

Bulbs

The bulbs recommended in this book are perennials that come up year after year and bloom in late winter or spring. After they flower, their leaves continue growing until sometime in summer, when they gradually turn yellow and die down to the ground. To get started, you must buy bulbs from a garden center or catalog as soon as the weather starts to cool off in fall (usually in October or November). Plant them promptly in a bed with well-prepared soil. In subsequent years, all you have to do is pick off the faded flowers in spring and remove (orignore, if you choose) the old leaves after they turn brown in summer. Most bulbs can be divided every few years if you want to make more. Dig them up as the foliage is turning yellow, shake or pull them apart, and replant them right away. For more information on specific bulbs, see box at left.

Butia capitata

PINDO PALM. This slow-growing palm of featherlike, blue-grey fronds can reach a height of 10 to 20 ft. and a spread of 8 to 10 ft. Along with foliage, the stout trunk provides attractive texture, with cut off old leaf fronds forming "boots" around the trunk. Old fronds can be trimmed close to the trunk to create a diamond pattern. Choose a young adult with at least 3 ft. of trunk height; a juvenile lacks the characteristic trunk, and once a trunk is visible, the growth rate slows to less than 1 ft. per year. In spring, pindo palm produces clusters of small creamy yellow flowers that mature into pineapple-scented fruits that are yellow to bright orange. Fruits can be eaten fresh or used to make jellies. Grows in full sun to light shade in a range of soils. Adapts to high rainfall or drought conditions and has a moderate salt tolerance. Hardy in Zones 8 to 10, this is a superior palm for the Southeast. Page: 77.

Buxus

BOXWOOD. Very popular and highly prized shrubs that form a dense mass of neat, small, glossy evergreen leaves. The leaves, and also the small flowers in spring, have a distinct fragrance. Boxwood forms soft mounded shapes if left alone or can be sheared into formal globes, cones, hedges, or topiary. There are many kinds of boxwood, differing in rate of growth, size of leaf, and natural habit (upright or spreading). Most cultivars of littleleaf boxwood, *B. microphylla* (pp. 22, 32, 105, 107), have small, bright green leaves and form compact globes up to 4 ft. tall. English boxwood, *B. sempervirens* (p. 31), has larger, darker green leaves and can grow quite large, up to 20 ft. tall. Boxwoods grow slowly, so buy the largest plants you can afford. They need well-drained soil covered with a layer of mulch. Shear in early summer, if desired.

Camellia

CAMELLIA. Evergreen shrubs with glossy foliage and lovely white, pink, or rose flowers. There are hundreds of cultivars, differing mostly in flower color, size, and form (single or double) as well as in overall plant habit, mature size, and hardiness. 'Magnoliaeflora' Japanese camellia, *C. japonica* (pp. 124, 127), is a compact plant about 6 ft. tall, hardy to Zone 7, with large lustrous leaves and pale pink semidouble flowers off and on throughout the winter and spring. 'Jean May' sasanqua camellia, *C. sasanqua* (pp. 56, 59, 127 grows about 6 ft. tall, is hardy to Zone 8, and has smaller leaves and large pink double flowers that bloom throughout the late fall. Camellias need moist, well-drained, acid soil with a layer of mulch, and a site that is shaded from midday sun. Prune immediately after flowering, if desired. Camellias are not recommended for colder regions of Zone 6 or 7, because freezing temperatures kill the flowers and buds. In cold areas, plant rhododendrons instead. Page: 55.

Campsis radicans

TRUMPET CREEPER. A vigorous vine with a stout woody trunk and thick stems, large compound leaves, and

Camellia sasanqua 'Jean May'

Canna 'Pretoria'
BENGAL TIGER CANNA

Campsis radicans
TRUMPET CREEPER

very showy clusters of coral-red flowers throughout the summer. Needs full sun. Once started, it can climb and cover a trellis with no further assistance or care. Grows at least 10 ft. tall; can reach 30 to 40 ft. Prune in early spring to control size, if desired. Page: 54.

Canna

CANNA. Big, bold perennials with smooth oval leaves up to 1 ft. wide and 2 ft. long and loose clusters of large red, orange, salmon, pink, or yellow flowers on stalks 3 to 6 ft. tall. The foliage can be either green or bronze (pp. 100, 111). 'Pretoria', often called the Bengal tiger canna (pp. 88, 91, 96), has bright yellow-and-green-striped leaves and orange flowers. Cannas need full sun. They spread by rhizomes to form a patch; divide every few years in early spring. In Zone 6, dig rhizomes in fall and store in a cool dry place; then replant in spring.

Carex morrowii
'Aureo-variegata'
VARIEGATED JAPANESE SEDGE

Carex morrowii 'Aureo-variegata'

VARIEGATED JAPANESE SEDGE. An evergreen perennial that looks like a windswept tuft of grass with slender green-and-gold leaves. Flowers are inconspicuous. Grows about 1 ft. tall, 1 to 2 ft. wide. Needs partial shade and moist, fertile soil. Trim off any tattered foliage in early spring. Divide every few years to make more plants. Pages: 69, 118, 120.

Caryopteris x clandonensis 'Longwood Blue'

'LONGWOOD BLUE' BLUEBEARD. A small deciduous shrub with soft gray foliage. Bears fluffy clusters of medium blue flowers for weeks in late summer and attracts many butterflies. Needs full sun and well-drained soil. Thrives in a warm dry spot. Cut it down close to the ground each spring for compact growth and maximum bloom. Grows about 3 ft. tall and wide by fall. Pages: 43, 51, 107.

Cephalotaxus harringtonia 'Prostrata'

PROSTRATE JAPANESE PLUM YEW. An evergreen conifer with shiny dark green needles. Spreads to form a low mound 2 to 3 ft. tall and wide. Grows slowly and needs little pruning. Adapts to sun or shade. An excellent conifer for the South, as it's very tolerant of hot weather. Pages: 120, 123.

Ceratostigma plumbaginoides

DWARF PLUMBAGO. A perennial ground cover with indigo blue flowers in summer and fall. Deciduous foliage is late to appear in spring, turns from dark green to maroon or crimson in fall. Needs full or partial sun. Cut old stems to the ground in early spring. Stays under 1 ft. tall, spreads 2 to 3 ft. wide. Pages: 117, 118.

Cercis canadensis

REDBUD. A small deciduous tree. Clusters of tiny bright pink-purple flowers line the bare branches in early spring. May reach 20 to 25 ft. tall and wide. Heart-shaped leaves are medium green all summer and turn gold in fall. Needs partial shade and well-drained soil. Available with single or multiple trunks. Grows quickly, so it's reasonable to start with a small plant. Prune every summer, removing limbs that hang too low and dead twigs that accumulate inside the crown. Page: 39.

Chasmanthium latifolium

NORTHERN SEA OATS. A native grass that forms erect leafy clumps about 3 ft. tall, topped with loose clusters of flat seed heads that dance in the breeze from midsummer through winter. All parts are green in summer, russet or tan in winter. Grows in sun or shade and adapts to amost any soil. Cut to the ground in spring. Divide every few years, if you want more plants. Pages: 113, 118.

Caryopteris x *clandonensis*
'Longwood Blue'
BLUEBEARD

Ceratostigma plumbaginoides
DWARF PLUMBAGO

Cercis canadensis
REDBUD

Chasmanthium latifolium
NORTHERN SEA OATS

Chionanthus virginicus
FRINGE TREE

Clematis x *jackmanii*
JACKMAN CLEMATIS

Clethra alnifolia
'Hummingbird'
SUMMERSWEET

Chionanthus virginicus

FRINGE TREE, GRANCY GRAY-BEARD. A deciduous small tree or large shrub with multiple trunks and a rounded or domed crown. Blooms in May, with loose clusters of fragrant white flowers dangling from every branch. Leaves are medium to dark green in summer and may turn an attractive yellow in fall. Needs full or partial sun. Nurseries usually sell it in small sizes because larger plants don't transplant well. Grows slowly, so use low-growing perennials, bulbs, or annuals to fill the space around it for the first few years. Eventually it will reach 20 ft. tall and wide. Page: 124.

Chrysanthemum x superbum 'Becky'

'BECKY' SHASTA DAISY. A popular cultivar of this favorite perennial, named for Atlanta garden designer Becky Stewart, who contributed several of the designs in this book. Blooms all summer despite heat and humidity, with large daisy blossoms on stalks 3 ft. tall. Forms a low mat of glossy foliage in winter. Needs full sun. Divide every year or two in early spring. Pages: 49, 51, 88, 91.

Clematis

CLEMATIS. Popular vines that climb or sprawl, forming a tangle of leafy stems adorned with masses of flowers, which can be tiny or large. All clematis need full or partial sun and good garden soil. If your soil is acid, add a cup or so of ground limestone to the planting area and mix it zinto the soil. Plant clematis in spring. Unlike for most plants, dig the hole deep enough to cover the root ball and base of the stem with about 2 in. of soil. Cut the stem back to the lowest set of healthy leaves to encourage the plant to branch out near the base. As new stems grow, secure them to a trellis, wire, or other support with twist ties.

Evergreen clematis, *C. armandii* (pp. 62, 88, 90), has glossy evergreen leaves, climbs 15 to 20 ft. tall, and bears fragrant white flowers in spring. Prune after it flowers to control its size, if desired, otherwise let it grow naturally.

Pink anemone clematis, *C. montana* 'Rubens' (p. 110), has deciduous leaves, climbs 20 ft. or taller, and bears fragrant pink flowers in late spring that resemble dogwood blossoms. Prune after it flowers to control its size, if desired.

Jackman clematis, *C.* x *jackmanii* (pp. 29, 35), has deciduous leaves, climbs about 10 ft. tall, and bears large violet-purple flowers in summer. Prune all stems down to 1 ft. tall in spring, just as the buds start to swell.

Clethra alnifolia 'Hummingbird'

'HUMMINGBIRD' SUMMERSWEET. A compact form of this popular native shrub, growing only 4 ft. tall instead of the normal 6 to 8 ft. Very sweet-scented white flowers bloom for weeks in midsummer. Deciduous leaves are glossy green in summer, golden yellow in fall. Very adaptable—tolerates sun or shade and damp soil. Prune each year in early spring, cutting some of the older stems to ground level and cutting new stems back by one-third. Sends up suckers around the base and gradually forms a patch. Page: 124.

Coreopsis verticillata 'Moonbeam'

'MOONBEAM' COREOPSIS. A long-blooming perennial that bears hundreds of small, daisylike, lemon yellow blossoms, starting in June and repeating until September if you shear off the old flowers from time to time. The dark green leaves are short and threadlike. Grows about 18 in. tall and wide. Spreads by underground runners but isn't invasive. Needs full sun. Pages: 49, 51, 118.

Coreopsis verticillata
'Moonbeam'

Cryptomeria japonica 'Yoshino'
JAPANESE CEDAR

Cotinus coggygria 'Royal Purple'
SMOKE TREE

Daphne odora 'Aureomarginata'
VARIEGATED WINTER DAPHNE

Dendranthema 'Sheffield'
HARDY CHRYSANTHEMUM

Cornus florida

DOGWOOD. A very popular native deciduous tree with showy flowers in spring, red berries that attract birds in fall, and crimson autumn foliage. Grows up to 25 ft. tall and wide, with a rounded crown. Typically has white flowers but can have pink flowers instead (p. 98). Adapts to full sun or partial shade. Small sizes transplant better than large specimens do. Plant when dormant in early spring or late fall, not in the heat of summer. Prune in early summer, right after it blooms, only to remove weak, crossing, or lower limbs. Pages: 30, 82, 102.

Cotinus coggygria 'Royal Purple'

'ROYAL PURPLE' SMOKE TREE. A deciduous shrub with rounded leaves that open red, turn dark purple for the summer, then turn gold or orange in fall. Fluffy pink flower plumes are showy for many weeks in summer and fall. Grows about 10 ft. tall and wide if unpruned, or you can prune it hard every year to have a smaller shrub with larger leaves. Needs full sun for good color; it will turn green if shaded. Pages: 54, 72, 109.

Cotoneaster salicifolius 'Repens'

CREEPING WILLOWLEAF COTONEASTER. A shrub often used as a ground cover, with glossy evergreen leaves that turn purple in cold weather, white flowers in spring, and red berries in fall. Grows about 1 ft. tall and spreads up to 6 ft. wide. Prune anytime. Needs full sun. If 'Repens' is unavailable, 'Scarlet Leader' is a good substitute. Pages: 29, 81.

Cryptomeria japonica 'Yoshino'

'YOSHINO' JAPANESE CEDAR. A fast-growing conifer that forms a neat cone-shaped tree with needle-like foliage that is bright green in summer, bronzy in winter. Grows to 30 ft. or taller. Needs full sun. Requires no care at all. Pages: 21, 98

Daphne odora 'Aureomarginata'

VARIEGATED WINTER DAPHNE. A compact, slow-growing shrub that reaches about 4 to 5 ft. tall and wide, with glossy evergreen leaves that have a thin gold stripe around the edge. Crimson buds open into small white flowers that have a powerful sweet fragrance. Blooms mostly in spring, but sometimes scattered flowers appear in fall. Needs full or partial sun and well-drained soil. Prune only to remove damaged shoots. In Zone 6, substitute *Daphne x burkwoodii* 'Carol Mackie', a similar-looking, but hardier, plant. Pages: 22, 120, 123.

Dendranthema

HARDY CHRYSANTHEMUM, DAISY. Popular perennials that bloom for several weeks in fall. Soft, gray-green, aromatic foliage is quietly attractive throughout the summer. The following cultivars all have single or semidouble daisylike flowers and are widely available in the Southeast. *D. rubellum* 'Clara Curtis' (pink flowers) and 'Mary Stoker' (yellow) bloom in September. *D. x grandiflorum* 'Sheffield' and 'Venus' both have pink flowers and bloom in October and November. All form rounded clumps about 2 to 3 ft. tall and wide; you can cut them back partway in early summer to make them bushier and more compact. Full sun. Divide every few years in early spring. (Nurseries often sell these plants under the name *Chrysanthemum*.) Pages: 99, 118.

Dianthus

DIANTHUS, PINK. Low-growing perennials with very fragrant flowers like small carnations, held on supple stalks 8 to 12 in. tall. 'Bath's Pink' (pp. 23, 44), with clear pink flowers in late spring, and 'Itsaul White' (pp. 66, 72), with white flowers in early summer, are unusually tolerant of the hot humid summers typical in the Southeast. They need full sun and well-drained soil. After they bloom, shear off the flower stalks and cut the leaves back halfway. Fresh new foliage will soon develop and form a grassy blue-green mat 1 to 2 ft. wide. Divide every few years in early spring.

Dichorisandra thyrsiflora

BLUE GINGER. This shade-loving evergreen perennial is a perfect jungle specimen for a tropical garden. Lustrous succulent leaves are arranged in spirals on stems, forming a dark green patchwork 5 to 8 ft. tall and 4 ft. wide. Dense clusters of deep violet flowers bloom at the top of the plant in autumn. Prefers well-drained, fertile soil. Water plentifully during warm months but sparingly in winter to avoid crown rot. Remove frost-damaged foliage in early spring and apply a balanced liquid fertilizer monthly. Root hardy in Zones 9 and 10. Page: 86.

Dietes vegeta

WHITE AFRICAN IRIS. An evergreen perennial grown as a ground cover. Forms clumps of stiff, blade-like, grey-green foliage 18 to 24 in. tall and wide. From spring through summer, branching flower stalks bear 2-in. diameter iris-like flowers with violet and yellow throat marks. Grows in full sun to partial shade, prefers well-drained soil, and is drought tolerant once established. Remove spent flower stalks to encourage repeat blooms. Divide clumps every 3 to 4 years in late summer or late winter by cutting rhizomes into several sections, each with a fan of foliage. Root hardy in Zones 9 and 10. Also known as *D. iridoides*. Pages: 79, 85, 125.

Distylium 'Emerald Heights'

A compact, dense, broadleaf, evergreen shrub. It makes an outstanding foundation plant with excellent resistance to pests and diseases. Features cascading green, glossy leaves in a layered pattern. In late winter through early spring, maroon-red flowers add a dash of color along the stems. This highly adaptable shrub is an excellent choice for mass plantings, hedges, and borders. Hardy in zones 6-9. Pages: 29, 34, 65, 66, 69, 109.

Echinacea purpurea

PURPLE CONEFLOWER. A prairie wildflower that thrives in gardens and blooms for several weeks in midsummer. Large pink daisylike blossoms are held on stiff branching stalks about 3 ft. tall, above a mound of dark green basal foliage about 2 ft. wide. Needs full sun. Cut back flower stalks if you choose, or let the seed heads ripen for winter interest. May self-sow but isn't weedy. Older plants can be divided in early spring. Pages: 49, 51, 88, 91, 99, 107, 113, 115.

Dianthus 'Bath's Pink'

Dichorisandra thyrsiflora
BLUE GINGER

Echinacea purpurea
PURPLE CONEFLOWER

Recommended ferns

Athyrium goeringianum 'Pictum', Japanese painted fern

A colorful fern that forms rosettes of finely cut fronds marked in shades of green, silver, and maroon. They look almost iridescent. Deciduous. Grows about 1 ft. tall, 2 ft. wide. Pages: 31, 56, 95, 123.

Cyrtomium falcatum, Holly fern

A showy evergreen fern with fronds divided into large, glossy, hollylike leaflets. Forms clumps about 2 ft. tall and 3 ft. wide. Hardy only to Zone 8; in colder regions, substitute another fern. Pages: 26, 59, 87, 95.

Dryopteris erythrosora, Japanese autumn fern

Beautiful glossy fronds start out coppery-colored, then turn dark green. Evergreen in mild winters but may freeze to the ground in cold years. Forms erect clumps 2 to 3 ft. tall, 1 ft. wide. Pages: 27, 87, 95, 122.

Osmunda cinnamomea, Cinnamon fern

A native fern that forms erect clumps of finely divided deciduous fronds. Grows 2 to 3 ft. tall and spreads to form a patch. Needs moist soil. In drier conditions, substitute the similar-looking interrupted fern, *O. claytoniana*. Page: 82.

Polystichum polyblepharum, Tassel fern

An evergreen fern with stiff, glossy, finely divided fronds. Needs moist soil. Forms a clump about 2 ft. tall, 3 to 4 ft. wide. Pages: 71, 122.

Athyrium goeringianum 'Pictum'
JAPANESE PAINTED FERN

Cyrtomium falcatum
HOLLY FERN

Osmunda cinnamomea
CINNAMON FERN

Festuca ovina var. *glauca*
BLUE FESCUE GRASS

Ferns

Ferns are carefree, long-lived perennials for shady sites. Despite their delicate appearance, they're among the most durable and trouble-free plants you can grow. Almost all ferns need shade from the midday and afternoon sun. They grow best in soil that's been amended with extra organic matter. You can divide them every few years in early spring if you want more plants, or leave them alone for decades. They need no routine care. See box at left for more information on specific ferns.

Festuca ovina var. glauca

BLUE FESCUE GRASS. A neat compact grass that forms a dense tuft, about 1 ft. tall and wide, of hair-thin, blue-green leaves. Slender flower spikes appear in early summer and soon turn tan. Needs full sun and well-drained soil. Cut old foliage to the ground in late winter. Divide every few years in early spring. Page: 111.

Forsythia x intermedia

FORSYTHIA. A large, fast-growing deciduous shrub whose arching limbs are covered with bright yellow flowers for a few weeks in early spring, followed in summer by soft green foliage that turns purple before dropping in late fall. Typically grows 6 to 8 ft. tall, 8 to 10 ft. wide; prune immediately after it flowers if you want to keep it smaller. Needs full or partial sun. Page: 81.

Gardenia jasminoides

GARDENIA. An evergreen shrub with intensely fragrant white flowers in summer. 'August Beauty' and 'Mystery' (pp. 34, 61, 107) are popular cultivars with double flowers up to 4 in. wide and an upright or rounded habit, reaching 5 ft. or taller and 3 to 5 ft. wide. 'Radicans' (p. 100) has 1-in. flowers and grows about 1 ft. tall and 2 to 3 ft. wide.

Gardenia jasminoides
GARDENIA

Gelsemium sempervirens
CAROLINA JASMINE

Geranium macrorrhizum
BIGROOT GERANIUM

All need full or partial sun and acid soil. Prune in winter to control size and shape. Subject to many insect pests, but most can be controlled by a few applications of horticultural oil spray. Not hardy in Zone 6; substitute azaleas there (see *Rhododendron*).

Gelsemium sempervirens

CAROLINA JASMINE. An evergreen vine native to the Southeast and beloved throughout the region for its showy display of fragrant yellow bell-shaped flowers in early spring. The neat small leaves are dark green all summer, maroon in winter. Can climb trees but is usually trained against a fence, trellis, or post and pruned annually (right after it blooms) to keep it under 10 ft. tall. Can also be used as a ground cover; prune annually to keep it within bounds. Needs full or partial sun. Not hardy in Zone 6; substitute clematis there. Pages: 29, 31, 43, 55, 109.

Geranium macrorrhizum

BIGROOT GERANIUM. A short, compact perennial that forms bushy clumps, about 12 in. tall and 18 to 24 in. wide, of fragrant semievergreen foliage. The large lobed leaves are medium green in summer, turning shades of red and purple in winter. Clusters of magenta or pink flowers last for a few weeks in late spring. Makes a good ground cover for partial shade and dry soil. Divide every few years in spring or early fall. Page: 100.

Hamamelis

WITCH HAZEL. Deciduous small trees or large shrubs that are often grown with multiple trunks. Growing up to 20 ft. tall and wide, *H. x intermedia* 'Arnold Promise' (p. 126) bears clusters of sweet-scented yellow flowers for several weeks in early spring. The vernal, or Ozark, witch hazel, *H. vernalis* (p. 34), reaches only about 10 ft. tall and wide and has smaller but equally fragrant reddish or gold flowers a few weeks earlier, in late winter. Both bloom before the leaf buds swell. The large rounded leaves are dull green in summer, bright gold in fall. Witch hazels prefer partial shade and moist soil and grow fairly slowly, so buy a big plant to start with. Prune in early summer.

Hamelia patens

FIREBUSH. A native Florida evergreen shrub that brings color, texture, and hummingbirds to the garden. Bright red, tubular flowers bloom from March to November and mature into glossy black berries. Large compound leaves acquire a red tinge as autumn approaches. Grows 6 to 8 ft. tall and 4 to 5 ft. wide. Prefers full sun but adapts to partial shade. Drought tolerant. Grow it in moderately to well-drained soil. Root hardy in Zones 9 and 10. Remove cold-damaged or dead branches prior to new spring growth.
Pages: 78, 85, 93.

Hamamelis x intermedia
'Arnold Promise'
WITCH HAZEL

Hamelia patens
FIREBUSH

Hemerocallis 'Stella d'Oro'
DAYLILY

Hibiscus syriacus 'Diana'
ROSE-OF-SHARON

Helleborus orientalis
LENTEN ROSE

Helleborus orientalis

LENTEN ROSE. A carefree, long-lived perennial with evergreen foliage and cup-shaped round flowers that bloom for many weeks in early spring. The flowers can be pink, rosy, white, or greenish. The leaves are large and deeply lobed. Forms a clump about 18 in. tall, 18 to 24 in. wide. Needs partial shade and rich, well-drained soil. Looks its best when you groom it once a year by cutting off any dead leaves when the flower buds appear. Pages: 31, 96, 120, 123.

Hemerocallis

DAYLILY. Among the most reliable and popular perennials, with large lilylike flowers in summer, held above dense clumps of grassy arching leaves. Each clump produces several flower stalks 2 to 4 ft. tall, bearing up to a dozen or more flowers apiece. Hundreds of cultivars produce flowers in shades of orange, gold, yellow, cream, pink, red, or purple (pp. 21, 41, 49, 51, 100), each blooming for a few weeks or more during June or July. 'Stella d'Oro' (pp. 21, 29, 37, 61, 89, 91, 107, 111) is especially popular because it blooms almost continuously from late spring until hard frost, with golden yellow flowers on stalks about 2 ft. tall. Daylilies prefer full sun. Cut off flower stalks after blooming is finished. Divide every few years in late summer.

Hibiscus syriacus 'Diana'

'DIANA' ROSE-OF-SHARON. A deciduous shrub with large, pure white, hollyhock-like flowers from July through September. Grows 8 to 10 ft. tall, 6 to 8 ft. wide. Needs full sun. Prune in early spring by cutting some of the oldest stems down to the ground. Japanese beetles may chew on the flowers; their damage looks ugly but doesn't really hurt the plant. Pages: 61, 124.

Hosta

HOSTA. Long-lived, carefree perennials with beautiful leaves in a wide variety of colors and sizes. The plants form dome-shaped clumps or spreading patches of foliage that looks good from spring to fall and dies down in winter. Stalks of lavender, purple, or white flowers appear in mid- to late summer. A few hostas tolerate full sun, but most grow better in partial or full shade. All need fertile, moist, well-drained garden soil. Cut off flower stalks before seedpods ripen. Clumps can be divided in early spring if you want to make more plants; otherwise, leave them alone. See box on facing page for more information on specific hostas.

Recommended hostas

'Antioch' *hosta*
Large leaves are medium green edged with a wide creamy white stripe. Lavender flowers. Forms a clump about 2 ft. tall, 3 ft. wide. Pages: 71, 74.

'Frances Williams' *hosta*
Very large, puckered leaves are iridescent blue-green in the center, gold around the edge. White flowers. Grows slowly but forms giant clumps over 2 ft. tall and 4 ft. wide. Pages: 120, 123.

'Halcyon' *hosta*
Leaves are solid-colored powder blue in spring, darker blue-green in summer. Forms low mounds, about 1 ft. tall and 2 ft. wide. Lilac flowers. Pages: 59, 74, 96.

Hosta sieboldiana 'Elegans'
Large, round, puckered leaves have a lovely blue-gray color and waxy texture. White flowers. Forms a very impressive clump, 2 to 3 ft. tall, up to 8 ft. wide. Pages: 31, 39, 71, 123.

'Piedmont Gold' *hosta*
Bright yellow-gold leaves are large and puckered, with wavy edges. White flowers. Grows about 2 ft. tall, 3 to 4 ft. wide. Page: 100.

'Royal Standard' *hosta*
Forms large clump of sizable medium green leaves. Large white flowers with a very sweet fragrance bloom in August. Forms a mound under 2 ft. tall, about 3 ft. wide. Pages: 74, 123.

Hosta 'Antioch'

Hosta 'Frances Williams'

Hosta 'Halcyon'

Hosta sieboldiana 'Elegans'

Hosta 'Royal Standard'

Hydrangea macrophylla
'Blue Wave'
HYDRANGEA

Hydrangea quercifolia
OAKLEAF HYDRANGEA

Ilex decidua
POSSUMHAW

*Iberis
sempervirens*
EVERGREEN
CANDYTUFT

Hydrangea macrophylla

HYDRANGEA. A bushy, rounded deciduous shrub with showy clusters of papery-textured flowers that look fresh and bright for several weeks in midsummer and smooth, glossy, heart-shaped leaves. 'Blue Wave' (p. 74) grows about 6 ft. tall and wide and has flat, lacy flower clusters about 8 in. wide. The flowers are blue if the plant is growing in acid soil, pink if growing in alkaline soil. The variegated lacecap hydrangea, 'Mariesii Variegata' (p. 122), has similar but smaller flowers and is a smaller plant, growing only 4 to 5 ft. tall and wide, with leaves edged with irregular white stripes. 'Nikko Blue' (pp. 22, 62, 127) has puffy, spherical, blue or pink flower heads and grows about 6 ft. tall and wide. Hydrangeas prefer partial shade and need well-drained soil. Flower color varies with soil pH, as noted above. Prune every year in early spring, removing stalks that flowered the previous summer by cutting them off at the ground. Trouble-free.

Hydrangea quercifolia

OAKLEAF HYDRANGEA. A deciduous shrub native to the Southeast and well adapted to hot humid weather. Large lobed leaves emerge pale green in spring, turn dark in summer, and display winelike shades of red and purple in fall. Grows fairly quickly, reaching at least 8 ft. tall and wide. The stems have peeling, cinnamon-colored bark that's attractive in winter. Clusters of papery white flowers top the stems in late spring, then turn beige or pink-tan and last through the summer and fall. 'Snow Queen' has larger-than-average flowers, and 'Snowflake' has double flowers. Adapts to sun or shade. Water regularly during long dry spells. Needs no other care. Pages: 69, 82, 102, 113, 115, 124, 127.

Iberis sempervirens

EVERGREEN CANDYTUFT. A bushy perennial that forms a low or sprawling mound, about 1 ft. tall and 2 to 3 ft. wide, of slender, glossy evergreen foliage, topped for several weeks in March or April with clusters of bright white flowers. Needs full or partial sun, well-drained soil. Shear off the top half of the plants after they bloom. Needs no other care. Don't try to divide it; buy new plants if you want more. Pages: 49, 51, 60, 65, 99.

Ilex, Evergreen hollies

A versatile group of evergreen shrubs and trees used for foundation plantings, hedges, and specimens. The stiff-textured leaves can be small or large, smooth or spiny, dull or glossy. Holly plants are either male or female. Females typically bear heavy crops of small round berries that ripen in fall and last through the next spring. See box on facing page for more information on specific hollies. All tolerate sun or shade. Prune or shear at any season to keep them at the desired size.

Ilex decidua

POSSUMHAW. Also known as winterberry holly. A native small tree or large shrub that grows fairly quickly, reaching 15 to 20 ft. tall. Usually trained with multiple trunks and a rounded crown. Small spineless leaves are deciduous and don't have much fall color, but the large red or orange berries look wonderful all fall and winter. Only females produce berries, and there has to be a male within a few hundred yards. A local nursery can advise whether there's likely to be a male growing wild in your vicinity or if you should plant your own. Needs full or partial sun. Page: 32.

Recommended evergreen hollies

Ilex x *attenuata* 'Foster #2'
FOSTER HOLLY

Ilex vomitoria
YAUPON HOLLY

Ilex cornuta
'Needlepoint'
HOLLY

Ilex
'Nellie R. Stevens'
HOLLY

Ilex x *attenuata*

A slim, columnar or conical tree, growing about 25 ft. tall and 10 to 15 ft. wide, with shiny leaves and lots of red berries. 'Foster #2' (pp. 22, 65, 66, 105, 107) is a popular cultivar with slender leaves. 'Savannah' (pp. 81, 82) is similar but has larger leaves and berries.

I. cornuta

A large, dense, bushy shrub with glossy foliage. 'Burfordii', or Burford holly (pp. 28, 113, 115), grows 15 to 20 ft. tall, has large leaves with few spines, and bears abundant crops of red berries. 'Needlepoint' (pp. 61, 105, 107) can reach 10 ft. tall and wide but is often kept smaller by shearing. It has lobed leaves with very sharp spines, and bright red-orange berries.

I. crenata, Japanese holly

A dense twiggy shrub with small dark green leaves and inconspicuous dark berries. 'Compacta' (pp. 22, 32, 53, 62) grows about 6 ft. tall and wide, with glossier-than-average leaves. 'Helleri' (pp. 23, 29, 32, 117) reaches only 4 ft. tall and wide and has dull leaves. Both are often sheared, but they don't need it, as their natural growth habit is very neat and compact. Japanese hollies need acid soil; where the soil is alkaline, plant dwarf yaupon holly instead.

I. 'Nellie R. Stevens'

A slim, columnar or conical tree with narrow shiny leaves and lots of red berries. Grows quickly, reaching 25 to 30 ft. tall, 10 to 15 ft. wide, but can be kept smaller. Pages: 109, 115.

I. opaca, American holly

A conical tree, native to the Southeast, with broad leaves that have a few spines. Foliage is typically olive green, but selected cultivars have bright green leaves. Berries are dark red. It can grow as much as 50 ft. tall and 30 ft. wide. Page: 115.

I. vomitoria, Yaupon holly

A native tree with small, shiny, spineless leaves and juicy red berries. Grows about 15 to 20 ft. tall, usually with multiple trunks, and is easily trained and pruned into a picturesque specimen (pp. 53, 94). 'Pendula' is a weeping form (p. 25). Dwarf yaupon holly, 'Nana' (pp. 23, 25, 34, 61), is a low, compact, shrubby form that grows 3 to 5 ft. tall and wide. It bears few berries. Yaupon hollies are very tough, adaptable, and easy to grow.

Ilex verticillata
WINTERBERRY HOLLY

Illicium parviflorum
YELLOW ANISE

Iris sibirica 'Caesar's Brother'
SIBERIAN IRIS

Iris sibirica 'White Swirl'
SIBERIAN IRIS

Ilex verticillata

WINTERBERRY HOLLY. A native deciduous shrub with many twiggy stems and soft spineless leaves that turn yellow in fall. Grows about 8 to 12 ft. tall, 6 to 8 ft. wide. Female cultivars such as 'Sparkleberry' and 'Winter Red' bear tremendous crops of small bright red berries, if there's a wild male or a male cultivar such as 'Apollo' or 'Southern Gentleman' growing within a few hundred yards. Slow-growing, so start with the largest, fullest plants you can find and prune only to remove dead or damaged shoots. Needs full or partial sun. Pages: 113, 115, 126.

Illicium parviflorum

YELLOW ANISE. A native evergreen shrub often grown as a hedge because of its dense uniform habit. The thick yellow-green matte foliage reaches 4 to 10 ft. high while staying full to the ground. Leaves release a licorice scent when cut or crushed. The flowers are inconspicuous. Yellow anise performs well in full sun or partial shade and tolerates wet soil and short periods of drought. It responds well to hand pruning. Trim the top narrower than the base to allow light to reach the lower limbs. Hardy in Zones 8 and 9. Pages: 26, 94.

Iris

GERMAN OR BEARDED IRIS. Popular perennials that bloom in midspring, with large elegant flowers in shades of blue, purple, pink, yellow, or white, on stalks 1 to 3 ft. tall. Irises form patches of stiff, bladelike, gray-green leaves about 1 ft. tall. They need full sun and well-drained soil. Divide every few years in late summer, cutting the thick finger-like rhizomes into sections with three or four buds or fans of foliage each. When planting, lay the rhizome horizontally right at the surface of the soil. Pages: 32, 46, 72.

Iris sibirica

SIBERIAN IRIS. A carefree perennial that forms a large, vase-shaped clump of slender green leaves up to 2 ft. long and bears scores of showy flowers in late spring on stalks 2 to 3 ft. tall. 'Caesar's Brother' (pp. 49, 96, 117) is a popular cultivar with very dark blue-purple flowers. 'White Swirl' (pp. 88, 91) has clear white flowers. Other cultivars have indigo, sky blue, or yellow flowers. Let the seedpods develop if you choose; they look interesting from summer through winter, and setting

Itea virginica 'Henry's Garnet'
VIRGINIA SWEETSPIRE

seed doesn't seem to reduce the next year's display of flowers. Needs full or partial sun. Divide clumps after several years, in early fall. Pages: 32, 69, 105.

Itea virginica 'Henry's Garnet'

'HENRY'S GARNET' VIRGINIA SWEETSPIRE. A native deciduous shrub that forms a clump of erect or arching stems 6 to 8 ft. tall, topped with clusters of fragrant white flowers in early summer. Smooth leaves are glossy green in summer, rich wine red or burgundy throughout the fall. Adapts to sun or shade. Prefers moist soil. Page: 126.

Juniperus chinensis 'Torulosa'

HOLLYWOOD JUNIPER. A small evergreen tree with an interesting irregular profile and bright green, fine-textured foliage. Grows 15 to 20 ft. tall, 4 to 8 ft. wide. Needs full sun. Prune only if needed to remove damaged shoots. Carefree. Pages: 21, 72.

Juniperus conferta 'Blue Pacific'

'BLUE PACIFIC' SHORE JUNIPER. An evergreen shrub that makes a good ground cover, staying under 1 ft. tall and spreading several feet wide, with short soft blue-green needles. Needs full sun. Prune only if needed to control its spread. Carefree. Page: 37.

Juniperus davurica 'Expansa'

PARSON'S JUNIPER. A low evergreen shrub with gray-green foliage. Grows about 2 ft. tall and can spread several feet wide but is often pruned to keep it narrower. One of the best shrubby junipers for southeastern gardens. Needs full sun. Page: 21.

Justicia carnea

JACOBINEA. An erect, sparsely branching, evergreen shrub grown for its irresistible hot-pink flowers. Known also as Brazilian plume or flamingo flower.

Juniperus conferta 'Blue Pacific'
SHORE JUNIPER

Juniperus davurica 'Expansa'
PARSON'S JUNIPER

Clusters of tubular flowers open in feathery plumes against a backdrop of dark green oblong leaves in summer. Grows 6 ft. tall and 3 ft. wide. Plant in bright filtered sunlight or partial shade, but always protect it from the hot sun. Prune the tips of young plants in spring to promote bushiness. Root hardy in Zones 8 to 10. Page: 87.

Kalimeris pinnatifida

DOUBLE JAPANESE ASTER. An easy-to-grow perennial that forms an upright clump about 3 ft. tall, with small neat leaves and masses of daisylike flowers. Blooms in the heat of summer; cut it back afterward and it will rebloom in fall. Needs full or partial sun. Page: 96.

Justicia carnea
JACOBINEA

Kalimeris pinnatifida
DOUBLE JAPANESE ASTER

Lantana montevidensis 'Weeping White'
TRAILING LANTANA

Lagerstroemia indica 'Natchez'
CRAPE MYRTLE

Lantana 'New Gold'

Leucothoe fontanesiana
DROOPING LEUCOTHOE

Lagerstroemia indica

CRAPE MYRTLE. Small, often multi-trunked, deciduous trees with handsome bark, rounded leaves, and clusters of frilly-edged flowers. Unlike old-fashioned crape myrtles, the cultivars listed below are resistant to powdery mildew and their foliage looks nice throughout the growing season. 'Natchez' (pp. 21, 23, 42, 59) grows 20 to 25 ft. tall and blooms all summer, bearing large clusters of papery-textured white flowers atop each stem. Leaves turn bright red, orange, or purplish in fall and flaking cinnamon-colored trunk bark is attractive in winter. 'Acoma' (*L. indica* x *fauriei*, p. 85) is a semi-dwarf slightly weeping cultivar, growing 10 to 12 ft. tall and 7 to 8 ft. wide. White flowers appear in late spring to early summer, followed by rounded seedpods. Removing pods as they develop encourages a second and even a third bloom. Crape myrtles need full sun and well-drained soil. Prune in spring, removing weak, broken, or crossing branches. Never commit "crape murder"; trim healthy branches only if they are smaller than the diameter of a pencil. Select multi-trunked trees if possible. Crape myrtles may suffer frost damage in severe winters but they soon recover. Zones 7 to 10.

Lantana montevidensis

TRAILING LANTANA. A low-growing, trailing, evergreen shrub that forms a dense mat 2 to 4 ft. wide and up to 3 ft. high of slender, hairy stems and dark green toothed leaves. Tiny lavender to violet flowers bloom in tight domed heads at the ends of the stems, making perfect sipping stations for butterflies and moths. The heaviest bloom is in summer, but it may bloom year-round in coastal areas and in mild winters elsewhere. A good choice for hot sites and poor soils. Prefers full sun and little water. Prune stem tips in early spring and fall to encourage bushiness and new blooms. Root hardy in Zones 8 to 10. Pages: 25, 93.

Lantana 'New Gold'

'NEW GOLD' LANTANA. A low-growing compact evergreen ground cover with dark green saw-toothed leaves. Clusters of tiny 5-petaled flowers are a rich, clear orange-yellow and provide a great source of nectar for butterflies and night moths. Grows 12 to 18 in. high and spreads 30 in. wide. Prefers full sun and well-drained soil. It is drought-tolerant once established. Prune lightly in early spring and again in early fall to encourage more flower production. Blooms almost year-round in Florida. Root hardy in Zones 8 to 10. Pages: 79, 85, 93.

Leucothoe

LEUCOTHOE. Evergreen shrubs with arching stems, glossy leaves, and clusters of fragrant white flowers in spring. Drooping leucothoe, *L. fontanesiana* (pp. 82, 103), grows up to 6 ft. tall and wide. It needs full or partial shade and moist soil and suffers in hot dry weather. Florida leucothoe, *L. populifolia*, sometimes listed as *Agarista populifolia* (p. 103), grows up to 16 ft. tall but can be pruned if you need to control its size. It tolerates hot summers and adapts to sunny or shady sites.

Liatris spicata

BLAZING STAR. A perennial prairie wildflower that blooms in midsummer, with dense spikes of small purple flowers on stiff stalks 3 to 4 ft. tall, arising from a basal tuft of grassy dark green foliage. Attracts butterflies. Needs full sun. Cut off the flower stalks after it blooms. Needs no other care. 'Kobold' is a smaller cultivar that grows only 2 to 3 ft. tall. Pages: 51, 105, 113, 115.

Ligustrum japonicum

JAPANESE OR WAX-LEAF LIGUSTRUM. A fast-growing evergreen shrub or small tree with very glossy bright green leaves, clusters of heavy-scented white flowers in early summer, and dark blue-black berries in fall and winter. Develops a graceful shape if you leave it alone and can reach 15 to 20 ft. tall, or you can prune it however (and whenever) you choose. Needs full or partial sun and well-drained soil. Not hardy in Zone 6; substitute sweet bay magnolia there. Pages: 25, 37, 56, 93.

Lilium

HYBRID LILY. There are hundreds of wonderful lily cultivars, all with large flowers on leafy stalks. Flower colors include white, yellow, gold, orange, pink, red, and magenta. Different kinds bloom in sequence from May through August. The so-called Asiatic hybrids (p. 41) typically have scentless flowers on stalks 2 to 4 ft. tall and bloom in early summer. Most Oriental hybrids such as 'Casablanca' (white flowers) and 'Stargazer' (pink) have sweet-scented flowers in late summer on stalks 3 to 5 ft. tall (pp. 88, 91). All lilies prefer full sun and deep, fertile, well-drained soil. Plant bulbs when they are available in late fall or early spring, burying them about 6 in. deep. Lilies multiply slowly and can remain in the same place for years (unless they get eaten by rodents). Sprinkle some bulb fertilizer on the soil each fall.

Liatris spicata
BLAZING STAR

Ligustrum japonicum
JAPANESE LIGUSTRUM

Lilium
ORIENTAL LILY

Liriope muscari
'Variegata'
VARIEGATED LILYTURF

Liriope muscari 'Super Evergreen Giant'
LILYTURF

Lonicera x *heckrottii*
GOLDFLAME HONEYSUCKLE

Loropetalum chinense
FRINGE FLOWER

Liriope muscari

LILYTURF. A perennial that forms clumps about 1 to 2 ft. tall and wide of grasslike evergreen leaves. Bears spikes of small violet, purple, or white flowers in late summer, followed by pea-size black berries. Often used as a ground cover. 'Super Evergreen Giant' (p. 79) is one of the largest cultivars, growing as much as 2 ft. tall and bearing ½-in.-wide dark green leaf blades. 'Silvery Sunproof' (p. 74) and 'Variegata' (p. 61) have leaves edged with narrow golden-yellow stripes that fade with age to creamy white. Lilyturf prefers partial sun or shade. Mow or shear off the old foliage in early spring. Can be divided every few years to make more plants. Pages: 35, 63, 105.

Liriope spicata

CREEPING LILYTURF. Resembles regular lilyturf but spreads fast by underground runners to form a dense patch of foliage, not just clumps. It also has narrower leaves and the flowers are less conspicuous than those of regular lilyturf. The grassy-looking foliage stays dark green throughout the year. Makes a good ground cover for shady sites but can spread into a lawn. Mow or shear off old foliage in early spring. Can be divided every few years to make more plants. Pages: 29, 118.

Lonicera

HONEYSUCKLE. Fast-growing vines with woody stems that twine around a support, climbing 10 to 15 ft. or higher. The smooth oval leaves are ev-ergreen or nearly so and are arranged in neat pairs on the stems. The native trumpet honeysuckle, *L. sempervirens* (pp. 100, 110), has coral, red, or sometimes yellow flowers that are scentless but are very attractive to hummingbirds. Blooms heavily in early summer and continues off and on until fall. Songbirds eat the bright red berries. Goldflame honeysuckle, *L.* x *heckrottii* (pp. 41, 74, 109), is similar but has fragrant pink-and-yellow flowers. Unlike Japanese honeysuckle, *L. japonica*, which is not recommended for the Southeast, these two species are not aggressive or invasive. Both need full or partial sun in order to bloom well. Prune in winter, thinning out some of the older stems.

Loropetalum chinense

LOROPETALUM. Also known as fringe flower, this small shrub bears fluffy clusters of lovely white flowers among layers of oval evergreen leaves. Blooms mostly in spring but occasionally in summer and fall. Grows about 5 ft. tall, up to 8 ft. wide, with arching limbs. In Zone 6, substitute 'Delaware Valley White' azalea. The cultivar 'Ruby' (*L. chinense* var. *rubrum*, pp. 25, 77) bears bright pink flowers and burgundy leaves. It is hardy in Zone 8 and above, reaching a height and spread of 4 to 5 ft. Loropetalum prefers partial shade and acid soil. Hand prune lightly after spring bloom to maintain a rounded shape and encourage flower bud development. Trouble-free. Pages: 32, 124.

Lysimachia nummularia

MONEYWORT. A creeping, clinging perennial that forms a carpet of round coin-size leaves. Cheerful yellow flowers last for a month or so in summer. Tolerates full sun if the soil is moist, but also does well in full shade. Buy one to start and divide it later if you want more plants. Spreads fast, up to 1 ft. per year. Normally has medium green leaves, but 'Aurea' (pp. 49, 120) has golden yellow leaves. Page: 117.

Magnolia

MAGNOLIA. Popular trees that has showy flowers in spring or summer. Saucer magnolia or tulip tree, *M. x soulangiana* (pp. 96, 109, 119), blooms in early spring, with upright, cup-shaped flowers in shades of pink, purple, or white. Its large oblong leaves are deciduous. It can grow 30 ft. tall and wide. Star magnolia, *M. stellata* (p. 32), also blooms in early spring, with fresh white flowers that have floppy petals. It is deciduous, with leaves smaller than those of other magnolias. It grows slowly but eventually reaches 15 to 20 ft. tall. Sweet bay magnolia, *M. virginiana* (pp. 56, 124), has fragrant round white flowers in early summer and glossy leaves with silver bottoms that flash in the breeze. Its leaves hang on partway through winter and sometimes year-round. It grows fairly quickly and reaches 30 ft. or taller. Magnolias prefer full or partial sun. Plant in spring, being careful not to break the roots, which are rather brittle. If you don't prune them, magnolias retain their lower limbs and form impressive specimens that are bushy all the way to the ground. If you want to shape them into a tree with a trunk and open up the space underneath the boughs, prune in midsummer.

Mahonia fortunei

CHINESE MAHONIA. Unlike invasive leatherleaf mahonia, *M. bealei*, Chinese mahonia is a well-behaved member of the barberry family. This handsome evergreen shrub produces multiple bushy cane-like stems, full of fern-like compound leaves. The narrow leaflets are spiny at the tips with darker green glossy surface and pale green undersides. Bright yellow flower spikes develop from late summer through early fall. Grows upright, 8 to 10 ft. tall and 3 to 4 ft. wide. Prefers partial shade and welldrained soil. Groom in early spring, removing tattered or discolored leaves. To prune, remove old, weak, or broken stems at ground level. Pages: 30, 74, 120, 126.

Magnolia stellata
STAR MAGNOLIA

Magnolia x soulangiana
SAUCER MAGNOLIA

Lysimachia nummularia
MONEYWORT

Mahonia fortunei
CHINESE MAHONIA

Myrica cerifera

WAX MYRTLE. An evergreen native shrub that grows upright and bushy, with slender twigs and glossy leaves that have a delicious spicy aroma. Clusters of small gray berries line the stems of female plants in fall and winter. Needs full or partial sun. Grows quickly and can reach 30 ft. tall; prune in winter if you want to keep it smaller or control its shape. Pages: 22, 59, 70, 96.

Nandina domestica

HEAVENLY BAMBOO. This evergreen shrub has lost favor thanks to invasive tendencies and massive clusters of toxic red berries. Non-fruiting cultivars offer an eco-friendly alternative. 'Gulf Stream' (pp. 29, 32, 61, 63, 65, 66, 100) produces multiple canes that grow to a compact 3 ft. high with lacy evergreen foliage in shades of bronze and orange, blue-green, gold, and red. 'Obsession' (pp. 25, 46, 62, 77, 96, 99) has a compact, upright growth habit. New growth emerges bright red, and the whole plant takes on rich maroon, gold, and orange tones in winter. It matures to 3 ft. tall and 3 ft. wide. 'Sienna Sunrise' features intensely red new foliage that changes to lush green in summer, with fiery red highlights developing in fall and winter. Nandina serves well as an informal hedge, foundation plant, or accent to large-leaved plants. Zones 6-11.

Myrica cerifera
WAX MYRTLE

Nandina domestica
'Gulf Stream'
HEAVENLY BAMBOO

Odontonema cuspidatum
FIRESPIKE

Ophiopogon japonicus
MONDO GRASS

Odontonema cuspidatum

FIRESPIKE. A tropical evergreen shrub for Zones 8 and higher, with rigid upright stems and glossy, deep green, wavy leaves. Each stem is topped with showy clusters of tubular crimson flowers in winter, in time for hummingbirds returning south. Blooms continue through spring. If left unpruned, firespike will grow 6 ft. tall or more and 4 ft. wide. Full sun or filtered light and well-drained soil. Remove dead or winter-damaged stems at ground level in spring to encourage new growth. Also sold as *O. strictum*. Root hardy in Zones 9 and 10. Page: 93.

Ophiopogon japonicus

MONDO GRASS. A perennial ground cover with shiny dark green leaves about 1/8 in. wide and up to 1 ft. long. Looks like unmown grass. The flowers are inconspicuous. Grows best in full or partial shade; foliage burns in the sun. A patch fills in better if you start with several small plants instead of a few large ones. Rake out dead foliage in early spring. Fresh new growth will look neat the rest of the year. Pages: 27, 43, 46, 56, 59, 87, 95, 117.

Ophiopogon planiscapus 'Ebony Knight'
BLACK MONDO GRASS

Osmanthus x *fortunei*
SWEET OLIVE

Osmanthus x *fortunei*
SWEET OLIVE

Ophiopogon planiscapus 'Ebony Knight'

BLACK MONDO GRASS. A small, slow-growing perennial with grassy evergreen foliage in an unusual shade of purple-black. Spreads gradually to form a patch, under 1 ft. tall and 1 to 2 ft. wide. Prefers partial sun and moist, well-drained soil. Cut the leaves back partway in early spring to remove any damaged tips. Needs no other care. Pages: 51, 65, 117, 118.

Osmanthus x fortunei

SWEET OLIVE. An evergreen shrub with hollylike leaves and white flowers that are tiny but very sweet-scented. Blooms in late summer and fall. The habit is dense and compact. Grows at least 6 ft. tall and wide. Adapts to sun or shade. Needs minimal pruning. Pages: 69, 105, 107, 126.

Pachysandra terminalis

JAPANESE SPURGE. An ideal ground cover for semi-shade or shady areas. It has a low, shrubby growth habit, reaching 8 to 12 in. high. It spreads by shallow lateral stems to form a dense mat of rich, deep green foliage. In early spring, tiny white flower spikes form at the branch tips. Unlike invasive English ivy, pachysandra does not climb trees or walls and generally stays in its place once established, with little care or attention. Zones 5-9. Pages: 39, 82.

Panicum virgatum

SWITCHGRASS. A dense clumping perennial grass with a fairly upright growth habit. It produces attractive wispy, pink-tinged flower panicles above the foliage in summer. Withstands seasonal flooding, and is also drought tolerant once established. 'Shenandoah' is a popular cultivar with a compact habit and purplish highlights in the foliage. 'Heavy Metal' is a stiff, metallic-blue cultivar that grows somewhat larger. The flower panicles turn beige in fall, while the foliage color intensifies before turning an attractive amber color in winter. Zones 4-9. Pages: 41, 88, 90, 99, 117.

Paspalum quadrifarium

EVERGREEN PASPALUM GRASS. A fine-textured ornamental grass with yellow-green leaf blades. It forms a graceful mound 3 to 4 ft. tall and wide and is attractive as a single specimen or in a mass planting. Slender flowerheads rise above the foliage. It is drought-resistant and moderately salt-tolerant. Foliage needs no winter pruning but may be cut back to 8 in. above the ground to rejuvenate. Page: 79.

Paspalum quadrifarium
EVERGREEN PASPALUM GRASS

Philodendron 'Xanadu'

Passiflora x 'Amethyst'

'AMETHYST' PASSION FLOWER. A favorite evergreen vine of butterfly enthusiasts. Climbs on slender stems and delicate tendrils to heights of 12 ft. or more. Star-shaped flowers with purple-blue centers and green anthers look spectacular against rich green lobed leaves from late spring through autumn. This vine attracts Gulf fritillary butterflies, who lay single golden eggs that hatch into orange-and-black-striped caterpillars. Well-established vines can easily support their voracious appetites. Vines may be stripped of foliage but will quickly recover. Resist the urge during the growing season to trim young growth, which will remove potential blooms and egg-laying sites. For renewed growth, cut back severely in early spring. Also sold as *P.* x 'Lavender Lady'. Root hardy in Zones 9 and 10. Page: 93.

Pennisetum alopecuroides 'Hameln'

DWARF FOUNTAIN GRASS. A grass that forms a hassocklike clump of arching leaves, green in summer and gold or tan in fall. Grows 2 ft. tall, 3 ft. wide. Blooms over a long season from midsummer to fall, with fluffy spikes on arching stalks. Needs full sun, garden soil. Cut old leaves to the ground in late winter, or sooner if storms knock them down. Can go many years without being divided. **Note:** Pennisetum alopecuroides is considered invasive; however 'Hameln' is a safe choice because it does not reseed itself. Pages: 37, 41, 51, 105, 109, 117.

Philodendron 'Xanadu'

'XANADU' PHILODENDRON. A well-behaved cousin of the familiar philodendron, this compact, nonvining shrub forms a slow-growing mound that won't overrun the landscape. Reaches a maximum height and spread of 4 ft. Deeply split evergreen leaves are smaller and narrower than those of common philodendron. Grows in full sun to partial shade and prefers moist well-drained soil. Remove dead or damaged growth in early spring. Root hardy in Zones 8 to 10. Pages: 26, 87.

Phlox paniculata 'David'

'DAVID' GARDEN PHLOX. A perennial with clusters of fragrant white flowers in late summer. Forms a clump or patch 3 to 4 ft. tall, 2 to 3 ft. wide. Unlike most cultivars of garden phlox, 'David' is resistant to powdery mildew and does well in heat and humidity, with foliage that stays green and healthy-looking all summer. Needs full or partial sun. Cut off flowers after they fade. Divide clumps every few years in spring. Pages: 49, 61.

Phlox stolonifera

CREEPING PHLOX. A low perennial with creeping stems, small evergreen leaves, and clusters of fragrant flowers in spring. 'Bruce's White' has white flowers. 'Blue Ridge' bears blue flowers. Other cultivars are good, too. Grows only a few inches tall but can spread 1 to 2 ft. in a year. Makes a good ground cover for sites with partial or full shade and fertile, moist, well-drained soil. Pages: 96, 103.

Passiflora x 'Amethyst'
PASSIONFLOWER

Phlox paniculata 'David'
GARDEN PHLOX

Pinus taeda
LOBLOLLY PINE

Phlox subulata

MOSS PHLOX. A low perennial that forms dense mats of prickly-textured evergreen foliage. Pink, magenta, lilac-blue, or white flowers completely cover the foliage for a few weeks in spring. Grows 6 in. tall and spreads to form a patch 2 to 3 ft. wide. Needs full or partial sun. Tolerates dry sites. Shear the plants back halfway after they bloom to promote neat, compact growth. Divide every few years in fall or early spring. Pages: 44, 53, 61.

Pinus

PINE. Several pines are native to the Southeast. All have evergreen needles and woody cones and grow upright with a thick central trunk and spreading limbs. Loblolly pine, *P. taeda* has green or yellow-green needles 6 to 9 in. long and thrives in warmer regions. Eastern white pine, *P. strobus*, has green or blue-green needles 2 to 4 in. long and prefers cooler regions. Both grow quickly (1 to $1\frac{1}{2}$ ft. per year) and soon provide shade and screening. Longleaf pine, *P. palustris*, has needles up to 18 in. long. Seedlings grow very slowly at first but mature into beautiful specimens with a tall trunk and open crown. (Buy plants with at least two lateral branches—this ensures that they are past the slowest stage of growth.) All pines need full sun. Young trees retain their lower limbs, but you can remove these when the trees reach 15 to 20 ft. or taller, to expose the trunk and to create a shady space for growing other plants. Pages: 113, 115.

Phlox stolonifera
CREEPING PHLOX

Phlox subulata
MOSS PHLOX

Pittosporum tobira

PITTOSPORUM. An evergreen shrub with tufts of glossy leaves, fragrant white flowers in early summer, and a rounded bushy habit. The most popular cultivars are 'Variegata', variegated pittosporum (p. 32), which has gray-green leaves with white edging and grows about 6 ft. tall and wide; and 'Wheeleri', dwarf pittosporum (pp. 21, 100), which has bright green leaves and grows only 3 to 4 ft. tall and wide. Both adapt to sun or shade and need only minimal pruning. Hardy only to Zone 8; in colder parts of the Southeast a good substitute is cherry laurel (*Prunus laurocerasus*).

Plumbago auriculata

PLUMBAGO. A semi-tropical semi-evergreen shrub that forms a rounded mound 3 to 5 ft. high and wide of slender whiplike stems and oblong leaves. In many parts of the Southeast it will be smothered in clusters of clear blue flowers from summer to frost. In Florida it blooms nearly year-round. Plumbago needs fertile well-drained soil and full sun. Lightly prune in early spring and early fall to rejuvenate tired plants. Remove dead stems in early spring after freezes. Root hardy in Zones 8 to 10. Page: 85.

Polygonatum odoratum 'Variegatum'

VARIEGATED SOLOMON'S SEAL. A perennial that forms a patch of upright or arching stems 2 to 3 ft. tall, with lovely green-and-white leaves and fragrant white flowers that dangle below the leaves in late spring. Needs full or partial shade; grows well under trees. Trouble-free. Can grow for years without needing division or other care. Page: 35.

Prunus

FLOWERING CHERRY. Small deciduous trees prized for their flowers. The autumn cherry or twice-blooming cherry, *P. subhirtella* 'Autumnalis' (p. 124), bears delicate pale pink flowers in late fall and again in early spring. It grows upright, 20 to 30 ft. tall, with a slender, vase-shaped habit. The Yoshino cherry, *P.* x *yedoensis* (p. 100), has fragrant flowers in early spring; they can be single or double, pink or white. There are many cultivars. Most form a rounded or weeping crown and grow to 25 ft. or taller. Cherry leaves are medium green in summer and typically turn yellow in fall. Full sun. These trees grow quickly but are subject to several pests and diseases and may be short-lived. Prune and train to avoid narrow crotches, which are liable to split apart.

Pittosporum tobira 'Wheeleri' DWARF PITTOSPORUM

Polygonatum odoratum 'Variegatum' VARIEGATED SOLOMON'S SEAL

Plumbago auriculata PLUMBAGO

Prunus x *yedoensis* YOSHINO CHERRY

Rhaphiolepis indica
INDIAN HAWTHORN

Prunus laurocerasus 'Zabeliana'
CHERRY LAUREL

Rhapis excelsa
LADY PALM

Prunus laurocerasus

CHERRY LAUREL. An adaptable evergreen shrub, often used for foundation plantings. Leathery leaves are glossy dark green. Spikes of heavy-scented white flowers stick up like birthday candles in late spring. Adapts to sun or shade. Prefers moist, well-drained soil but tolerates dry sites. 'Zaebeliana' (p. 81) grows 4 to 6 ft. tall and 8 to 10 ft. wide, and has narrower leaves. Stays compact even if you don't prune it and looks fine if you leave it alone, but can be pruned at any time if you prefer a tidy, formal look.

Rhaphiolepis indica

INDIAN HAWTHORN. A low, spreading evergreen shrub with thick-textured dull green leaves, small pink or white flowers in spring, and blue berries that last through the summer and fall. Grows 2 to 4 ft. tall, 3 to 6 ft. wide. There are many fine cultivars. Needs full sun. Requires minimal pruning or care. Hardy only to Zone 8; substitute 'Crimson Pygmy' Japanese barberry (*Berberis thunbergii*) in colder areas. Page: 21.

Rhapis excelsa

LADY PALM. A small palm with delicate handlike fronds. Grows slowly, forming a clump of slender, reedlike stems and deeply lobed, lustrous, dark green leaves, often a foot long. Well-established clumps may achieve a height of 7 ft. Panicles of tiny cream-colored flowers bloom among the foliage in summer. Lady palm prefers filtered light or partial shade. Grows in moderately fertile moist but well drained soil. Root hardy in Zones 9 and 10. Pages: 26, 86, 94.

Recommended azaleas and rhododendrons

PINK GUMPO EVERGREEN AZALEA (left);
WHITE EVERGREEN AZALEA (right)

'Amagasa' Satsuki azalea
A spreading shrub, 3 to 4 ft. tall, with small evergreen leaves and large, rosy pink flowers in late spring. Page: 71.

'Delaware Valley White' azalea
An upright shrub, 4 to 6 ft. tall, with medium-size evergreen leaves and masses of single white flowers in midspring. Pages: 59, 124.

'Fiedlers White' azalea
A vigorous evergreen shrub, 7 to 8 ft. tall, with lovely single white flowers in midspring. Hardy to Zone 8; in colder regions substitute 'Delaware Valley White'. Page: 70.

'George Lindley Taber' azalea
A vigorous evergreen shrub, 7 to 8 ft. tall, with beautiful pale pink flowers in midspring. Hardy to Zone 8; in colder regions substitute a pink Glen Dale azalea. Pages: 56, 70.

Glen Dale azaleas
A group of azaleas that grow about 3 to 6 ft. tall, with evergreen foliage and large white, pink, red, or orange flowers in midspring. Unusually cold-hardy, they are especially valuable in Zones 7 and 6, where other evergreen azaleas might freeze. Page: 61

Gumpo azaleas
Low, spreading shrubs, 2 to 3 ft. tall and wide, with small evergreen leaves and large pink or white flowers in late spring. Pages: 31, 39, 53, 71, 103, 118.

'George Lindley Taber' AZALEA

**Rhododendron canescens,
Piedmont azalea**
A deciduous native azalea with clove-scented white or pink flowers in midspring. Grows 10 to 15 ft. tall and spreads to form a colony. Page: 126.

R. prunifolium, Plumleaf azalea
A deciduous native azalea that bears its orange-red flowers in midsummer, long after other azaleas have finished blooming. Grows 8 to 10 ft. tall and wide. Page: 56.

'Roseum Elegans' rhododendron
A fast-growing shrub with large glossy evergreen leaves and rounded clusters of pink or pink-purple flowers in late spring. Grows about 6 ft. tall and wide. Pages: 30, 82, 102.

Rhododendron canescens
PIEDMONT AZALEA

Rhododendron
'Roseum Elegans'

Rhododendron

RHODODENDRON AND AZALEA. An especially diverse and popular group of shrubs with very showy flowers in spring or summer. The leaves can be small or large, deciduous or evergreen. The plants can be short, medium, or tall, with spreading, mounded, or erect habits. All rhododendrons and azaleas do best with partial shade and need fertile, moist, well-drained soil. Mix a 3-in. layer of peat moss into the soil to prepare a bed for these plants.

Plant rhododendrons and azaleas in spring or early fall. Don't plant them too deep—the top of the root ball should be level with, or a little higher than, the surrounding soil. Azaleas are usually sold in containers. When planting them it's very important that you make a few deep cuts down the root ball and tease apart some of the roots; otherwise, azaleas typically do not root well into the surrounding soil. Treat container-grown rhododendrons the same way. Large rhododendron plants are often sold balled-and-burlapped. The roots were cut when the plants were dug and need no further attention. They will grow through the burlap in time.

Use a layer of mulch to keep the soil cool and damp around your azaleas and rhododendrons, and water the plants during any dry spell for the first few years. Prune or shear off the flower stalks as soon as the petals fade, to prevent seed formation and to neaten the plants. Prune or shear to control plant size and shape at the same time (in early summer). See the facing page for more information on specific varieties.

Rohdea japonica

JAPANESE SACRED LILY, LILY OF CHINA. An evergreen perennial with broad, arching, straplike leaves about 2 ft. long, 3 in. wide. Spreads slowly to form a patch with many clumps of foliage. The short-stalked yellow flowers are insignificant, but the red berries that follow look nice. Needs full or partial shade and rich, moist soil. Carefree. In Zone 6, substitute a hosta. Page: 120.

Rosa

ROSE. Vigorous shrubs with thorny woody stems and deciduous compound leaves. Hybrid tea roses (p. 105), the most popular group of cultivars, typically have stiff upright stems 3 to 6 ft. tall. They bear exquisite long-stalked red, orange, pink, yellow, or white flowers from late spring until hard frost. The plants need regular fertilizing, spraying, and pruning; ask local rose enthusiasts for advice.

Rohdea japonica
JAPANESE SACRED LILY

Rosa 'Blaze'

So-called climbing roses are really shrubs, not vines, and they don't climb without assistance—you have to fasten them to a trellis or other support. 'Blaze' (pp. 21, 72) is an old favorite with semidouble red flowers that bloom in June and continue through the summer. Its canes grow about 12 ft. long. Lady Bank's rose, *R.* x *banksiae* (p. 54), has long flexible canes that are almost thornless, small leaves that are almost evergreen, and puffy clusters of double yellow flowers in spring.

All roses grow best in full sun and fertile, well-drained soil topped with a few inches of mulch. Prune them every in spring, before new growth starts. (See p. 222 for rose-pruning instructions.)

Rosmarinus officinalis 'Arp'

'ARP' ROSEMARY. An evergreen shrub with gray-green needlelike leaves that combine a lovely fragrance with a tasty flavor. Small blue, lilac, or white flowers bloom in late winter and early spring. Grows upright and bushy, 3 to 4 ft. tall. 'Arp' is the hardiest cultivar of this popular herb and survives outdoors throughout the Southeast; other cultivars are hardy only to Zone 8. Needs full sun and well-drained soil. Prune or shear in spring or summer. Pages: 63, 88, 90.

Rosa
HYBRID TEA ROSE

Sabal palmetto
SABAL PALM

Rudbeckia fulgida 'Goldsturm'
CONEFLOWER

Rudbeckia fulgida 'Goldsturm'

'GOLDSTURM' CONEFLOWER. An improved form of a popular perennial wildflower. Bears hundreds of gold-and-brown flowers, which are often called black-eyed Susans, for several weeks in late summer. Forms a robust clump about 3 ft. tall and wide, with large dark green leaves at the base and stiff branching flower stalks. Needs full or partial sun. Cut down the flower stalks in fall or spring, as you choose. Divide every few years in early spring. Pages: 41, 44, 55, 113, 115.

Sabal palmetto

SABAL PALM. A popular native palm of the Southeast. Grows slowly (about 6 in. a year), reaching a mature height of 100 ft. and a spread of 8 ft. Leaf stalks bear impressive fan-shaped leaves up to 6 ft. long. Frond bases remain on the trunk after they die, forming characteristic "boots." For a cleaner look, you can remove them with a sharp shovel. Large clusters of small cream-colored flowers bloom among the leaves in summer. They can be removed before the seeds mature to prevent sprouting palm seedlings. Sabal palm grows in full sun and in a range of soils from well to poorly drained. Hardy in Zones 8 to 10. Pages: 78, 85.

Salvia coccinea

SCARLET SAGE. A perennial Texas wildflower that grows about 2 ft. tall and wide, with a bushy habit, heart-shaped green leaves, and flower stalks at the top of every stem. Blooms for months throughout the summer and fall. 'Lady in Red' is a popular cultivar with bright red flowers; although sold as a bedding plant, it often overwinters in the Southeast. Needs full sun. Carefree. Page: 105.

Salvia coccinea
SCARLET SAGE

Salvia farinacea
MEALY BLUE SAGE

Salvia farinacea

MEALY BLUE SAGE. Another perennial Texas wild-flower. Grows 2 to 3 ft. tall and wide, with a bushy habit and slender, glossy green leaves. Blooms all summer and fall, with dense spikes of violet, blue, or white flowers on slender stiff stalks. Often sold as a bedding plant but frequently overwinters in the Southeast. Cut down old stalks in fall or spring. Needs full sun. Carefree. Pages: 72, 109.

Salvia greggii

AUTUMN SAGE. A shrubby perennial with small semievergreen leaves. Grows about 2 to 3 ft. tall and wide. Blooms throughout the summer and fall. Flowers are typically bright red, but they can be pink, salmon, or white. 'Cherry Chief' (pp. 44, 46) has cherry red flowers. Needs full sun. In spring, prune or shear off any weak, damaged, or frozen stems. In Zone 6, substitute scarlet sage (*Salvia coccinea*). Pages: 21, 23, 49, 71, 117.

Salvia leucantha

MEXICAN BUSH SAGE. This shrubby perennial blooms best in autumn and in the spring, producing hundreds of spikes of purple-and-white flowers above its gray-green foliage. The nectar-rich blossoms attract bees, butterflies, and occasionally hummingbirds. Grows into a fuzzy" mound 3 to 4 ft.

high and 2 to 3 ft. wide. Young stems and leaves are covered with a downy growth and even the flowers sport soft, velvety hairs. Requires full sun and good drainage. It has very few pests and needs little watering. To rejuvenate, cut back to 8 in. above the ground in late summer and again in early spring. Page: 93.

Sarcococca hookeriana 'Humilis'

SWEET BOX. A slow-growing evergreen shrub with small, leathery, pointed leaves that are glossy green all year. Grows 12 to 18 in. tall and spreads 2 to 3 ft. wide. Can be used as a ground cover. Blooms in February or March, with small white flowers that are very sweet-scented. Needs full or partial shade. Carefree. Page: 74.

Scabiosa columbaria 'Butterfly Blue'

'BUTTERFLY BLUE' PINCUSHION FLOWER. A compact perennial that forms a neat clump of bright green foliage. It will bloom continuously from May to hard frost if you keep picking off the old flowers. The round, sky blue flowers really do attract butterflies, and they make good cut flowers, too. Grows about 1 ft. tall and wide. Needs full sun and well-drained soil. Divide every few years in early spring. Pages: 51, 89, 96.

Scabiosa columbaria 'Butterfly Blue'
PINCUSHION FLOWER

Salvia leucantha
MEXICAN BUSH SAGE

Sarcococca hookeriana 'Humilis'
SWEET BOX

Sedum 'Autumn Joy'

Sedum 'Vera Jameson'

Sedum

SEDUM. Perennials that form clumps of succulent foliage on thick stems topped with flat clusters of flowers. 'Autumn Joy' (pp. 44, 46, 66, 99, 111) grows 2 to 3 ft. tall, with erect stems, gray-green foliage, and flowers that change color from pale to deep salmon-pink to rusty red over a span of many weeks in late summer and fall as they open, mature, and go to seed. 'Vera Jameson' (p. 51) grows about 1 ft. tall, with floppy stems, rounded leaves in an unusual shade of purple-gray, and pink flowers in August. Sedums need full sun. Cut down old stalks in winter or spring. Divide clumps every few years in early spring.

Spiraea japonica

JAPANESE SPIREA. A very popular deciduous shrub that forms a low mound of thin, graceful, arching stems with small toothed leaves and round flat clusters of tiny flowers in summer. 'Goldflame' (p. 110) has bright gold leaves that are tinged with orange in spring and turn red in fall, and pink-red flowers. This cultivar is sometimes listed under the species *S. x bumalda*. 'Little Princess' (pp. 37, 65, 66) has dark green leaves and rosy pink flowers. Both grow about 2 to 3 ft. tall and wide and need full or partial sun. To keep plants looking their best, prune every year in early spring, removing some of the older stems at ground level and cutting others back partway. In summer, shear off faded flowers to promote reblooming. Trouble-free.

Spiraea nipponica 'Snowmound'

'SNOWMOUND' SPIREA. A deciduous shrub that forms a dense rounded clump of arching branches covered with fine-textured, dark blue-green foliage. Grows about 4 ft. tall and wide. Clusters of pure white flowers line the stems in spring. Needs full or partial sun. To keep the plant compact and healthy, prune right after it flowers, cutting off some of the stems at ground level and shearing the rest back partway. Pages: 42, 96.

Choosing Eco-Friendly Plants

The time and expense of installing new landscaping can do more than just make your yard look great. With the right plant selection, you have a chance to improve the outlook for migratory birds, pollinators, and other backyard wildlife; you can take pleasure watching them rest, feed, nest, and raise their young in the garden you planted. While hundreds of beautiful, easy-to-grow, exotic plants exist in the nursery trade, those with invasive tendencies outcompete native plants without adding habitat value for local wildlife. In large numbers, these plants damage local ecosystems. The best eco-friendly plant selections for any landscape are often those native to the region.

Native species are those that evolved in the local area. For instance, if you live near the coast, along the piedmont, or in the mountains, consider the unique palette of plants that naturally grow there. Planting native trees, shrubs, vines, perennials, and annuals turns your property into a haven for resident wildlife and contributes essential food and shelter for migratory species. As a bonus, these plants are almost always the least needy in terms of water, fertilizer, and pest prevention. Choose 70 percent or more native plants for a diverse landscape that offers flowers, foliage, and fruits all year long.

If you want to plant native species to support wildlife, take a little time to learn about the plants and animals that originated where you live. Sometimes, the most common native landscape plants are sold alongside exotic species without fanfare. Other times, plants are labeled "native" but may not have originated in your bioregion or ecosystem. If you are not sure where to start your research, check with local nature centers, botanical gardens, your state's Department of Natural Resources, or the National Forest Service. The best places to buy native plants are independent garden centers and online nurseries.

Spiraea japonica 'Goldflame'
SPIREA

Spiraea japonica 'Little Princess'
SPIREA

Spiraea nipponica 'Snowmound'
SPIREA

Stachytarpheta jamaicensis

BLUE PORTERWEED. A low, sprawling native shrub with light-blue flowers on long spikes. Flowers attract butterflies. Grows 1 to 2 ft. tall and spreads 3 to 4 ft. wide. The gray-green leaves may have a purplish blush and the leaf surfaces are flat. (Avoid planting a non-native porterweed that has dark blue flowers with white centers, dark green leaves and raised leaf surfaces. It can invade natural areas and hybridize with native populations.) Prefers full sun and well-drained soil. Root hardy to Zone 9. Page: 93.

Stokesia laevis

STOKE'S ASTER. A native perennial wildflower that blooms from June until frost, with flowers like large flat bachelor's buttons; they make excellent long-lasting cut flowers. 'Blue Danube' has sky blue flowers on stalks 12 to 18 in. tall. The basal foliage is evergreen. Adapts to full sun or partial shade. Needs well-drained soil. Pick the flowers regularly to promote continuous bloom. Divide every few years in spring or fall. Page: 44.

Stokesia laevis
STOKE'S ASTER

Ternstroemia gymnanthera

CLEYERA. A neat, compact evergreen shrub with glossy leaves in changeable colors; they can be red, gold, green, or purple, depending on stage of growth, season, and light level. Red berries that ripen in fall are attractive, too. Grows about 4 ft. tall and 3 ft. wide. 'Bronze Beauty' (p. 25) has bronzy new foliage that turns a dark glossy green and a mature height of 8 ft. Cleyera prefers full or partial shade and acid soil. Needs minimal pruning. Trouble-free. Not hardy in Zone 6; substitute 'Roseum Elegans' rhododendron there. Pages: 25, 110.

Ternstroemia gymnanthera
CLEYERA

Teucrium chamaedrys
GERMANDER

*Trachelospermum
asiaticum*
ASIAN JASMINE

Teucrium chamaedrys

GERMANDER. A low, mounded shrub with small, glossy, dark evergreen leaves and pink-purple flowers in late summer. Grows about 1 ft. tall and 2 ft. wide. Needs full or partial sun and well-drained soil. Shear stems back partway every spring to keep it compact and bushy. Pages: 41, 118.

Trachelospermum asiaticum

ASIAN JASMINE. A creeping, nonflowering vine commonly used as a ground cover. Grows less than 1 ft. tall and spreads to about 3 ft., forming a thick mat of small, shiny evergreen leaves. Many variegated cultivars display mahogany to cream-colored young growth. Asian jasmine only requires watering when it's dry and the leaves turn dull green. Semi-drought tolerance makes this a good choice to compete with tree roots. Plant in full sun or in the shade of tree canopies. Fills in completely in two to three years, keeping out most weeds. Shear the foliage as needed to keep the plant tidy. Root hardy in Zones 9 and 10. Pages: 25, 77, 85.

Trachelospermum jasminoides

STAR JASMINE. An evergreen vine. The woody twining stems are lined with pairs of small leathery oval leaves. Bears dangling clusters of cream-colored, sweet-scented flowers in early summer. Climbs 10 to 15 ft. tall. Prefers partial shade. Prune at least once a year, cutting out older stems and cutting new ones back partway. Take care when pruning; the stems contain a milky sap that can stain clothes and surfaces. Normally hardy only to Zone 8, but 'Madison' is hardy in Zone 7. In Zone 6, substitute a clematis. Pages: 32, 35, 54, 85.

Verbena bonariensis

PURPLE VERBENA. A perennial that thrives in hot weather and blooms from June or July until frost. Forms a low mound of basal foliage topped by a thicket of stiff, erect, much-branched but almost leafless flower stalks, 3 to 4 ft. tall. Bears countless small clusters of small purple flowers that butterflies love. Needs full sun. Carefree; simply cut down old stalks in winter or spring. May self-sow but isn't weedy. Pages: 21, 53, 55, 85, 93.

Trachelospermum jasminoides
STAR JASMINE

Verbena canadensis 'Homestead Purple'

'HOMESTEAD PURPLE' VERBENA. A perennial with sprawling stems, evergreen leaves, and round clusters of purple flowers. Blooms nonstop from late spring until hard frost if regularly deadheaded. Grows about 1 ft. tall, spreads 3 ft. or wider. Needs full sun. Prune any damaged or frosted shoots in early spring. Pages: 49, 51 99, 88.

Veronica 'Sunny Border Blue'

'SUNNY BORDER BLUE' VERONICA. A perennial that blooms from early summer until frost if regularly deadheaded, with spikes of blue-purple flowers on stalks 18 to 24 in. tall. The leaves are green and glossy, with a crisp texture. Needs full sun. Divide every few years, in spring or fall. Pages: 49, 99.

Vinca minor

VINCA. An evergreen ground cover that spreads by long runners to form dense patches. Planted 1 ft. apart, soon forms a solid mass. The small leathery leaves are shiny green. Round blue-purple flowers bloom for a few weeks in spring. Adapts to most soils, in partial sun or shade. Once established, needs absolutely no care. If you want something special, look for the lovely variegated or white-flowered forms of this plant. They are just as easy to grow as the common type. **Note:** This plant exhibits invasive characteristics in parts of the Southeast. Pages: 31, 55, 103.

Verbena canadensis 'Homestead Purple'

Veronica 'Sunny Border Blue'

Vinca minor

Water plants

Most big garden centers have a small collection of water plants. Mail-order water-garden specialists offer several dozen kinds. Most water plants are fast-growing, even weedy, so you need only one of each kind to start with.

There are two main categories of water lilies (*Nymphaea*). Hardy water lilies survive outdoors from year to year and bloom in midsummer. Tropical water lilies bloom from summer through fall, but in most of the Southeast they need to be stored indoors in winter or treated as annuals. Both hardy and tropical water lilies are available in dwarf-size plants, suitable for small pools, with fragrant or scentless flowers in shades of white, yellow, and pink; tropicals also come in shades of blue and purple. All water lilies need full sun. Plant in a container of heavy, rich garden soil, and set it in the pool so about 6 in. of water covers the soil. (See p. 185 for more on planting water plants.)

Lotuses (*Nelumbo*) grow like water lilies but hold their leaves and flowers above the water. They have fragrant yellow, pink, or white flowers and interesting seedpods. Most kinds are hardy, but only dwarf cultivars are suitable for small ponds. Full-size lotuses get to be huge plants.

Marginal or emergent water plants grow well in containers covered with 2 in. or more of water; their leaves and flower stalks stick up into the air. For example, dwarf papyrus (*Cyperus haspan*) is a popular marginal with leaves that branch out like umbrella spokes; it grows 18 in. tall. Floating plants have leaves that rest on the water and roots that dangle down into it. Water lettuce (*Pistia stratiotes*) is a floater that forms saucer-size rosettes of iridescent pale green leaves. Oxygenating or submerged plants grow underwater; they help keep the water clear and provide oxygen, food, and shelter for fish. Anacharis (*Elodea canadensis*) is a popular oxygenator with tiny dark green leaves. Page: 117.

Wisteria frutescens

AMERICAN WISTERIA. A very vigorous vine with woody stems that twine around any support, deciduous compound leaves, and long drooping clusters of very fragrant blue-purple, lilac, or white flowers in late spring. Sometimes reblooms a little in summer. Needs full sun. Provide a very sturdy trellis or support. Wisteria can climb to 40 ft., and you will need to prune it hard once or twice every summer to keep it smaller. It's worth spending extra to buy a named cultivar; these bloom at an early age. With inexpensive seed-raised plants, you may wait years before seeing a flower. Page: 53.

Nymphaea 'Perry's Fire Opal'
HARDY WATER LILY

Wisteria frutescens
AMERICAN WISTERIA

Yucca filamentosa 'Golden Sword'

'GOLDEN SWORD' YUCCA. An unusual shrub or perennial with evergreen daggerlike leaves, 2 ft. long, that stick out in all directions from a short thick trunk. Leaves have a broad yellow stripe down the middle and green edges; although lovely, this cultivar does grow more slowly than the common all-green form. Blooms in June, with large creamy white flowers on stiff branching stalks 4 to 6 ft. tall. The woody seedpods are decorative, too. Needs full or partial sun. Cut down the old flower stalks whenever you choose, and peel dead leaves from around the base of the plant in spring. Once established, it lives for decades and can't be moved, although you can dig up the baby plants that form around the base and transplant them. Pages: 41, 44, 46.

Zamia maritima

CARDBOARD PLANT. This prehistoric cycad, also known as cardboard palm, makes a dramatic specimen in a tropical garden. It produces a rosette of thick, palmlike, evergreen leaves 3 to 4 ft. high and 6 to 8 ft. in diameter. The new leaves appear to be covered in red felt and unfurl from an underground trunk, stiffening and turning green as they mature. Male or female cones appear at the base of the clump in summer. It grows in full sun to partial shade and is drought tolerant, preferring moderate to well-drained soil. Give it plenty of room and keep it tidy by removing unsightly fronds from the base of the plant. Root hardy in Zones 9 and 10. Also sold as *Z. furfuracea*. Page: 78.

Zamia pumila

COONTIE. A Florida native cycad and smaller cousin to the cardboard plant (*Z. maritima*). It has a mounding habit and is often grown as a ground cover, reaching a height and spread of 4 ft. Stiff feather-like fronds emerge from an underground stem, unfurling in the spring like fern fiddleheads. Bears either male or female cones in summer. Grows in full sun or partial shade and well-drained soil. Drought tolerant. Also known as *Z. floridana*. Root hardy in Zones 8 to 10. Page: 77.

Zamioculcas zamiifolia

ZZ. An African jewel that resembles a cycad and performs equally well indoors and out, in a container, or as a tropical accent in the landscape. Thick underground rhizomes bear large stemless leaves that are glossy and evergreen. Grows 3 ft. tall and wide. Requires well-drained soil and shade from the hot sun but not much else. Tolerates very low light and low watering. Succulent leaves store water. Divide the plant with a sharp shovel or soil knife when it becomes crowded or if you want more plants. Root hardy in Zones 9 and 10. Page: 87.

Yucca filamentosa 'Golden Sword'

Zamioculcas zamiifolia
ZZ

Zamia pumila
COONTIE

Guide *to* Installation

In this section, we introduce the hard but rewarding work of landscaping. Here you'll find information on all the tasks you need to install any of the designs in this book, organized in the order in which you'd most likely tackle them. Clearly written text and numerous illustrations help you learn how to plan the job; clear the site; construct paths, patios, ponds, fences, arbors, and trellises; prepare the planting beds; and install and maintain the plantings. Roll up your sleeves and dig in. In just a few weekends, you can create a landscape feature that will provide years of enjoyment.

Organizing Your Project

If your gardening experience is limited to mowing the lawn, pruning the bushes, and growing some flowers and vegetables, the thought of starting from scratch and installing a whole new landscape feature might be intimidating. But in fact, adding one of the designs in this book to your property is completely within reach, if you approach it the right way. The key is to divide the project into a series of steps and take them one at a time. This is how professional landscapers work. It's efficient and orderly, and it makes even big jobs seem manageable.

On this and the facing page, we'll explain how to think your way through a landscaping project and anticipate the various steps. Subsequent topics in this section describe how to do each part of the job. Detailed instructions and illustrations cover all the techniques you'll need to install any design from start to finish.

The step-by-step approach
Choose a design and adapt it to your site. The designs in this book address parts of the home landscape. In the most attractive and effective home landscapes, all the various parts work together. Don't be afraid to change the shape of beds; alter the number, kinds, and positions of plants; or revise paths and structures to bring them into harmony with their surroundings.

To see the relationships with your existing landscape, you can draw the design on a scaled plan of your property. Or you can work on the site itself, placing wooden stakes, pots, tricycles, or whatever is handy to represent plants and structures. With a little imagination, either method will allow you to visualize basic relationships.

Lay out the design on site. Once you've decided what you want to do, you'll need to lay out the paths and structures and outline the beds. Some people are comfortable laying out a design "freehand," pacing off distances and relying on their eye to judge sizes and relative positions. Others prefer to transfer the grid from the plan full size onto the site in order to place elements precisely. (Garden lime, a grainy white powder available at nurseries, can be used like chalk on a blackboard to "draw" a grid or outlines of planting beds.)

Clear the site. (See pp. 174–175.) Sometimes you have to work around existing features—a nice big tree, a building or

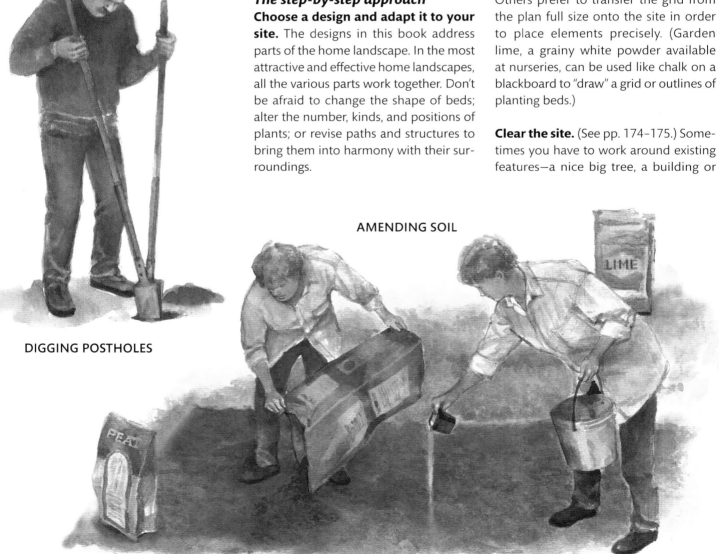

DIGGING POSTHOLES

AMENDING SOIL

fence, a sidewalk—but it's usually easiest to start a new landscaping project if you clear as much as possible, down to ground level. That means removing unwanted structures or pavement and killing, cutting down, or uprooting all the plants. Needless to say, this can generate a lot of debris, and you'll need to figure out how to dispose of it all. Still, it's often worth the trouble to make a fresh start.

Build the "hardscape." (See pp. 176–207.) "Hardscape" means anything you build as part of a landscape—a fence, trellis, arbor, retaining wall, walkway, edging, outdoor lighting, or whatever. If you're going to do any building, do it first, and finish the construction before you start any planting. That way you won't have to worry about stepping on any of the plants, and they won't be in the way as you work.

Prepare the soil. (See pp. 208–211.) On most properties, it's uncommon to find soil that's as good as it should be for growing plants. Typically, the soil around a house is shallow, compacted, and infertile. It may be rocky or contain buried debris. Some plants tolerate such poor conditions, but they don't thrive. To grow healthy, attractive plants, you need to improve the quality of the soil throughout the entire area that you're planning to plant.

Do the planting and add mulch. (See pp. 212–216.) Putting plants in the ground usually goes quite quickly and provides instant gratification. Spreading mulch over the soil makes the area look neat and "finished" even while the plants are still small.

Maintain the planting. (See pp. 217–229.) Most plantings need regular watering and occasional weeding for the first year or two. After that, depending on the design you've chosen, you'll have to do some routine maintenance—pruning, shaping, cutting back, and cleaning up—to keep the plants looking their best. This may take as little as a few hours a year or as much as an hour or two every week throughout the growing season.

TRANSPLANTING

SETTING FLAGSTONES

Clearing the Site

The site you've chosen for a landscaping project may or may not have any man-made objects (fences, old pavement, trash, etc.) to be removed, but it will almost certainly be covered with plants.

Before you start cutting plants down, try to find someone—a friend or neighbor who enjoys gardening—to identify these plants for you. As you walk around together, make a sketch that shows which plants are where, and attach labels to the plants, too. Determine if there are any desirable plants worth saving—mature shade trees that you should work around, shapely shrubs that aren't too big to dig up and relocate or give away, worthwhile perennials and ground covers that you could divide and replant, healthy sod that you could lay elsewhere. Likewise, decide which plants have to go—diseased or crooked trees, straggly or overgrown shrubs, weedy brush, invasive ground covers, tattered lawn.

You can clear small areas yourself, bundling the brush for pickup and tossing soft-stemmed plants on the compost pile, but if you have lots of woody brush or any trees to remove, you might want to hire someone else to do the job. A crew armed with power tools can turn a thicket into a pile of wood chips in just a few hours. Have them pull out the roots and grind the stumps, too. Save the chips; they're good for surfacing paths or you can use them as mulch.

Working around a tree

If there are any large, healthy trees on your site, be careful as you work around them. It's okay to prune off some of a tree's limbs, as shown on the facing page, but respect its trunk and its roots. Never cut or wound the bark on the trunk (don't nail things to a tree), as that exposes the tree to disease organisms. Don't pile soil or mulch against the trunk, since that keeps the bark wet and can cause rot.

Killing perennial weeds

Some common weeds that sprout back from perennial roots or runners are bedstraw, bindweed, blackberry and other briers, ground ivy, poison ivy, quack grass, and sorrel. Garden plants that can become weedy include ajuga, akebia, bamboo, bishop's weed, English ivy, Japanese honeysuckle, Japanese knotweed, lily-of-the-valley, loosestrife, sundrops, and tansy. Once they get established, perennial weeds are hard to eliminate. You can't just cut off the tops, because they keep sprouting back. You have to dig the weeds out, smother them with mulch, or kill them with an herbicide, and it's better to do this before rather than after you plant a bed.

Smothering weeds

This technique is easier than digging, particularly for eradicating large infestations, but much slower. First mow or cut the tops of the weeds as close to the ground as possible ❶. Then cover the area with sections from the newspaper, overlapped like shingles ❷, or flattened-out cardboard boxes and top with a layer of mulch, such as straw, grass clippings, tree leaves, wood chips, or other organic material spread several inches deep ❸.

Smothering works by excluding light, which stops photosynthesis. If any shoots reach up through the covering and produce green leaves, pull them out immediately. Wait a few months, until you're sure the weeds are dead, before you dig into the smothered area and plant there.

SMOTHERING WEEDS

❶ Smothering kills weeds by depriving them of light. Cut the tops off close to the ground.

❷ Cover with thick newspaper or cardboard.

❸ Top with several inches of mulch. Wait a few months to be sure weeds are dead, then till rotted newspaper and mulch into the soil.

Digging. In many cases, you can do a pretty good job of removing a perennial weed if you dig carefully where the stems enter the ground, find the roots, and follow them as far as possible through the soil, pulling out every bit of root that you find. Some plant roots go deeper than you can dig, and most plants will sprout back from the small bits that you miss, but these leftover sprouts are easy to pull.

Spraying. Herbicides are easy, fast, and effective weed killers when chosen and applied with care. Look for those that break down quickly into more benign substances, and make sure the weed you're trying to kill is listed on the product label. Apply all herbicides exactly as directed by the manufacturer. After spraying, you usually have to wait from one to four weeks for the weed to die completely, and some weeds need to be sprayed a second or third time before they give up. Some weeds just "melt away" when they die, but if there are tough or woody stems and roots, you'll need to dig them up and discard them.

Replacing turf

If the area where you're planning to add a landscape feature is currently part of the lawn, you have a fairly easy task ahead. How to proceed depends on the condition of the turf and on what you want to put in its place. If the turf is healthy, you can "recycle" it to replace, repair, or extend the lawn elsewhere.

The drawing below shows a technique for removing relatively small areas of strong healthy turf for replanting. First, with a sharp shovel, cut it into squares or strips about 1 to 3 ft. square (these small pieces are easy to lift) ❶. Then slice a few inches deep under each square and lift the squares, roots and all, like brownies from a pan ❷. Quickly transplant the squares to a previously prepared site; water them well until the roots are established.

If you don't need the turf, or if it's straggly or weedy, leave it in place and kill the grass. Spraying with an herbicide kills most grasses within one to two weeks. Or cover it with a tarp or a sheet of black plastic for two to four weeks during the heat of summer (it takes longer in cool weather). Then dig or till the bed, shredding the turf, roots and all, and mixing it into the soil.

Removing large limbs

If there are large trees on your property now, you may want to remove some of the lower limbs so light can reach your plantings. Major pruning of large trees is a job for a professional arborist, but you can remove limbs smaller than 4 in. in diameter and less than 10 ft. above the ground yourself with a simple bow saw or pole saw.

Use the three-step procedure shown below to remove large limbs safely. First, saw partway through the bottom of the limb, approximately 1 ft. out from the trunk ❶. This keeps the bark from tearing down the trunk when the limb falls. Then make a corresponding cut down through the top of the limb ❷—be prepared to get out of the way when the limb drops. Finally, remove the stub ❸. Undercut it slightly or hold it as you finish the cut, so it doesn't fall away and peel bark off the trunk. Note that the cut is not flush with the trunk but is just outside the thick area at the limb's base, called the branch collar. Leaving the branch collar helps the wound heal quickly and naturally. Wound dressing is considered unnecessary today.

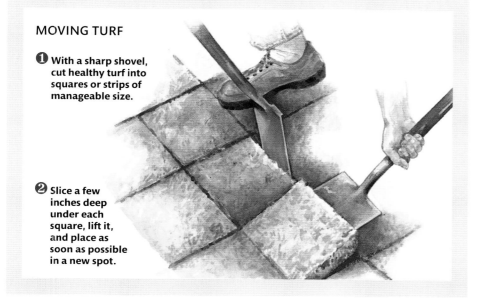

MOVING TURF

❶ With a sharp shovel, cut healthy turf into squares or strips of manageable size.

❷ Slice a few inches deep under each square, lift it, and place as soon as possible in a new spot.

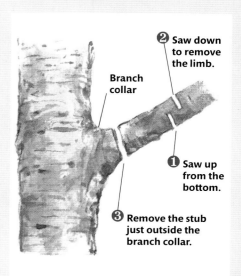

❷ Saw down to remove the limb.

Branch collar

❶ Saw up from the bottom.

❸ Remove the stub just outside the branch collar.

Making Paths and Walkways

Every landscape needs paths and walkways if for no other reason than to keep your feet dry as you move from one place to another. A path can also divide and define the spaces in the landscape, orchestrate the way the landscape is viewed, and even be a key element enhancing its beauty.

Whether it is a graceful curving garden path or a utilitarian slab leading to the garage, a walk has two main functional requirements: durability and safety. It should hold up through seasonal changes. It should provide a well-drained surface that is easy to walk on and to maintain.

A path's function helps determine its surface and its character. In general, heavily trafficked walkways leading to a door, garage, or shed need hard, smooth (but not slick) surfaces and should take you where you want to go fairly directly. A path to a backyard play area could be a strip of soft wood bark, easy on the knees of impatient children. A relaxed stroll in the garden might require only a hop-scotch collection of flat stones meandering from one prized plant to another.

Before laying out a walk or path, spend some time observing existing traffic patterns. If your path makes use of a route people already take (particularly children), they'll be more likely to stay on the path and off the lawn or flowers. Avoid areas that are slow to drain. When determining width, consider whether the path must accommodate rototillers or several strollers walking abreast, or just provide access for plant maintenance.

Dry-laid paths

You can make a path simply by laying bricks or spreading wood chips on top of bare earth. While quick and easy, this method has serious drawbacks. Laid on the surface, with no edging to contain them, loose materials are soon scattered, and solid materials are easily jostled out of place. If the earth base doesn't drain very well, the path will be a swamp or sheet of ice after rain or snowmelt. And in cold-winter areas, repeated expansion and contraction of the soil will heave bricks or flagstones out of alignment, making the path unsightly and dangerous.

The method we recommend—laying surface material on an excavated sand-and-gravel base—minimizes these problems. The sand and gravel improve drainage and provide a cushion against the freeze-thaw movement of the soil. Excavation can place the path surface at ground level, where the surrounding soil or an installed edging can contain loose materials and prevent hard materials from shifting.

All styles, from a "natural" wood-bark path to a formal cut-stone entry walk, and all the materials discussed here can be laid on an excavated base of gravel and sand.

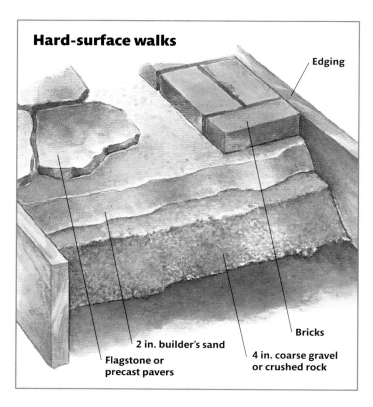

Hard-surface walks

Edging

2 in. builder's sand

Flagstone or precast pavers

Bricks

4 in. coarse gravel or crushed rock

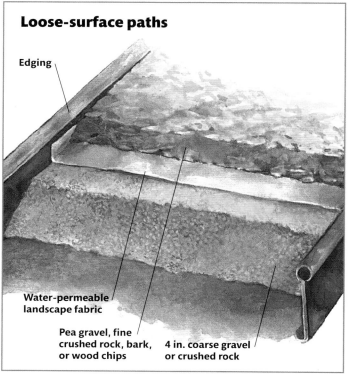

Loose-surface paths

Edging

Water-permeable landscape fabric

Pea gravel, fine crushed rock, bark, or wood chips

4 in. coarse gravel or crushed rock

Choosing a surface

Walkways and paths can be made of either hard or soft material. Your choice of material will depend on the walkway's function, your budget, and your personal preferences.

Soft materials, including bark, wood chips, pine needles, and loose gravel, are best for informal and low-traffic areas. Inexpensive and simple to install, they settle, scatter, or decompose and must be replenished or replaced every few years.

Hard materials, such as brick, flagstone, and concrete pavers, are more expensive and time-consuming to install, but they are permanent, requiring only occasional maintenance. (Compacted crushed stone can also make a hard-surface walk.) Durable and handsome, they're ideal for high-traffic, "high-profile" areas.

Bark, wood chips, and pine needles

Perfect for a "natural" look or a quick temporary path, these loose materials can be laid directly on the soil or, if drainage is poor, on a gravel bed. Bagged materials from a nursery or garden center will be cleaner, more uniform, and considerably more expensive than bulk supplies bought by the cubic yard. Check with local tree services to find the best prices on bulk material.

Gravel and crushed rock

Loose rounded gravel gives a bit underfoot, creating a "soft" but messy path. The angular facets of crushed stone eventually compact into a "hard" and tidier path that can, if the surrounding soil is firm enough, be laid without an edging. Gravel and stone type and color vary from area to area. Buy materials by the ton or cubic yard.

Concrete pavers

Precast concrete pavers are versatile, readily available, and often the least expensive hard-surface material. They come in a range of colors and shapes, including interlocking patterns. Precast edgings are also available. Most home and garden centers carry a variety of precast pavers, which are sold by the piece.

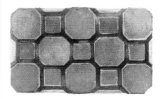

PRECAST PAVERS

Brick

Widely available in a range of sizes, colors, and textures, brick complements many design styles. When carefully laid on a well-prepared sand-and-gravel base, brick provides an even, safe, and long-lasting surface. Buy paving brick instead of the softer "facing" brick, which may break up after a few freeze-thaw cycles. (If you buy used brick, pick the hardest.) Avoid glazed brick; the glaze traps moisture and salts, which will damage the brick.

RUNNING BOND

TWO-BRICK BASKET WEAVE

HERRINGBONE

DIAGONAL HERRINGBONE

Flagstone

"Flagstone" is a generic term for stratified stone that can be split to form pavers. Limestone, sandstone, and bluestone are common paving materials. The surfaces of marble and slate are usually too smooth to make safe paving. Cut into squares or rectangles, flagstone can be laid as individual stepping-stones or in interesting patterns. Flagstones come in a range of colors, textures, and sizes. Flags for walks should be at least 2 in. thick. Purchased by weight, surface area, or pallet load, flagstones are usually the most expensive paving choice.

CUT FLAGSTONE

CUT AND IRREGULAR FLAGSTONE

IRREGULAR FLAGSTONE

Drainage

Few things are worse than a path dotted with puddles or icy patches. To prevent these from forming, the soil around and beneath the path should drain well. The path's location and construction should ensure that rainwater and snowmelt do not collect on the surface. Drainage also affects frost heaving. In cold-winter areas, the soil expands and contracts as the water in it freezes and thaws. As the soil moves, so do path and walkway materials laid on it. The effect is minimal on loose materials such as wood chips or gravel, but frost heaving can shift brick and stone significantly.

Before you locate a path, observe runoff and drainage on your property during and after heavy rains or snowmelt. It is best to avoid routing a path where water courses, collects, or is slow to drain.

While both loose and hard paving can sometimes be successfully laid directly on well-drained soil, laying surface materials on a base of gravel and sand will help improve drainage and minimize frost heaving. In most situations, a 4-in. gravel bed topped with 2 in. of sand will be sufficient. Water moves through these materials quickly, and they "cushion" the surface materials from the expansion and contraction of the underlying soil. Very poorly drained soils may require more gravel, an additional layer of coarse rock beneath the gravel, or even drain tiles—if you suspect your site has serious drainage problems, consult a specialist for advice.

Finally, keep water from pooling on a walk by making its surface higher in the center than at the edges. The center of a 4-ft.-wide walk should be at least ½ in. higher than its edges. If you're using a drag board to level the sand base, curve its lower edge to create this "crown." Otherwise crown the surface by eye.

Edgings

All walk surfaces need to be contained in some fashion along their edges. Where soil is firm or tightly knit by turf, neatly cut walls of the excavation can serve as edging. An installed edging often provides more effective containment, particularly if the walk surface is above grade. It also prevents damage to bricks or stones on the edges of paths. Walkway edgings are commonly made of 1- or 2-in.-thick lumber, thicker landscaping timbers, brick, or stone.

Wood edging

Wood should be rot-resistant redwood, cedar, or cypress, or pressure-treated for ground-contact use. If you're working in loose soils, fix a deep wooden edging to support stakes with double-headed nails. When the path is laid, pull the nails, and fill and tamp behind the edging. Then drive the stakes below grade. In firmer soils, or if the edging material is not wide enough, install it on top of the gravel base. Position the top of the edging at the height of the path. Dimension lumber 1 in. thick is pliable enough to bend around gradual curves.

Treated dimensional lumber with support stakes

Landscape timbers with crossties laid on gravel base

Brick and stone edging

In firm soil, a row of bricks laid on edge and perpendicular to the length of the path adds stability. For a more substantial edging, stand bricks on end on the excavated soil surface, add the gravel base, and tamp earth around the base of the bricks on the outside of the excavation. Stone edgings laid on end can be set in the same way. "End-up" brick or stone edgings are easy to install on curved walks.

Bricks on edge, laid on gravel base

Bricks on end, laid on soil

Preparing the base

Having decided on location and materials, you can get down to business. The initial steps of layout and base preparation are much the same for all surface materials.

Layout

Lay out straight sections with stakes and string, turning 90-degree corners with batter boards (see illustration below). You can plot curves with stakes and "fair" the curve with a garden hose, or outline the curve with hose alone, marking it with lime or sand ❶.

Excavation

The excavation depth depends on how much sand-and-gravel base your soil's drainage calls for, the thickness of the surface material, and its position above or below grade ❷. Mark the depth on a stake or stick and use this to check depth as you dig. Walking surfaces are most comfortable if they are reasonably level across their width. Check the bottom of the excavation with a level as you dig. If the walk cuts across a slope, you'll need to remove soil from the high side and use it to fill the low side to produce a level surface. If you've added soil or if the subsoil is loose, compact it by tamping.

Edging installation

Some edgings can be installed immediately after excavation; others are placed on top of the gravel portion of the base ❸. (See the sidebar "Edgings" on the facing page.) If the soil's drainage permits, you can lay soft materials now on the excavated, tamped, and edged soil base. To control weeds, and to keep bark, chips, or pine needles from mixing with the subsoil, spread water-permeable landscape fabric over the gravel or the excavated base.

Laying the base

Now add gravel (if required), rake it level, and compact it ❹. Use gravel up to 1 in. in diameter or ¼- to ¾-in. crushed stone, which drains and compacts well. You can rent a hand tamper (a heavy metal plate on the end of a pole) or a machine compactor if you have a large area to compact.

If you're making a loose-gravel or crushed-stone walk, add the surface material on top of the base gravel. (See "Loose materials" page 180.) For walks of brick, stone, or pavers, add a 2-in. layer of builder's sand, not the finer sand masons use for mixing mortar.

Rake the sand smooth with the back of a level-head rake. You can level the sand with a wooden drag board, also known as a screed ❺. Nail together two 1x4s or notch a 1x6 to place the lower edge at the desired height of the sand, and run the board along the path edging. To settle the sand, dampen it thoroughly with a hose set on fine spray. Fill any low spots, rake or drag the surface level, then dampen it again.

PREPARING THE BASE

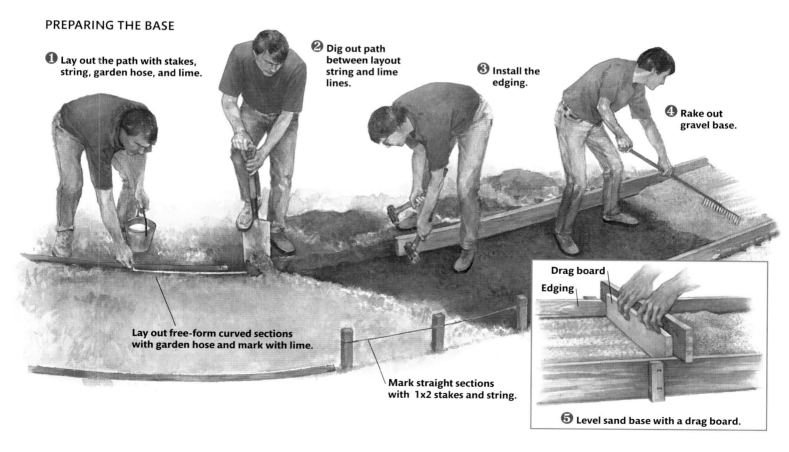

❶ Lay out the path with stakes, string, garden hose, and lime.

❷ Dig out path between layout string and lime lines.

❸ Install the edging.

❹ Rake out gravel base.

Lay out free-form curved sections with garden hose and mark with lime.

Mark straight sections with 1x2 stakes and string.

Drag board

Edging

❺ Level sand base with a drag board.

Laying the surface

Whether you're laying a loose or hard material, take time to plan your work. Provide access for delivery trucks, and have material deposited as close to the worksite as possible.

Loose materials

Install water-permeable landscape fabric over the gravel base to prevent gravel from mixing with the surface material. Spread bark or wood chips 2 to 4 in. deep. For a pine-needle surface, spread 2 in. of needles on top of several inches of bark or chips. Spread loose pea gravel about 2 in. deep. For a harder, more uniform surface, add ½ in. of fine crushed stone on top of the gravel. You can let traffic compact crushed-rock surfaces, or compact them by hand or with a machine.

Bricks and precast pavers

Take time to figure out the pattern and spacing of the bricks or pavers by laying them out on the lawn or driveway, rather than disturbing your carefully prepared sand base. When you're satisfied, begin in a corner, laying the bricks or pavers gently on the sand so the base remains even ❶. Lay full bricks first; then install cut bricks to fit as needed at the edges. To produce uniform joints, space bricks with a piece of wood cut to the exact joint width. You can also maintain alignment of the bricks with a straightedge or with a string stretched across the path between

nails or stakes. Move the string as the work proceeds.

As you complete a row or section, bed the bricks or pavers into the sand base with several firm raps of a rubber mallet or a hammer on a scrap 2x4. Check with a level or straightedge to make sure the surface is even ❷. (You'll have to do this by feel or eye across the width of a crowned path.) Lift low bricks or pavers carefully and fill beneath them with sand; then reset them. Don't stand on the walk until you've filled the joints.

When you've finished a section, sweep fine, dry mason's sand into the joints, working across the surface of the path in all directions ❸. Wet thoroughly with a fine spray and let dry; then sweep in more sand if necessary. If you want a "living" walk, sweep a loam-sand mixture into the joints and plant small, tough, ground-hugging plants, such as thyme, in them.

Rare is the brick walk that can be laid without cutting something to fit. To cut brick, mark the line of the cut with a dark pencil all around the brick. With the brick resting firmly on sand or soil, score the entire line by rapping a wide mason's chisel called a "brickset" with a heavy wooden mallet or a soft-headed steel hammer as shown on the facing page. Place the brickset in the scored line across one face and give it a sharp blow with the hammer to cut the brick.

If you have a lot of bricks to cut, or if you want greater accuracy, consider renting a masonry saw. Whether you work by hand or machine, always wear safety glasses.

LOOSE MATERIALS

Cover gravel base with water-permeable landscape fabric and add 2 to 4 in. of bark or wood chips.

BRICKS AND PRECAST PAVERS

To turn square corners, align the edging board with a carpenter's square.

❸ Sweep fine, dry sand into the joints to fix the bricks or pavers in place.

❶ Begin laying in a corner.

❷ Check the surface with a level or straightedge. Fill under low bricks; tamp down high ones. Use a plank to distribute your weight if you must work on the path.

Stepping-stones

A stepping-stone walk set in turf creates a charming effect and is very simple to lay. You can use cut or irregular flagstones or fieldstone, which is irregular in thickness as well as in outline. Arrange the stones on the turf; then set them one by one. Cut into the turf around the stone with a sharp flat shovel or trowel, and remove the stone; then dig out the sod with the shovel. Placing stones at or below grade will keep them away from mower blades. Fill low spots beneath the stone with earth or sand so the stone doesn't move when stepped on.

Cut around stepping-stone with shovel or trowel.

Remove sod and soil.

Set in place, filling with sand or soil to bed stone firmly.

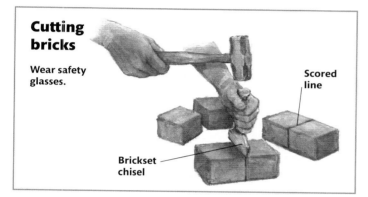

Cutting bricks

Wear safety glasses.

Scored line

Brickset chisel

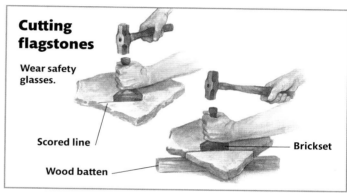

Cutting flagstones

Wear safety glasses.

Scored line

Wood batten

Brickset

Flagstones

Install cut stones of uniform thickness as described for bricks and pavers. Working out patterns beforehand is particularly important—stones are too heavy to move around more than necessary. To produce a level surface with cut or irregular stones of varying thickness, you'll need to add or remove sand for each stone. Set the stone carefully on sand; then move it back and forth to work it into place ❶. Lay a level or straightedge over three or four stones to check the surface's evenness ❷. When a section is complete, fill the joints with sand or with sand and loam as described for bricks and pavers.

You can cut flagstone with a technique similar to that used for bricks. Score the line of the cut on the top surface with a brickset and hammer. Prop the stone on a piece of scrap wood, positioning the line of the cut slightly beyond the edge of the wood. Securing the bottom edge of the stone with your foot, place the brickset on the scored line and strike sharply to make the cut.

FLAGSTONES

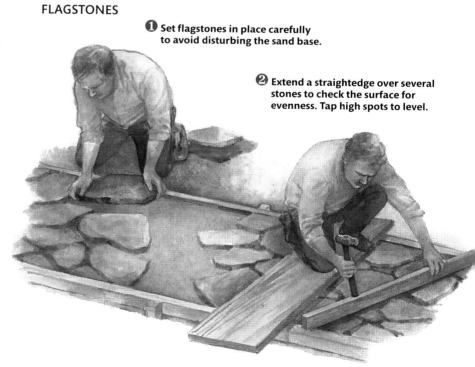

❶ Set flagstones in place carefully to avoid disturbing the sand base.

❷ Extend a straightedge over several stones to check the surface for evenness. Tap high spots to level.

Laying a Patio

You can make a simple patio using the same techniques and materials we have discussed for paths. To ensure good drainage, an even surface, and durability, lay hard surfaces such as brick, flagstone, and pavers on a well-prepared base of gravel, sand, and compacted soil. (Crushed-rock and gravel surfaces likewise benefit from a sound base.) Make sure the surface drains away from any adjacent structure (house or garage); a drop-off of ¼ in. per foot is usually adequate. If the patio isn't near a structure, make it higher in the center to avoid puddles.

Establish the outline of the patio as described for paths; then excavate the area roughly to accommodate 4 in. of gravel, 2 in. of sand, and the thickness of the paving surface. (Check with a local nursery or landscape contractor to find out if local conditions require alterations in the type or amounts of base material.) Now grade the rough excavation to provide drainage, using a simple 4-ft. grid of wooden stakes as shown in the drawings.

Drive the first row of stakes next to the house (or in the center of a freestanding patio), leveling them with a 4-ft. builder's level or a smaller level resting on a straight 2x4. The tops of these stakes should be at the height of the top of the sand base (finish grade of the patio less the thickness of the surface material) **❶**. Working from this row of stakes, establish another row about 4 to 5 ft. from the first. Make the tops of these stakes 1 in. lower than those of the first row, using a level and spacer block, as shown in the box below. Continue adding rows of stakes, each

LAYING A SIMPLE PATIO

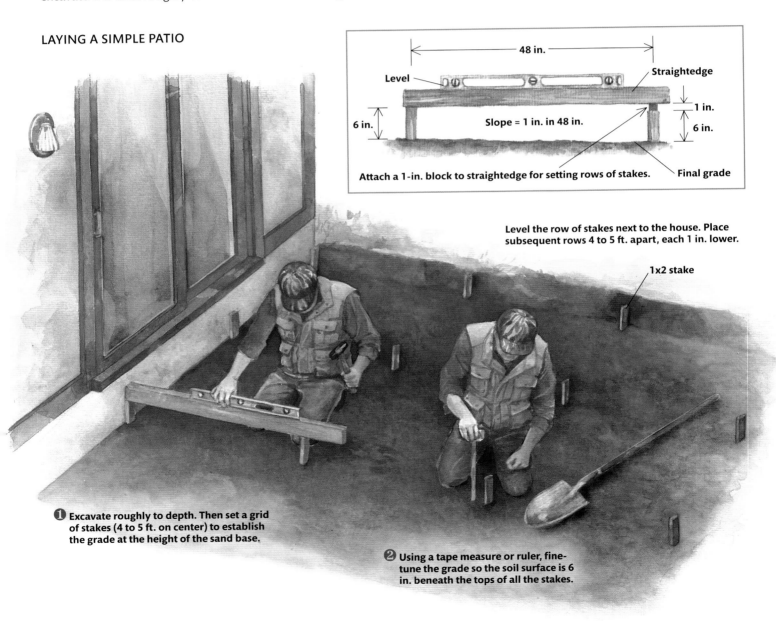

48 in.

Level

Straightedge

1 in.

6 in.

Slope = 1 in. in 48 in.

6 in.

Attach a 1-in. block to straightedge for setting rows of stakes.

Final grade

Level the row of stakes next to the house. Place subsequent rows 4 to 5 ft. apart, each 1 in. lower.

1x2 stake

❶ Excavate roughly to depth. Then set a grid of stakes (4 to 5 ft. on center) to establish the grade at the height of the sand base.

❷ Using a tape measure or ruler, fine-tune the grade so the soil surface is 6 in. beneath the tops of all the stakes.

1 in. lower than the previous row, until the entire area is staked. Then, with a tape measure or ruler and a shovel, fine-tune the grading by removing or adding soil until the excavated surface is 6 in. (the thickness of the gravel-sand base) below the tops of all the stakes ❷.

When installing the sand-and-gravel base, you'll want to maintain the drainage grade you've just established and produce an even surface for the paving material. If you have a good eye or a very small patio, you can do this by sight. Otherwise, you can use the stakes to install a series of 1x3 or 1x4 "leveling boards," as shown in the drawing below. (Before adding gravel, you may want to cover the soil with water-permeable landscape fabric to keep perennial weeds from growing; just cut slits to accommodate the stakes.)

Add a few inches of gravel ❸. Then set leveling boards along each row of stakes, with the boards' top edges even with the top of the stakes ❹. Drive additional stakes to sandwich the boards in place (don't use nails). Distribute the remaining inch or so of gravel and compact it by hand or machine, then the 2 in. of sand. Dragging a straight 2x4 across two adjacent rows of leveling boards will produce a precise grade and an even surface ❺. Wet the sand and fill low spots that settle.

You can install the patio surface as previously described for paths, removing the leveling boards as the bricks or pavers reach them ❻. Disturbing the sand surface as little as possible, slide the boards out from between the stakes and drive the stakes an inch or so beneath the level of the sand. Cover the stakes and fill the gaps left by the boards with sand, tamped down carefully. Then continue laying the surface. Finally, sweep fine sand into the joints.

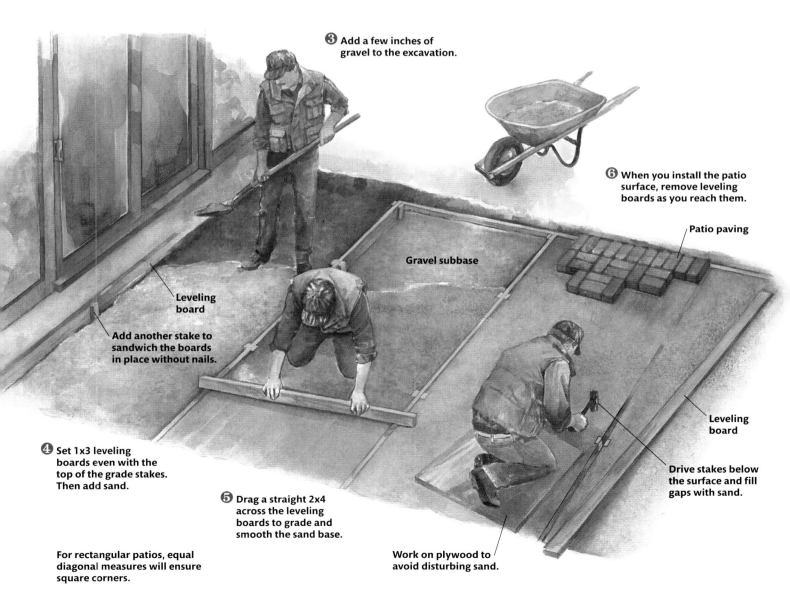

❸ Add a few inches of gravel to the excavation.

❻ When you install the patio surface, remove leveling boards as you reach them.

Patio paving

Gravel subbase

Leveling board

Add another stake to sandwich the boards in place without nails.

Leveling board

Drive stakes below the surface and fill gaps with sand.

❹ Set 1x3 leveling boards even with the top of the grade stakes. Then add sand.

❺ Drag a straight 2x4 across the leveling boards to grade and smooth the sand base.

For rectangular patios, equal diagonal measures will ensure square corners.

Work on plywood to avoid disturbing sand.

Installing a Pond

It wasn't so long ago that a garden pond like the one in this book required yards of concrete, an expert mason, and deep pockets. Today's strong, lightweight, and long-lasting synthetic liners and rigid fiberglass shells have put garden pools in reach of every homeowner. Installation does require some hard labor, but little expertise: just dig a hole, spread the liner or seat the shell, install edging, and plant. We'll discuss installation of a linered pond in the main text; see below for installing a smaller, fiberglass pool.

Liner notes

More and more nurseries and garden centers are carrying flexible pond liners; you can also buy them from mail-order suppliers specializing in water gardens. Synthetic rubber liners are longer lasting but more expensive than PVC liners. (Both are much cheaper than rigid fiberglass shells.) Buy only liners specifically made for garden ponds—don't use ordinary plastic sheeting. Many people feel that black liners look best; blue liners tend to make the pond look like a swimming pool.

Before you dig

First, make sure you comply with any rules your town may have about water features. Then keep the following ideas in mind when locating your pond. Avoid trees whose shade keeps sun-loving water plants from thriving; whose roots make digging a chore; and whose flowers, leaves, and seeds clog the water, making it unsightly and inhospitable to plants or fish. Avoid the low spot on your property; otherwise your pond will be a catch basin for runoff. Select a level spot; the immediate vicinity of the pond must be level, and starting out that way saves a lot of work. (Remember that you can use excavated soil to help level the site.)

Using graph paper, enlarge the outline of the pond provided on the site plan on p. 117, altering it as you wish. If you change the size or depth of the pond, or are interested in growing a wider variety of water plants or in adding fish, remember that

Small fiberglass pool

A fiberglass shell 2 to 3 ft. wide, 4 to 5 ft. long, and 2 to 3 ft. deep is ideal for the small pools on pp. 93, 95, and 118. Garden centers often stock pond shells in a variety of shapes.

Dig a hole about 6 in. wider on all sides than the shell; its depth should equal that of the shell plus 1 in. for a sand base, plus the thickness of the fieldstone edging. Compact the bottom of the hole and spread the sand; then lower the shell into place. Add temporary wedges or props level the shell. Slowly fill the shell with water, backfilling around it with sand or sifted soil, keeping pace with the rising water. Excavate a wide relief for the edging stones, laying them on a firm base, slightly overhanging the rim of the shell.

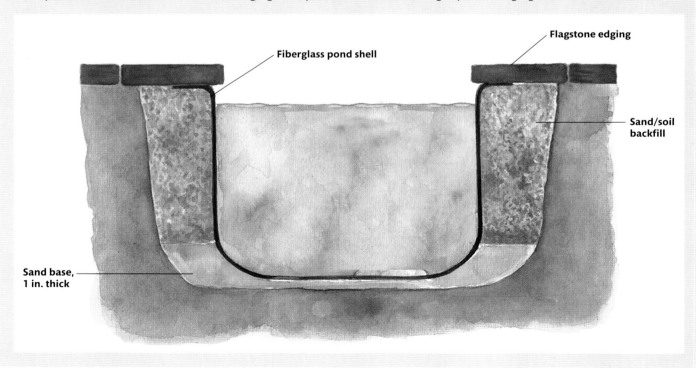

Fiberglass pond shell

Flagstone edging

Sand/soil backfill

Sand base, 1 in. thick

a healthy pond must achieve a balance between the plants and fish and the volume, depth, and temperature of the water. Even if you're not altering size or pond plants and fish, it's a good idea to consult with a knowledgeable person at a nursery or pet store specializing in water-garden plants and animals.

Calculate the liner width by adding twice the maximum depth of the pool plus an additional 2 ft. to the width. Use the same formula to calculate the length. So, for a pond 2 ft. deep, 6 ft. wide, and 17 ft. long, the liner width would be 4 ft. plus 6 ft. plus 2 ft. (or 12 ft.). The length would be 4 ft. plus 17 ft. plus 2 ft. (or 23 ft.).

Pond Aeration and Filtration

It is possible to have a rustic pond with no mechanical systems if you do not intend to have fish. But in a fishpond without proper treatment, fish waste and plant debris accumulate, creating an unhealthy, unsustainable, smelly environment. To establish a healthy, balanced ecosystem with plants, fish, and clear water, garden ponds must include systems to filter and aerate the water. All-in-one pond kits, available at water gardening stores, include all the materials you need to get started along with detailed setup instructions. The most important factor is that you must have a GFCI outlet close by to power the pump.

In small ponds, a simple system consisting of a centrally located aeration pump with a fountain head creates a splash that breaks the water's surface tension, infuses oxygen, and circulates the oxygen through the body of water. These ponds must be pumped down regularly to remove built-up debris.

Larger landscape ponds typically include a debris skimmer at one end and a filtering waterfall box at the other. The two are connected by a powerful filter pump. The pump pulls water through the debris skimmer, where leaves and other large particles collect in a net, and then pushes the water up through a porous biofiltration media in the waterfall box. The filter media, along with rocks and gravel in the pond itself, is colonized by beneficial bacteria that neutralize fish waste and other microscopic debris. Ongoing maintenance of this system entails simply cleaning the skimmer net regularly and monitoring water quality.

Growing pond plants

One water lily, a few upright-growing plants, and a bundle of submerged plants (which help keep the water clean) are enough for a medium-size pond. An increasing number of nurseries and garden centers stock water lilies and other water plants. For a larger selection, your nursery or garden center may be able to recommend a specialist supplier.

These plants are grown in containers filled with heavy garden soil (not potting soil, which contains ingredients that float). You can buy special containers designed for aquatic plants, or simply use plastic pails or dishpans. Line basketlike containers with burlap to keep the soil from leaking out the holes. A water lily needs at least 2 to 3 gal. of soil; the more, the better. Most other water plants, such as dwarf papyrus, need 1 to 2 gal. of soil.

After planting, add a layer of gravel on the surface to keep soil from clouding the water and to protect roots from marauding fish. Soak the plant and soil thoroughly. Then set the container in the pond, positioning it so the water over the soil is 6 to 18 in. deep for water lilies, 0 to 6 in. for most other plants.

For maximum bloom, push a tablet of special water-lily fertilizer into the pots once or twice a month throughout the summer. Most water plants are easy to grow and carefree, although many are tropicals that die after hard frost, so you'll have to replace them each spring.

PLANTING WATER PLANTS

Set water plants in a container of heavy garden soil. Then cover soil surface with gravel to keep soil from floating away.

Gravel

1- to 3-gal. dishpan or special container

Heavy garden soil

Excavation

If your soil isn't too compacted or rocky, a good-size pond can be excavated with a shovel or two in a weekend ❶. (Energetic teenagers are a marvelous pool-building resource.) If the site isn't level, you can grade it using a stake-and-level system like the one described on pp. 182–183 for grading the patio.

Outline the pond's shape with garden lime, establishing the curves freehand with a garden hose or by staking out a large grid and plotting from the graph-paper plan. The pond has two levels. The broad end, at 2 ft. deep, accommodates water lilies and other plants requiring deeper water as well as fish. Make the narrow end 12 to 16 in. deep for plants requiring shallower submersion. (You can put plant pots on stacks of bricks or other platforms to vary heights as necessary.) The walls will be less likely to crumble as you dig and the liner will install more easily if you slope them in about 3 to 4 in. for each foot of depth. Make the walls smooth, removing roots, rocks, and other sharp protrusions.

Excavate a shallow relief about 1 ft. wide around the perimeter to contain the liner overlap and stone edging. (The depth of the relief should accommodate the thickness of the edging stones.) Somewhere along the perimeter, create an overflow channel to take runoff after a heavy rain. This can simply be a 1- to 2-in. depression 1 foot or so wide spanned by one of the edging stones. Lengths of PVC pipe placed side by side beneath the stone (as shown in the drawing on p. 187) will keep the liner in place. The overflow channel can open onto a lower area of lawn or garden adjacent to the pond or to a rock-filled dry well.

Fitting the liner

When the hole is complete, cushion the surfaces to protect the liner ❷. Here we show an inch-thick layer of sand on the bottom surfaces and carpet underlayment on the sloping walls. Fiberglass batting insulation also works well, as do old blankets or even heavy landscaping fabric.

Stretch the liner across the hole, letting it sag naturally to touch the walls and bottom but keeping it taut enough so it does

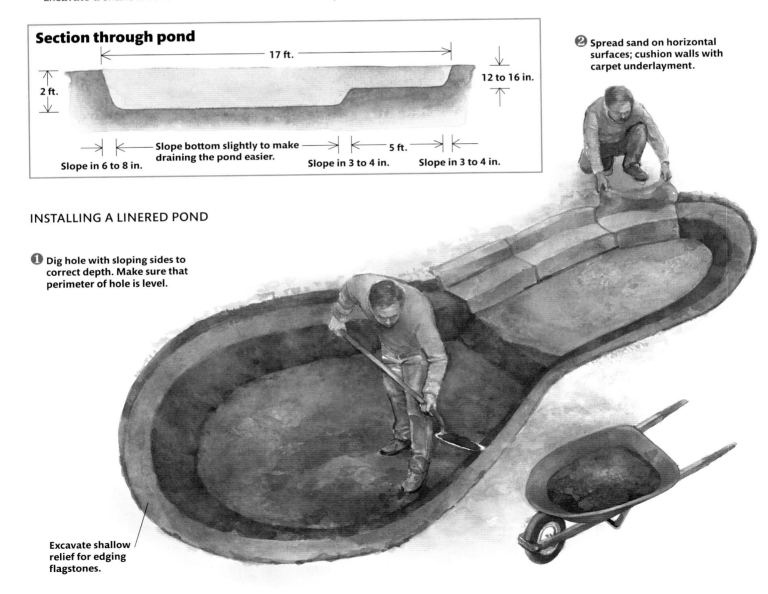

Section through pond

17 ft.

2 ft.

12 to 16 in.

Slope in 6 to 8 in.

Slope bottom slightly to make draining the pond easier.

5 ft.

Slope in 3 to 4 in.

Slope in 3 to 4 in.

❷ Spread sand on horizontal surfaces; cushion walls with carpet underlayment.

INSTALLING A LINERED POND

❶ Dig hole with sloping sides to correct depth. Make sure that perimeter of hole is level.

Excavate shallow relief for edging flagstones.

not bunch up. Weight its edges with bricks or stones; then fill it with water ❸. The water's weight will push the liner against the walls; the stones will prevent it from blowing around. As it fills, tuck and smooth out as many creases as you can; the weight of the water makes this difficult to do after the pond is full. If you stand in the pond to do so, take care not to damage the liner. Don't be alarmed if you can't smooth all the creases. Stop filling when the water is 2 in. below the rim of the pond, and cut the liner to fit into the overlap relief ❹. Hold it in place with a few long nails or large "staples" made from coat hangers while you install the edging.

Edging the pond

Finding and fitting flagstones so there aren't wide gaps between them is the most time-consuming part of this task. Cantilevering the stones an inch or two over the water will hide the liner somewhat.

The stones can be laid directly on the liner, as shown ❺. Add sand under the liner to level the surface where necessary so that the stones don't rock. Such treatment will withstand the occasional gingerly traffic of pond and plant maintenance but not the wear and tear of young children or large dogs regularly running across the edging. (The liner won't go long without damage if used as a wading pool.)

Water work

Unless you are a very tidy builder, the water you used to fit the liner will be too dirty to leave in the pond. Siphon or pump out the water, clean the liner, and refill the pond. If you're adding fish to the pond, you'll need to let the water stand for a week or so to allow any chlorine (which is deadly to fish) to dissipate. Check with local pet stores to find out if your water contains chemicals that require commercial conditioners to make the water safe for fish.

Installing the pond and plants is only the first step in water gardening. It takes patience, experimentation, and usually some consultation with experienced water gardeners to achieve a balance between plants, fish, and waterborne oxygen, nutrients, and waste that will sustain all happily while keeping algae, diseases, insects, and predators at acceptable levels.

Elevation detail of pond overflow

Flagstone edging, 12 in. or more wide

Pond liner

Cover pipe with flagstone.

To overflow area

PVC pipe, 1- or 2-in.-dia., about 12 in. long

Garden bed or lawn

Carpet underlayment (walls)

1-in. layer of sand (horizontal surfaces)

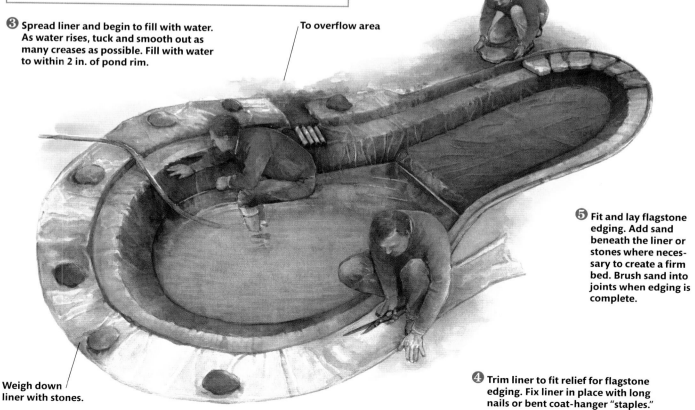

❸ Spread liner and begin to fill with water. As water rises, tuck and smooth out as many creases as possible. Fill with water to within 2 in. of pond rim.

To overflow area

Weigh down liner with stones.

❺ Fit and lay flagstone edging. Add sand beneath the liner or stones where necessary to create a firm bed. Brush sand into joints when edging is complete.

❹ Trim liner to fit relief for flagstone edging. Fix liner in place with long nails or bent coat-hanger "staples."

Building a Retaining Wall

Contours and sloping terrain can add considerable interest to a home landscape. But you can have too much of a good thing. Two designs in this book employ retaining walls to alter problem slopes. The wall shown on p. 48 eliminates a small but abrupt grade change, producing two almost level surfaces and the opportunity to install attractive plantings on them. On p. 80 two low retaining walls help turn a steep slope into a showpiece.

Retaining walls can be handsome landscape features in their own right. Made of cut stone, fieldstone, brick, landscape timbers, or concrete, they can complement the materials and style of your house or nearby structures. However, making a stable, long-lasting retaining wall of these materials can require tools and skills many homeowners do not possess.

For these reasons we've instead chosen retaining-wall systems made of precast concrete for designs in this book. Readily available in a range of sizes, sur-

face finishes, and colors, these systems require few tools and no special skills to install. They have been engineered to resist the forces that soil, water, freezing, and thawing bring to bear on a retaining wall. Install these walls according to the manufacturer's specifications, and you can be confident that they will do their job for many years.

A number of systems are available in the region through nurseries, garden centers, and local contracting suppliers (check the internet listings). But they all share basic design principles. Like traditional dry-stone walls, these systems rely largely on weight and friction to contain the weight of the soil. In many systems, interlocking blocks or pegs help align the courses and increase the wall's strength. In all systems, blocks must rest on a solid, level base. A freely draining backfill of crushed stone is essential to avoid buildup of water pressure (both liquid and frozen) in the retained soil, which can buckle even a heavy wall.

The construction steps shown here are typical of those recommended by most system manufacturers for retaining walls up to 3 to 4 ft. tall; be sure to follow the manufacturer's instructions for the system you choose. (Some installation guides are excellent; others are less helpful. Weigh the quality of instructions in your decision of which system to buy.) For higher walls, walls on loose soil or heavy clay soils, and walls retaining very steep slopes, it is prudent to consult with a landscape architect or contractor.

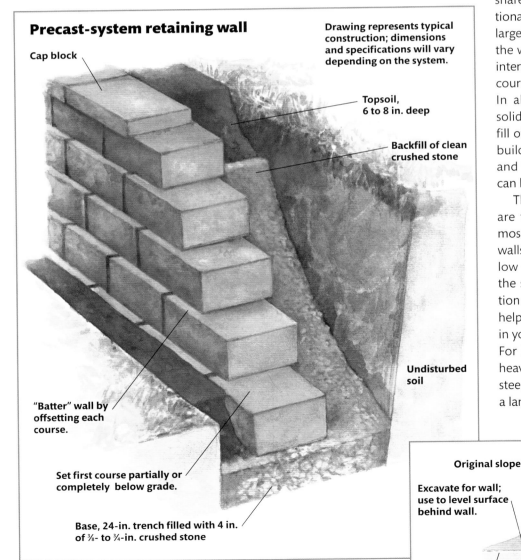

Precast-system retaining wall

Drawing represents typical construction; dimensions and specifications will vary depending on the system.

Cap block

Topsoil, 6 to 8 in. deep

Backfill of clean crushed stone

Undisturbed soil

"Batter" wall by offsetting each course.

Set first course partially or completely below grade.

Base, 24-in. trench filled with 4 in. of ⅜- to ¾-in. crushed stone

Original slope

New grade level

Excavate for wall; use to level surface behind wall.

30–45° from plumb

New grade

Building a wall

Installing a wall system is just about as simple as stacking up children's building blocks. The most important part of the job is establishing a firm, level base. Start by laying out the wall with string and hose (for curves) and excavating a base trench.

As the boxed drawing shows, the position of the wall in relation to the base of the slope determines the height of the wall, how much soil you move, and the leveling effect on the slope. Unless the wall is very long, it is a good idea to excavate along the entire length and fine-tune the line of the wall before beginning

the base trench. Remember to excavate back far enough to accommodate the stone backfill. Systems vary, but a foot of crushed-stone backfill behind the blocks is typical. (For the two-wall design, build the bottom wall first, then the top.)

Systems vary in the width and depth of trench and type of base material, but in all of them, the trench must be level across its width and along its length. We've shown a 4-in. layer of ⅜- to ¾-in. crushed stone (blocks can slip sideways on rounded aggregate or pea gravel, which also don't compact as well). Depending on the system and the circumstances, a portion or all of the first course lies below grade, so the soil helps hold the blocks in place.

Add crushed stone to the trench, level it with a rake, and compact it with a hand tamper or mechanical compactor. Lay the first course of blocks carefully ❶. Check frequently to make sure the blocks are level across their width and

along their length. Stagger vertical joints as you stack subsequent courses. Offset the faces of the blocks so the wall leans back into the retained soil. Some systems design this "batter" into their blocks; others allow you to choose from several possible setbacks.

As the wall rises, shovel backfill behind the blocks ❷. Clean crushed rock drains well; some systems suggest placing a barrier of landscaping fabric between the rock and the retained soil to keep soil from migrating into the fill and impeding drainage.

Thinner cap blocks finish the top of the wall ❸. Some wall systems recommend cementing these blocks in place with a weatherproof adhesive. The last 6 to 8 in. of the backfill should be topsoil, firmed into place and ready for planting.

BUILDING A WALL

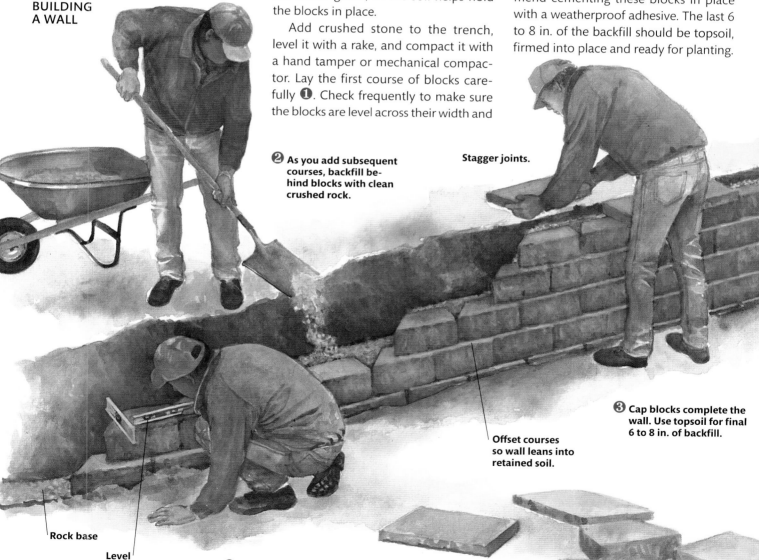

❷ As you add subsequent courses, backfill behind blocks with clean crushed rock.

Stagger joints.

❸ Cap blocks complete the wall. Use topsoil for final 6 to 8 in. of backfill.

Offset courses so wall leans into retained soil.

Rock base

Level

❶ After digging and leveling the trench, spread, level, and compact the base materials; then lay the blocks. Check frequently to see that they are level across their width and length.

Wall parallel with a slope: Stepped base

Construct walls running parallel to a slope in "steps," each with a level base.

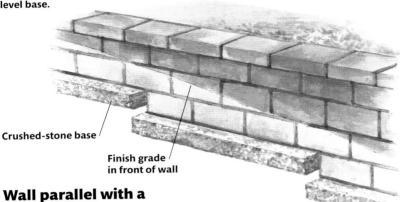

Backfill so grade behind finishes level with top of wall.

Crushed-stone base

Finish grade in front of wall

Wall parallel with a slope: Stepped cap

Sometimes the top of a wall needs to step up or down to accommodate grade changes in the slope behind.

Cap block

A "return" corner

Where you want the slope to extend beyond the end of the wall, make a corner that cuts into the slope.

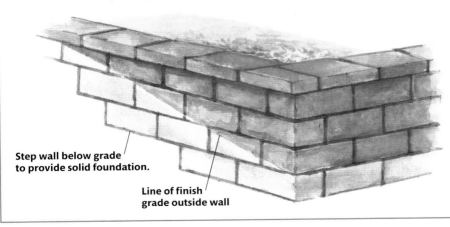

Step wall below grade to provide solid foundation.

Line of finish grade outside wall

Sloped sites

If your site slopes along the wall's length, you'll need to "step" the bottom of the wall, as shown at top left. Create a length of level trench along the lowest portion of the site; then work up the slope, creating steps as necessary.

The top of the wall can also step if the slope dissipates at one end. Such slopes are common on sites such as the one shown on p. 68, which slopes away from the house and toward the driveway. Here the base of the wall will rest on level ground, but the slope behind the wall decreases along the wall's length. The design on p. 68 shows one solution to this dilemma—a wall of uniform height with \a "return" corner at the street end (see bottom left), backfilled to raise the grade behind to the top of the wall. Another solution, shown at center left, is to step the wall down as the slope decreases, which saves material, produces a different look, but still works with the planting design.

Curves and corners

Wall-system blocks are designed so that curves are no more difficult to lay than straight sections. Corners may require that you cut a few blocks or use specially designed blocks, but they are otherwise uncomplicated. If your wall must fit a prescribed length between corners, consider working from the corners toward the middle (after laying a base course). Masons use this technique, which also avoids exposing cut blocks at the corners.

You can cut blocks with a mason's chisel and mallet or rent a mason's saw. Chiseling works well where the faces of the blocks are rough textured, so the cut faces blend right in. A saw is best for smooth-faced blocks and projects requiring lots of cutting.

Where the wall doesn't run the full length of the slope, the best-looking and most structurally sound termination is a corner constructed to cut back into the slope, as shown at bottom left.

Steps

Steps in a low retaining wall are not diffi-cult to build, but they require forethought and careful layout. Systems differ on construction details. The drawing below shows a typical design where the blocks and stone base rest on "steps" cut into firm subsoil. If your soil is less stable or is recent fill, you should excavate the entire area beneath the steps to the same depth as the wall base and build a foundation of blocks, as shown in the boxed drawing.

These steps are independent of the adjacent "return" walls, which are verti-cal, not battered (stepped back). In some systems, steps and return walls are in-terlocked. To match a path, you can face the treads with the same stone, brick, or pavers, or you can use the system's cap blocks or special treads.

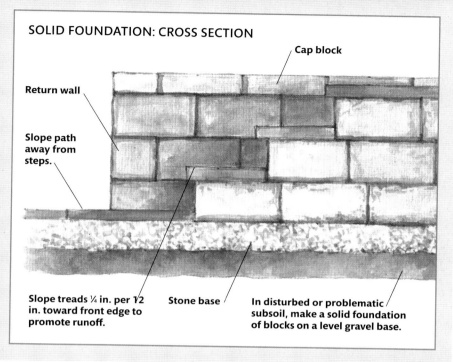

SOLID FOUNDATION: CROSS SECTION

Cap block

Return wall

Slope path away from steps.

Slope treads ¼ in. per 12 in. toward front edge to promote runoff.

Stone base

In disturbed or problematic subsoil, make a solid foundation of blocks on a level gravel base.

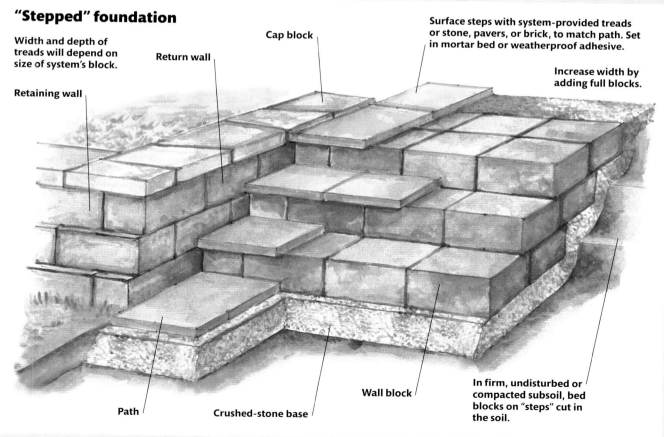

"Stepped" foundation

Width and depth of treads will depend on size of system's block.

Cap block

Return wall

Retaining wall

Surface steps with system-provided treads or stone, pavers, or brick, to match path. Set in mortar bed or weatherproof adhesive.

Increase width by adding full blocks.

Path

Crushed-stone base

Wall block

In firm, undisturbed or compacted subsoil, bed blocks on "steps" cut in the soil.

Fences, Arbors, and Trellises

Novices who have no trouble tackling a simple flagstone path often get nervous when it comes time to erect a fence, an arbor, or even a trellis. While such projects can require more skill and resources than others in the landscape, the ones in this book have been designed with less-than-confident do-it-yourself builders in mind. The designs are simple, the materials are read-ily available, and the tools and skills will be familiar to anyone accustomed to ordinary home maintenance.

First we'll introduce you to the materials and tools needed for the projects. Then we'll present the small number of basic opera-tions you'll employ when building them. Finally, we'll provide drawings and comments on each of the projects.

Tools and materials

Even the least-handy homeowner is likely to have most of the tools needed for these projects: claw hammer, crosscut handsaw, brace-and-bit or electric drill, adjustable wrench, combination square, tape measure, carpenter's level, and sawhorses. You may even have Grandpa's old posthole digger. Many will have a handheld power circular saw, which makes faster (though noisier) work of cutting parts to length. A cordless drill/screwdriver is invaluable if you're substituting screws for nails. If you have more than a few holes to dig, consider renting a gas-powered posthole dig-ger. A 12-in.-diameter hole will serve for 4x4 posts; if pos-sible, get a larger-diameter digger for 6x6 posts.

Materials

Of the materials offering strength, durability, and attractive-ness in outdoor settings, wood is the easiest to work and affords the quickest results. While almost all commercially available lumber is strong enough for landscape structures, most decay quickly when in prolonged contact with soil and water. Cedar, cypress, and redwood, however, contain natural preservatives and are excellent for landscape use. Alternatively, a range of softwoods (such as pine, fir, and hemlock) are pressure-treated with preservatives and will last for many years. Parts of structures that do not come in contact with soil or are not continually wet can be made of ordinary construction-grade lumber, but unless they're regularly painted, they will not last as long as treated or naturally decay-resistant material.

In addition to dimension lumber, several of the designs incorporate lattice, which is thin wooden strips crisscrossed to form patterns of diamonds or squares. Premade lattice is widely available in sheets 4 ft. by 8 ft. and smaller. Lattice comes in decay-resistant woods as well as in treated and untreated softwoods. Local supplies vary, and you may find lattice made of thicker or narrower material.

Fasteners

For millennia, even basic structures such as these would have been assembled with complicated joints. Today, with simple nailed, bolted, or screwed joints, a few hours' practice swinging a hammer or wielding a cordless electric screwdriver is all the training necessary.

All these structures can be assembled using nails. But screws are stronger and, if you have a cordless screwdriver, make assembly easier. Buy common or box nails that are galvanized to prevent rust. Self-tapping screws ("deck" screws) require no pilot holes. For rust resistance, buy galva-nized screws or screws treated with zinc dichromate.

Galvanized metal connectors are available to reinforce the joints used in these projects. For novice builders, con-nectors are a great help in aligning parts and making assem-bly easier. (Correctly fastened with nails or screws, the joints are strong enough without connectors.)

Finishes

Cedar, cypress, and redwood are handsome when left unfinished to weather, when treated with clear or colored stains, or when painted. Pressure-treated lumber is best painted or stained.

Outdoor stains are becoming increasingly popular. Clear or lightly tinted stains can preserve or enhance the rich red-dish browns of cedar, cypress, and redwood. Stains also come in a range of colors that can be used like paint. Because they penetrate the wood rather than forming a film, stains don't form an opaque surface, but stains won't peel or chip like paint and are therefore easier to touch up and refinish.

When choosing a finish, take account of what plants are growing on or near the structure. It's a lot of work to remove yards of vines from a trellis or squeeze between a large shrub and a fence to repaint; consider an unfinished decay-resistant wood or an initial stain that you allow to weather.

Setting posts

All the projects are anchored by firmly set, vertical posts. In general, the taller the structure, the deeper the post should be set. For the arbors and the tallest fences, posts should be at least 3 ft. deep. Posts for fences up to 4 ft. tall can be set 2 ft. deep. To avoid post movement caused by expansion and contraction of the soil during freeze-thaw cycles, it's a good idea to set all arbor posts below the frost line. This depth is greater in colder climates; check with local building authorities.

The length of the posts you buy depends, of course, on the depth at which they are set and their finished heights. When calculating lengths of arbor posts, remember that the tops of the posts must be level. The easiest method of achieving this is to cut the posts to length after installation. For example, buy 12-ft. posts for an arbor finishing at 8 ft. above grade and set 3 ft. in the ground. The convenience is worth the expense of the foot or so you cut off. The site and personal preference can determine whether you cut fence posts to length after installation or buy them cut to length and add or remove fill from the bottom of the hole to position them at the correct heights.

Arbor posts

Be sure to take extra care when positioning and installing arbor posts. The corners of the structure must be right angles, and the sides must be parallel with one another. Locating the corners with batter boards and string is fussy but accurate. Make the batter boards by nailing 1x2 stakes to scraps of 1x3 or 1x4, and position them about 1 ft. from the approximate location of each post as shown in the boxed drawing at right. Locate the exact post positions with string; adjust the string so the diagonal measurements are equal, which ensures that the corners of the structure will be at right angles.

At the intersections of the strings, locate the postholes by eye or with a plumb bob ❶. Remove the strings and dig the holes; then reattach the strings to position the posts exactly ❷. Plumb and brace the posts carefully. Check positions with the level and by measuring between adjacent posts and across diagonals. Diagonal braces between adjacent posts will stiffen them and help align their faces ❸. Then add concrete ❹ and let it cure for a day.

To establish the height of the posts, measure up from grade on one post, then use a level and straightedge to mark the heights of the other posts from the first one. Where joists will be bolted to the faces of the posts, you can install the joists and use their top edges as a handsaw guide for cutting the posts to length.

SETTING ARBOR POSTS

❶ **Position the posts with batter boards, taut string, and a plumb bob.**

Batter board

Taut string

Plumb bob

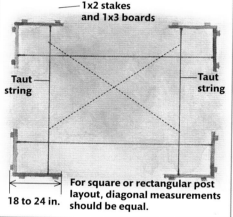

BATTER BOARDS
Set L-shaped batter boards at each corner and stretch string to position the posts exactly.

1x2 stakes and 1x3 boards

Taut string

Taut string

18 to 24 in.

For square or rectangular post layout, diagonal measurements should be equal.

❷ **Remove the string to dig the holes; then reattach it and align the outer faces of the posts with the string while you plumb and brace them.**

❸ **Check distances between posts at top. Add diagonal bracing between posts to fix positions.**

❹ **Cement posts in place.**

Fence posts

Lay out and set the end or corner posts of a fence first, then add the intermediate posts. Dig the holes by hand or with a power digger ❶. To promote drainage, place several inches of gravel at the bottom of the hole for the post to rest on. Checking with a carpenter's level, plumb the post vertically and brace it with scrap lumber nailed to stakes ❷. Then add a few more inches of gravel around the post's base.

If your native soil compacts well, you can fix posts in place with tamped earth. Add the soil gradually, tamping it continu-ously with a heavy iron bar or 2x4. Check regularly with a level to see that the post doesn't get knocked out of plumb. This technique suits rustic or informal fences, where misalignments caused by shifting posts aren't noticeable or damaging.

For more formal fences, or where soil is loose or fence panels are buffeted by winds or snow, it's prudent to fix posts in concrete ❸. Mix enough concrete to set the two end posts; as a rule of thumb, figure one 80-lb. bag of premixed concrete per post. As you shovel it in, prod the concrete with a stick to settle it, particularly if you've added rubble to extend the mix. Build

SETTING A FENCE POST

❷ **Plumb the post, checking on adjacent faces with a level. Hold it in position with stakes and braces.**

❶ **Position the end or corner posts; then dig holes for them.**

❸ **Fill the hole with concrete and rubble.**

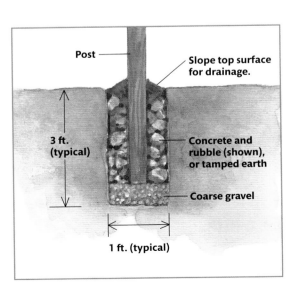

Post — / Slope top surface for drainage.

3 ft. (typical)

Concrete and rubble (shown), or tamped earth

Coarse gravel

1 ft. (typical)

the concrete slightly above grade and slope it away from the post to aid drainage.

Once the end posts are set, stretch a string between the posts. (The concrete should cure for 24 hours before you nail or screw rails and panels in place, but you can safely stretch string while the concrete is still wet.) Measure along the string to position the intermediate posts; drop a plumb bob from the string at each intermediate post position to gauge the center of the hole below ❹. Once all the holes have been dug, again stretch a string between the end posts, near the top. Set the intermediate posts as described previously; align one face with the string and plumb adjacent faces with the carpenter's level ❺. Make sure to check positions of intermediate posts a final time with a tape measure.

If the fence is placed along a slope, the top of the slats or panels can step down the slope or mirror it (as shown in the drawings below). Either way, make sure that the posts are plumb, rather than leaning with the slope.

❹ Stretch a string between the tops of the two end posts. Then locate positions of intermediate posts with a plumb bob.

❺ After digging the holes, stretch a string between the end posts to align intermediate posts. Use a level to plumb adjacent faces.

Fencing a slope

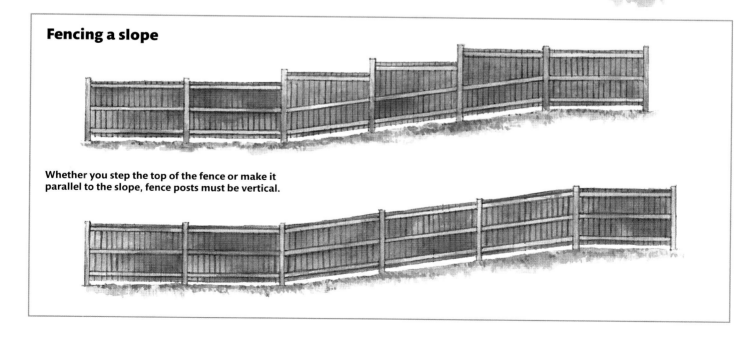

Whether you step the top of the fence or make it parallel to the slope, fence posts must be vertical.

Joints

The components of the fences, arbors, and trellises used in this book are attached to the posts and to each other with the simple joints shown below. Because all the parts are made of dimensioned lumber, the only cuts you'll need to make are to length. For strong joints, cut ends as square as you can, so the mating pieces make contact across their entire surfaces. If you have no confidence in your sawing, many lumberyards will cut pieces to length for a modest fee.

Novices often find it difficult to keep two pieces correctly positioned while trying to drive a nail into them, particularly when the nail must be driven at an angle, called "toenailing." If you have this problem, consider assembling the project with screws, which draw the pieces together, or with metal connectors, which can be nailed or screwed in place on one piece and then attached to the mating piece.

For several designs, you need to attach lattice panels to posts. The panels are made by sandwiching store-bought lattice be-

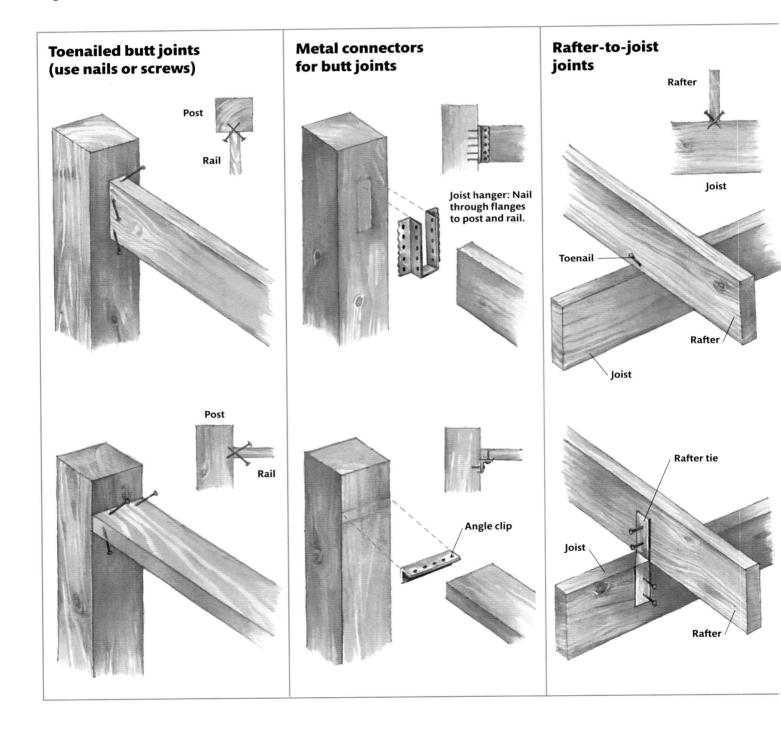

Toenailed butt joints (use nails or screws)

Post

Rail

Post

Rail

Metal connectors for butt joints

Joist hanger: Nail through flanges to post and rail.

Angle clip

Rafter-to-joist joints

Rafter

Joist

Toenail

Rafter

Joist

Rafter tie

Joist

Rafter

tween frames of dimension lumber (construction details are given on the following pages). While the assembled panels can be toenailed to the posts, novices may find that the job goes easier using one or more types of metal connector, as shown in the drawing below and right. Attach the angle clips or angle brackets to the post; then position the lattice panel and fix it to the connectors. For greatest strength and ease of assembly, attach connectors with self-tapping screws driven by an electric screwdriver.

In the following pages, we'll show construction details of the fences, arbors, and trellises presented in the Portfolio of Designs. (The page number indicates the design.) Where the basic joints discussed here can be used, we have shown the parts but left choice of fasteners to you. Typical fastenings are indicated for other joints. We have kept the constructions shown here simple and straightforward. They are not the only possibilities, and we encourage experienced builders to adapt and alter constructions as well as designs to suit differing situations and personal preferences.

Frame corner with metal connector

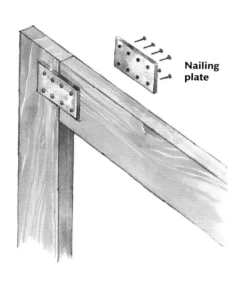

Nailing plate

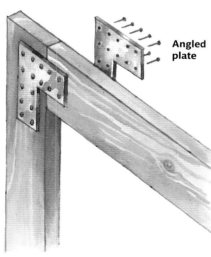

Angled plate

Attaching framed lattice panels to posts

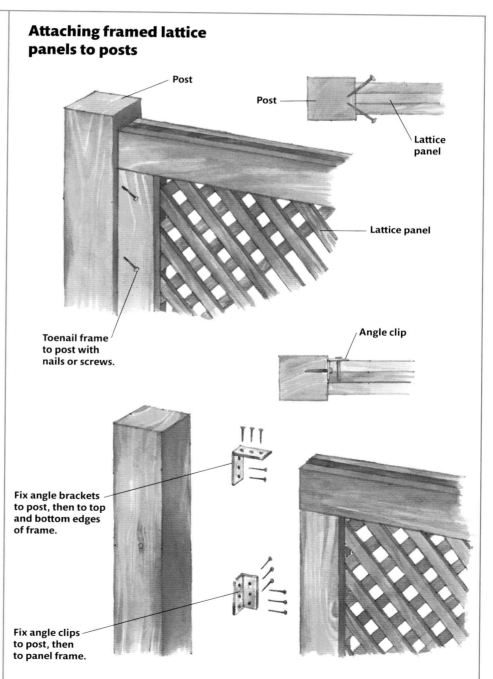

Post

Post

Lattice panel

Lattice panel

Toenail frame to post with nails or screws.

Angle clip

Fix angle brackets to post, then to top and bottom edges of frame.

Fix angle clips to post, then to panel frame.

Screen
(pp. 28–31)

This easy-to-build screen helps create a sense of intimacy and enclosure for greeting guests. At 7 ft. tall and wide, it forms a vine-covered extension of the small alcove that shelters the front door.

The screen is a snap to build. After setting the posts (see pp. 194–195), add the top and bottom rails. Trim the ends of the "pickets" at a 45° angle and fix them with a nail or screw into each rail. Position the pickets before fastening them to ensure even spacing. If you want a more solid-looking screen, offset the pickets so that those on one side fill the gaps left by those on the other. You can vary the size of the screen and the materials shown here. Keep in mind that the proportions are what make this simple design look good.

4x4 post

2x8 top rail

2x2 picket

2x8 bottom rail

PLAN VIEW

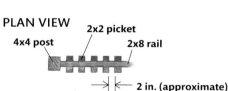

4x4 post

2x2 picket

2x8 rail

2 in. (approximate)

FRONT ELEVATION

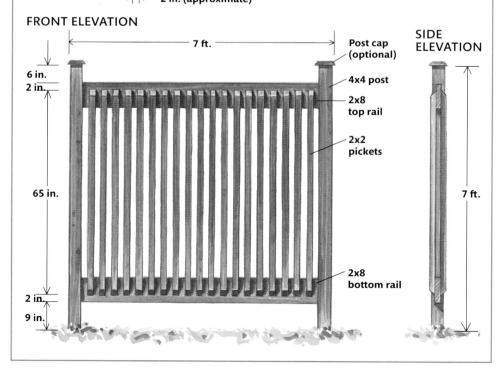

7 ft.

6 in.

2 in.

65 in.

2 in.

9 in.

Post cap (optional)

4x4 post

2x8 top rail

2x2 pickets

2x8 bottom rail

SIDE ELEVATION

7 ft.

Picket fence
(pp. 20-23)

This fence, a modest embellishment of the traditional picket fence, adds a familiar touch to a formal design for a front yard. It is most convenient to build the fence in sections and then space the posts (pp. 194–195) accordingly. Sections are easier to handle if they are no longer than 8 ft.

Work will proceed quickly if you set up a small assembly line. Cut all the rails and pickets to length; then form the "arrow" ends on the pickets with two 45° saw cuts. Assemble the sections on a flat surface (a garage floor is ideal), fixing each picket with two nails or screws to each rail. The gate is just a short section of fence with a diagonal brace to keep it from sagging. Nail or screw the 2x4 rails of the assembled sections to the posts; then add a wide picket to cover the joint where the 2x4 rails butt together on a post.

STYLIZED PICKETS

This alternative uses 1x4s and 1x2s and requires a middle rail to support the tops of the shorter "pickets".

GRIDWORK FENCE

A more unconventional design incorporates a lightweight gridwork made of 1x2s. This fence is best made in 4- to 8-ft. panels, assembled on a flat surface, and then nailed or screwed to 4x4 posts. Proportion the fence to suit your situation. Here, the vertical members are spaced 8 in. apart. From bottom to top, the horizontal members are spaced 4 in., 6 in., and 12 in. apart.

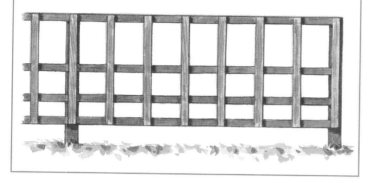

DETAIL: RAIL-TO-POST JOINT

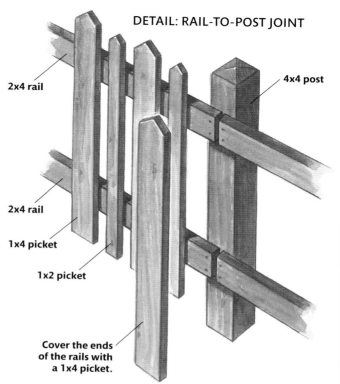

2x4 rail

2x4 rail

1x4 picket

1x2 picket

4x4 post

Cover the ends of the rails with a 1x4 picket.

PLAN VIEW

Gate

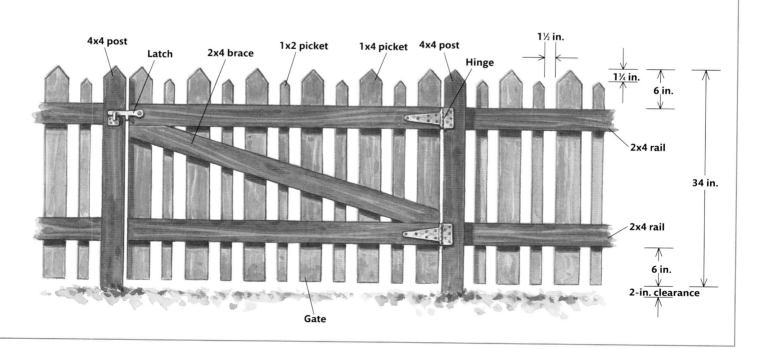

4x4 post

Latch

2x4 brace

1x2 picket

1x4 picket

4x4 post

Hinge

1½ in.

1¾ in.

6 in.

2x4 rail

34 in.

2x4 rail

6 in.

2-in. clearance

Gate

Planter
(pp.64–67)

This planting box brings colorful annuals onto a small patio. Commercially made planters are available in a wide range of sizes, shapes, and materials. But a do-it-yourselfer can make this one in just an hour or so.

The design can be resized to suit your needs. For longevity, use cedar, cypress, redwood, or pressure-treated lumber. You can nail the box together, but the box will be stronger and the job easier if you use screws and an electric screwdriver. (Whether you opt for nails or screws, be sure to use fasteners treated against rust.)

Begin by assembling battens and boards to make the pair of long sides and the box bottom ❶. Note that the ends of the 1x2 battens on the box sides stop short of the two edges. Position the box bottom against the bottom ends of these battens ❷ and fix the sides to the bottom. (The top ends stop short so you can cover them with soil, which results in a neater appearance inside the box.) Complete the box by fastening the end boards to the edges of the battens on the ends of the sides and bottom ❸.

Bore ¾-in. drainage holes in the box bottom on a 6-in. grid. Cover the holes with pieces of window screen, fill the boxes with damp potting soil, and plant.

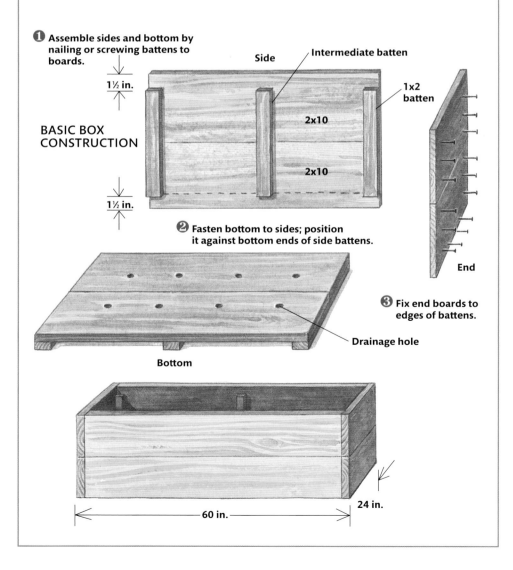

❶ Assemble sides and bottom by nailing or screwing battens to boards.

1½ in.

BASIC BOX CONSTRUCTION

Side

Intermediate batten

1x2 batten

2x10

2x10

End

1½ in.

❷ Fasten bottom to sides; position it against bottom ends of side battens.

❸ Fix end boards to edges of battens.

Drainage hole

Bottom

60 in.

24 in.

Arbor and fence
(pp. 62–63)

These structures work together to enhance the passage from driveway to back door. The fence separates the ball games and autos on the driveway from backyard activities, while the vine-covered arbor makes the journey a shady pleasure.

Build the arbor first. Position the posts to suit the dimensions of your property and set them in concrete as described on pp. 193–195. Cut the joists and crossties to length and fix them to the posts with galvanized carriage bolts. Tack the 2x8s in place with nails; then bore holes with a long electrician's auger bit. (Use crossties on all pairs of posts spanning the walk.) You can fix the rafters by toenailing or using metal rafter ties.

This fence is similar in construction to the one shown on p. 207. Note that the rails are fixed between the posts so that the faces of the pickets are flush with those of the posts. This fence, too, can be constructed by assembling sections, then positioning the posts to fit the sections. This ensures uniform spacing between the posts and adjacent pickets.

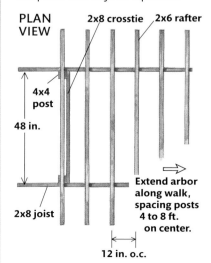

PLAN VIEW

2x8 crosstie   2x6 rafter

4x4 post

48 in.

2x8 joist

Extend arbor along walk, spacing posts 4 to 8 ft. on center.

12 in. o.c.

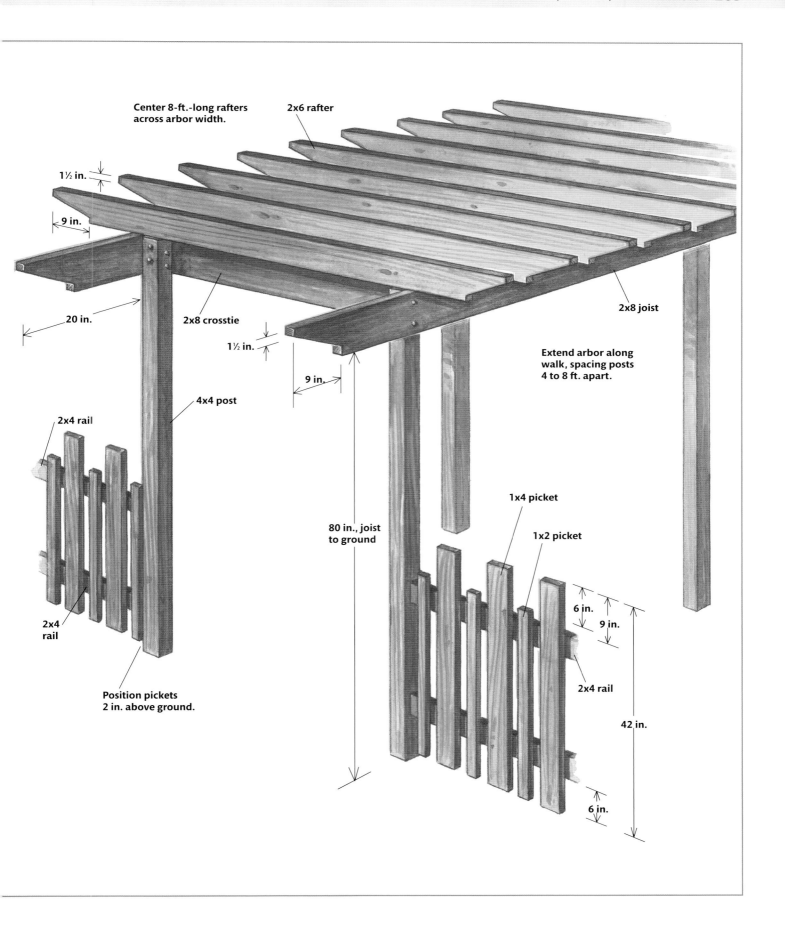

Center 8-ft.-long rafters across arbor width.

2x6 rafter

1½ in.

9 in.

20 in.

2x8 crosstie

1½ in.

9 in.

4x4 post

2x4 rail

2x4 rail

Position pickets 2 in. above ground.

2x8 joist

Extend arbor along walk, spacing posts 4 to 8 ft. apart.

80 in., joist to ground

1x4 picket

1x2 picket

6 in.

9 in.

2x4 rail

42 in.

6 in.

Homemade lattice trellis
(pp. 72–74 and 86–87)

The trellis shown here supports climbing plants to make a vertical garden of a blank wall. The design can be altered to fit walls of different sizes. The three 32-in.-wide modules, hung on L-hangers, are simpler to make than a single large trellis and easy to remove when you need to paint the wall. (If you're in a hurry, you can just attach ready-made lattice to 2x2 frameworks of the same dimensions as shown here.)

Start by cutting all the pieces to length. (Here we'll call the horizontal members "rails" and the vertical members "stiles.") Working on a large flat surface, nail or screw the two outer stiles to the top and bottom rails, checking the corners with a framing square. The 2x2 rails provide ample material to house the L-hangers.

Carefully attach the three intermediate stiles, then the 1x2 rails. Cut a piece of scrap 6 in. long to use as a spacer. Fix the L-shaped hangers to 2x4 studs inside the wall. Buy hangers long enough to hold the trellis several inches away from the wall.

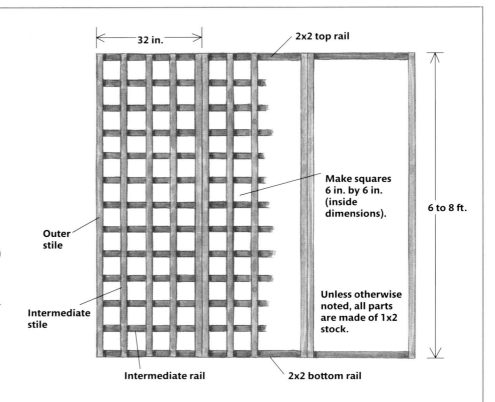

32 in. · 2x2 top rail

Make squares 6 in. by 6 in. (inside dimensions).

6 to 8 ft.

Outer stile

Intermediate stile

Unless otherwise noted, all parts are made of 1x2 stock.

Intermediate rail · 2x2 bottom rail

TRELLIS HANGER

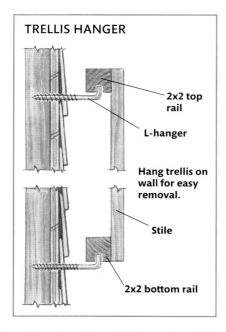

2x2 top rail

L-hanger

Hang trellis on wall for easy removal.

Stile

2x2 bottom rail

CONSTRUCTION DETAILS

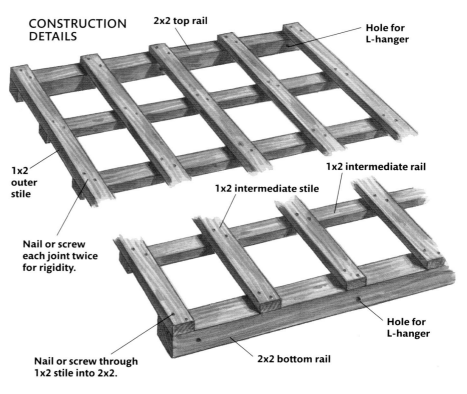

2x2 top rail

Hole for L-hanger

1x2 outer stile

1x2 intermediate rail

1x2 intermediate stile

Nail or screw each joint twice for rigidity.

Nail or screw through 1x2 stile into 2x2.

2x2 bottom rail

Hole for L-hanger

Hideaway arbor
(pp. 76–77 and 108–111)

This cozy enclosure shelters a bench and supports vines to shade the occupants. Once the posts are set in place, this project can be finished in a weekend.

Build the arbor before laying the pavers under it. After setting the posts (see pp. 193-195), attach the 2x10 joists with carriage bolts. (The sizes of posts and joists have been chosen for visual effect; 4x4 posts and 2x6 or 2x8 joists will work, too.) Tack the joists in place with nails; then bore holes for the bolts through post and both joists with a long electrician's auger bit. Fix the rafters by toenailing or using rust-protected metal rafter ties. Nail or screw the rafters at each end to the posts for added stability.

Sandwich store-bought lattice between 1x3s to make the trellis panels for the vines, and fix them to the posts with metal connectors. Offset the corner joints, as shown in the drawing, or reinforce them with metal brackets, or both.

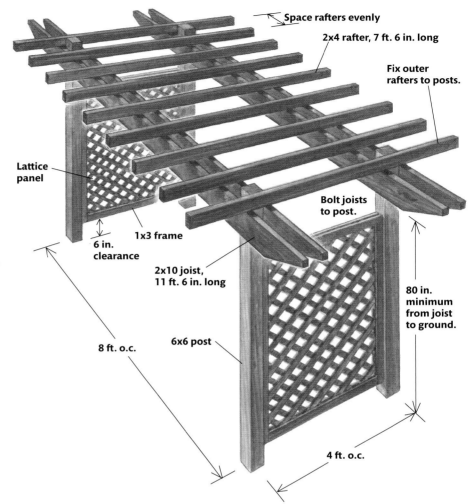

Space rafters evenly

2x4 rafter, 7 ft. 6 in. long

Fix outer rafters to posts.

Lattice panel

1x3 frame

6 in. clearance

Bolt joists to post.

2x10 joist, 11 ft. 6 in. long

80 in. minimum from joist to ground.

8 ft. o.c.

6x6 post

4 ft. o.c.

TRELLIS-PANEL CONSTRUCTION

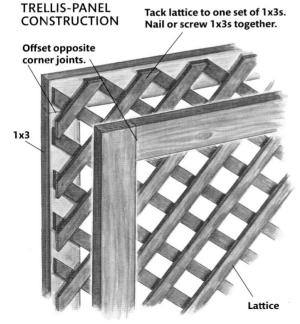

Tack lattice to one set of 1x3s. Nail or screw 1x3s together.

Offset opposite corner joints.

1x3

Lattice

POST-TO-JOIST DETAIL

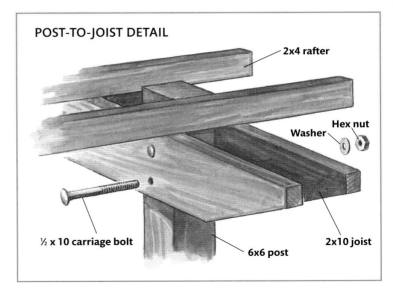

2x4 rafter

Hex nut

Washer

½ x 10 carriage bolt

6x6 post

2x10 joist

Patio screens
(pp. 100–101)

Made of vertical slats spaced a small distance apart, a pair of these 6-ft.-tall screens allow air circulation to plants and people near the patio while providing privacy. Be sure to check local codes about height and setback from property lines.

The slats are supported by three rails. The top and middle rails are 2x4s; a 2x6 bottom rail adds visual weight to the design. Set the posts (see pp. 194–195). Then cut and fix the rails to their back faces. Position the 1x6 slats with a spacer block 1½ in. wide. (To ensure uniform spacing, position all the slats before assembly.) Alternatively, assemble the slats and rails on a flat surface first, and then set the posts at a distance determined by the assembly. Add the 1x6 cap piece to complete the screen.

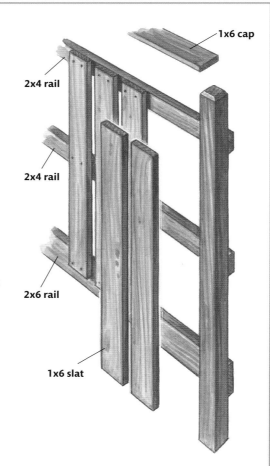

Scene-setting fence
(pp. 88–91)

This design provides privacy and an attractive backdrop for a perennial border. If the fence is used on a property line, be sure to check local codes for restrictions on placement and height.

This is a simple fence to construct. Assemble the panels on a flat surface, nailing or screwing the slats to the three 2x4 rails. You can lay out the arc at the top of each panel by "springing" a thin strip of wood, as shown on the facing page. Place the strip against a nail driven into a slat at the highest point of the arc in the center of the panel ❶. Enlist a couple of assistants to bend each end of the strip down to nails near each edge of the panel indicating the lowest points of the arc ❷. Pencil in the arc against the strip ❸; then cut to the line. (A handheld electric jigsaw does the job quickly, but the curve is gentle enough to cut with a handsaw.)

FRONT ELEVATION

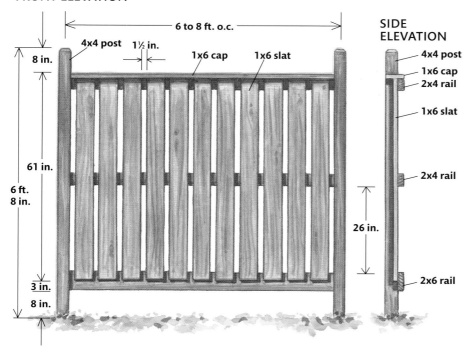

SIDE ELEVATION

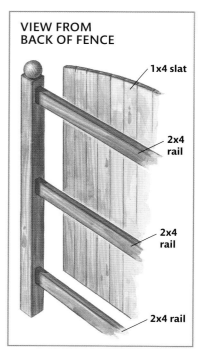

VIEW FROM BACK OF FENCE

Set the posts (see pp. 194–195) according to the widths of the finished panels. The 6x6 posts shown here add an eye-pleasing heft to the fence, an effect emphasized by setting the face of the panel 1 in. back from the faces of the posts. (Posts made of 4x4s will work just as well.) Metal fasteners are the easiest means of attaching the completed panels to the posts. To allow yourself access to the rails when mounting the metal fasteners, leave the last slats at each end off when you assemble the panels. We've shown a spherical finial attached to the end of each post; you can buy finials of various types at home centers.

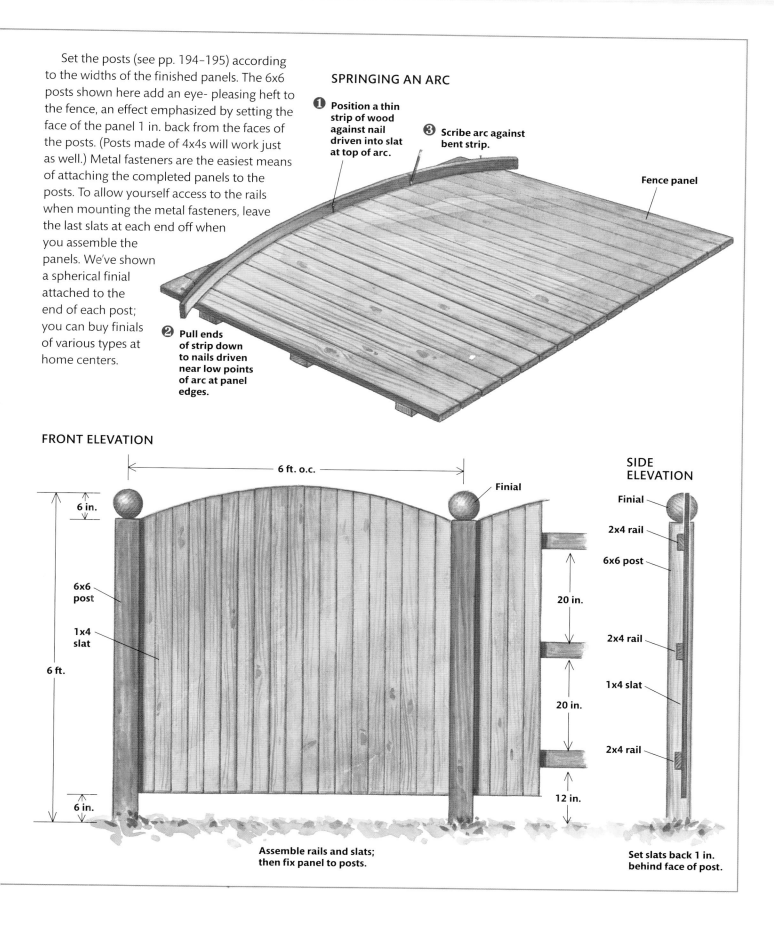

SPRINGING AN ARC

❶ Position a thin strip of wood against nail driven into slat at top of arc.

❸ Scribe arc against bent strip.

Fence panel

❷ Pull ends of strip down to nails driven near low points of arc at panel edges.

FRONT ELEVATION

6 ft. o.c.

Finial

6 in.

6x6 post

1x4 slat

6 ft.

6 in.

Assemble rails and slats; then fix panel to posts.

SIDE ELEVATION

Finial

2x4 rail

6x6 post

20 in.

2x4 rail

20 in.

1x4 slat

2x4 rail

12 in.

Set slats back 1 in. behind face of post.

Lattice skirting for a deck
(pp. 68–71)

The wide lattice gridwork shown here gives the base of a tall deck an airy but substantial look and creates (with a planting of shrubs and trees) a sense of enclosure for a storage area beneath the deck.

The gridwork can be easily nailed or screwed together on a large flat area, then attached to the deck posts. If you want to assemble the gridwork on the deck posts, first fix the horizontal members. Then screw the vertical members to them using an electric screwdriver. (Nailing these unsupported pieces would be difficult.) To ensure equal spacing, lay out the vertical members before assembly.

We've shown a grid of 2x2s fixed to deck posts spaced 7 ft. apart. A lightweight grid made of 1x2s could be used for decks with posts spaced 4 to 6 ft. apart. Alter the size of the gridwork squares to ensure a uniform gridwork pattern between posts.

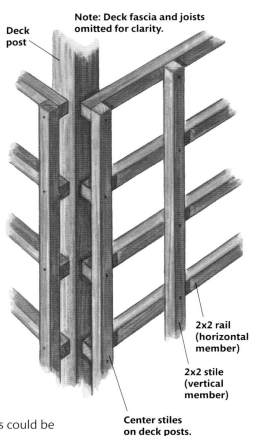

Note: Deck fascia and joists omitted for clarity.

Deck post

2x2 rail (horizontal member)

2x2 stile (vertical member)

Center stiles on deck posts.

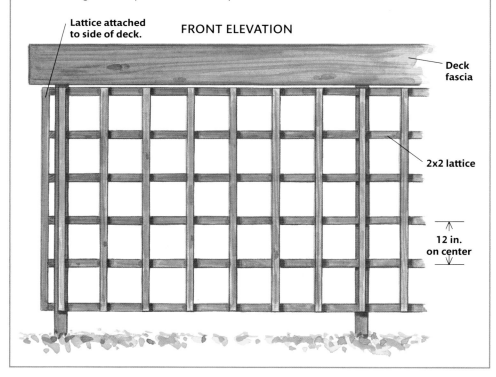

Lattice attached to side of deck.

FRONT ELEVATION

Deck fascia

2x2 lattice

12 in. on center

Entry arbor and fence
(pp. 52–55)

This arbor makes an event of the passage from one part of your property to another. Two versions are shown in the Portfolio. One features the arbor and a holly hedge, the other replaces the hedge with a fence.

As with the other arbors in this book, once the posts are set (see pp. 193–195), assembly is easy. Nail the 2x6 joists to the posts or fix them with carriage bolts. (Clamp or tack the joists to the posts; then bore holes for the bolts with a long electrician's auger bit.) Short sections of fence attached between the posts on the sides of the arbor give young vines support. Heavier rafters attached to the arbor joists stabilize the structure.

The fence is easily made by nailing or screwing the slats to the rails. If you'd prefer to set the posts first and build fence panels to fit, ensure uniform spacing by laying out and adjusting the position of the slats on the rails before fastening them in place.

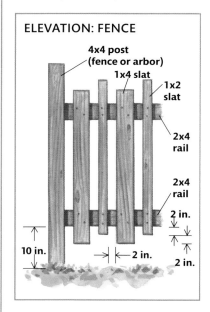

ELEVATION: FENCE

4x4 post (fence or arbor)

1x4 slat

1x2 slat

2x4 rail

2x4 rail

2 in.

10 in.

2 in.

2 in.

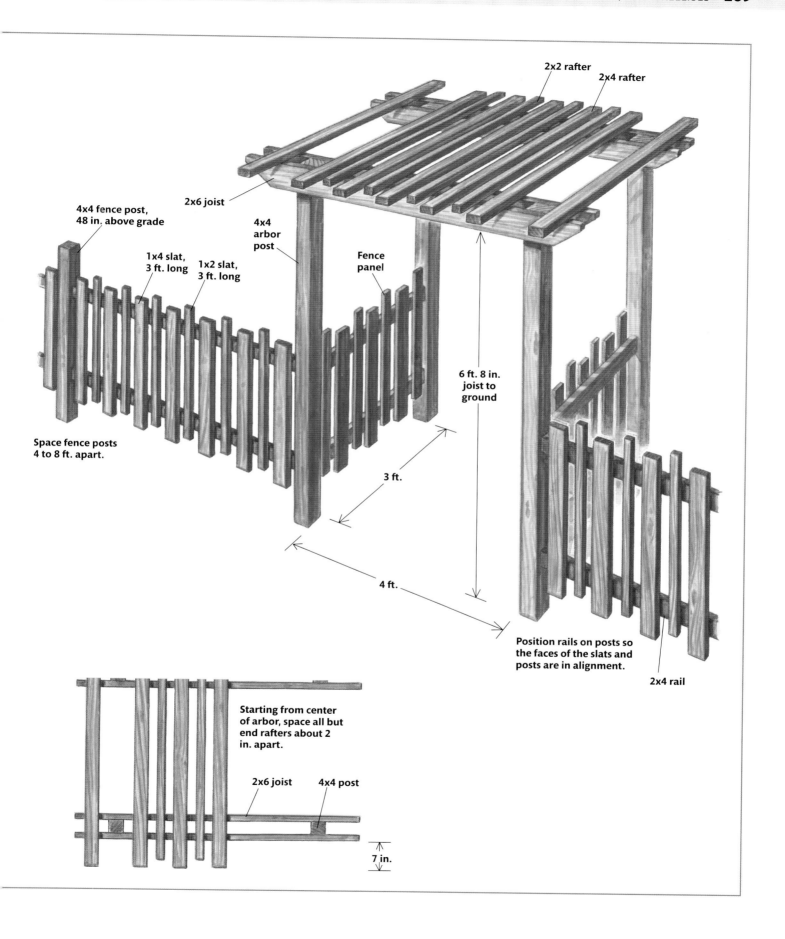

2x2 rafter

2x4 rafter

2x6 joist

4x4 fence post, 48 in. above grade

4x4 arbor post

1x4 slat, 3 ft. long

1x2 slat, 3 ft. long

Fence panel

6 ft. 8 in. joist to ground

Space fence posts 4 to 8 ft. apart.

3 ft.

4 ft.

Position rails on posts so the faces of the slats and posts are in alignment.

2x4 rail

Starting from center of arbor, space all but end rafters about 2 in. apart.

2x6 joist

4x4 post

7 in.

Preparing the Soil for Planting

The better the soil, the better the plants. Soil quality affects how fast plants grow, how big they get, how good they look, and how long they live. But on many residential lots, the soil is shallow and infertile. Unless you're lucky enough to have a better-than-average site where the soil has been cared for and amended over the years, perhaps for use as a vegetable garden or flower bed, you should plan to improve your soil before planting in it.

If you were planting just a few trees or shrubs, you could prepare individual planting holes for them and leave the surrounding soil undisturbed. However, for nearly all the plantings in this book, digging individual holes is impractical,

and it's much better for the plants if you prepare the soil throughout the entire area that will be planted. (The major exception is when you're planting under a tree, which we'll discuss on p. 210.)

For most of the situations shown in this book, you could prepare the soil with hand tools—a spade, digging fork, and rake. The job goes faster, though, if you use a rototiller, and a rototiller is better than hand tools for mixing amendments into the soil. Unless you grow vegetables, you probably won't use a rototiller often enough to justify buying one yourself, but you can easily borrow or rent a rototiller or hire someone with a tiller to come and prepare your site.

Loosen the soil

After you've removed any sod or other vegetation from the designated area (see pp. 174–175), the first step is digging or tilling to loosen the soil ❶. Do this on a day when the soil is moist—not so wet that it sticks to your tools or so dry that it makes dust. Start at one end of the bed and work back and forth until you reach the other end. Try to dig down at least 8 in., or deeper if possible. If the ground is very compacted, you'll have to make repeated passes with a tiller to reach 8 in. deep. Toss aside any large rocks, roots, or debris that you encounter. When you're working near a house or other buildings, watch out for buried wires, cables, and pipes. Most town and city governments have a number you can call to request that someone help you locate buried utilities.

After this initial digging, the ground will probably be very rough and lumpy. Farmers used to plow in the fall and let frost break the clods apart over the winter. That's still a good system; if you plan ahead and do the initial digging in fall, it's easy to finish preparing the soil in spring. But you can do the whole job in one day, too, if you want to. Whump the clods with the back of a digging fork or make another pass with the tiller. Continue until you've reduced all the clumps to the size of apples.

Loosening the existing soil comes first, because that's when you can dig as deep as possible. Then add some topsoil and rake it around if you want to fill in some low spots, refine the grade, or raise the planting area above the surrounding grade for improved visibility and better drainage. Unless you need just a few bags of it, order screened topsoil by the cubic yard from a landscape contractor.

Add organic matter

Common dirt (and purchased topsoil, too) consists mainly of rock and mineral

Common fertilizers and soil amendments

The following materials serve different purposes. Follow soil-test recommendations or the advice of an experienced gardener in choosing which amendments would be best for your soil. If so recommended, you can apply two or three of these amendments at the same time, using the stated rate for each one.

Material	Description	Amount for 100 sq. ft.
Bagged steer manure	A weak all-purpose fertilizer.	6–8 lb.
Dried poultry manure	A high-nitrogen fertilizer.	2 lb.
5-5-5 all-purpose fertilizer	An inexpensive and popular synthetic fertilizer.	2 lb.
Superphosphate or rock phosphate	Supplies phosphorus. Work into the soil as deep as possible.	2–4 lb.
Greensand	Supplies potassium and many trace elements.	2–4 lb.
Regular or dolomitic limestone	Used primarily to sweeten acid soil.	5 lb.
Gypsum	Helps loosen clay soil. Also helps reduce salt buildup in roadside soil.	2 lb.
Wood ashes	Supply potassium, phosphorus, and lime.	2–4 lb.

fragments of various sizes—which are mostly coarse and gritty in sandy soil, and dust-fine in clay soil. One of the best things you can do to improve any kind of soil for garden plants is to add some organic matter. Sold in bags or in bulk at nurseries and garden centers, organic materials include all kinds of composted plant parts and animal manures.

How much organic matter should you use? Spread a layer 2 to 3 in. thick across the entire area you're working on ❷. At this thickness, a cubic yard (about one heaping pickup-truck load) of bulk material, or six bales of peat moss, will cover 100 to 150 sq. ft. If you're working on a large area and need several cubic yards of organic matter, have it delivered. Ask the driver to dump the pile as close to your project area as possible; it's worth allowing the truck to drive across your lawn to get there. You can spread a big truckload of material in just a few hours if you don't have to cart it very far.

Add fertilizers and mineral amendments

Organic matter improves the soil's texture and helps it retain water and nutrients, but it doesn't actually supply many nutrients. To provide the nutrients that plants need, you need to use organic or synthetic fertilizers and powdered minerals. It's most helpful if you mix these materials into the soil before you do any planting, putting them down into the root zone as shown in the drawing ❸, but you can also sprinkle them on top of the soil in subsequent years to maintain a planting.

Getting a sample of soil tested (a service that's usually available free or at low cost through your County Extension Service) is the most accurate way to determine how much of which nutrients is needed. Less precise, but often adequate, is asking the advice of an experienced gardener in your neighborhood. Test results or a gardener's advice will point out any significant deficiencies in your soil, but these are uncommon. Most soil just needs a moderate, balanced dose of nutrients.

Most important is to avoid using too much of any fertilizer or mineral. Don't guess at this; measure and weigh carefully. Calculate your plot's area. Follow your soil-test results, instructions on a commercial product's package, or the general guidelines given in the chart above, and weigh out the appropriate amount, using a kitchen or bathroom scale. Apply the material evenly across the plot with a spreader or by hand.

PREPARING THE SOIL FOR PLANTING

❶ Use a spade, digging fork, or tiller to dig at least 8 in. deep and break the soil into rough clods. Discard rocks, roots, and debris. Watch out for underground utilities.

❷ Spread a 2- to 3-in. layer of organic matter on top of the soil.

❸ Sprinkle measured amounts of fertilizer and mineral amendments evenly across the entire area, and mix thoroughly into the soil.

Mix and smooth the soil

Finally, use a digging fork or tiller and go back and forth across the bed again until the added materials are mixed thoroughly into the soil and everything is broken into nut-size or smaller lumps ❹. Then use a rake to smooth the surface ❺.

At this point, the soil level may look too high compared with adjacent pavement or lawn, but don't worry. It will settle a few inches over the next several weeks and end up close to its original level.

Working near trees

Plantings under the shade of old trees can be cool lovely oases, like the ones shown on pp. 120–123. But to establish the plants, you'll need to contend with the tree's roots. Contrary to popular belief, most tree roots are in the top few inches of the soil, and they extend at least as far away from the trunk as the limbs do. If you dig anyplace in that area, you'll probably cut or bruise some of the tree's roots. When preparing for planting beneath a tree, therefore, it is important to disturb as few roots as possible.

It is natural for a tree's trunk to flare out at the bottom and for the roots near the trunk to be partly above ground. Don't bury them. However, if the soil has eroded away from roots farther out from the trunk, it's okay to add a layer of soil up to several inches deep and top the new soil with a thinner layer of mulch. Adding some soil like this makes it easier to start ground covers or other plants underneath a tree. (See p. 217 for planting instructions.) Just don't overdo it—covering roots with too much soil can starve them of oxygen, damaging or killing them, and piling soil close to the trunk can rot the bark.

❹ Use a tiller or digging fork to mix everything together, again working as deep as possible.

❺ Finish by smoothing the surface with a rake.

Making neat edges

All but the most informal landscapes look best if you define and maintain neat edges between the lawn and any adjacent plantings. There are several ways to do this, varying in appearance, effectiveness, cost, and convenience. For the Southeast region, the best methods are cut, brick or stone, and plastic strip edges. Several other prefab edging systems that you may see in catalogs work well only in warmer climates; they tend to frost-heave in cold winters. In any case, the time to install an edging is after you prepare the soil but before you plant the bed.

Cut edge

Lay a hose or rope on the ground to mark the line where you want to cut. Then cut along the line with a sharp spade or edging tool. Lift away any grass that was growing into the bed (or any plants that were running out into the lawn). Use a rake or hoe to smooth out a shallow trench on the bed side of the cut. Keep the trench empty; don't let it fill up with mulch.

Pros and cons: Free. Good for straight or curved edges, level or sloped sites. You have to recut the edge at least twice a year, in spring and late summer, but you can cut 50 to 100 ft. in an hour or so. Don't cut the trench too deep; if a mower wheel slips down into it, you scalp the lawn. Crabgrass and other weeds may sprout in the exposed soil.

Brick mowing strip

Dig a trench about 8 in. wide and 4 in. deep around the edge of the bed. Fill it halfway with sand; then lay bricks on top, setting them level with the soil on the lawn side. You'll need three bricks per foot of edging. Sweep extra sand into any cracks between the bricks. You'll probably have to reset a few frost-heaved bricks each spring. You can substitute cut stone blocks or concrete pavers for bricks.

Pros and cons: Good for straight or curved edges on level or gently sloped sites. Looks good in combination with brick walkways, or brick house. Fairly easy to install and maintain. Some kinds of grass and plants will grow under, between, or over the bricks.

Plastic strip edging

Garden centers and home-improvement stores sell heavy-duty plastic edging in strips 5 or 6 in. wide and 20 or 50 ft. long. To install it, use a sharp tool to cut straight down through the sod around the edge of the bed. Hold the edging so the round lip sits right at soil level, and drive the stakes through the bottom of the edging and into the undisturbed soil under the lawn. Stakes, which are supplied with the edging, should be at least 8 in. long and set about 3 ft. apart.

Pros and cons: Good for straight or curved edges, but only on relatively level sites. Neat and carefree when well installed, but installation is a two- or three-person job. If the lip isn't set right on the ground, you're likely to hit it with the mower blade. Liable to frost-heave unless it's very securely staked. Hard to drive stakes in rocky soil. Some kinds of grass and ground covers can grow across the top of the edging.

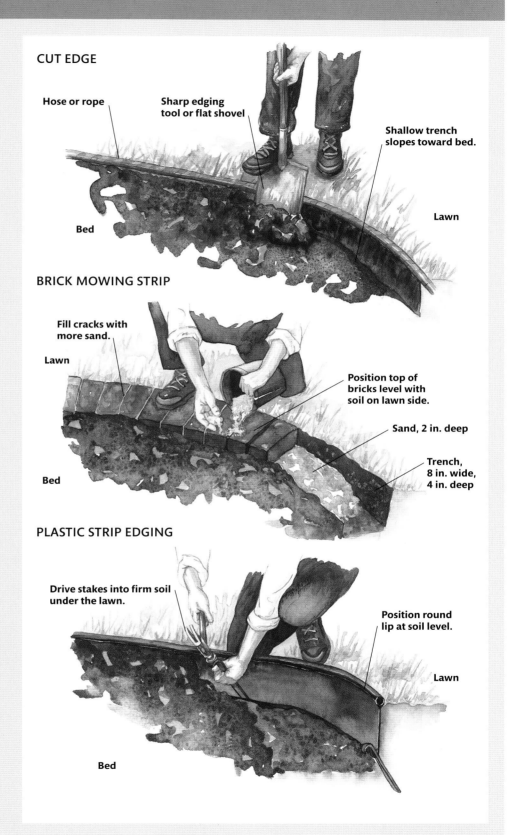

CUT EDGE

Hose or rope

Sharp edging tool or flat shovel

Shallow trench slopes toward bed.

Bed

Lawn

BRICK MOWING STRIP

Fill cracks with more sand.

Lawn

Position top of bricks level with soil on lawn side.

Sand, 2 in. deep

Trench, 8 in. wide, 4 in. deep

Bed

PLASTIC STRIP EDGING

Drive stakes into firm soil under the lawn.

Position round lip at soil level.

Lawn

Bed

Buying Plants

Once you have chosen and planned a landscape project, make a list of the plants you want and start thinking about where to get them. You'll need to locate the kinds of plants you're looking for, choose good-quality plants, and get enough of the plants to fill your design area.

Where and how to shop

You may already have a favorite place to shop for plants. If not, check internet listings under Nursery Stock, Nurserymen, Garden Centers, and Landscape Contractors, and choose a few places to visit. Take your shopping list, find a salesperson, and ask for help. The plants in this book are commonly available in the Southeast region, but you may not find everything you want at one place. The salesperson may refer you to another nursery, offer to special-order plants, or recommend similar plants as substitutes.

If you're buying too many plants to carry in your car or truck, ask about delivery—it's usually available and sometimes free. Some nurseries offer to replace plants that fail within a limited guarantee period, so ask about that, too.

The staff at a good nursery or garden center will usually be able to answer most of the questions you have about which plants to buy and how to care for them. If you can, go shopping on a rainy weekday when business is slow so staff will have time to answer your questions.

Don't be lured by the low prices of plants for sale at supermarkets or discount stores unless you're sure you know exactly what you're looking for and what you're looking at. The salespeople at these stores rarely have the time or knowledge to offer you much help, and the plants are often disorganized, unlabeled, and stressed by poor care.

If you can't find a plant locally or have a retailer order it for you, you can always order it yourself from an online nursery. Most online nurseries produce good plants and pack them well, but if you haven't dealt with a business before, be smart and place a minimum order first. Judge the quality of the plants that arrive; then decide whether or not to order larger quantities from that firm.

Timing

It's a good idea to plan ahead and start shopping for plants before you're ready to put them in the ground. That way, if you can't find everything on your list, you'll have time to keep shopping around, place special orders, or choose substitutes. Most nurseries will let you "flag" an order for later pickup or delivery, and they'll take care of the plants in the meantime. Or you can bring the plants home; just remember to check the soil in the containers every day and water if needed.

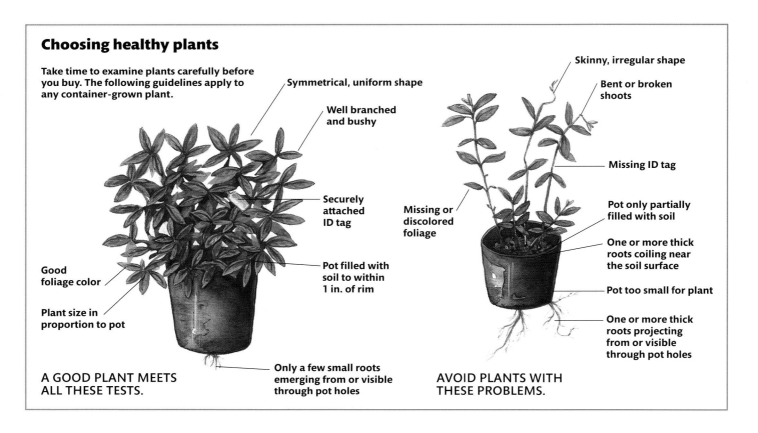

Choosing healthy plants

Take time to examine plants carefully before you buy. The following guidelines apply to any container-grown plant.

Symmetrical, uniform shape

Well branched and bushy

Securely attached ID tag

Good foliage color

Plant size in proportion to pot

Pot filled with soil to within 1 in. of rim

Only a few small roots emerging from or visible through pot holes

A GOOD PLANT MEETS ALL THESE TESTS.

Skinny, irregular shape

Bent or broken shoots

Missing ID tag

Missing or discolored foliage

Pot only partially filled with soil

One or more thick roots coiling near the soil surface

Pot too small for plant

One or more thick roots projecting from or visible through pot holes

AVOID PLANTS WITH THESE PROBLEMS.

Choosing particular plants

If you need, for example, five mugo pines and the nursery or garden center has a whole block of them, how do you choose which five to buy? The sales staff may be too busy to help you decide; you often have to choose by yourself.

Most plants nowadays are grown in containers, so it's possible to lift them one at a time and examine them from all sides. Following the guidelines shown in the drawings below, evaluate each plant's shape, size, health and vigor, and root system.

Trees and shrubs are frequently sold "balled-and-burlapped," that is, with a ball of soil and roots wrapped tightly in burlap. For these plants, look for strong limbs with no broken shoots, an attractive profile, and healthy foliage. Then press your hands against the burlap-covered root ball to make sure that it feels firm, solid, and damp, not loose or dry. (If the ball is buried within a bed of wood chips, carefully pull the chips aside; then push them back after inspecting the plant.)

To make the final cut when you're choosing a group of plants, line them up side by side and select the ones that are most closely matched in height, bushiness, and foliage color. If your design includes a hedge or mass planting where uniformity is very important, it's a good idea to buy a few extra plants as potential replacements in case of damage or loss. It's easier to plan ahead than to find a match later. Plant the extras in a spare corner and you'll have them if you need them.

Sometimes a plant will be available in two or more sizes. Which is better? That depends on how patient you are. The main reason for buying bigger plants is to make a landscape look impressive right away. If you buy smaller plants and set them out at the same spacing, the planting will look sparse at first, but it will soon catch up. A year after planting, you can't tell if a perennial came from a quart- or gallon-size pot: they look the same. For shrubs, the difference between one size pot and the next usually represents one year's growth.

The Planting Process

Throughout the Southeast region, spring is the best season for planting. You can start planting as soon as the soil thaws and the nurseries open, and continue through May with good results. Planting in spring gives the plants a whole growing season to send out roots and get established before facing the rigors of winter. The second-best time for planting is from mid-September to early November, after the heat of summer but before hard frosts. If you want to plant during the summer, do it on a cloudy day when rain is forecast for the next day or so.

Compared with preparing the soil, putting plants in the ground goes quite quickly. If you're well prepared, you can plant a whole bed in just an hour or two.

Try to stay off the soil

Throughout the planting process, do all you can by reaching in from outside the bed—don't step on the newly prepared soil if you can help it. Stepping or walking in the bed compacts the soil and makes it harder to dig planting holes. Use short boards or scraps of plywood as temporary steppingstones if you do need to walk around on the soil. As soon as you can decide where to put them, you might want to lay permanent steppingstones for access to plants that need regular maintenance.

Check placement and spacing

The first step in planting is to mark the position of each plant. The simplest way to do this is to arrange the plants themselves on the bed. Use an empty pot or a stake to represent any plant that's too heavy to move easily. Use a yardstick to check the spacing, and set the plants in place.

Then step back and take a look. Walk around and look from all sides. Go into the house and look out the window. What do you think? Should any of the plants be adjusted a little? Don't worry if the planting looks a little sparse now—it should. Plants almost always grow faster and get bigger than you can imagine when you're first setting them out, and it's almost always better to allow space and wait a few years for them to fill in than to crowd them too close together at first and have to keep pruning and thinning them later.

PLANTING POINTERS

When working on top of prepared soil, kneel on a piece of plywood to distribute your weight.

Use empty pots or stakes to mark positions of plants not yet purchased or too heavy to move frequently.

Moving through the job

When you're satisfied with the arrangement, mark the position of each plant with a stake or stone, and set the plants aside out of the way, so you won't knock them over or step on them as you proceed. Start planting in order of size. Do the biggest plants first, then move on to the medium-size and smaller plants. If all the plants are about the same size, start at the back of the bed and work toward the front, or start in the center and work to the edges.

Position trees and shrubs to show their best side

Most trees and shrubs are slightly asymmetric. There's usually enough irregularity in their branching or shape that one side looks a little fuller or more attractive than the other sides do. After you've set a tree or shrub into its hole, step back and take a look. Then turn it partway, or try tilting or tipping it a little to one side or the other. Once you've decided which side and position looks best, start filling in the hole with soil. Stop and check again before you firm the soil into place.

The fine points of spacing

When you're planting a group of the same kind of plants, such as perennials or ferns, it normally looks best if you space them informally, in slightly curved or zigzag rows, with the plants in one row offset from those of the next row. Don't arrange plants in a straight row unless you want to emphasize a line, such as the edge of a bed. After planting, step back and evaluate the effect. If you want to adjust the placement or position of any plant, now is the time to do so.

Rake, water, and mulch

Use a garden rake to level out any high and low spots that remain after planting. Water enough to settle the soil into place around the roots. Mulch the entire planting area with 1 to 3 in. of composted bark, wood chips, or other organic matter. Mulch is indispensable for controlling weeds and regulating the moisture and temperature of the soil. If you're running out of time, you don't have to spread the mulch right away, but try to get it done within the next week or so.

Using annuals as fillers

The plants in our designs have been spaced so they will not be crowded at maturity. Buying more plants and spacing them closer may fill things out faster, but in several years (for perennials; longer for shrubs) you'll need to remove plants or prune them frequently.

If you want something to fill the gaps between newly planted perennials, shrubs, or ground covers for that first year or two, use some annuals. The best annual fillers are compact plants that grow only 6 to 10 in. tall. These will hide the soil or mulch and make a colorful carpet. Avoid taller annuals, because they can shade or smother your permanent plantings.

The following annuals are all compact, easy to grow, readily available, and inexpensive. Seeds of those marked with a symbol (✿) can be sown directly in the garden about the time of last frost. For the others, buy six-packs or flats of plants. Thin seedlings or space plants 8 to 12 in. apart.

Annual phlox ✿: Red, pink, or white flowers. Good for hot dry sites.
China pink ✿: Red, pink, white, or bicolor flowers. Blooms all summer.
Dusty miller: Silvery foliage, often lacy-textured. No flowers.
Edging lobelia: Dark blue, magenta, or white flowers. Likes afternoon shade.

Flossflower: Fluffy blue, lavender, or white flowers. Choose dwarf types.
Garden verbena: Bright red, pink, purple, or white flowers. Good for hot dry sites.
Globe candytuft ✿: Pink or white flowers. Grows and blooms fast, then goes to seed.
Moss rose: Bright flowers in many colors. Ideal for hot dry sites.
Pansy and viola: Multicolored flowers. Grow best in cool weather.
Sweet alyssum ✿: Fragrant white or lilac flowers. Blooms for months. Very easy.
Wax begonia: Rose, pink, or white flowers. Good for shady sites but also takes sun.

Planting Basics

Most of the plants that you buy for a landscaping project today are grown and sold in individual plastic containers, but large shrubs and trees may be balled-and-burlapped. Mail-order plants may come bare-root. And ground covers are sometimes sold in flats. In any case, the basic concern is the same: Be careful what you do to a plant's roots. Spread them out; don't fold or coil them or cram them into a tight hole. Keep them covered; don't let the sun or air dry them out. And don't bury them too deep; set the top of the root ball level with the surrounding soil.

Planting container-grown plants

The steps are the same for any plant, no matter what size container it's growing in. Dig a hole that's a little wider than the container but not quite as deep ❶. Check by setting the container into the hole—the top of the soil in the container should be slightly higher than the surrounding soil. Dig several holes at a time, at the positions that you've already marked out.

Remove the container ❷. With one hand, grip the plant at the base of its stems or leaves, like pulling a ponytail, while you tug on the pot with the other hand. If the pot doesn't slide off easily, don't pull harder on the stems. Try whacking the pot against a hard surface; if it still doesn't slide off, use a strong knife to cut or pry it off.

Examine the plant's roots ❸. If there are any thick, coiled roots, unwind them and cut them off close to the root ball, leaving short stubs. If the root ball is a mass of fine, hairlike roots, use the knife to cut three or four slits from top to bottom, about 1 in. deep. Pry the slits apart and tease the cut roots to loosen them. This cutting or slitting may seem drastic, but it's actually good for the plant because it forces new roots to grow out into the surrounding soil. Work quickly. Once you've taken a plant out of its container, get it in the ground as soon as possible. If you want to prepare several plants at a time, cover them with an old sheet or tarp to keep the roots from drying out.

Set the root ball into the hole ❹. Make sure that the plant is positioned right, with its best side facing out, and that the top of the root ball is level with or slightly higher than the surface of the bed. Then add enough soil to fill in the hole, and pat it down firmly.

PLANTING CONTAINER-GROWN PLANTS

❶ Dig a hole a little wider than the container but not as deep.

❷ Remove the plant from the container.

❸ Unwind any large, coiled roots and cut them off short. Cut vertical slits through masses of fine roots.

❹ Position the plant in the hole and fill in around it with soil.

Planting a balled-and-burlapped shrub or tree

Nurseries often grow shrubs and trees in fields, then dig them with a ball of root-filled soil and wrap a layer of burlap snugly around the ball to keep it intact. The problem is that even a small ball of soil is very heavy. A root ball that is a foot wide is a two-person job. For larger root balls, ask the nursery to deliver and plant it. Here's how to proceed with plants that are small enough that you can handle them.

Dig a hole several inches wider than the root ball but not quite as deep as the root ball is high. Firm the soil so the plant won't sink. Set the plant into the hole, and lay a stick across the top of the root ball to make sure it's at or a little higher than grade level. Be sure to remove any twine or wire cage from the trunk and root ball. Fold the burlap down around the sides of the ball. Don't try to pull the burlap out altogether—roots can grow out through it, and it will eventually decompose. Fill soil all around the sides of the ball and pat it down firmly. Spread only an inch of soil over the top of the ball.

The top of the ball should be level with the surrounding soil. Cut twine that wraps around the trunk. Fold down the burlap, but don't remove it.

Planting bare-root plants

Mail-order nurseries sometimes dig perennials, roses, and other plants when the plants are dormant, cut back the tops, and wash all the soil off the roots, to save space and weight when storing and shipping them. If you receive a plant in bare-root condition, unwrap it, trim away any roots that are broken or damaged, and soak the roots in a pail of water for several hours.

To plant, dig a hole large enough that you can spread the roots across the bottom without folding them. Start covering the roots with soil, then lay a stick across the top of the hole and hold the plant against it to check the planting depth, as shown in the drawing. Raise or lower the plant if needed in order to bury just the roots, not the buds. Add more soil, firming it down around the roots, and continue until the hole is full.

Dig a hole wide enough that you can spread out the roots. A stick helps position the plant at the correct depth as you fill the hole with soil.

Planting ground covers from flats

Sometimes ground covers are sold in flats of 25 or more rooted cuttings. Start at one corner, reach underneath the soil, and lift out a portion of the flat's contents. Working quickly, because the roots are exposed, tease the cuttings apart, trying not to break off any roots, and plant them individually. Then lift out the next portion and continue planting.

Remove a clump of little plants, tease their roots apart, and plant them quickly.

Planting bulbs

Plant spring-blooming bulbs in October and November. If the soil in the bed was well prepared, you can use a trowel to dig holes for planting individual bulbs; where you have room, you can dig a wider hole or trench for planting a group of bulbs all at once. The perennials, ground covers, shrubs, and trees you planted earlier in the fall or in the spring will still be small enough that you won't disturb their roots. As a rule of thumb, plant small (grape- or cherry-size) bulbs about 2 in. deep and 3 to 5 in. apart, and large (walnut- or egg-size) bulbs 4 to 6 in. deep and 6 to 10 in. apart.

Plant bulbs with the pointed end up, at a depth and spacing determined by the size of the bulb.

Planting under a tree

When planting beneath a mature tree, as for the design on pp. 120–123, remember that most tree roots are in the top few inches of the soil, and they extend at least as far away from the trunk as the limbs do. For areas of ground cover and most container-grown perennials, you can add topsoil and organic amendments up to about 6 in. deep over the entire area; then set the plants out in the new soil. Larger plants need deeper holes. Whether you dig their planting holes in existing soil or through a layer of added topsoil, dig carefully, disturbing as few tree roots as possible. If you encounter a large root, move the planting hole rather than sever the root.

Confining perennials

Yarrow, bee balm, artemisia, and various other perennials, grasses, and ferns are described as invasive because they spread by underground runners. To confine these plants to a limited area, install a barrier when you plant them. Cut the bottom off a 5-gal. or larger plastic pot, bury the pot so its rim is above the soil, and plant the perennial inside. You'll need to lift, divide, and replant part of the perennial every second or third year.

Position rim above soil surface.

Remove bottom of pot.

Basic Landscape Care

The landscape plantings in this book will grow increasingly carefree from year to year as the plants mature, but of course you'll always need to do some regular maintenance. Depending on the design you choose, this ongoing care may require as much as a few hours a week during the season or as little as a few hours a year. No matter what you plant, you'll have to control weeds, use mulch, water as needed, and do spring and fall cleanups. Trees, shrubs, and vines may need staking or training at first and occasional pruning or shearing afterward. Perennials, ground covers, and grasses may need to be cut back, staked, deadheaded, or divided. Performing these tasks, which are explained on the following pages, is sometimes hard work, but for many gardeners it is enjoyable labor, a chance to get outside in the fresh air. Also, spending time each week with your plants helps you identify and address problems before they become serious.

Mulches and fertilizers

Covering the soil in all planted areas with a layer of organic mulch does several jobs at once: it improves the appearance of your garden while you're waiting for the plants to grow, reduces the number of weeds that emerge, reduces water loss from the soil during dry spells, moderates soil temperatures, and adds nutrients to the soil as it decomposes. Inorganic mulches such as clear or black plastic, landscape fabric, and gravel also provide some of these benefits, but their conspicuous appearance and the difficulty of removing them if you ever want to change the landscape are serious drawbacks.

Many materials are used as mulches; the box on p. 218 presents the most common, with comments on their advantages and disadvantages. Consider appearance, availability, cost, and convenience when you're comparing different products. Most garden centers have a few kinds of bagged mulch materials, but for mulching large areas, it's easier and cheaper to have a landscape contractor or other supplier deliver a truckload of bulk mulch. A landscape looks best if you see the same mulch throughout the entire planting area, rather than a patchwork of different mulches. You can achieve a uniform look by spreading a base layer of homemade compost, rotten hay, or other inexpensive material and topping that with a neater-looking material such as bark chips, shredded bark, or cocoa hulls.

It takes at least a 1-in. layer of mulch to suppress weeds, but there's no need to spread it more than 3 in. deep. As you're spreading it, don't put any mulch against the stems of any plants, because that can lead to disease or insect problems. Put most of the mulch between plants, not right around them. Check the mulch each spring when you do an annual garden inspection and cleanup. Be sure it's pulled back away from the plant stems. Rake the surface of the mulch lightly to loosen it, and top it up with a fresh layer if the old material has decomposed.

Fertilizer

Decomposing mulch frequently supplies enough nutrients to grow healthy plants, but using fertilizer helps if you want to boost the plants—to make them grow faster, get larger, or produce more flowers. There are dozens of fertilizer products on the market—liquid and granular, fast-acting and slow-release, organic and synthetic. Choose whichever you prefer; they all give good results if applied as directed. And observe the following precautions: Don't overfertilize, don't fertilize when the soil is dry, and don't fertilize after midsummer, because plants need to slow down and finish the season's growth before cold weather comes.

Mulch materials

Bark products

Bark nuggets, chipped bark, shredded bark, and composted bark, usually from conifers, are available in bags or in bulk. All are attractive, long-lasting, medium-price mulches.

Chipped tree trimmings

The chips from utility companies and tree services are a mixture of wood, bark, twigs, and leaves. These chips cost less than pure bark products (you may be able to get a load for free), but they don't look as good and you have to replace them more often, because they decompose fast.

Sawdust and shavings

These are cheap or free at sawmills and woodshops. They make good path coverings, but they aren't ideal mulches, because they tend to pack down into a dense, water-resistant surface.

Hulls and shells

Cocoa hulls, buckwheat hulls, peanut shells, and nut shells are available for pickup at food-processing plants and are sometimes sold in bags or bulk at garden centers. They're all attractive, long-lasting mulches. Price varies from free to quite expensive, depending on where you get them.

Tree leaves

A few big trees may supply all the mulch you need, year after year. You can just rake the leaves onto the bed in fall, but they'll probably blow off it again. It's better to chop them up with the lawn mower, pile them in compost bins for the winter, and spread them on the beds in late spring. If you have the space for two sets of compost bins, give leaves an extra year to decompose before spreading them. Pine needles make good mulch, too, especially for rhododendrons, mountain laurels, and other acid-loving shrubs. You can spread pine needles in fall, because they cling together and don't blow around.

Grass clippings

A 1- to 2-in. layer of dried grass clippings makes an acceptable mulch that decomposes within a single growing season. Don't pile clippings too thick, though. If you do, the top surface dries and packs into a water-resistant crust, and the bottom layer turns into nasty slime.

Hay and straw

Farmers sell hay that's moldy, old, or otherwise unsuitable for fodder as "mulch" hay. This hay is cheap, but it's likely to include weed seeds, particularly seeds of weedy grasses such as barnyard grass. Straw—the stems of grain crops such as wheat—is usually seed-free but more expensive. Both hay and straw are more suitable for mulching vegetable gardens than landscape plantings because they have to be renewed each year. They are bulky at first but decompose quickly. They also tend to attract rodents.

Gravel

A mulch of pea gravel or crushed rock, spread 1 to 2 in. thick, helps keep the soil cool and moist, and many plants grow very well with a gravel mulch. However, compared with organic materials such as bark or leaves, it's much more tiring to apply a gravel mulch in the first place; it's harder to remove leaves and litter that accumulate on the gravel or weeds that sprout up through it; it's annoying to dig through the gravel if you want to replace or add plants later; and it's extremely tedious to remove the gravel itself, should you ever change your mind about having it there.

Landscape fabrics

Various types of synthetic fabrics, usually sold in rolls 3 to 4 ft. wide and 20, 50, or 100 ft. long, can be spread over the ground as a weed barrier and topped with a layer of gravel, bark chips, or other mulch. Unlike plastic, these fabrics allow water and air to penetrate into the soil. It's useful to lay fabric under paths, but not in planted areas. In a bed, it's a two-person job to install the fabric in the first place, it's inconvenient trying to install plants through holes cut in the fabric, and it's hard to secure the fabric neatly and invisibly at the edges of the bed. The fabric lasts indefinitely, and removing it—if you change your mind—is a messy job.

Clear or black plastic

Don't even think about using any kind of plastic sheeting as a landscape mulch. The soil underneath a sheet of plastic gets bone-dry, while water accumulates on top. Any loose mulch you spread on plastic slips or floats around and won't stay in an even layer. No matter how you try to secure them, the edges of plastic sheeting always pull loose, appear at the surface, degrade in the sun, and shred into tatters.

Watering

Watering is less of a concern for gardeners in the Southeast region than in other parts of the country, but even here there are dry spells and droughts when plants could use some extra water. New plantings, in particular, almost always need water more often than rain provides it.

Deciding whether water is needed

Usually only experienced gardeners can judge whether plants need water simply by looking at their leaves. Their appearance can be misleading. Moreover, you can't go by your own feelings about the weather. One of the ironies of the Southeast climate is that the air can be very humid, making us humans feel all wet, even though at the same time the soil is so dry that the plants around us are suffering from drought.

Fortunately, there are two very reliable ways of deciding whether you should water. One is to check the soil. Get a paint stirrer or similar piece of unfinished, light-colored wood and use it like a dipstick. Push it down through the mulch and a few inches into the soil, leave it there for an hour or so, and pull it out to see whether moisture has discolored the wood. If so, the soil is moist enough for plants. If not, it's time to water. You have to let the stick dry out before you can use it again; it's handy to have several of these sticks around the garden shed.

The other method is to make a habit of monitoring rainfall by having your own rain gauge or listening to the weather reports, and marking a calendar to keep track of rainfall amounts. In the Southeast region, most landscape plants thrive if they get 3 to 4 in. of rain a month. You should make every effort to water new plantings if there's been less than 1 in. of rain in two weeks. In subsequent years, after the plants have had time to put down roots, they can endure three or more weeks with no rain at all; even so, you should water them if you can. In this region, established plants rarely die from drought, but they do show many signs of stress—wilting leaves, premature leaf drop, failure to bloom or to set fruit, and increased susceptibility to insect and disease attacks.

Pay attention to soil moisture or rainfall amounts from March through December, because plants can suffer from dryness throughout that entire period, not just in the heat of summer,

and water whenever the soil is dry. As for time of day, you can water whenever the plants need it and you get the chance. Gardening books sometimes warn against watering plants late in the day, saying that plants are more vulnerable to fungal infections if the leaves stay wet at night. That's true, but plants get wet with dew most nights anyway.

How much to water

It's easy to overwater a houseplant but hard to overwater a plant in the ground. Outdoors, you're much more likely to water too little than too much. You could spend an hour with hose in hand, watering the plants in a flower bed, and supply the equivalent of ¼ in. of rain or less. Holding a hose or carrying a bucket is practical for watering new plantings only where the plants are few, small, or relatively widely spaced. To thoroughly water an area that's filled with plants, you need a system that allows you to turn on the water, walk away, and come back later. An oscillating sprinkler on the end of a hose works fine, or you can weave a soaker hose through the bed.

No matter how you water, you should monitor how much water you have applied and how evenly it was distributed. If you're hand-watering or using a soaker hose, the watering pattern may be quite uneven. Put several wooden "dipsticks" in different parts of the bed to make sure that all areas have received enough water to moisten the sticks. Monitor the output of a sprinkler by setting tuna-fish cans around the bed and checking to see how much water they catch, like measuring rainfall. Let the sprinkler run until there's about an inch of water in each can.

CHECKING SOIL MOISTURE

Stick a paint stirrer or similar piece of light-colored, unfinished wood down through the mulch and into the soil. Pull it up after an hour. If the bottom of the stick looks and feels damp, the soil is moist enough for plants.

MONITORING A SPRINKLER

Set several tuna-fish cans throughout the area, and let the sprinkler run until about 1 in. of water has collected in each can.

Controlling weeds

Weeds are not much of a problem in established landscapes. Once the "good" plants have grown big enough to merge together, they tend to crowd or shade out all but the most persistent weeds. But weeds can be troublesome in a new landscape unless you take steps to prevent and control them.

There are two main types of weeds: those that mostly sprout up as seedlings and those that keep coming back from perennial roots or runners. Try to identify and eliminate any perennial weeds before you start a landscaping project. Then you'll only have to deal with new seedlings later.

Annual and perennial weeds that commonly grow from seeds include crabgrass, chickweed, dandelions, plantain, purslane, ragweed, and violets. Trees and shrubs such as silver maple, wild cherry, cottonwood, willow, black locust, buckthorn, and honeysuckle produce weedy seedlings, too. For any of these weeds that grow from seeds, the strategy is twofold: try to keep the weed seeds from sprouting, and eliminate any seedlings that do sprout as soon as you see them, while they are still small.

Almost any patch of soil includes weed seeds that are ready to sprout whenever that soil is disturbed. You have to disturb the soil to prepare it before planting, and that will probably cause an initial flush of weeds, but you'll never see that many weeds again if you leave the soil undisturbed in subsequent years. You don't have to hoe, rake, or cultivate around perennial plantings. Leave the soil alone, and fewer weeds will appear. Using mulch helps even more; by shading the soil, it prevents weed seeds from sprouting. And if weed seeds blow in and land on top of the mulch, they'll be less likely to germinate there than they would on bare soil.

Pull or cut off any weeds that appear while they're young and small. Don't let them mature and go to seed. Most weed seedlings emerge in late spring and early summer.

Using herbicides

Two kinds of herbicides can be very useful and effective in maintaining home landscapes, but only if used correctly. You have to choose the right product for the job and follow the directions on the label regarding dosage and timing of application exactly.

Preemergent herbicides. Usually sold in granular form, these herbicides are designed to prevent weed seeds, particularly crabgrass and other annual weeds, from sprouting. One application is typically enough to last through the growing season, but you need to apply the product quite early in spring, at the time forsythias start blooming. If you wait until later, many weeds will already have sprouted, and a preemergent herbicide will not stop them then.

WEEDS THAT SPROUT FROM SEEDS

Simple root systems can be easily pulled while still small.

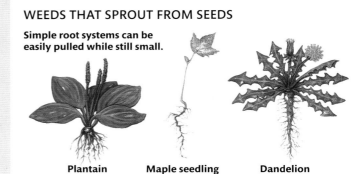

Plantain   **Maple seedling**   **Dandelion**

WEEDS THAT SPROUT BACK FROM PERENNIAL ROOTS OR RUNNERS

Connected by underground runners, the shoots of these weeds need to be pulled repeatedly, smothered with a thick mulch, or killed with an herbicide.

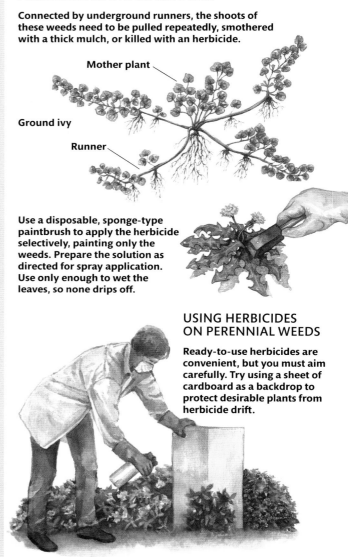

Mother plant

Ground ivy

Runner

Use a disposable, sponge-type paintbrush to apply the herbicide selectively, painting only the weeds. Prepare the solution as directed for spray application. Use only enough to wet the leaves, so none drips off.

USING HERBICIDES ON PERENNIAL WEEDS

Ready-to-use herbicides are convenient, but you must aim carefully. Try using a sheet of cardboard as a backdrop to protect desirable plants from herbicide drift.

Caring for Woody Plants

Read the label carefully, and make sure the herbicide you buy is registered for use around the kinds of ground covers, perennials, shrubs, or other plants you have. Measure the area of your bed, weigh out the appropriate amount of granules, and sprinkle them as evenly as possible across the soil. Wear heavy rubber gloves that are rated for use with farm chemicals, not common household rubber gloves, and follow the safety precautions on the product label.

Postemergent herbicides. These chemicals are used to kill plants. Some kinds kill only the aboveground parts of a plant; other kinds are absorbed into the plant and kill it, roots and all. Postemergent herbicides are typically applied as sprays, which you can buy ready-to-use or prepare by mixing a concentrate with water. Look for those that break down quickly, and read the label carefully for registered applications, specific directions, and safety instructions.

Postemergent herbicides work best if applied when the weeds are growing vigorously. You usually have to apply enough to thoroughly wet the plant's leaves, and do it during a spell of dry weather. Applying an herbicide is an effective way to get rid of a perennial weed that you can't dig or pull up, but it's really better to do this before you plant a bed, as it's hard to spray herbicides in an established planting without getting some on your good plants. Aim carefully, and don't spray on windy days. Brushing or sponging the herbicide on the leaves avoids damaging adjacent plants.

Using postemergent herbicides in an established planting is a painstaking job, but it may be the only way to get rid of a persistent perennial weed. For young weed seedlings, it's usually easier and faster to pull them by hand than to spray them.

A well-chosen garden tree, such as the ones recommended in this book, grows naturally into a neat, pleasing shape; won't get too large for its site; is resistant to pests and diseases; and doesn't drop messy pods or other litter. Once established, these trees need very little care from year to year.

Regular watering is the most important concern in getting a tree off to a good start. Don't let it suffer from drought for the first few years. To reduce competition, don't plant ground covers or other plants within 2 ft. of the tree's trunk. Just spread a thin layer of mulch there.

Arborists now dismiss other care ideas that once were common practice. According to current thinking, you don't need to fertilize a tree when you plant it (in fact, most landscape trees never need fertilizing). Keep pruning to a minimum at planting time; remove only dead or damaged twigs, not healthy shoots. Finally, if a tree is small enough that one or two people can carry and plant it, it doesn't need staking and the trunk will grow stronger if unstaked. Larger trees that are planted by a nursery may need staking, especially on windy sites, but the stakes should be removed within a year.

Pruning to direct growth

Pruning shapes plants not only by removing stems, branches, and leaves but also by inducing and directing new growth. All plants have a bud at the base of every leaf. New shoots grow from these buds. Cutting off the end of a stem encourages the lower buds to shoot out and produces a bushier plant. This type of pruning makes a hedge fill out and gives an otherwise lanky perennial or shrub a better rounded shape.

The same response to pruning also allows you to steer the growth of a plant. The bud immediately below the cut will produce a shoot that extends in the direction the bud was pointing. To direct a branch or stem, cut it back to a bud pointing in the direction you want to encourage growth. This technique is useful for shaping young trees and shrubs and for keeping their centers open to light and air.

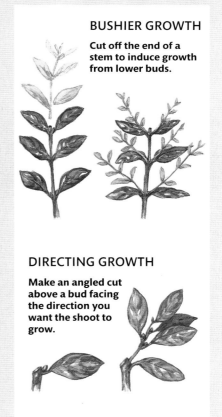

BUSHIER GROWTH

Cut off the end of a stem to induce growth from lower buds.

DIRECTING GROWTH

Make an angled cut above a bud facing the direction you want the shoot to grow.

Pruning roses

Roses are vigorous, fast-growing shrubs that need regular pruning to keep them shapely and attractive. Most of this pruning is done in early spring, just as the buds start to swell but before the new leaves start to unfold. Always use sharp pruning shears and cut back to a healthy bud, leaving no stub. Right after pruning is a good time to add fresh mulch around the plant.

Prune hybrid tea roses to keep them neat, compact, and shapely. Remove any extremely skinny or weak stems plus a few of the oldest stems (you can tell by looking at their bark, which is tan or gray instead of green) by cutting them off at the ground. Prune off any shoots that got frozen or broken during the winter, remove old or weak shoots and crossing or crowded stems, and trim back any asymmetric or unbalanced shoots. Don't be afraid of cutting back too hard; it's better to leave just a few strong shoots than a lot of weak ones. If you cut old stems off at ground level, new ones will grow to replace them. Cut damaged or asymmetric stems back partway and they will branch out.

Hybrid tea roses bloom on new growth, so if you prune in spring you aren't cutting off any flower buds. During the growing season, make a habit of removing the flowers as soon as they fade. This keeps the plant neat and makes it bloom more abundantly and over a longer season. At least once a week, locate each faded flower, follow down its stem to the first or second five-leaflet leaf, and prune just above one of those leaves. (Follow the same steps to cut roses for a bouquet.)

Climbing roses don't need as much spring pruning as hybrid tea roses do. Remove any weak, dead, or damaged shoots by cutting them back to the ground or to healthy wood. You may need to untie and untangle the canes in order to do this spring pruning.

Climbing roses need regular attention throughout the summer, because their stems or canes can grow a foot or more in a month. Check regularly and tie this new growth to the trellis while it's still supple and manageable. When the canes grow long enough to reach the top of the trellis or arbor, cut off their tips and they will send out side shoots, which are where the flowers form. Remove the individual roses or clusters of roses as the petals fade by cutting the stems back to the nearest healthy five-leaflet leaf.

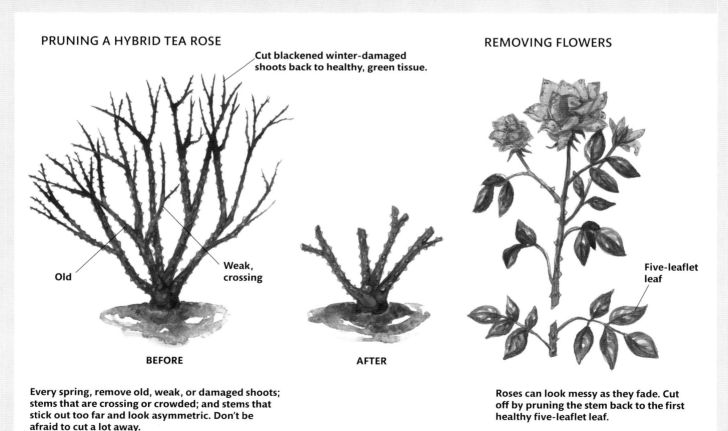

PRUNING A HYBRID TEA ROSE

Cut blackened winter-damaged shoots back to healthy, green tissue.

Old

Weak, crossing

BEFORE

AFTER

Every spring, remove old, weak, or damaged shoots; stems that are crossing or crowded; and stems that stick out too far and look asymmetric. Don't be afraid to cut a lot away.

REMOVING FLOWERS

Five-leaflet leaf

Roses can look messy as they fade. Cut off by pruning the stem back to the first healthy five-leaflet leaf.

Shaping young trees

As a tree grows, you can direct its shape by pruning once a year, in winter or summer. (See the box on page 221.) Take it easy, though. Don't prune just for the sake of pruning; that does more harm than good. If you don't have a good reason for making a cut, don't do it. Follow these guidelines:

- **Use sharp pruning shears, loppers, or saws,** which make clean cuts without tearing the wood or bark.
- **Cut branches back** to a healthy shoot, leaf, or bud, or cut back to the branch collar at the base of the branch, as shown at right. Don't leave any stubs; they're ugly and prone to decay.
- **Remove any dead or damaged** branches and any twigs or limbs that are very spindly or weak.
- **Where two limbs cross over or rub** against each other, save one limb—usually the thicker, stronger one—and prune off the other one.
- **Prune or widen narrow crotches.** Places where a branch and trunk or two branches form a narrow V are weak spots, liable to split apart as the tree grows. Where the trunk of a young tree exhibits such a crotch or where either of two shoots could continue the growth of a branch, prune off the weaker of the two. Where you wish to keep the branch, insert a piece of wood as a spacer to widen the angle, as shown below. Leave the spacer in place for a year or so.

One trunk or several?

If you want a young tree to have a single trunk, identify the leader or central shoot and let it grow straight up, unpruned. The trunk will grow thicker faster if you leave the lower limbs in place for the first few years, but if they're in the way, you can remove them. At whatever height you

WHERE TO CUT

When removing the end of a branch, cut back to a healthy leaf, bud, or side shoot. Don't leave a stub. Use sharp pruning shears to make a neat cut that slices the stem rather than tears it.

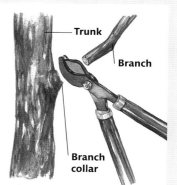

Trunk

Branch

Branch collar

When removing an entire branch, cut just outside the slightly thickened area, called the branch collar, where the branch grows into the trunk.

choose—usually about 8 ft. off the ground if you want to walk or see under the tree—select the shoots that will become the main limbs of the tree. Be sure they are evenly spaced around the trunk, pointing outward at wide angles. Remove any lower or weaker shoots. As the tree matures, it will only need an annual pruning to remove dead, damaged, or crossing shoots.

Most of the trees in this book are often grown with multiple (usually two to four) trunks, for a graceful, clumplike appearance. When buying a multiple-trunk tree, what's most important is that the trunks should diverge at the base. The more space between them, the better, so they can grow without squeezing each other. Prune multiple-trunk trees as previously described for single-trunk trees, and remove some of the branches that are growing toward the center of the clump, so the center doesn't get too dense and tangled.

AVOIDING NARROW CROTCHES

A tree's limbs should spread wide, like outstretched arms. If limbs angle too close to the trunk or to each other, there isn't room for them to grow properly and they may split apart after a few years, ruining the tree.

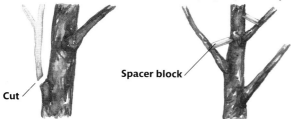

Cut

Spacer block

Spacer

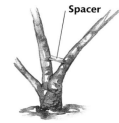

Spacer

SINGLE-TRUNK TREES: Correct narrow crotches on a young tree by removal or by widening the angle with a wooden spacer block. Choose well-spaced shoots to become the main limbs of a shade tree.

MULTIPLE-TRUNK TREES: Whether the stems of a multiple-trunk tree emerge from the ground or from a single trunk near the ground, widen angles if necessary to keep the trunks from touching.

Pruning shrubs

Shrubs are generally carefree plants, but they almost always look better if you do some pruning at least once a year. As a minimum, remove dead twigs from time to time, and if any branches are broken by storms or accidents, remove them as soon as convenient, cutting back to a healthy bud or to the plant's crown. Also, unless the shrub produces attractive seedpods or berries, it's a good idea to trim off the flowers after they fade.

Beyond this routine pruning, some shrubs require more attention. (The entries in Plant Profiles, pp. 130–169, give more information on when and how to prune particular shrubs.) Basically, shrub pruning falls into three categories: selective pruning, severe pruning, and shearing.

Selective pruning means using pruning shears to remove or cut back individual shoots, in order to refine the shape of the bush and maintain its vigor, as well as limit its size. (See the drawing at left.) This job takes time but produces a very graceful and natural-looking bush. Cut away weak or spindly twigs and any limbs that cross or rub against each other, and cut all the longest shoots back to a healthy, outward-facing bud or to a pair of buds. You can do selective pruning on any shrub, deciduous or evergreen, at any time of year.

Severe pruning means using pruning shears or loppers to cut away most of a shrub's top growth, leaving just short stubs or a gnarly trunk. This kind of cutting back is usually done once a year in late winter or early spring. Although it seems drastic, severe pruning is appropriate in several situations.

It makes certain fast-growing shrubs such as bluebeard and butterfly bush flower more profusely. It keeps others, such as lavender and spirea, compact and bushy, and it stimulates Siberian dogwood to produce canelike stems with bright red bark.

One or two severe prunings done when a shrub is young can make it branch out at the base, producing a bushier specimen or a fuller hedge plant. Nurseries often do this pruning as part of producing a good plant, and if you buy a shrub that's already bushy you don't need to cut it back yourself.

Older shrubs that have gotten tall and straggly sometimes respond to a severe pruning by sprouting out with renewed vigor, sending up lots of new shoots that bear plenty of foliage and flowers. This strategy doesn't work for all shrubs, though—sometimes severe pruning kills a plant. Don't try it unless you know it will work (check with a knowledgeable person at a nursery) or are willing to take a chance.

Shearing means using hedge shears or an electric hedge trimmer to trim the surface of a shrub, hedge, or tree to a neat, uniform profile, producing a solid mass of greenery. Both deciduous and evergreen shrubs and trees can be sheared; those with small, closely spaced leaves and a naturally compact growth habit usually look best. A good time for shearing most shrubs is early summer, after the new shoots have elongated but before the wood has hardened, but you can shear at other times of year, and you may have to shear some plants more than once a year.

If you're planning to shear a plant, start when it is young and establish the shape—cone, pyramid, flat-topped hedge, or whatever. Looking at the profile, always make the shrub wider at the bottom, otherwise the lower limbs will be shaded and won't be as leafy. Shear off as little as needed to maintain the shape as the shrub grows. Once it gets as big as you want it, shear as much as necessary to keep it that size.

SELECTIVE PRUNING. Remove weak, spindly, bent, or broken shoots (red). Where two branches rub on each other, remove the weakest or the one that's pointing inward (orange). Cut back long shoots to a healthy, outward-facing bud (blue).

SEVERE PRUNING. In late winter or early spring, before new growth starts, cut all the stems back close to the ground.

SHEARING. Trim with hedge clippers to a neat profile.

Making a hedge

To make a hedge that's dense enough that you can't see through it, choose shrubs that have many shoots at the base. If you can only find skinny shrubs, prune them severely the first spring after planting to stimulate bushier growth.

Hedge plants are set in the ground as described on pp. 215–216 but are spaced closer together than they would be if planted as individual specimens. We took that into account in creating the designs and plant lists for this book; just follow the spacings recommended in the designs. If you're impatient for the hedge to fill in, you can space the plants closer together.

A hedge can be sheared, pruned selectively, or left alone, depending on how you want it to look. Slow-growing, small-leaved plants such as boxwood and Japanese holly make rounded but natural-looking hedges with no pruning at all, or you can shear them into any profile you choose and make them perfectly neat and uniform. (Be sure to keep them narrower at the top.) Choose one style and stick with it. Once a hedge is established, you can neither start nor stop shearing it without an awkward transition that may last a few years before the hedge looks good again.

Getting a vine off to a good start

Nurseries often sell clematis, honeysuckle, and other vines as young plants with a single stem fastened to a bamboo stake. To plant them, remove the stake and cut off the stem right above the lowest pair of healthy leaves, usually about 4 to 6 in. above the soil ❶. This forces the vine to send out new shoots low to the ground. As soon as those new shoots have begun to develop (normally within four to six weeks after planting), cut them back to their first pairs of leaves ❷. After this second pruning, the plant will become bushy at the base. Now, as new shoots form, use sticks or strings to direct them toward the base of the support they are to climb ❸.

Once they're started, both clematis and honeysuckle can scramble up a lattice trellis, although it helps if you tuck in any stray ends from time to time. The plants can't climb a smooth surface, however. For them to cover a fence or post, you have to provide something the vine can wrap around.

Screw a few eyebolts to the top and bottom of such a support and stretch wire, nylon cord, or polypropylene rope between them. (The wires or cords should be a few inches out from the fence, not flush against it.)

Other vines need different treatments. 'Golden Showers' and other so-called climbing roses don't really climb at all by themselves—you have to fasten them to a support. Twist-ties are handy for this job. Roses grow fast, so you'll have to tie in the new shoots every few weeks from spring to fall. Climbing hydrangea is a slow starter, but once under way, it can climb any surface to any height by means of their clinging rootlets and so need no further assistance or care.

After the first year, the vines in this book don't need pruning on a regular basis, but you can cut them back whenever they get too big, and you should remove any dead or straggly stems from time to time.

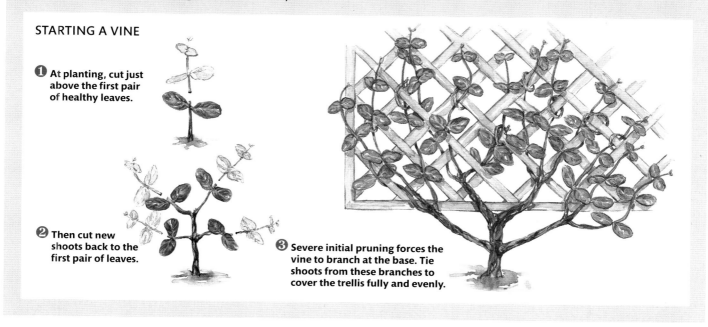

STARTING A VINE

❶ At planting, cut just above the first pair of healthy leaves.

❷ Then cut new shoots back to the first pair of leaves.

❸ Severe initial pruning forces the vine to branch at the base. Tie shoots from these branches to cover the trellis fully and evenly.

Caring for Perennials

Perennials are simply plants that send up new growth year after year. A large group, perennials include flowering plants such as daylilies and astilbes as well as grasses, ferns, and hardy bulbs. Although some perennials need special conditions and care, most of the ones in this book are adaptable and easygoing. Get them off to a good start by planting them in well-prepared soil, adding a layer of mulch, watering as often as needed throughout the first year, and keeping weeds away. After that, keeping perennials attractive and healthy typically requires just a few minutes per plant each year.

Routine annual care

Some of the perennials that are used as ground covers, such as lily-of-the-valley, moneywort, pachysandra, periwinkle, sweet woodruff, and sweet violet, need virtually no care. On a suitable site, they'll thrive for decades even if you pay them no attention at all.

Most garden perennials, though, look and grow better if you clean away the old leaves and stems at least once a year. When to do this depends on the plant.

Perennials such as aster, daylily, dwarf fountain grass, hosta, interrupted fern, iris, and peony have leaves and stalks that turn tan or brown after they're frosted in fall. Cut these down to the ground in late fall or early spring; either time is okay.

Perennials such as beach wormwood, bigroot geranium, blue oat grass, Christmas fern, dianthus, Lenten rose, lilyturf, and moss phlox have foliage that is more or less evergreen, depending on the severity of the winter. For those plants, wait until early spring; then cut back any leaves or stems that are discolored or shabby-looking. Don't leave cuttings lying on the soil, because they may contain disease spores. Do not compost diseased stems or leaves.

Right after you've cleared away the dead material is a good time to renew the mulch on the bed. Use a fork, rake, or cultivator to loosen the existing mulch, and add some fresh mulch if needed. Also, if you want to sprinkle some granular fertilizer on the bed, do that now, when it's easy to avoid getting any on the plants' leaves. Fertilizing perennials is optional, but it does make them grow bigger and bloom more than they would otherwise.

Remove faded flowers

Removing flowers as they fade (called "deadheading") makes the garden look neater, prevents unwanted self-sown seedlings, and often stimulates a plant to continue blooming longer than it would if you left it alone, or to bloom a second time later in the season. (This is true for shrubs and annuals as well as for perennials.)

Pick large flowers such as daisies, daylilies, lilies, peonies, and tulips one at a time, snapping them off by hand. Use pruning shears on perennials such as astilbe, bee balm, hosta, lady's mantle, phlox, and yarrow that produce tall stalks crowded with lots of small flowers, cutting the stalks back to the height of the foliage. Use hedge shears on bushy plants that are covered with lots of small flowers on short stalks, such as basket-of-gold, catmint, dianthus, and evergreen candytuft, cutting the stems back by about one-half.

Instead of removing them, you may want to let the flowers remain on coneflower, purple coneflower, false indigo, Siberian iris, 'Autumn Joy' sedum, and the various grasses. These plants all bear conspicuous seedpods or seed heads on stiff stalks that remain standing and look interesting throughout the fall and winter.

Pruning and shearing perennials

Some perennials that bloom in summer or fall respond well to being pruned earlier in the growing season. Bee balm, boltonia, chrysanthemum, garden phlox, gaura, New England aster, Nippon daisy, and 'Autumn Joy' sedum all form tall clumps of stems topped with lots of little flowers. Unfortunately, tall stems are liable to flop over in stormy weather, and even if they don't, too-tall clumps can look leggy or top-heavy. To prevent floppiness, prune these plants when the stems are about 1 ft. tall. Remove the weakest stems from each clump by cutting them off at the ground, then cut all the remaining, strong stems back by about one-third. Pruning in this way keeps these plants shorter, stronger, and bushier, so you don't have to bother with staking them.

Southernwood and 'Valerie Finnis' artemisia are grown more for their foliage than for their flowers. You can use hedge shears to keep them neat, compact, and bushy, shearing off the tops of the stems once or twice in spring and summer.

PRUNING A PERENNIAL

Prune to create neater, bushier clumps of some summer- and fall-blooming perennials such as phlox, chrysanthemums, New England aster, and bee balm. When the stalks are about 1 ft. tall, cut them all back by one-third. Remove the weakest stalks at ground level.

Dividing perennials

Most perennials send up more stems each year, forming denser clumps or wider patches. Dividing is the process of cutting or breaking apart these clumps or patches. This is an easy way to make more plants to expand your garden, to control a plant that might otherwise spread out of bounds, or to renew an old specimen that doesn't look good or bloom well anymore.

Most perennials can be divided as often as every year or two if you're in a hurry to make more plants, or they can go for several years if you don't have any reason to disturb them. You can divide them in early spring, just as new growth is starting, or in late summer and fall, up until a month before hard frost.

There are two main approaches to dividing perennials, as shown in the drawings at right. You can leave the plant in the ground and use a sharp shovel to cut it apart, like slicing a pie, then lift out one chunk at a time. Or you can dig around and underneath the plant and lift it out all at once, shake off the extra soil, and lay the plant on the ground or a tarp where you can work with it.

Some plants, such as boltonia, yarrow, and most ferns, are easy to divide. They almost fall apart when you dig them up. Others, such as astilbe, daylily, and most grasses, have very tough or tangled roots and you'll have to wrestle with them, chop them with a sharp butcher knife, pry them apart with a strong screwdriver or garden fork, or even cut through the roots with a hatchet or pruning saw. However you approach the job, before you insert any tool, take a close look at the plant right at ground level, and be careful to divide *between*, not *through*, the biggest and healthiest buds or shoots. Using a

hose to wash loose mulch and soil away makes it easier to see what you're doing.

Don't make the divisions too small; they should be the size of a plant that you'd want to buy, not just little scraps. If you have more divisions than you need or want, choose just the best-looking ones to replant and discard or give away the others. Replant new divisions as soon as possible in freshly prepared soil. Water them right away, and water again

whenever the soil dries out over the next few weeks or months, until the plants are growing again.

Divide hardy bulbs such as daffodils and crocuses every few years by digging up the clumps after they have finished blooming but before the foliage turns yellow. Shake the soil off the roots, pull the bulbs apart, and replant them promptly, setting them as deep as they were buried before.

DIVIDING PERENNIALS

You can divide a clump or patch of perennials by cutting down into the patch with a sharp spade, like slicing a pie or a pan of brownies, then lifting out the separate chunks.

Or you can dig up the whole clump, shake the extra soil off the roots, then pull or pry it apart into separate plantlets.

Problem Solving

Some plants are much more susceptible than others to damage by severe weather, pests, or diseases. In this book, we've recommended plants that are generally trouble-free, especially after they have had a few years to get established in your garden. But even these plants are subject to various mishaps and problems. The challenge is learning how to distinguish which problems are really serious and which are just cosmetic, and deciding how to solve—or, better yet, prevent—those problems that are serious.

Pests, large and small

Deer, rabbits, and woodchucks are liable to be a problem if your property is surrounded by or adjacent to fields or woods. You may not see them, but you can't miss the damage they do—they bite the tops off or eat whole plants of hostas, daylilies, and many other perennials. Deer also eat the leaves and stems of maples, azaleas, arborvitae, and many other trees and shrubs. Commercial or homemade repellents that you spray on the foliage may be helpful if the animals aren't too hungry. (See the box below for plants that deer

seem to avoid.) But in the long run, the only solution is to fence out deer and to trap and remove smaller animals.

Chipmunks and squirrels are cute but naughty. They normally don't eat much foliage, but they do eat some kinds of flowers and several kinds of bulbs, they dig up new transplants, and they plant nuts in your flower beds and lawns. Voles and field mice can kill trees and shrubs by stripping the bark off the trunk, usually in the winter when the ground is covered with snow, and they eat away at many perennials, too. Moles don't eat plants, but their digging makes a mess of a lawn or flower bed. Persistent trapping is the most effective way to control all of these little critters.

Insects and related pests can cause minor or devastating damage. Most plants can afford to lose part of their foliage or sap without suffering much of a setback, so don't panic if you see a few holes chewed in a leaf. However, whenever you suspect that insects are attacking one of your plants, try to catch one

Identify, then treat

Don't jump to conclusions and start spraying chemicals on a supposedly sick plant before you know what (if anything) is actually wrong with it. That's wasteful and irresponsible, and you're likely to do the plant as much harm as good. Pinpointing the exact cause of a problem is difficult for even experienced gardeners, so save yourself frustration and seek out expert help from the beginning.

If it seems that there's something wrong with one of your plants—for example, if the leaves are discolored, have holes in them, or have spots or marks on them—cut off a sample branch, wrap it in damp paper towels, and put it in a plastic bag (so it won't wilt). Take the sample to the nursery or garden center where you bought the plant, and ask for help. If the nursery can't help, contact the nearest office of your state's Cooperative Extension Service or a public garden in your area and ask if they have a staff member who can diagnose plant problems.

Meanwhile, look around your property and around the neighborhood, too, to see if any other plants (of the same or different kinds) show similar symptoms. If a problem is widespread, you shouldn't have much trouble finding someone who can identify it and tell you what, if anything, to do. If only one plant is affected, it's often harder to diagnose the problem, and you may just have to wait and see what happens to it. Keep an eye on the plant, continue with watering and other regular maintenance, and see if the problem gets worse or goes away. If nothing more has happened after a few weeks, stop worrying. If the problem continues, intensify your search for expert advice.

Plant problems stem from a number of causes: insect and animal pests, diseases, and poor care, particularly in winter. Remember that plant problems are often caused by a combination of these; all the more reason to consult with experts about their diagnosis and treatment.

Deer-resistant plants

Deer may nibble these plants, but they're unlikely to strip them bare. If you live in an area where deer populations are high, consider substituting some of these plants for others that are specified in a design.

Trees and Shrubs

Andromeda	Dogwood	Magnolia
Barberry	Forsythia	Pine
Boxwood	Holly	Spirea
Daphne	Lilac	Spruce

Perennials

Astilbe	Geranium	Lenten rose
Bee balm	Grasses	Peony
Blazing star	Heuchera	Russian sage
Bluebeard	Iris	Sage
Daffodil	Lamb's ears	Veronica
Ferns	Lavender	Yarrow

DEER-CONTROL FENCING Deer have been known to jump very tall fences, so a wide fence is one of the best ways to protect your landscape plants from deer. This fence is suitable for a larger property. It is about 6 ft. wide and 5 ft. high, and consists of angled poles fixed to posts spaced about 10 ft. apart. Attach electric wires at 12 in. intervals to the poles. For advice on deer fences that work best in your area, consult your Cooperative Extension agent.

of them in a glass jar and get it identified, so you can decide what to do.

There are several new kinds of insecticides that are quite effective but much safer to use than the older products. You must read the fine print on the label to determine whether an insecticide will control your particular pest. Carefully follow the directions for how to apply the product, or it may not work.

Diseases

Several types of fungal, bacterial, and viral diseases can attack garden plants, causing a wide range of symptoms such as disfigured or discolored leaves or petals, powdery or moldy-looking films or spots, mushy or rotten stems or roots, and overall wilting. As with insect problems, if you suspect that a plant is infected with a disease, gather a sample of the plant and show it to someone who can identify the problem before you do any spraying.

In general, plant diseases are hard to treat, so it's important to take steps to prevent problems. These steps include choosing plants adapted to your area, choosing disease-resistant plants, spacing plants far enough apart so that air can circulate between them, and removing dead stems and litter from the garden.

Perennials that would otherwise be healthy are prone to fungal infections during spells of hot humid weather, especially if the plants are crowded together or if they have flopped over and are lying on top of each other or on the ground. Look closely for moldy foliage, and if you find any, prune it off and discard (don't compost) it. It's better to cut the plants back severely than to let the disease spread. Plan to avoid repeated problems by dividing the perennials, replanting them farther apart, and pruning them early in the season so they don't grow so tall and floppy again. Crowded shrubs are also subject to fungal problems in the summer and should be pruned so that air can flow around them.

Winter damage

More plants are damaged or killed in the winter than in any other season. Shrubs, trees, and woody vines may get broken by heavy, wet snows or ice storms. When this happens, prune off the broken limbs, cutting them back to a main trunk or branch, sometime before new growth starts in spring. Severe cold spells or a sudden change from mild to freezing weather can kill the tops of woody plants. In this case, wait until early spring to assess the severity of the damage; then prune off any limbs that are definitely brown and dead. In most cases, new growth will sprout out from the surviving stems; if no buds appear by late spring, replace the plant.

Even in midwinter, evergreen trees, shrubs, vines, and perennials lose moisture through their leaves on warm, sunny, breezy days. Normally, rain wets the soil enough to meet these plants' water needs, but you should give them a deep watering if there's a long dry spell. Deciduous plants rarely need watering in winter.

In mountainous regions or the upper Southeast, any small or medium-size perennial or shrub that is planted in the fall is liable to be pushed up out of the ground, or frost-heaved, as the soil repeatedly freezes and thaws, and that means its roots get dried out. To prevent this, cover the ground around these plants with loose mulch as soon as the soil has frozen hard, and don't remove until midspring.

Glossary

Amendments. Organic or mineral materials such as peat moss, perlite, or compost that are used to improve the soil.

Annual. A plant that germinates, grows, flowers, produces seeds, and dies in the course of a single growing season; a plant that is treated like an annual and grown for a single season's display.

Antitranspirant. A substance sprayed on the stems and leaves of evergreen plants to protect them from water loss caused by winter winds.

Balled-and-burlapped. Describes a tree or shrub dug out of the ground with a ball of soil intact around the roots; the ball is then wrapped in burlap and tied for transport.

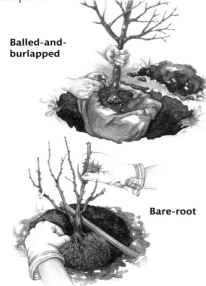

Balled-and-burlapped

Bare-root

Bare-root. Describes a plant dug out of the ground and then shaken or washed to remove the soil from the roots.

Compound leaf. A leaf with two or more leaflets branching off a single stalk.

Container-grown. Describes a plant raised in a pot that is removed before planting.

Crown. That part of a plant where the roots and stem meet, usually at soil level.

Cultivar. A cultivated variety of a plant, often bred or selected for some special trait such as double flowers, compact growth, cold hardiness, or disease and pest resistance.

Deadheading. Removing old flowers during the growing season to prevent seed formation and to encourage the development of new flowers.

Deciduous. Describes a tree, shrub, or vine that drops all its leaves in winter.

Division. Propagation of a plant by separating it into two or more pieces, each of which has at least one bud and some roots. Used mostly for perennials, grasses, ferns, and bulbs.

Drainage. The movement of water down through the soil. With good drainage, water disappears from a planting hole in just a few hours. If water remains standing overnight, the drainage is poor.

Drip line. An imaginary line on the soil around a tree that mirrors the circumference of the canopy above. Many of the tree's roots are found in this area.

Dry-laid. Describes a masonry path or wall that is installed without mortar.

Edging. A shallow trench or physical barrier of steel, plastic, brick, or boards used to define the border between a flower bed and adjacent turf.

Exposure. The intensity, duration, and variation in sun, wind, and temperature that characterize any particular site.

Feeder roots. Slender branching roots that spread close to the soil surface and absorb most of the nutrients for a tree or shrub.

Formal. Describes a style of landscaping that features symmetrical layouts, with beds and walks related to adjacent buildings, and often with plants sheared to geometric or other shapes.

Foundation planting. Traditionally, a narrow border of evergreen shrubs planted around the foundation of a house. Contemporary foundation plantings often include deciduous shrubs, grasses, perennials, and other plants as well.

Frost heaving. A disturbance or uplifting of soil, pavement, or plants caused when moisture in the soil freezes and expands.

Full shade. Describes a site that receives no direct sun during the growing season.

Full sun. Describes a site that receives at least eight hours of direct sun each day during the growing season.

Garden soil. Soil specially prepared for planting to make it loose enough for roots and water to penetrate easily. Usually requires digging or tilling and the addition of some organic matter.

Grade. The degree and direction of slope on a piece of ground.

Ground cover. A plant such as ivy, liriope, or juniper used to cover the soil and form a continuous low mass of foliage. Often used as a durable substitute for turfgrass.

Habit. The characteristic shape or form of a plant, such as upright, spreading, or rounded.

Hardiness. A plant's ability to survive the winter without protection from the cold.

Hardiness zone. A geographic region where the coldest temperature in an average winter falls within a certain range, such as between 0° and –10°F.

Hardscape. Parts of a landscape constructed from materials other than plants, such as walks, walls, and trellises made of wood, stone, or other materials.

Herbicide. A chemical used to kill plants. Preemergent herbicides are used to kill weed seeds as they sprout, and thus to prevent weed growth. Postemergent herbicides kill plants that are already growing.

Hybrid. A plant resulting from a cross between two parents that belong to different varieties, species, or genera.

Interplant. To combine plants with different bloom times or growth habits, making it possible to fit more plants in a bed, thus prolonging the bed's appeal.

Invasive. Describes a plant that spreads quickly, usually by runners, and mixes with or dominates adjacent plantings.

Landscape fabric. A synthetic fabric, sometimes water-permeable, spread under paths or mulch to serve as a weed barrier.

Lime, limestone. White mineral compounds used to combat soil acidity and to supply calcium for plant growth.

Loam. An ideal soil for gardening, containing plenty of organic matter and a balanced range of small to large mineral particles.

Microclimate. Local conditions of shade, exposure, wind, drainage, and other factors that affect plant growth at any particular site.

Mowing strip. A row of bricks or paving stones set flush with the soil around the edge of a bed, and wide enough to support one wheel of the lawn mower.

Mulch. A layer of bark, peat moss, compost, shredded leaves, hay or straw, lawn clippings, gravel, paper, or other material, spread over the soil around the base of plants. During the growing season, a mulch can help retard evaporation, inhibit weeds, and moderate soil temperature. In the winter, a mulch of evergreen boughs, coarse hay, or leaves is used to protect plants from freezing.

Native. Describes a plant that occurs naturally in a particular region and was not introduced from some other area.

Nutrients. Nitrogen, phosphorus, potassium, calcium, magnesium, and other elements needed by plants. Nutrients are supplied by the minerals and organic matter in the soil and by fertilizers.

Organic matter. Plant and animal residues such as leaves, trimmings, and manure in various stages of decomposition.

Peat moss. Partially decomposed mosses and sedges, mined from boggy areas and used to improve garden soil or to prepare potting soil.

Perennial. A plant that lives for a number of years, generally flowering each year. By "perennial," gardeners usually mean "herbaceous perennial," although woody plants such as vines, shrubs, and trees are also perennial.

Pressure-treated lumber. Softwood lumber treated with chemicals that protect it from decay.

Propagate. To produce new plants by sowing seeds, rooting cuttings, dividing plant parts, layering, grafting, or other means.

Retaining wall. A wall built to stabilize a slope and keep soil from sliding or eroding downhill.

Rhizome. A horizontal underground stem, often swollen into a storage organ. Both roots and shoots emerge from rhizomes. Rhizomes generally branch as they creep along and can be divided to make new plants.

Root ball. The mass of soil and roots dug with a plant when it is removed from the ground; the soil and roots of a plant grown in a container.

Rosette. A low, flat cluster of leaves arranged like the petals of a rose.

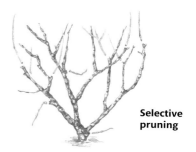

Selective pruning

Severe pruning

Selective pruning. Using pruning shears to remove or cut back individual shoots, in order to refine the shape of a shrub, maintain its vigor, or limit its size.

Severe pruning. Using pruning shears or loppers to cut away most of a shrub's top growth, leaving just short stubs or a gnarly trunk.

Shearing. Using hedge shears or an electric hedge trimmer to shape the surface of a shrub, hedge, or tree and produce a smooth, solid mass of greenery.

Specimen plant. A plant placed alone in a prominent position, to show it off.

Spike. An elongated flower cluster, with individual flowers borne on very short stalks or attached directly to the main stem.

Tender. Describes a plant that is damaged by cold weather.

Underplanting. Growing short plants, such as ground covers, under a taller plant, such as a shrub.

Variegated. Describes foliage that is marked, striped, or blotched with color other than green.

234

Index

Mark Wolfe is a garden and landscape content specialist based in Georgia, with an extensive background in the green industry. He works as an industry expert and commerce writer at BobVila.com, while contributing content and editing services for many other outlets. Mark graduated from Northland College in Ashland, Wisconsin with a degree in outdoor education. Early in his career, Mark fell in love with plants. Working on stream restoration and wetlands construction projects, he marveled at the willow's ability to quickly grow from a stem fragment and heal a sorely eroded streambank, and the ways that aquatic plants transform a suburban retention pond into a wildlife oasis. Over the next two decades, trees, shrubs, annuals, and perennials would dominate his working life as a landscaper and nursery manager. In the mid-twenty-teens, Mark co-founded a garden blog, ThePrudentGarden.com, and soon began contributing freelance work for dozens of lawn and garden websites and consumer brands. As a writer, his favorite topics are those that help those who are new to plants and gardening find success and helping seasoned plant people find new inspiration. As a gardener, he is passionate about establishing backyard habitats for wild birds and pollinators and growing his collection of native azaleas.

Photo Credits

Front Cover: *(main image)* Saxon Holt; *top left* Jerry Pavia; *top center* Shutterstock.com (NPvancheng55); *top right* Carole Ottesen **Back Cover:** *all* Jerry Pavia **page 1:** Jerry Pavia **page 7:** Saxon Holt **pages 20–21:** Jerry Pavia **page 25:** *both* Jerry Pavia **page 29:** *top* Karen Bussolini, design: Wayne Renaud; *center* Stephen Pategas **page 32:** *top* Stephen Pategas; *bottom right* Jerry Pavia; *bottom left* Karen Bussolini **page 37:** *all* Jerry Pavia **page 40:** *top & bottom right* Jerry Pavia; *bottom left* Charles **Mann page 44:** *top & center* Jerry Pavia; *bottom* Charles Mann, design: Joan Brink **page 49:** *all* Jerry Pavia **page 53:** *top & center* Jerry Pavia; *bottom* Karen Bussolini, design: Wesley Rouse **pages 56–64:** *all* Jerry Pavia **page 69:** *top both* Jerry Pavia; *bottom* Karen Bussolini **page 72**: *top & bottom left* Karen Bussolini, *(bottom left)* design: Dickson DeMarche; *bottom right* Jerry Pavia **page 77:** *top* Karen Bussolini, design: Juanita Flagg; *bottom both* Jerry Pavia **page 80:** *top* Karen Bussolini; *bottom* Stephen Pategas **page 85:** *top* Jerry Pavia; *bottom both* Karen Bussolini **page 89:** *top* Karen Bussolini; *bottom* Saxon Holt **page 93:** *top both* Jerry Pavia; *bottom* Saxon Holt **page 97:** *top & center* Jerry Pavia; *bottom* Karen Bussolini, design: Cynthia Rice **page 101:** *top & bottom* Jerry Pavia; *center* Karen Bussolini **page 104:** *top & bottom* Jerry Pavia, *(bottom)* courtesy of Marlene King; *center* Karen Bussolini, design: Juanita Flagg **pages 109–121:** *all* Jerry Pavia **page 124:** *top* Saxon Holt; *bottom both* Jerry Pavia **page 129:** *all* Jerry Pavia **pages 130–131**: Shannon Barnes/Dreamstime.com **pages 132:** *left* Saxon Holt; *right* Galen Gates **page 133:** *top* Dency Kane; *right center* Jerry Pavia; *left center* Rita Buchanan; *bottom right* Charles Mann; *bottom left* Saxon Holt **page 134:** *top both* Stephen Pategas; *bottom* Carole Ottesen **page 135:** *top* Charles Mann; *center* Rita Buchanan; *bottom right* Saxon Holt; *bottom left* Stephen Pategas **page 136**: *top left* Stephen Pategas; *top right* Galen Gates; *center* Rita Buchanan; *bottom* Jerry Pavia **page 137:** *top* Stephen Pategas; *center* Karen Bussolini; *bottom* Charles Mann **page 138:** *bottom both* Jerry Pavia; *top right* Stephen Pategas **page 139:** *top left* Rita Buchanan; *top right* Karen Bussolini; *bottom* Charles Mann **page 140:** *top & bottom left* Saxon Holt; *center both* Charles Mann; *bottom right* Jerry Pavia **page 141:** *top left* Galen Gates; *top center & bottom right* Charles Mann; *top right* Rita Buchanan **page 142:** *top left* Charles Mann; *top right* Jerry Pavia; *bottom both* Lauren Springer **page 143:** *top* Galen Gates; *center* Stephen Pategas; *bottom* Charles Mann **page 144:** *left all* Jerry Pavia; *top right* Lauren Springer **page 145:** *top left, top center & bottom right* Jerry Pavia; *top right* Charles Mann; *middle right* Karen Bussolini **page 146:** *top left and bottom left* Charles Mann; *top right* Galen Gates **page 147:** *top left* Jerry Pavia; *top right* Karen Bussolini; *center* Galen Gates; *bottom right* Lauren Springer; *bottom left* Rick Mastelli **page 148:** *top both* Charles Mann; *middle left* Jerry Pavia; *bottom left* John Elsley **page 149:** *top left* Lauren Springer; *top center & top right* Michael Dirr; *bottom right* Jerry Pavia **page 150:** *top left* Karen Bussolini; *top right* Stephen Pategas; *bottom right* Rick Mastelli; *bottom left* Charles Mann **page 151:** *top left* Karen Bussolini; *top center* Saxon Holt; *top right* Rita Buchanan; *middle right* Stephen Pategas; Carole Ottesen **page 152:** *top left & center* Jerry Pavia; *top right* Richard Shiell; *bottom* Carole Ottesen **page 153:** *top* Charles Mann; *center* Michael Dirr; *bottom* Saxon Holt **page 154:** *top left* Greg Grant; *center & top right* Jerry Pavia; *bottom left* John Elsley **page 155:** *top left* Saxon Holt; *top right* Dency Kane; *bottom right* Jerry Pavia; *bottom left* Rita Buchanan **page 156:** *top right* Galen Gates; *center right* Shutterstock.com (NPvancheng55); *center left* Stephen Pategas; *bottom left* Charles Mann **page 157:** *bottom right* Stephen Pategas; *top left* Charles Mann; *top right* Michael Dirr; *center right* Shutterstock.com (MacBen) **page 158:** *top left* Galen Gates; *top right & bottom* Stephen Pategas **page 159:** *top left* Carole Ottesen; *top right* Michael Dirr; *bottom both* Saxon Holt **page 160:** *top* Rita Buchanan; *top right* Richard Shiell; *left center* Saxon Holt; *bottom* Jerry Pavia **page 161:** *top left* Jerry Pavia; *top right* Rita Buchanan; *bottom* Stephen Pategas **page 162:** *top* Karen Bussolini; *middle left* Jerry Pavia; *middle right* Carole Ottesen; *bottom* Galen Gates **page 163:** *top* Cole Burrell; *center* Charles Mann; *bottom* Saxon Holt **page 164:** *top left* Stephen Pategas; *top right & bottom both* Charles Mann **page 165:** *top right* Galen Gates; *bottom right* Jerry Pavia; *bottom left* Ruth Rogers Clausen **page 164:** *top left* Charles Mann; *top right* Karen Bussolini; *bottom right* Jerry Pavia **page 167:** *top left* Charles Mann; *top right* Galen Gates; *right center* Saxon Holt; *bottom* Michael Dirr **page 168:** *top* Charles Mann; *center* Greg Grant; *bottom* Jerry Pavia **page 169:** *top & bottom right* Charles Mann; *bottom left* Jerry Pavia **page 170:** *top* Galen Gates; *bottom* Shutterstock.com (MaryAnne Campbell) **page 171:** *top* Jerry Pavia; *center & bottom* Stephen Pategas **pages 172–173:** Vanessagifford/Dreamstime.com